# CONFESSIONS OF
# AN OPTIMIST

Peregrine,

You may find some of this amusing

Woodrow

# CONFESSIONS OF AN OPTIMIST

Woodrow Wyatt

COLLINS
8 Grafton Street, London W1
1985

William Collins Sons & Co. Ltd
London · Glasgow · Sydney · Auckland
Toronto · Johannesburg

First published 1985
© Woodrow Wyatt 1985

BRITISH LIBRARY CATALOGUING IN PUBLICATION DATA

Wyatt, Woodrow
Confessions of an optimist.
1. Wyatt, Woodrow    2. Politicians—Great
Britain—Biography
I. Title
941.085′092′4        DA591.W9

ISBN 0 00 217170 8

Photoset in Linotron Sabon by
Rowland Phototypesetting Ltd
Bury St Edmunds, Suffolk
Made and printed in Great Britain by
Robert Hartnoll, Bodmin, Cornwall

For Pericles and Petronella
who are my bid for immortality

"A non-starter? I'll ride and ride and ride again, to save the <u>parties</u> I love...!"

# Acknowledgements

My thanks are due to Mrs Mavis Johnson and Miss Valerie Rutherford for their patient and careful typing of the pages which follow; to Mrs Miranda Wood who worked for me for many years for her suggestions and for compiling the Index; to Jeff Hodson, a young American who made the first and essential foray into sorting out my papers which had been carefully filed by Miss Marjorie Cummins, my secretary for fourteen years; to Philip Ziegler of Collins for his first class editing; and to Sir Penderel Moon for allowing me to consult him on the passages about India.

Some of the incidents referred to here have been mentioned in abbreviated, unconnected form elsewhere, particularly in *To the Point*, a short collection of some reflections on life published by Weidenfeld and Nicolson, to whom my thanks.

# CONTENTS

# ILLUSTRATIONS

# CHAPTER I

———— ❧❦❧ ————

# The Beginnings Breed
# Ambition

THE FIVE-TO-ONE WARNING BELL for lunch had just rung as I started emerging into the world. I was there in time for the second bell at one o'clock, and have rarely been late for a meal since. As it was English summer time it was noon by Greenwich Mean Time, which has enabled astrologers to pinpoint my moment of birth when casting my horoscopes, in which I have always half believed, being credulous of supernatural grand designs shaped for me alone though sceptical of the existence of any supernatural Supreme Being.

I was born on 4 July 1918 in my parents' bedrooom at a private school, Milbourne Lodge, which my father had started in 1915 at Esher. Esher was almost in the country, but becoming increasingly a superior suburb for prosperous business and professional men working in London. Their new houses were already beginning to change the character of the area.

My father, with one of his few flashes of business shrewdness, foresaw they would need a day school for their sons. This they did, but not as quickly as he would have wished. For years the school teetered near bankruptcy with some thirty day boys and a handful of boarders. It is still there, three times the size, with a high success rate of scholarships and entries into the grander public schools as well as the lesser ones. My father would have been surprised that after a sickly start the acorn he planted grew so well.

When I showed my third wife the house where I was born she said it looked common, but I do not think so. It was built in late Victorian times with big windows, roofed in dark-grey slate and topped by pointed gabling with interesting neo-Gothic detail. It was a good house for children, particularly out of term time when there were no other children there: arches under the kitchen in which one could scramble and hide; stables, from which the horses had vanished, next to the garage with a long room above it, reached by an outside staircase. My father used this room for carpentry. After he died in March 1932 I took it over for books and the manufacture of fantasies.

My father was fifty-one when I was born. His name was Robert Harvey Lyle Wyatt. The Lyle came from his mother, Annie Lyle, a Cornish lady whose brother Joseph inherited a substantial property in Cornwall. My father became the presumptive heir to it when Great-Uncle Joseph left only an unmarried daughter, Molly, unlikely to bear children. My father never lived to inherit Bonython, near Helston, with its farms and woods, lands at the Lizard, including the freehold of the most southerly lighthouse in England, and a share of the headland at Kynance Cove. That was a pity. Bonython would have suited him, with its country pursuits (he was a very good shot), its opportunities to collect and polish local serpentine, and to play golf at Gunwalloe, and an end of the need to work. He always did as little as possible of that, unless gardening or weeding, mowing and rolling his perfectly kept grass tennis-court counted as work.

We happily spent most of our holidays at Bonython while Great-Uncle Joseph lived in New Zealand. He had gone there after selling his life interest in Bonython to repair some of the losses caused by a classically mis-spent youth. Great-Uncle Joseph was at Cambridge with my grandfather, Robert Harvey Wyatt, who subsequently became his brother-in-law.

Joseph while at Cambridge had got entangled with a tobacconist's daughter. She extracted a sensational amount of money from him in an early breach of promise action in the 1850s. Having made a mess of his love-life he made another of the family property. So it was New Zealand for him. Fortunately on the ship taking him there he met a Miss Lucy Dundas, who had money of her own, and married her. She never stopped thinking him splendid, dashing and brilliantly intelligent, despite the evidence. Without her money they could not have sustained themselves on their marginal sheep-farm, but he made her happy.

We visited Bonython so often in part because my father wanted to ensure that the life tenants, a strange and dirty couple

14

called Skewes, did not wreck the place beyond the legal bounds. The best way to do that was for us to stay there frequently as lodgers, either in the big house or elsewhere on the estate. This did not prevent Mr Skewes keeping the Home Farm so filthy that I and my brother, older than I by three and a quarter years, got tubercular glands from drinking his milk. He might have pleaded in exoneration that he had not expected us day after day to lie on our backs under the cows in the dirty cowshed, clutching their udders and putting their teats straight into our mouths. It was an agreeable way of drinking milk, but it led to my brother having an operation to his neck and to my spending periods of many months lying in bed flat on my back forbidden to move my stomach or my neck until the swelling of my glands subsided. Partly as a result of this I got through much indiscriminate reading around the ages of eight, nine and ten, proclaiming priggishly to an astonished aunt that I read everything from Edgar Wallace to Sir Walter Scott.

Cousin Molly determinedly believed that the Lyles were Scottish and referred mysteriously to the name meaning 'Lords of the Isles'. This inspired me with the desire to be one too. I would go round in a happy glow repeating to myself 'Lord of the Isles'. Actually, the Lyles were only Lords of the Lizard, a title by local custom shared with three other joint owners of land around the Lizard and acquired by purchase. They were as Cornish as could be, with a common Cornish name. They had made their money in tin mines in the early nineteenth century, and not always scrupulously. When some of his ventures failed in the 1830s, Samuel Lyle escaped from his creditors to France, taking with him £8000, 'of which the greater part was in sovereigns'. His brother Joseph, who had become rich out of a mine called West Wheal Basset and others nearby, tried to help Samuel. Together they made a joint offer to pay Samuel's creditors twenty shillings in the pound after the sudden success of another of Samuel's tin mines had made Samuel feel safe to return to Cornwall. He was wrong. His creditors were too angry at his past behaviour to stop the bankruptcy proceedings.

At the end of the worst day of a nasty examination lasting many weeks before the bankruptcy commissioners Samuel bolted from the hotel where the examination was being held, on the top of a mail-coach in his slippers. He was chased by attorneys in a carriage and four, leaving houses and hotels by the back door like Dick Turpin as the attorneys came in by the front. For a time he was thought to have got back to France, but he was caught in London by the police and put in Devon County Gaol.

These were Wild West days in the Cornish tin mines. Samuel Lyle was one among many who speculated, lost, swindled to gain time and struck tin again. We heard none of these exciting tin adventures from Cousin Molly. But from them came the purchase of Bonython in 1837 by Joseph Lyle. The property passed to Captain John Lyle (the rank was not military but meant Captain of the Mines), the father of Great-Uncle Joseph.

Cousin Molly's story was that the Lyles, a grand family in Scotland, had decided to emigrate to Cornwall in the distant past. Crossing Bodmin Moor on a dark stormy night they lost nearly all their money when one of the wagons got swallowed in a bog. They had only enough left for the buying of Bonython, which she put vaguely somewhat earlier than 1837. Cousin Molly must have come to believe that her account was true. When she died in 1949 aged eighty-four she had stipulated in her Will that if he were to take up his inheritance, my brother must change his name and quarter her arms with his. The first bit was easy. The second was impossible. The College of Arms found she had no coat of arms. The myth of the Cornish Lyles being Scottish was exposed, mercifully after her death.

But she was half-Scottish, her mother being a genuine Dundas whose armorial bookplate is in some of the eighteenth-century books Cousin Molly left me. She left me all her books but nothing else. She was shocked by my becoming a Labour MP in 1945, which was clearly less respectable than the things scally-wag Samuel Lyle, and other Lyles, got up to with their tin mines. As the entail had been broken she could have left me, or at least my brother, a charming house with a little land called Franchis, on the road to the Lizard. It had a pretty wood behind it, through which ran a fast-moving stream with occasional fairy-tale water-falls breaking over and around mossy rocks. I dreamed by it as the sun was reflected in its splashes when we stayed at Franchis as children.

Instead she left Franchis to Jones, a rough Cornish farm-hand with a dark, threatening face and frightening manner, whom she had promoted to Farm Manager. Gradually she gave him control of her finances. Had she lived much longer she might have left Jones everything. Old women who have never married and live by themselves are often like that. Cousin Molly was alone after her mother died in 1933, aged ninety-one. I never much liked Jones. He was one of those Cornishmen, of whom there are too many, who sullenly and seriously regard all those not born Cornish as foreigners and I was a mere quarter-Cornish. I liked him still less when he was left Franchis.

Cousin Molly was short and rotund, nearly as wide as she was tall. She ate heroically. She began her breakfast with a large helping of porridge, sprinkled with salt in the Scottish way, of course, and surmounted with spoonfuls of Cornish clotted cream. She then ate a fair-sized steak with fried potatoes. Afterwards came slices of bacon, several eggs and quantities of toast and marmalade. Her appetite was good at lunch, too. But she had been up since seven working in her old granite-walled garden, warm even in winter, kept for flowers and fruit rather than vegetables. My brother has put a swimming-pool in it, which would have displeased her. However, she might grudgingly have admired the way he has resurrected the place, run down in her father's and her own time, establishing a model farm.

On the other hand, she might not. Cousin Molly, armed with a little learning procured in New Zealand from Great-Uncle Joseph, was violently opinionated. She was convinced she knew everything better than anyone else. She would make vehement statements such as, 'No good ever came from any -ism', and glaring at me, 'particularly socialism.' 'Not even Conservatism?' I once ventured. 'That's not a real word', she snapped. If I had known she would leave me nothing but her books I might have argued with her more strenuously.

She was strongly religious. No cards or newspapers were allowed in the house on Sundays before the war, though the *News of the World* sometimes strayed into the kitchen. On Sundays we walked a mile and a half to Cury Church. In the graveyard was the gruesome family vault: when it was opened to put in Cousin Molly, bones were protruding from the collapsed coffins. Or we walked three miles, anguish for me, to the little church built almost on the beach at Gunwalloe by shipwrecked sailors in thanks for their rescue. Above on the cliff was Poldhu, where a device originated that was to save many thousands of sailors' lives. From there Marconi sent the first radio message across the Atlantic. Occasionally we went to church in a pony-trap, which was fun when my cousin let me take the reins.

On Sunday evenings Cousin Molly would play hymns on a harmonium in the corner of the dining-room. As she was tone-deaf she played for religious not musical reasons. Bibles and prayer-books were always to hand, as were simple aphorisms from them. She told me that on the ship from New Zealand she was deeply worried at her sinfulness in being full of fury and vindictiveness. She explained to a bishop on board why. He said, 'My dear, don't you know that in the Bible there is such a thing as righteous anger?' She never explained to me why venom had entered her soul, but I found out later. When her father died, his sister, my Great-Aunt Mary, declared that her niece was illegitimate and therefore not entitled to Bonython. Great-Aunt Mary wanted Bonython to go to her favourite, Uncle John, my father's younger brother. Mary would be next in line to Great-Uncle Joseph if his daughter could be proved illegitimate. Mary, who had dissipated her own inheritance in ostentatious arrogance, had some of the optimistic skullduggery of the old tin miners in her. Answering the false charges delayed Cousin Molly's departure from New Zealand several years.

I loved Bonython, as did my father, his three brothers and his sister and Great-Uncle Joseph and his sisters when they were young in the 1870s and 1880s. In the holidays they would produce an oleographed magazine called *Buzzings from Bonython*, to be read by those relations, friends and neighbours who could be persuaded to pay up. It was full of jokes, rhymes and accounts of shooting, hunting (my Great-Grandfather Lyle was MFH of the undistinguished Cury Hunt, which still exists), and of drawings, some original and others copied from magazines like *Punch* (my father had a talent for drawing and painting water-colours and his mother painted exact and beautiful bird pictures).

I still think of Bonython as my anchor home, far more so than the other houses I have lived in, though I have not been there much in the last thirty-five years. Glorious places such as Coverack, Cadgwith, Kynance, Mullion, St Just-in-Roseland, Marazion, Helford, Gweek, were all within easy reach. There was once a king of Gweek. I used to wonder about him as I bicycled down the great sweeping road, glimpsing the sea through the tall trees on the slopes, to the centre of his kingdom at the bottom of the hill. Struggling on the way up, I would think what a fool I had been to be deluded by carefree joy as I coasted speedily down. I have never liked physical effort.

In my first car, costing £10 second-hand, I nearly killed myself whirling down to Gweek. I was reading a letter while holding the steering-wheel and absent-mindedly did not notice I was leaving the road. It was a letter from a girl which distracted me because it began with 'Darling' and ended 'With all my love'. I have always been absent-minded. In those days it was ascribed to the inconsiderateness of youth. Now it is taken as a sign of early senility. Yet it is precisely the same defect as I have endured all my life.

My first memories of Bonython are of the quarter of a mile dark drive, dominated by tall, unkempt trees with untended hydrangea bushes at their feet blooming plentifully in the gloom, and surrounded by daffodils in the spring, which also flourished despite the scarcity of light. Self-seeding high trees had crept close to the house during decades of neglect, destroying a tennis-court in their passage, and resounding with the cawing of rooks in the evening. At the sides and back of the house there was no view and the rooms were dim.

The back of the house was very old, dating from the fourteenth or fifteenth century, perhaps earlier. A large stone-flagged kitchen, where the farm-hands ate, had a huge pump from which exceptionally pure water flowed when the long, heavy handle was vigorously manipulated. There was no electric light until the 1930s when an uncertain generator was installed. We went to bed as children with candles, which threw sinister, flickering shadows on the walls. Though the granite façade of the house was Georgian, early eighteenth century, plain but light and pleasing with nearly a touch of elegance, there simply had to be ghosts.

19

One sunny Sunday I was left lying on my back in a room at the front, still trying to get rid of my tubercular glands, when everyone else went to church in my father's car. A little earlier than I expected I heard the crunch of wheels as they rode over the deep layer of tiny pebbles from Gunwalloe beach which covered the drive and the square in front of the house. I heard the wheels pass round to the back of the house. I waited expectantly for the churchgoers to come in, but there was silence. Twenty minutes afterwards I heard another set of wheels move over the pebbles and disappear round the back.

'I thought I heard you come some time ago,' I said to my father. 'Did you go out again by the back drive?'

My father asked me what I had heard. Gravely he enquired from the kitchen whether a van or car had gone to the back door or past it and was told nothing had. He was silent, perhaps afraid of frightening me. Then he said, 'You may have heard the ghost carriage. Lots of people have. It can come any time of the day, and goes round to the stables at the back. Sometimes they hear the jingling of the horses being unharnessed.'

Seeing my pleased alarm he went on, 'It could be some trick of the atmosphere. The wind in the right direction lifts the sound of a vehicle in the dip of the Lizard road and brings it to the house. But it has happened too often, so I don't think it's that.'

Nor did I. The Lizard road was three-quarters of a mile away below the hill, sloping down from the front of the house. You could listen outside the front door for days and not hear the sound of traffic, even in mid-August when the tourists drove by.

Cousin Molly steadfastly pooh-poohed any talk of ghosts. She did not want servants or visitors frightened. Once I woke to see a strangely dressed woman gliding towards me and was terrified – too terrifed to move until she vanished, and too terrified to say anything about it in the morning for fear of Cousin Molly's anger.

One breakfast the solid-looking companion my cousin had at the time said, 'Miss Lyle, I had an extraordinary experience last night. I woke up and saw a woman with a beautiful face dressed like a nun coming towards me. I lit my candle and it disappeared. Are there ghosts in the house?'

'Nonsense woman,' my cousin said angrily. 'You're imagining things. Please don't talk in such a silly way.'

She stroked her little grey moustache rapidly, which she did whenever she was annoyed and trying to control herself. I said nothing. Shortly afterwards the companion departed for ever. She too looked angry.

Perhaps it was our imagination, or in my case a nightmare brought on by apprehension; or perhaps Cousin Molly was so put out because she had seen the same ghost as we had and was determined to censor all news of it. The coming of electric light seems to have ended the ghostly era, if ever there was one. Subsequently there were noises in the night, but they were much more likely to have been rats running between the wide double walls than poltergeists.

I grew fond of Cousin Molly. When I was at Oxford I spent large slices of my holidays with her and would bring friends to stay, treating the house as my home as she clearly wished. We would read together or talk animatedly, delicately stepping around topics which might cause friction. She was not a fool, though she could be foolish. Her pretensions about her Scottish descent harmed no one and gave her satisfaction. In the best Victorian tradition she tried to be a good Christian. She was as generous and hospitable as she could be within her diminishing means, which she would try to replenish not by putting up rents, as she should have done, but by selling more bits of the property at knock-down prices to people who took advantage of her.

At Bonython I made my first tentative attempt to form an attachment with a girl. She was the vicar's daughter, slight and pallidly pretty. The vicar was suspicious of my intentions. He need not have been. We walked by the sea, mostly in the rain, my clumsy endearments competing unsuccessfully with the wind and the wet and the noise of the waves. Timidly she would let me hold her cold, damp hand which I would manoeuvre into my mackintosh pocket and squeeze, getting no more than a tiny, hesitating response, as was proper from a vicar's daughter. But it was enough to give me plenty to think about at eighteen. I was less advanced than my son Pericles, who began his adventures with girls at sixteen, or maybe earlier.

The Harvey in my father's name came in zigzag fashion. William Wyatt (b. 1701) was the son of John Wyatt (b. 1675), who owned and farmed land at Weeford in Staffordshire like his ancestors for hundreds of years before him. William married Mary Harvey. One of William's younger brothers was Benjamin, founder of the great Wyatt architectural dynasty. Benjamin's eldest son, another William, was an architect who in the 1750s helped his father build the first important Wyatt buildings (Egginton Hall in Derbyshire and Swinfen Hall near Weeford). Benjamin's son William married his first cousin, Sarah, daughter of his uncle William. Sarah's third son was called Robert Harvey, after his grandmother. In turn Robert Harvey married his first cousin, Harriet Wyatt, daughter of Samuel Wyatt, Sarah's brother, and granddaughter of the William born in 1701. Thereafter the eldest sons of this branch down to my father were given Harvey as one of their names.

This Wyatt habit of marrying first cousins (thirteen did) or cousins (twenty-one did) kept the architectural, painting, sculpting, stained glassmaking, manufacturing and inventing genes going for nearly two hundred years. It also means a wet towel around the head is needed when one examines the family tree. My father was descended from or closely related to all the notable Wyatts, numerous ways up and sideways. There they were in rows.

John (b. 1700) invented the spinning-jenny and spun the first thread of cotton yarn ever produced by mechanical means twenty-five years before Arkwright (for proof, go to the City Library at Birmingham) but did not have the money or business sense to develop it. Among other devices he did perfect was a compound lever weighing-machine, which is still used with modifications by British Rail. He was the first to design a suspension bridge. When imprisoned for debt in 1740 and 1744 he occupied himself by making gadgets to ease the work-load on the warders, who reciprocated by treating him with great consideration.

Job (b. 1719), youngest of the seven sons of our common ancestor John, in 1760 patented his invention for the mechanical cutting of screws, which was the earliest recorded application of machine tools to manufacturing. Charles (b. 1750) was responsible for a new type of cement: stucco, of the kind now on many houses in London and elsewhere. Wyatts built factories and canals across England, developed slate quarries and great estates. Wyatts were there at the start of the Industrial Revolution; were prime movers in its development, and profited by or went bankrupt because of it.

And glittering in their glory were the architects. Samuel, James, Sir Jeffry (Wyatville), Benjamin Dean, Lewis, Thomas Henry, Sir Matthew Digby: twenty-eight in all, the last one of any merit dying in 1920, though his son, Humphrey, who died in 1946, might have resented that statement. There were at least two remarkable sculptors. Matthew Cotes (b. 1777), James's third son, was a good painter as well as a sculptor (see the bronze equestrian statue of George III at the start of Pall Mall); Richard James (b. 1795) was an assistant of Canova and his *Musidora* is at Chatsworth. Once, on a visit to Chatsworth, the Queen remarked, slightly puzzled, 'It so reminds me of Windsor.' Not so surprising. Sir Jeffry Wyatville, with George IV as his friendly and instructing partner, built most of Windsor Castle as it now is, and all that you can see on the skyline, and a great part of the present Chatsworth, including the library and staterooms, is his.

The purpose of referring to all these Wyatts, apart from showing off and establishing some more of my origins, is to introduce an astonishing fact. My father hardly ever mentioned them, and if he did so, it was glancingly and depreciatingly. It was not until the 1950s that I began to understand and learn who they all were. It was long after I became an MP that I discovered that I was not the first Weeford Wyatt to be in the House of Commons. Charles (1758–1819), eldest brother of the original Robert Harvey Wyatt, became MP for Sudbury after a military career in the East India Company. When Lord Wellesley, Governor-General, wanted in 1798 a grand new Government House to impress the maharajas, Charles casually tossed one off for him in Calcutta, somewhat in the manner of Kedleston in Derbyshire. It is still in use, the finest eighteenth-century building in India. Charles could have been one of the best Wyatt architects but he made too much money in India to bother.

In the nineteenth century the Wyatt family got the Cousin

23

Molly bug. It was probably Horace Walpole's fault. He fell in love with the Pantheon in Oxford Street, the first major building of James Wyatt. Walpole thought it 'the most beautiful edifice in England'. He could not believe that its brilliant twenty-five-year-old creator, despite the fact that James's brothers were already well-known architects, could have leaped so suddenly into such genius from farming stock. There must be hereditary artistic talent. So in July 1772 Walpole wrote to James, asking him whether he were descended from Sir Thomas Wyatt, the celebrated Tudor poet about whom he was writing a book.

James very properly replied: 'The knowledge I have of my family is derived from oral traditions only, and goes no farther back than my great-grandfather, who, as I have been told, was a farmer in Staffordshire where I myself was born, whether therefore we are descendants of Sir Thomas Wyatt or not is a subject I am not in the least acquainted with. . . .' If James had troubled to look in the Parish Register at Weeford Church, he could have been more informative. He would have found there his great-great-great-great-great-grandfather Humphrey, born in 1540, whose family held a front pew in the church.

But he would not have found any connection with Sir Thomas Wyatt. It is faintly possible that there may have been a link centuries before. The Thomas Wyatts went to Kent in the fifteenth century from Yorkshire, which I suppose was not far from Staffordshire, despite the difficulties of travel. Perhaps once they were all one family, but the probabilities are against it.

But Horace Walpole had started something. My nineteenth-century ancestors converted his innocent enquiry into the statement of an indisputable fact. They were encouraged by the strong similarities between the Kent Wyatt coat of arms and crest and those registered in 1780 by James Wyatt and his elder brother John (a Fellow of the Royal Society and the Founder of the Royal College of Surgeons). Thomas, Henry and Digby, the names of Kent Wyatt knights, became our family names, some members having two at once like Thomas Henry Wyatt, the prolific Victorian architect born in 1807. Drawings and copies of pictures of Sir Thomas Wyatt (described as after Holbein) and of his son Sir Thomas, whose mad rebellion against Bloody

Mary nearly cost Elizabeth I her head and her throne, appeared in our halls and dining-rooms.

Farmers, builders, architects were out. Aristocratic Wyatts were in. Crests and armorial bearings abounded. I have a school prize, Campbell's *Poems*, won by my grandfather at Harrow in 1850, on the cover of which he had, aged fifteen, his crest embossed in gold. My father always stamped his writing-paper with a large black crest. He would complacently repeat a story of how he visited a newly rich man who proudly pointed out a freshly painted coat of arms above the fireplace. 'Do you like them?' 'Yes,' my father replied. 'They're mine.' It was appropriate that my grandfather, bogus descendant of Sir Thomas Wyatt, should marry a Cornish Lyle, bogus member of a grand Scottish family.

Naturally I fell for all this rubbish about Sir Thomas Wyatt. I was spurred on by my sweet old Aunt Sis. She had a storehouse of verses extolling the glories of our imaginary Wyatt ancestors and would declaim with enthusiasm the younger Sir Thomas Wyatt's battlecry: 'No popery. No Spanish match. A Wyatt, a Wyatt!' It was all she had to keep up her morale, having much come down in the world. She married a handsome but dissolute physical training instructor and ended up living in a sordid little flat in Tavistock Square. She would have died with shock had she known the truth. However, she filled my youth, and beyond, with dreams of grandeur and hopes of becoming famous like the two Sir Thomas Wyatts, excluding serious interest in the accomplishments of my real family. Disillusionment did not set in until 1952 when I mentioned my alleged descent in a book. I heard that one of the true Kent Wyatts had complained crossly about it. I apologize to him. But it might have been more gracious of him to have acknowledged the relationship or to have expressed sorrow at the absence of it. None of *his* Wyatts did anything of merit after Sir Thomas Wyatt, the elder, became the first poet to write sonnets in English. After all, James Wyatt is buried in Poets' Corner at Westminster Abbey, which is more than Sir Thomas is. This rebuff to my pride set me off investigating my antecedents more thoroughly. The more I learned about them, the better I liked them.

My father was an excellent sportsman if not so good as his

younger brother John. When they were at Oxford they were both in the shooting team in a two-day match against Cambridge. My father was Captain of his side. On the first day his score broke the inter-University record. The next day his brother John broke my father's record. John was good at cricket and was the father of R. E. S. Wyatt who, as an amateur, scored more runs in first-class cricket than any other amateur except W. G. Grace, more centuries than any other amateurs except W. G. Grace and C. B. Fry, and took many wickets, even in Test Matches. Uncle John gave his son his initial coaching, supplemented by my father, who was a sound, medium-standard club player.

Uncle John was held up to us as the ultimate in slowness and laziness. We would watch fascinatedly at breakfast as he slowly ate his porridge. He would raise his spoon between long pauses, revolving the porridge in his mouth as many times as Mr Gladstone advocated chewing prior to swallowing (I think thirty-two times) before it went down his throat. According to one count I made, it took him twenty-five minutes to finish a plateful of porridge. Curiously he was a fast driver. I was thrilled when he drove me at sixty-five miles an hour along the Oxshott Road, a tremendous speed in those days. He was clever, and his interest in cars got him a job running motor journals for the Iliffe Group, but he was so lazy that he repeatedly failed to get the journals ready by publication date, losing them circulation and advertising. The exasperated management summoned him to a board meeting, at which his consistent dilatoriness and his future were the subjects. After a two-hour discussion the Chairman turned to him and said, 'Mr Wyatt, we are decided, then, to give you one more chance.' Uncle John was fast asleep and had been for most of the meeting.

After returning to the Bonython he loved to see Cousin Molly, who had overcome her resentment at Aunt Mary's attempt to bastardize her in his favour, he was found dead sitting by a gate-post at the end of the drive. That, in his fashion, represented his last words. They were more apposite than most people's.

I was frightened of my father. His entrance into a room clouded it. He despised me because I was no good at games and disliked most outdoor activities. He also thought me a coward.

He was right on both counts. But it was not cowardice alone which made me run away screaming when he tried to push me, aged seven or eight, into the six-foot waves as they broke on the Cornish beaches. Those Atlantic breakers hit scaringly hard and knocked you over; they were freezing cold, liked pieces of ice mashed in electric gadgets for iced drinks. I have always recoiled from cold baths and showers.

I saw my father, over half a century older than I, as a Jehovah-like figure descending from his pedestal of wrath to deal out punishments and disapproval. When I was nine he caught me running about naked, innocent of malice, at the top of the house. 'Disgusting,' he cried, as he hauled me over his knee and thrashed me. Yet he would think nothing of wandering naked round the swimming-pool he built in the vegetable garden as an attraction to the parents. I must have inherited this characteristic, as I prefer to swim and sunbathe with nothing on, enjoying the freedom of being without clinging swimming-shorts and the warmth of the sun all over me.

In my father's presence I was too full of awe to do anything but make a fool of myself. One evening, when my mother was out to dinner, my brother and I were told that as a treat we were to have dinner with my father. He sat at the head of an old, polished oak refectory table with the grooves of age in it. On it were two heavy candelabra made by Matthew Boulton – a friend and associate of his Wyatt contemporaries – with candles alight. This, I thought, must be like sitting on the right hand of God, an awesome experience to which my father would refer when he taught us Scripture at the school. Actually I was on his left and my brother was on his right but the sensation was the same. As the meal progressed, my father turned to me.

'What did you do today, Woodrow?'

I mumbled incoherently about reading or walking. My reply evoked no critical response so I plunged on.

'What did you do today, Daddy?'

'I played golf with Mr Gibson.'

The Reverend Mackenzie Gibson was the elderly and very dignified curate. I had never seen him dressed other than in his surplice and vestments in church. My next question was inevitable.

'What did Mr Gibson wear to play golf in?'

'Oh, bloomers of some sort,' my father said, giving no significance to his answer. In his Victorian speech, bloomers were a familiar plus-four style garment worn by men, fastening under the knees and tucked into long stockings. To us they could mean only one thing: the voluminous, brightly coloured red or blue knickers worn by housemaids in the 1920s which flew filled with wind curving upwards and downwards on the washing-line, occasionally heeling right over, emanating a hint of the naughtiness and mystery of sex. The idea of Mr Gibson striding across the golf-course arrayed in gaudy knickers with nothing on top of them and nothing beneath them till his socks and shoes was funnier than anything in Laurel and Hardy. The more I tried not to laugh, the more the spluttering and giggling rose in me, till they became unbearable, and I burst out hysterically.

'Whatever's the matter with you, boy?'

My fear of my father was such that I could not possibly tell him. Eventually and desperately I stammered, 'Robert's-spilt-the-salt,' which he had not.

'You're a liar,' my father said.

He frequently called me that and I would be silent in terror. This time nothing could stop the maniac laughter which possessed me. Tears streamed down. Whenever I briefly stopped my laughing by trying to think of something else, the vision of Mr Gibson brandishing a golf-club, with a bright red or blue pair of knickers flowing round his bottom as he bent down to take aim, came back to me. I was off again.

'You're a very silly little boy,' my father said unsmilingly. 'You're too young to stay up to dinner. Go to bed.'

My silliness made meals with my father hazardous. One morning, again out of term, my father at breakfast asked the kind of blanket question I dreaded.

'What are you going to do today, Woodrow?'

I was day-dreaming about whether it were possible to talk through a mouthful of food. What a moment to choose. Carefully I filled my mouth up with runny porridge and milk. With what I hoped to be precision I began to answer him. A milky, porridgy mess spurted across the table and down my front. What I did that day was to spend it alone in my room without books.

28

My father, oddly for a schoolmaster, was suspicious of my non-stop reading in bed, in the backs of cars when we were supposed to be admiring the view, in corners, on the stairs. Depriving me of books, he judged incorrectly, as he did not appreciate the depth of my physical cowardice, would be a more effective punishment than the thrashings he administered more often to my brother than to me. My brother, nevertheless, got on with my father much better than I did. He was tolerant of the thrashings he received, believing they were prompted by my mother's wish to prove that no boy was worse treated at the school than her elder son.

As I thought my father omniscient as well as omnipotent I was particularly broken when he was unfair, which unintentionally he could be. There was a potting-shed at a distant corner of the garden with dirt-grimed windows and interesting objects inside, made more mysterious by the dim light. Among them was a large container with tar in it. When I was about five, my brother thought it would be amusing to spatter me with it from head to foot. I readily concurred. Happily I trotted off down the garden and met my father.

'What have you been doing to yourself?'

'I didn't do it, Robert did it.'

Robert, not far behind, was interrogated. For once he let me down and denied his part in the tarring. For being a liar I was severely punished. How could my all-knowing father, I wailed inside, not recognize the difference between when I was lying and telling the truth? To my fear was added the conviction that he was unjust, a conviction that persisted with me.

My father may not have known it but cribbing was prevalent at school. Boys not allowed out to play at the end of the day until they had finished the problems set them, whispered the answers to each other or surreptitiously passed around written solutions to them. I could never manage mathematics. Seeing I was stuck hopelessly with a difficult question, a friendly boy gave me the correct answer. Relieved, I took my exercise-book to my father. It seemed a passport to freedom.

'How did you work this out?'

Fumblingly and footlingly I tried to explain.

'You have cheated,' my father thundered.

I was in the greatest disgrace I had been in so far, and publicly. The stains of my guilt remained. Two months later we were at Bonython. My father had gone out to play golf for the afternoon. I played cribbage with Great-Aunt Lucy, then in her eighties. When my father returned he asked if she had enjoyed the game.

'Very much,' my great-aunt said. 'Woodrow is a very nice companion to play with.'

My father stood stationary in the middle of the room. He looked hard at me and at her. Slowly and loudly he asked, 'Did he cheat?'

The shame is still with me.

My father was reputed to be very clever. My mother thought so. Parents thought so. Others in the family thought so. The phrase 'double first' was widely used about him. A man called Walter Scott-Elliott first put a doubt in my mind.

Scott-Elliott was my brother's godfather and quite rich. In 1977 he and his wife were murdered by their butler, who carried their bodies around Scotland in the boot of their car. Walter Scott-Elliott was senile at the time and his wife's judgement was not at its peak. My brother had dinner with them in London not long before they were murdered. He remarked to Mrs Scott-Elliott on the strange behaviour of their new butler. Worried, he asked if she intended to keep him. 'Oh yes,' she said. 'He is the best butler we've had for a very long time.'

Walter Scott-Elliott was some years younger than my father, who when at Oxford coached him during the holidays in Scotland. After the Second World War Scott-Elliott, by now a grave and elderly person with decided views on the sanctity of property including his own, eccentrically became Labour MP for Accrington. He fitted into the Parliamentary Labour Party distinctly less well than I did. One evening I was sitting with him at one of those appalling charity dinner-dances, neither of us caring to dance, when he said, 'Your father was a kind and amiable man. He was a very good shot.' I liked him very much, but I'm afraid he was rather stupid.'

I sat up with a jerk at this sensational news. Was nothing in my life as it had originally seemed? The Lyles were not Scottish, we were not descended from Sir Thomas Wyatt, and now my father, generally admired for his brains, was 'rather stupid'. For a long while I disbelieved this unwelcome information. A few years ago I decided to settle the matter and wrote to the Oxford University Archives, enquiring about my father's scholastic record. That efficient organization supplied extensive details of his examination performances of almost a hundred years before.

The central point was clear. My father had taken four years to scrape a pass degree, the lowest you could get without failing altogether. After the statutory years of waiting he was able to convert his lucky BA into an MA. Thereafter he always put the initials after his name. Presumably he went into schoolmastering because he would have been unable to pass examinations for any other profession, although he might have made a good architect with his skill at drawing and perspective and eye for how things should look.

I am sure he was full of kindness, but the distance between us clogged its passage to me. 'Come quickly and listen to this on the wireless,' he called to me and a friend playing draughts. Foolishly I insisted on our carrying the board, pieces and table into his study. By the time we got there the last moments of 'Changing Guard at Buckingham Palace' were floating away, draughtsmen were falling all over the floor, and my father was thoroughly annoyed. 'Confound you! Why did you have to bring all that in here? You've missed it all now, anyway.' Another disaster.

My father adored my mother, twenty-four years younger than he was. When he was away on one of his shooting or fishing expeditions he wrote her sentimental letters interspersed with verses intended to be in the manner of Edward Lear. He tunelessly sang jingles –

> Oh dear what can the matter be,
> Poor dear Mr Chatterjee
> Is stuck up in the apple-tree.

– as he shaved with his cut-throat razor, carefully sharpening it on a long brown leather strop when he had finished. Another favourite he sang was Lear's 'The Owl and the Pussycat'. I caught this idiosyncrasy from him and have never got rid of it.

Perhaps my father's fondness for this type of singing was the

31

reason that, early one morning, I found a funny little man with big ears standing in the bathroom. He told me he was on a walk to Brighton and had stopped by for the night. His name was Charlie Coburn. He gave the world those glorious songs, 'Two Lovely Black Eyes' and 'The Man Who Broke the Bank at Monte Carlo'. Actually his name was not Coburn at all, it was McCallum. His family, who were friends of my father's, made him change his name when he embarrassed them by going on the music-halls. His son, a Conservative MP called Sir Duncan McCallum, was in the Commons with me. He never seemed pleased to see me and less so when I asked him, sitting among Tory MPs in the Smoking Room, for anecdotes about his father. He had little sense else he would have been proud of him.

My father's approach to politics was simple. He detested Socialists. The local MP was Sir Archibald Boyd-Carpenter. When I was twelve a public meeting was arranged for him in the school gymnasium. At the last moment Sir Archibald could not come but sent his son John, President of the Oxford Union and now Lord Boyd-Carpenter. He used to be known as Spring Heel Jack because of his habit of going up and down on his heels as he spoke. He made a speech highly charged with patriotism about the Empire, and the need for more destroyers and battleships, elevating and lowering himself as he made his rollicking points. I have often told him that his speech started me towards socialism, which he accepts with good humour. However, it was not his speech but my father's which prompted my first tentative political thoughts.

'It is confounded cheek of the Socialists,' he shouted vigorously, 'to think they're fit to govern the country. They are traitors and they haven't even got any money.'

If my father disapproved of people so strongly, there must be some good in them. And we had no money either.

'Confound' was one of my father's stock words. Whenever he ran into another car, in his heavy old Rover with the spare petrol tank on the wide running-board, as he did on a rainy day in Exeter, he would lean out of the window and bellow, 'Confound you, Sir, can't you learn to drive?' The other driver always was confounded by this angry roar, despite the damage usually being my father's fault.

'Confound you, Sir, get out of the way,' he cried, after hitting his ball ferociously off the fairway from the tee towards someone who thought he was taking a harmless country walk but was instead in danger of serious injury.

My father wore braces when he played golf. They were not ordinary, fixed, unyielding braces constricting his movements as he swung a club but a construction of his own design, suspended on an intricate system of pulleys so that the equipment swayed smoothly with the body without troubling the wearer. Before he put on a coat or a cardigan they were a joy to watch. He had devised similar machinery for a large touring bicycle he used for travels on the Continent before the First World War. The great saddle hung on springs. I used to climb on to it in an outhouse where it was kept in honoured retirement. It was very comfortable.

My father was prone to petty economies. He drank beer only at lunch on Sundays and hardly ever drank whisky or port. There was wine at Christmas and, bizarrely, cherry brandy, of which we were blissfully allowed a tiny glass when quite small. My father was very good at Christmas, decorating every picture with berried holly from the garden, hanging coloured streamers and inserting threepenny and sixpenny bits into the pudding (the making of it began ceremonially in September). He unbent to play charades and led sessions of consequences.

He wrote with pencil-stubs the length of a thumbnail. It was a puzzle how he accumulated so many. His unimportant correspondence was written on both sides of opened-up, used envelopes from which he had extracted the letters. When he went for walks he returned with screws, bolts or pieces of iron he had found by the wayside in case they came in useful.

One economy caused me torment. He hated buying new golf-balls. A short hole on the Gunwalloe course crossed Dollar Cove on its brief journey from tee to green. Many golfers mishit their balls into the cove, and a high proportion gave up the search for their lost balls among the rocks and stones. My brother and I were deputed to find them. If there were not a tally of four or five by the end of an afternoon, my father would look black. I loathed scrambling among the rocks and peering under them for golf-balls. My score was repeatedly below par.

33

'You're too lazy,' my father would say in his disappointment. He harped on my laziness, which was acute, especially in things physical like gardening or walking. It was to my laziness that my father attributed my inability to read the scoreboard at the Oval where I had been taken by my governess to watch my cousin play. Nor did he apologize when an oculist reported that the vision in my left eye was bad and in my right eye very bad. I have worn spectacles ever since and lost all but 2 per cent of the already poor sight of my right eye as a consequence of a motor accident.

My father correctly attacked me for my laziness at school work, too, convinced, incorrectly, that I could win a scholarship if I tried. Before he went into hospital where he died, when I was thirteen going on fourteen, he told Mr Bull, the friend who took over in his absence, that he was contemplating beating me into working harder. He recommended this course to his friend, who, though well-named for the task, thankfully did not follow it.

I assume my father recognized his own laziness in me. School began at nine and ended at three-thirty. The holidays were long. My father did little that taxed his brain in his acres of spare time. His bookcases were stacked with trash, apart from a few standard classics and *The Hundred Best Books*, and I am not sure he read those. He read extensively detective stories, being an early fan of Agatha Christie's *Murder of Roger Ackroyd*, and undemanding fiction placed on an old music-reading stand with brass pegs to hold the pages in position. I still have the cast-iron base, but the essential top has been lost during my many moves. I am sorry. Now I am growing more like my father I should like to use it.

I was frequently press-ganged into standing behind his arm-chair and stroking his bald head by the hour as he read or did the crossword. It was tiring but I came to map out all the mottled age marks on that round, brown surface. He enjoyed being stroked. When very small I would be told on many mornings to join my parents in the four-poster bed they slept in. My mother and I took turns to stroke my father's back. It had pink, black, brown and other coloured moles and bumps on it. In church it was my function to stroke his hand during the sermon, which meant that I had to stay awake while he half dozed in a sensual heaven more of the Muslim than the Christian kind.

One of my godfathers was a Muslim. This was never explained to me. He was Lord Headley, who had something to do with railways and was involved with building the Woking Mosque. I still have the christening-mug he gave me. It is very small. When I was born my mother wrote to President Woodrow Wilson asking him to be my godfather. He was told that, born on American Independence Day, I had been named after him. Surprisingly this idiotic letter brought a long reply from the President. He felt that at such a long distance he could not adequately perform the important duties of a godfather. He also mentioned some of his current responsibilities to which he had to devote considerable attention, such as, no doubt, the war against Germany and his Fourteen Points.

My mother had confidently expected a girl, to be named Diana. She lost interest when she found she had another boy. The choice of name was left to her elder sister, Aunt Annie, a turbulent lady who wore false blonde curls. When she was drunk a curl or two would slowly detach and fall between us as we sat together on the sofa. I would wait for this, partly hoping it would happen and partly that it would not. 'You've dropped a curl, Aunt Annie' was not a statement to be made with poise by a boy of seven to an intimidating lady who seemed older than the Tower of London.

It would be untrue to say that my fear of my father made me an unhappy child. I had ways of dodging my father. He could be very pleasant, as he was when he drove me over to Horsham to see his nephew, my hero, play for Warwickshire against Sussex, or when he took us mackerel fishing off the Cornish coast or rowing on the Helford estuary. He was an accomplished oarsman like his father, who stroked the Trinity crew to Head of the River and whose oar hung emblazoned with the names of the crew in the dining-room. Once when a violent squall hit us it was my father's strenuous, expert rowing that saved our lives. In retrospect I see I owe a lot to him. Unintentionally he made me question authority and its conventionally traditional assumptions. His Victorian values of truth and honesty and his Scripture readings made their mark, and they still

35

act as a brake when I am tempted to do something he would think dishonourable. His chaotically chosen collection of books sharpened my curiosity. Despite his own laziness, he instilled in me a horror of that vice. This does not prevent me from being lazy, but I am filled with guilt by a wasted hour if I cannot justify it as earned and needed recreation. Despite my nervousness of his all-pervasiveness, which began in the bathroom before breakfast, augmented by the smell of St Julien tobacco he smoked after breakfast coming through the door as he sat in his lavatory (I was not allowed to use it), I had a happy childhood. Having a father not as other fathers is stimulating. Osbert Sitwell, who was kind to me, asked me after the war, 'Have you killed your father yet?' I knew exactly what he meant. It took him a quantity of writing to kill his. I do not think either of us could extinguish the hovering shadow, however much we wrote.

My mother's maiden name was Ethel Morgan. Her father was an indigent tea merchant in Cardiff. His antecedents were obscure: his family came from around Tredegar. He died long before I was born. His wife died after the birth of their youngest son (when my mother was about ten). My other grandfather died at fifty-one in 1886, his widow dying of a broken heart within a year, so I have no notion of what having grandparents is like.

Aunt Annie lived for nothing but pleasure and cared about no one. The responsibility for managing the household fell on my tiny mother, whose tigress spirit was equal to it. Her eldest brother, Arthur, never forgot it. His gratitude to her stayed till his death, and for a crucial period I was a beneficiary of it.

My mother was pretty. Blue eyes, fair hair and delicate, light, Welsh colouring shine out of a pastel portrait of her. When, dressed for a dinner party, she leaned over me in bed to kiss me good night, she was a cloud of loveliness. She had an eagerness for life which won her less than a fair reward. She met my father because he was her elder sister's brother-in-law. 'I hated him when I first met him. I wouldn't speak to him, he was so old.'

The more she turned from him, the more my father wanted this strange, almost untutored and self-taught fairy. She met few young men and when she accepted him she did not love him.

The marriage was made in heaven. She worshipped him as the kindest, most considerate and cleverest man she ever knew. She saw in him the wonderful father she had never had. He never said a cross word to her except when she bought some curtains he did not like. Once when washing I said, 'Mummy is very silly.' My father rushed across the bathroom and gave my head so heavy a clout that I fell down. 'Never say that again about your mother.' I did not when he was there.

My mother's marriage lasted eighteen years, then her happiness was gone. She could never consider marrying any other man; it would have been an inconceivable insult to my father. Any suggestion from me that there might have been flaws in his perfection was treated as treachery. In March 1965 I wrote a newspaper article in a series in which the contributors described the impact their fathers had made on them. It was one of my major blunders. In my article I made a few mild jokes about my father, referred to my awe of him, and compared his Victorian virtues favourably with those of Mr Attlee. Most people would have thought my father came out well, but not my mother. She altered her Will. Instead of leaving me half of everything, including my father's furniture, possessions and other items, she left the lot to my brother. True, arteriosclerosis was already advancing on her brain and she soon had to go to a nursing home as loss of memory attacked her. If she had lingered longer with her senses intact it is possible she would have reinstated me. She enjoyed changing her Will and its permutations and did it a number of times. However, I have no complaint of my brother, who became High Sheriff of Cornwall (that would have delighted Cousin Molly), and voluntarily settled some of my mother's money on my children, besides helping me on several occasions.

My mother was worth a staff of five at the school. She organized the boarders, the lunch for which the day boys stayed, and the rest of the meals. She recruited the young maids from Wales, trained and supervised them. She cooked efficiently and ensured that the cooks we had were good. (You could get a good cook for £50 a year before the war: I was fond of one called Rowntree whose speciality was a thick tapioca pudding with white blobs in it which we called Rowntree's Clear Gums, a popular sweet of the period.) My mother taught the bottom form far better than any qualified teacher, knowing how to help the boys along because her academic knowledge was not much greater than theirs. She read a book only once: it was *The Constant Nymph* and she was at it for weeks, to the concern of the household at this unwonted activity. The title, combined with my mother's enthusiasm, made me think it must be a kitchen-maid book. I waited till I was over sixty to try it and found it one of the best novels I ever read.

Most important, my mother conducted the business side of the school, which baffled or bored my father. It was she who badgered reluctant parents into paying their fees. She urged the raising of them whenever the market would stand it. She fought off creditors. Without her, my father would have foundered several times. When he died she installed a new headmaster, made him a partner and in a few years sold the school to him for a satisfactory sum, living in reasonable comfort on the proceeds for the rest of her life. My father had not thought of anything so mundane as an insurance policy with a pension fund and would not have been able to pay for it if he had. All the time she was keeping the school alive my mother gave my father the credit for it. To her he was the rightly undisputed head of the household.

My mother's manifold activities did not allow her time to look after us directly as she would have liked. We had governesses. Miss Winterbon was mine when I was four and a half. We had tea in the nursery at the top of the house when she arrived. She made me start with bread and butter before I ate a cake. (She had another rule: leave something on the plate for shipwrecked sailors. How they were to get it was never disclosed.) In a few months she had taught me to read fluently from *Reading Without Tears*, much better than the ludicrous methods invented by those pseudo-intellectuals who now increase the flow of illiterates leaving our schools. And there were no tears.

Miss Winterbon was my surrogate mother. She poured love over me and never punished me. She had a romantic background. Her parents lived in disused railway-carriages converted to living quarters at Blackwater in Essex. Opening and slamming the doors and blowing whistles was encouraged by her elderly parents, who understood children. Miss Winterbon's indulgences were thought bad for me by my father. He was annoyed that she would not make me eat cabbage, a vegetable I hated unless I could mash it up with shepherd's pie. I do that now and reject carrots, swedes, turnips, secure from my father's disapproval and hoping that Miss Winterbon is somewhere smiling on me.

Miss Winterbon would read and tell stories and give painless instruction limitlessly, never caring what my father said. He wanted her to go. She had an ally in my mother who was fond of her and saw that she made me happy. Eventually my father prevailed. Whether he was saving my soul or his pocket I do not know, but Miss Winterbon went. The most dreadful moment of my life was standing on the bridge of Claygate Station watching the dwindling flutter of her handkerchief as the train carried her away for ever. I sobbed for days. She was the last person for many years to whom I could talk freely and confide my doubts and hopes, and from whom I felt warmth.

I never had a conversation with my mother which was not superficial. Her love was real but demonstrated in an overly sentimental and mechanically gushing form. It jangled. We were not sympathetic. I was ashamed of my response to her and tried many times to make a genuine bond. Occasionally I felt a faint connection was almost there, but it faded before it meant anything. She never told me I had done anything well. Her comment on my becoming an MP in 1945 was that my father would have been shocked at my joining those dreadful Socialists, and her friends in Esher were not impressed either. My becoming Under-Secretary of State for War when I was thirty-two was received with silence, tinged with ridicule. Maybe her attitude was right but it was not maternal.

I disliked Esher. The people were not the kind who roused my imagination as the characters did in the books I read. There was nothing wrong with them, but their minds hardly soared in a way such as to draw out a young boy full of dreams of conquering the world. I heard no conversation above the commonplace, no sentiments above the ordinary. Esher was a cultural wasteland. It was too near London to be country, despite its common lands and woods, its large gardens and its fields,

39

which were continually ravaged for new houses. Behind us was a farm, full-blown when we were very young; its fields gradually disappearing one by one. Esher was too far from London to be metropolitan. It had nothing but a provincial, middle-class approach spread thick. There were a few Liberals about but they were shunned as dangerous allies of the Socialists.

Esher determined me to seek fame and the famous in a wider, more exciting world where people made witty remarks and great decisions. There was a large car used by the school and driven by the gardener. When my father was away in hospital, I would sit in the back and look disdainfully at the appalling people. There were exceptions. A middle-aged bachelor known as Hock from the initials of his name, H. O. Crowther, had a pleasant house, library and butler on The Green. He was harmlessly interested in the young and mad about cricket. He was no good at it, so he acted as Secretary of the Esher Cricket Club and went in last. He was a lifeline to me. So was a well-known journalist who had worked for Northcliffe. His name escapes me but not his advice on how to write a newspaper article.

My ambition to be someone was fed by the exploits of my cricketing cousin. He was coming to the peak of his renown as I was approaching my teens. I was probably as thrilled as he was when he made a century in his first Test Match, or when he was chosen to captain England at the Oval for the fifth Test against Australia in 1930 (J.B. Hobbs's last Test). Perhaps I was more thrilled: he was always a modest, phlegmatic man with little outward emotion.

His first English captaincy was a national sensation. In those days only an amateur could captain England. A. P. F. Chapman, the previous captain, a flashing but erratic batsman, too fond of drinking, was dropped. My cousin was the only amateur good enough to replace him. For days the Press attacked Chapman's replacement by my cousin. *The Times* had its customary portentous leading article humming and hawing before deploring the selection. The peccadilloes of Ramsay MacDonald's Labour Government were forgotten. My cousin was pursued everywhere by photographers and reporters. It was heady stuff.

The attacks on my cousin were so virulent and unfair that a reaction set in. When he came out to bat in his first Test against

Australia, with English wickets tumbling, the whole crowd stood and cheered him till he finished his slow and lonely journey to the crease and the bowler, the great Grimmett, started his run to bowl to him. It was possibly the most vociferous reception ever given to a batsman on his way to the wicket. Even my unflappable cousin was shaken. He told me his head was so buffeted by the roars of applause that his eyes were swimming. His nerve had gone as he faced the remaining five balls of Grimmett's over. The fifth ball missed his off-stump by a quarter of an inch and he nearly collapsed. He went on to score 64 and joined with Sutcliffe in a record sixth wicket partnership against Australia of 170 in two hours and thirty-five minutes.

With a cousin like that, the first route to fame I saw was as Captain of England. I played many great matches in my imagination, scoring fabulous winning centuries and taking the wickets of celebrated Australian batsmen. I spent many days throwing tennis-balls at walls, trying to play the correct stroke as they bounced back. Despairing of my Test potential as an overarm bowler I practised underarm breaks to emulate Simpson Hayward, who played for Worcestershire and England. I learned to bowl fairly straight overarm without doing anything significant with the ball, and I sometimes hit the ball correctly with my bat (my cousin once said he saw me execute a perfect cover drive, claiming he was not joking, which may be true as he is short on jokes). But, alas, I was never better than the lower end of mediocre. A poor eye, weak wrists, small hands, indifferent balance, do not make a cricketer, practise though he may for fifty years. Yet there are few sweeter moments than when that hard red ball comes fearsomely towards you and you find that you have hit it with the full face of a straight bat along the ground to the boundary. I would rather have scored a century against Australia at Lord's than anything I have done in my life.

My cousin was a liberating force, showing me the way out of the confined Esher atmosphere. He was unaware of his influence on me and probably still is. I never ceased to be proud of him and confess that, when a conversation turns to cricket, I still continue to introduce a reference to him. Even now it brings me gratifyingly respectful looks, particularly from men, and sometimes women, familiar with the halcyon cricket years of the twenties and thirties.

My mother's youngest brother, Trevor, lived with us. He travelled up and down daily to work at Kitcat and Aitken, the stockbrokers, where he had a lowly position and where my clever stepson, Nicholas Banszky, now works in far more elevated style. Feckless and looking a little like the Prince of Wales, Uncle Trevor never made it. He was an early casualty of the Slump, being considered not bright enough to keep on. Whatever his commercial ineptitude he was a bright light to us as children. He had been a sub-lieutenant in submarines in the war and told highly coloured stories about it. He did not earn much but generously gave us each sixpence a week pocket-money. Money was not plentiful in our house. Without his aid I should not have been able to buy delicious slabs of liquorice called Black Jacks at a ha'penny a time and pink aniseed balls which changed to white as you sucked them. My gratitude to him has not dimmed.

It was my mother's eldest brother, Arthur, who dished out real money. On his visits he would hand over ten shillings or pound notes, staggering sums to small boys in the twenties. He also helped my father in his periodic financial crises, swallowing the general belief in my father's academic genius. He stepped in when my father's youngest brother Horace suddenly demanded back the money he had put into the school; this, though my father had used his own money to get Horace through Oxford after their father's early death. Nothing divides a family more than money.

My Uncle Arthur was short and plump with a large head and stubby legs. He lay on his back on a sofa and waved them in the air when in a merry mood, to the amazement of my brother and myself who could not believe an elderly man could behave so childishly. Children's views of age are elongated. Anyone over thirty is immensely old. Uncle Arthur was barely forty at the time. When my father died he acted as my guardian.

# CHAPTER II

———— ❃ ————

# The Headmaster
# Dislikes Me

IT HAD BEEN INTENDED, for what reason I do not know, that my brother and I should go to Marlborough. My brother failed the Common Entrance. It was not his fault; his work had been dislocated by another attack of tubercular glands. During the critical preparatory period he had an operation and was laid up for some weeks.

What was to be done? Opposite us lived a Mrs Foot. Her son, Stephen Foot, was a housemaster at Eastbourne College. A florid, voluble man, a bit like a motor-car salesman, he set out to persuade my father and mother that Eastbourne was the place. He guaranteed there would be no problem over the entrance examination. Mr Box, the solemn, high-collared tubercular specialist, whose cool, clean, strong hands we felt too often pressing on our stomachs and necks searching for swollen glands, concurred. Eastbourne was a very healthy town, he declared. Sea air should finally clear up the tubercular trouble.

When my turn came I joined my brother, now a senior boy, in September of the year my father died.

'Take your hands out of your pockets,' an unpleasant-looking boy shouted when I had been there a few minutes.

'Why?'

'Because you're only a first termer and you're not allowed to put your hands in your pockets till your second term.'

There were a number of similarly silly rules.

That evening after house prayers I was taken aside by the same boy and given a severe warning. I had looked towards the senior boys during prayers. This was strictly forbidden to me in my chrysalis stage.

'Where did your father go to school?'

'Repton, and his father went to Harrow, and now I'm here. We're going downhill.'

Not a tactful reply, as I was speedily made aware.

Eastbourne was founded in 1867. It was created in imitation of the more famous schools. It had all the trimmings: fagging; beatings by house and school prefects; a ludicrous school song in Latin; Big School; a Victorian chapel; cloisters; a tower; petty, 'traditional' restrictions which were lifted seriatim at the end of the first and second years; compulsory watching of first team matches. Almost anything which could be borrowed from some well-established school was put into ours, so we were an accumulation of the worst from everywhere. We wore straw boaters, stiff white collars, dark coats and blue ties.

'Never forget how much you hated being here,' I wrote in gigantic letters on every page of a diary for a complete term. I have kept that pledge. My initial dislike was sparked by simple snobbishness. Who had ever heard of Eastbourne? If you must be sent to a public school, why not to a decent one? The fees at Eastbourne were no cheaper. A Tory MP, Malcolm Bullock, must have shared my attitude. He married a daughter of the Earl of Derby and left Eastbourne out of his *Who's Who* entry. I never went as far as that.

The Headmaster, G. V. Carey, forbade all contact with girls at Eastbourne's numerous girls' schools. Girls were so abhorred that no school plays were permitted. Some boys might have had to act the part of girls. Hair-oil was publicly denounced in Big School. 'You are not imitation men, as they pretend at some schools. You are boys and will behave as such.' At Eastbourne during the term I used hair-oil. I never used it in the holidays and nor have I done so since.

Alcoholic drinks were prohibited, even if you were out with your parents or friends in an hotel. There was a boy, or young man, of eighteen and a half, a school prefect. Though two and a half years older than I, he was friendly to me, as we were in the Classical Sixth together. In his last term he was reported to the Headmaster by a miserable prep school master who had seen him in the Grand Hotel having a glass of sherry with friends who had come to take him out. The whole school was summoned to Big School to hear his public humiliation by the Headmaster. The evils of drinking, the betrayal of trust as a school prefect, the disgracing of the school's name, nothing that could be dredged from a hypocritical and sanctimonious mind was left out. The criminal was stripped of his office and privileges and reduced to the status of the most junior boy, and ordered to go to bed at 9.45 every night. He stood on the platform as stunned as if he had been sentenced to prison for a shameful crime. The Headmaster's face shone red with triumph. Mine had tears on it.

My friend was dazed with shock in the classroom. 'Don't worry,' I said to him. 'The whole school thinks you're marvellous. Everyone knows Carey is a swine. They're boiling at the injustice of it all.'

It was impossible to console him. I hope that headmaster did not do him irreparable damage. He would have liked to do me some. We were incompatible.

Every Friday in the late afternoon the school assembled in the chapel to practise the hymns and psalms to be sung on Sunday. It was pointless torture. The congregation on Sundays was ourselves, apart from the visiting preacher and a handful of masters' wives. But the Headmaster thought it good for the school and conducted the singing practice himself from the pulpit. Some of us sang different words to those on the printed page, passing obscenities, jokes and messages along the line by this means. It was possible if you were seated advantageously to obscure the Headmaster's view of you by getting behind a column, which permitted more adventurous antics. I used to make signals like a bookie's tic-tac man or jig up and down to amuse myself and my friends. Trying to start waves of giggling I would go further than that. I would tuck my handkerchief under my chin, suspending it by the ends from the sides of my spectacles. Pretending to be an old man, I would imitate the Headmaster's extravagant gestures as he pompously conducted the singing. It was a performance that brought the house down, or that part of it which could see it.

One Friday, aware that all was not as it should be in my area, the Headmaster cunningly changed his line of vision and joined the audience. The singing stopped. The House of God had been desecrated by a shameless exhibition, and so on. The consequences of my buffoonery were disagreeable.

Occasionally I would find myself in the Headmaster's class-room, where he taught Scripture. He was hot on this. We exchanged hostile glances and, so far as I dared, hostile remarks; the sequel to which was usually my doing early morning detentions half asleep before breakfast.

It was public knowledge that I despised the games ethos which was so important to the Headmaster. I was suspected of dodging the watching of school matches so that I could spend Saturday afternoons reading – a deplorable, unboylike pastime. I was also known to avoid being in representative teams for the same reason.

'If you tackled harder, you could be in the 2nd XV. Don't you want to be, Wyatt?' Mr Howell, the master in charge of games asked me.

'No, Sir. It interferes with my reading.'

The answer rattled round an incredulous school. I should have liked to have been in the cricket teams, but I opted for the alternative of shooting in my last two years. I was sulking because I had made a top score of 85 not out in a Colts trial game and was still not included in the side. Another injustice for me to stack up against authority. It was silly of me; I adored cricket and loathed shooting on the flat, dreary ranges by the sea near the scene of a famous murder. Useless as I was at it, my pride made me stick to it, though sadness overwhelmed me when I heard bat against ball. The last of the cricketing dreams had gone.

The Headmaster sent for me when I was just seventeen. 'You are the sort of person who will spend his life propping up bars, a waster,' he began.

Presumably he guessed I went to pubs in little villages away from Eastbourne and far out of bounds to drink an adventurous half pint of beer. But he had no hard evidence. I had learned from what happened to my friend the school prefect not to drink in the town.

'You are a bad influence in the school. I'm thinking of asking for you to be taken away at the end of the term. Go away and consider your behaviour. When you've thought about it, come back and tell me how you're going to improve it.'

I talked to some of the boys in my form and in School House.

I went to see my housemaster, H. J. Belk, the only civilized master in the school. He had not been consulted by the Headmaster and was puzzled as to what he meant. Mr Belk liked me. He sympathized when I told him I would not become a house prefect if I had to administer barbaric beatings and appointed me one just the same.

I returned to the Headmaster. 'I have discussed what you said with various people,' I began.

With flushed face the Headmaster interrupted me. 'I shouldn't have thought it was something to talk to other people about.'

I went on: 'And they don't think my behaviour is particularly awful. I've thought about what you said to me, Sir, and I don't see how I can improve it.'

The Headmaster was flummoxed. He was not used to being defied. He had expected a contrite boy anxious to placate him. Maddeningly for him he could not cite enough facts to clothe his understandable conviction that I revolted against everything the Eastbourne he had moulded stood for. He stifled the explosion showing behind his face. 'Go away,' he muttered, 'and remember I am watching you.'

I was cautiously elated. It was the first time I had scored off authority. There seemed some potential in further exploitation of this talent.

Sex. Adolescent boys' thoughts are swamped in it. Or at least mine were. Before I went to Eastbourne I had fantasies about it. I imagined a world temporarily made unconscious by a science-fiction gas which, mysteriously, had no effect on me. I went around making love to all the pretty girls I could find and to whom I would never have dared make the most trivial advances had they been awake. It was wonderful.

My real-life experiences were less spectacular. There was a gorgeous girl of twenty-three who used to watch cricket at the Esher cricket ground when I was fourteen. She had her own glamorous sports car in which she drove me or let me sit with her. As we talked (she would not have done so if she had known what was in my mind, or maybe she would: she had a generous, understanding mouth), I gazed at her beautiful hands on the

47

steering-wheel and thought how perfect they were for her lovely face.

A pretty little boy boarder sometimes lay naked over my lap in the dormitory at Milbourne Lodge when I was thirteen. One summer afternoon I felt a delicious sensation as I lay across the step of the school gymnasium, but I was not certain how to account for it. Staying in the holidays with a boy from Milbourne Lodge when I was twelve I talked to his fifteen-year-old sister, mildly ill in bed. Her nightdress slipped to show a delicate but full bust. I exulted in the memory of it for weeks.

I asked a boy whose brother was a doctor whether there were any girls without pubic hairs. He gravely brought back the news: 'I'm sorry to disappoint you. My brother says it's impossible unless she's some kind of albino.'

One of our stock jokes at the time, which we thought the height of obscenity, was: 'Where does a girl's hair grow short and curly?' Answer: 'In the Fiji Islands.'

Naturally we discussed the mechanics and got them roughly right, though there was some confusion about peeing into a girl to make a baby. I could not imagine my father doing anything so undignified. I supposed my mother had put up with it, or my brother and I would not be there. She sometimes spoke of the 'marvellous miracle' of how babies came into the world, as though her consciousness was limited to virgin births. One way or another I had just about got the hang of the process by the time I went to Eastbourne. Despite my fantasies I had never masturbated, but I had wet dreams and was aware of a dampness in the sheets in the morning which I furtively dried out. I was too ashamed to mention it to anyone for fear of being thought a late bed-wetter.

Stephen Foot, housemaster at the School House when I arrived, was a suppressed homosexual. After he left he wrote in a book that he was subject to wicked thoughts about some of the boys in his charge. He must have enjoyed the talks he gave to those of us he judged to have reached puberty (his timing was badly awry). His talks were called 'The Facts of Life'. They were delivered with him sitting down and you standing up in his study. They began curiously: 'What time each day do you have your bowel movement?' What had this to do with sex? He

48

might have been the school doctor enquiring whether I were constipated. I hoped we were not going on to Christian Science, as my mother had when I was constipated as a child. She called in a Christian Scientist lady who set me daily Christian Science readings. My constipation ended, but I think from other causes. I knew Foot was cranky: he was an ardent Buchmanite or Moral Rearmer, and urged us to have Quiet Times every morning during which God would issue his instructions for the day to us.

'Different times, Sir. Sometimes in the morning, sometimes after tea, sometimes at night. Whenever it comes on me, Sir.'

'That's no good. You know the laws of the Medes and the Persians. Their rules were very strict. Everything had to be done at exactly the same time every day. No variation was allowed.'

After negotiation, and consultation of the school and house schedules, a quarter to six every evening was fixed on for me. I manoeuvred for that. It was when the lavatory I liked best for its solid wooden Victorian comfort was least used. It was near the entrance to the house and was reserved for masters during school hours.

'Good. That's settled. It's the basis of having a sound mind in a sound body. Help you no end.'

Then we attacked the relationship between men and women. Men must always respect women. They were the mothers of the race. Indispensable, in fact. They must be honoured and never treated lightly. 'There is a certain act,' he boomed in his loud voice. 'It's called procreation. It's in the Bible. It's necessary before anyone can have children.'

He paused to give time for this concept to sink in. I smiled modestly, looking at my feet to encourage him through this embarrassing passage. I debated whether to tell him I knew about it already but decided it would be better not to.

'Did your father ever explain this act to you? No. You were too young.' (My father wouldn't have if he had lived to be ninety.) 'Well,' he shouted, '*I'm* going to explain it to you.'

He did it very badly. The poor man had never done it himself. At the conclusion of his lame sex lesson he said, 'This is between us. It's very serious and not to be talked about.' I was mystified. Not even to the sacred girl at the sacred moment?

49

As I moved with grave mien to the door, privileged possessor of information without which the race could not continue, he called out, 'Don't forget the Medes and Persians.'

I did not masturbate until I was twenty. I remember the occasion well. I was lying in a bath in a hotel at Vitznau in Switzerland where I was spending part of the summer holidays with my Uncle Arthur. I was mad with longing for the golden girl with whom I was having my first serious affair and whom I married just before the war. There was what is called in massage parlours 'relief', but it was not satisfactory. I had known since I was about fifteen that other boys masturbated, but had shied from the idea, thinking it must be sticky and unpleasant. I could not even get an erection when I lay naked on my bed and other boys looked at me. 'You're bound to get one if we stare at you long enough.' I did not. They thought it was my impressive self-control. They were wrong.

But wet dreams troubled me before I had even heard of masturbation. The elderly, waspish matron at School House asked me to see her in her room.

'The maids have been complaining to me that your sheets always have a horrible wet mess on them. You are abusing yourself. It's a disgusting habit. You must stop it or I'll report you.'

I was crucified with horror. 'It's not true. I don't do whatever you say it is.' The matron looked nasty and unbelieving. I had been getting up so near to breakfast that I had left no time to dry the sheets. What could I do about something I disliked as much as she did?

In matters of sex the Headmaster was sitting on a volcano. His orders forbade any contact with the girls at their many schools in Eastbourne. Had the inhuman Carey ever been a boy? If so, he must have been a very odd one. He relied on the Dr Arnold of Rugby method: exercise and games all the time and sodden runs round Beachy Head when the pitches were not fit for play. With over three hundred lusty boys compelled to look at and talk exclusively to each other, it was surprising that homosexuality was not the norm instead of the exception.

I saw little of it, though maybe it was swinging in some of the other houses. And maybe a lot went on I did not know about. At sixteen or thereabout I was infatuated with another boy of the same age. I once walked sixteen miles to see him in the holidays. He was fair-haired and pleasing to look at, athletic and graceful. I wanted to call him by his Christian name, and vice versa, a dramatic departure from the invariable cold surnames. Though we got on well, for weeks he held out. There must have been a little of the coquette in him.

From there I increased the pressure. I wanted to see him naked, alone. There was stiffer resistance. We had a fight which he won, being stronger than I was. I persisted. He gave in, perhaps to shut me up or because the idea shocked him into some arousal. We went secretly in the early morning to an attic room at the top of the main block. He quickly undressed, revealing the physique of an Ancient, but boy, Greek about to take part in an athletic contest. Quivering with excitement I held his balls and gently stroked him, stopping short of a conclusion. He showed no interest in my private parts and that was all there was to it. After several of these dangerous meetings which, if discovered, would have got us expelled, we gave it up. He was bored, and the satisfying of my curiosity as to how other boys reacted damped down my fires.

That is the total of my homosexual experience as a schoolboy, or indeed thereafter. It would never have happened if there had been some contact with girls, not necessarily physical, to let the most powerful emotions of all have an airing. Shut up in a box they were bound to struggle and twist, turning if only in thought, to what is known as perversion. Only blind idiots like Carey could fail to see that. Boys pushed by urges it was impossible for them to control into homosexual experiences suffered no permanent damage, I think. Heterosexuality is what they were really interested in. A very few may have got a taste for homosexuality they would otherwise have been unaware of. Some were confirmed in their inclinations. My record is anaemic. It must compare tepidly with that of most boys of spirit and inquisitiveness.

I have never recoiled from homosexuals save when I had to ward off embarrassing approaches from some when I was younger. Tom Driberg, a well-known homosexual, was one of my earliest political friends. I met him during the war. He treated me as an elder brother might; instructed me how to use the Commons procedure, to improve my halting speeches, to write better newspaper articles. He introduced me to a new world of culture containing people like Constant Lambert, the conductor, forever mourning the rejection of his love by Margot Fonteyn. He took me to restaurants and places previously unknown to me. For a brief period, by making it sound full of magic mysteries, he talked me into believing in religion again. But he never made advances to me, perhaps thinking it would be the end of our friendship or that I was unattractive.

Jim Callaghan was not so lucky. One day in the Commons he said to me, 'I have had a very odd experience. I was driving back to London at night with Tom after a meeting we'd been to. We stopped to have a pee on the verge. While I was peeing Tom came up to me and took hold of my penis. "You've got a very pretty one there," he said. I got away as quick as I could. What do you make of that?'

What could I make of that? Rather him than me.

At Eastbourne my form master, soon to be my housemaster, did me some good services and one disservice. H. J. Belk was a beacon in the desolation. While pretending the contrary, he disliked school games. He noticed boys who thought there were other more rewarding interests. The Festival at Glyndebourne had not long started. He would sometimes take a select group to dress rehearsals, crammed into his little car with a dickey at the back. Opera is beyond me, but I would not have hurt his feelings by saying so, or missed any outing from dismal Eastbourne. I actually got to like *Figaro* and still hum a few bars from it inaccurately. On the way home we would stop at a wood he knew and wait for the nightingales to sing. Not only the birds were happy as they sang out on a soft summer night.

Belk tried to teach me the Ancient Greek moderation. He thought Jane Austen the exemplar of English moderation. When I told him I had never read her he said, 'How lucky you are. Such a pleasure to come.' I wish his teaching had stuck.

I often sat next to him at lunch. Thursday was a bright spot: roast pork, apple sauce and white butter beans, followed by bananas and custard or strawberries and cream for a period in the summer term. There were a few second helpings for those who finished first so long as the supply lasted. The agonizing decision was whether to eat fast in the hope of winning a prize but run the risk of gobbling without getting one, or eat slowly to prolong the enjoyment without frenzy.

Belk would talk to me as if I were an adult, the only master who did. We discussed the world and what I hoped to do in it and he smiled tolerantly. Sometimes I had tea with him. He drank Earl Grey and ate nothing, saying it would spoil his dinner. I thought that fascinating.

The disservice Belk did me unwittingly was to encourage my laziness. I had done well in the School Certificate Examinations at the end of my first year. Science, physics, maths, were out of my range; so were modern languages. Tone-deaf, there was no future in my trying to understand or speak them. Dead languages, of which no one was certain of the correct pronunciation, were the answer. I joined Belk's Classical Sixth.

It was not like other classrooms. It had no desks. It was long and narrow with two pleasantly polished tables running down the middle, chairs on either side. Photographs of Greek temples and celebrated Greek sites (Belk was not so keen on the harsh Romans) hung on the walls. The classroom was next to the school library, which was handy for the quick illicit read, as Belk was aware: there were some complicated rules about when it was lawful to use the library, the Headmaster thinking that books could be bad for morals. Wearing his gown Mr Belk sat at a non-regulation master's desk of his own on a tiny raised dais at the end of the classroom by the window. On the first morning of term he said, 'Now you have reached this form I regard you as mature enough to know whether you want to work and learn or merely pass the time. I'm not going to drive you. The choice is yours.'

For the next two and a half years I idled along, doing just sufficient to get by. I took in the spirit of Belk's teaching but not the letters. He even forgot to take us through one of the set books for Higher Certificate. I assume that he knew I was doing the minimum but thought it did not matter. He would say, 'Some people believe in forcing boys beyond their capacity into winning scholarships. Sometimes they peter out before they take their degrees. Sometimes they fade away afterwards, their brains burned out. You should go at your own pace if you are going to last.'

Any moment I could get, during the lunch-hour, fifteen minutes after breakfast, I read, so that I could be carried away from Eastbourne. At nights I read in my cubicle by torchlight until two or three in the morning. I dozed or slept with my head on the table in class during the afternoons, my neighbour cutting off Belk's vision. Two afternoons a week there were one-and-a-half-hour periods of unseen translation. I would arrange for the boy next to me to prod me awake when there was half an hour left and then scramble through the translation.

I was reading once at 2.30 a.m. when Belk suddenly appeared at the entrance to my cubicle. 'I was walking in the garden and saw a light. Now I know why you are always asleep in the afternoons.' He did not tell me to stop reading late into the night or ever refer to the incident again.

Playing billiards one evening a boy complained of some action of Belk's. To be friendly I called out, 'Oh, Belk's a bloody old fool', which I did not mean. Looking up from my cue I saw Belk, my one friend in authority, passing in front of me. I was shattered. Always a coward, I dreaded our next meeting. I forced myself to get it over with and, my heart drooping, went to see him. He looked up with faint interest as I came in.

I blurted out, 'I'm sorry I called you a bloody old fool by the billiard-tables, Sir. I don't think so at all really. It was just something to say.'

'I didn't hear you.'

But I think he did.

A friend of mine, a thoughtful boy called Christopher Benwell, and I, read *Cry Havoc* by Beverley Nichols, a popular pacifist tract on the evils of war. His message was that, if we all refused to fight, there could be no new war. We became instant pacifists and asked to see Mr Belk.

'We understand the OTC is voluntary. We would like permission to leave it,' one of us said.

'Yes,' said Belk. 'The OTC is about as voluntary as being at school.'

I met Beverley Nichols later. He minced around his fussily over-cultivated garden and made twee remarks in an affected voice about the objects in his drawing-room, which resembled a lady's boudoir. I understood why pacifism had seized him.

Poor Belk. He looked so young with his fair hair, blue eyes, unwrinkled face, short, boyish figure edging a little towards stoutness. He died in 1946 aged forty-four, of constipation after enduring several unpleasant operations. It was ungracious of Fate. Since 1965 I have given an annual prize in his memory (I am surprised Eastbourne lets me in view of what I thought of the place). It is awarded for the best description of the conditions the entrant considers he (and now she) needs for a happy life – a favourite Belk topic. I try to give the prize to the entry I think would most please Belk. The entries are becoming cheekier and brighter: some ideas must be getting into Eastbourne.

There was a way of getting out of the OTC. If you passed a War Office examination called Certificate A, you could opt to join the Boy Scouts. A group of us decided to act. We were among the most slovenly ever to wear uniform, but thought we could do well in the written examination if we could smuggle cribs in. The examination was held in Big School. Long lines of desks went from front to back; half the OTC were there, keen soldiers to a boy aspiring for higher military honours. Before we began, the school porter came in with school notices to be read out by the War Office invigilator, a frail and ancient retired colonel. He was so deaf he could not hear what the porter said to him. An excellent start. The next plus was that the manner in which he read the notices, when he eventually understood what the porter wanted, indicated he was very short-sighted. He held the notices right up to his nose with his spectacles off. Confirmation came when we started to write and he walked up and down the platform, peering hopelessly at the rows of boys below.

We flourished the cribs openly. We passed the answers up and down. There were ancient cannonballs on pedestals at the side of Big School. We took them off and rolled them along the wooden floor. Even the good and serious boys joined in the cribbing when they saw how safe it was. They were not going to let us get higher marks than they did: they were genuinely keen on the OTC, the asses. The invigilator was unaware that he was presiding over a near-riot. It was the most enjoyable examination of my life.

55

After a few weeks the Headmaster said, 'I have a gratifying announcement to make which should make us proud to be Eastbournians. The War Office have written to congratulate Eastbourne on the highest number of passes in Certificate A achieved by any school in the country. Not one failure. We also got the highest ever average percentage marks. Some—' – he must have been looking towards my place, there was a tiny hesitation – 'some of the results are surprising. Congratulations to everyone concerned.'

In the Scouts you had to tie silly knots and cook and one week-end a term sleep in a tent even if it were raining. I have never enjoyed that. But it was better than the OTC, with buttons and boots to polish, belts to blanco, puttees to wind, and its imitation Caterham drilling. And we all dishonoured the pledge to become scoutmasters when we left school. Very lucky for whichever Baden-Powell was running the Boy Scouts at the time.

Confirmation was a great event at Eastbourne. I prepared for it partly because the day you were confirmed you were given the rest of the day off and could go anywhere you liked out of bounds to contemplate your soul. But I was not unaffected. The day I was confirmed I donned a holy mood and elevated myself above earthly thoughts. But the best part was taking the bus to Hailsham, where I had tea in an 'olde worlde' tea-shop. My religion lasted until I left school. I regularly examined my attitudes and tried to improve them to a Christian standard. They wobbled somewhat.

There was no debating society at Eastbourne; no mention of politics or any questioning of society as it existed. But we were allowed newspapers in the house reading-room. When Franco began his rebellion I followed his advance enthusiastically as a splendid attack on authority, and hoped he would win. Anyone prepared to fight authority had my backing. If it had been the start of the Bolshevik Revolution in Russia I should have reacted the same way.

Eastbourne was Esher magnified. I was even more eager to get away from it than I was from Esher. My ambition blazed away. I would be a barrister, a politician (what kind I had not decided, though I sent for the programmes of the three main parties) and a distinguished writer. This last prospect was enhanced by the father of one of my school friends whom I visited at Willesden. He had read a short story of mine in the school magazine. 'Only one in a hundred could have written that at your age.' I was very flattered. Subsequently I thought one in a hundred too high a proportion to give me fame.

Originally I was down to go to Christ Church, Oxford, in the October after my nineteenth birthday. I wrote to Uncle Arthur, my guardian, asking him to let me go a year earlier. I was on good terms with him still. My mother could not afford to pay for me through Oxford and he had offered to pay for my university education. I think he saw me as the bright, malleable son he would have liked to have had in place of his disappointing daughter Margaret, who became a Communist.

When I told Margaret some time in the 1970s that my falling out with her father troubled me for the ingratitude it implied after his generosity to me at Oxford, she said, 'Anyone would have done it in his position and after what your mother did for them as children.'

# CHATPER III

## Paradise Is Oxford

IT WAS A BEAUTIFUL JUNE DAY as the train carried me, not quite eighteen, into Oxford for the first time. I was undismayed at seeing gasometers as the train slowed down before the station. I knew it was the city of dreaming spires and the gateway to the world.

Since I was too late to get a place at Christ Church in October 1936, J. C. Masterman, subsequently Provost of Worcester, a kind man beaming with intelligence, had arranged for me to be interviewed by the current Provost of Worcester, the Reverend F. J. Lys. I walked the dingy back streets till I reached the wall of Worcester College and, following it round, came to the fine entrance gazing nobly at wide Beaumont Street.

The porter was enormous, with a goatee grey beard, an ex-Guards sergeant-major called Bryant. Intimidated, I felt I should call him Sir. Instead he bellowed 'Sah?' at me in a respectfully disrespectful way.

I was directed to the Provost's lodgings at the end of the handsome Georgian buildings on the right side of the grassed quadrangle. They faced the ancient thirteenth-century monastery cottages of Gloucester Hall, supporting Worcester's claim to be one of the oldest foundations, if not the oldest, in Oxford. The front doors of the cottages had been taken off, giving rise to the staircase system. The cottages themselves nearly went when the Georgian buildings were put up, but fortunately the money ran out before both sides could be completed. To the left of the porter's lodge was the Hall, which in my ignorance I did not realize had been designed by James Wyatt, as had several other buildings in Oxford, including such notable ones as the Radcliffe Observatory and Oriel College Library. As I stood looking to either side it was love at first sight. I had sat no entrance examination for Oxford or anywhere else. What would the Provost say? His butler led me into his study.

He was frail, white-haired and immensely old. He held out a small shrivelled hand, palm down. 'Good morning, Mr Wyatt.'

No one of such grandeur had ever called me 'Mr Wyatt' before. Just about no one of any status had. After years of Carey's 'You are not imitation men, you are boys' the breath-taking salutation conveyed its message. At Oxford I was a man.

'I understand you want to come here in October. I think if you don't mind we should have some idea of your intellectual attainments. Perhaps you would be kind enough to write down your thoughts on Hyde Park. If you would go outside the front door you will see to the left a sign saying "Junior Bursary". Go down the steps and in the office you will find a table with some paper. Perhaps you would be good enough to come back in about twenty minutes.'

My future life depended on it. I could think of nothing about Hyde Park that was not banal. I wrote despairingly.

The Provost read the paper I gave him, his hands shaking slightly. After a worrying pause he looked up. 'I think that will do very well. So we'll see you in October, Mr Wyatt.'

Worcester was a small, unfashionable college. Not all the places for the 170 or so undergraduates had been filled. Worcester liked a full complement if it could get one.

Uncle Arthur was delighted. I went to see him at the London Assurance, an insurance company he ran. He had also started one, the Guildhall, and maybe another. He understood insurance, including marine insurance, as well as anyone in the City. During the last war he invented a system by which no foreign merchant ship could put to sea without, through his international insurance connections, its whereabouts and destination being known to us. That was a grievous blow to German merchant shipping. The Germans never understood how we were so accurate in locating and sinking their ships. Uncle Arthur was knighted for this. He was undoubtedly master of his business.

Uncle Arthur's office was large and imposing. I was shown to it by several uniformed flunkeys. He sat behind a huge desk, too big for his body but not for his impressive head.

'I shall give you an allowance of £450 a year. I will pay it a year at a time in advance. Out of it you will have to pay your fees and other expenses and for whatever you do in the holidays. Whatever you can save, you can keep for yourself.'

It was a colossal amount for an eighteen-year-old in 1936, especially for one who had been used to pocket-money of ten shillings a week, recently raised to one pound. In 1985 terms it was worth around £10,000. The average allowance for an Oxford undergraduate was £150 to £200, many scraping by on around £130. My uncle was expert in great financial matters but he did not understand the psychology of eighteen-year-olds with dreams of glory circling in their heads. He should have given me the munificent allowance divided into three and once a term. Then I might have controlled it better and the breach which came later might have been avoided. Meanwhile I had an unexpected fortune.

My first night at dinner in Hall I sat opposite Anthony Whitefoord. He had been at Eton and thought those who had not were inferior, without strong contrary evidence. That included most of the Worcester undergraduates. A friend of his in the same year, Tommy Clyde, had been at school with him, but otherwise he looked set for a lonely time. 'Look at their bottoms in the showers,' he would say of other Worcester undergraduates. 'You can see how common they are.'

I never mastered this method of social grading, unable to detect the difference between upper-class and lower-class behinds, but I did not admit that to him. Though I had been to a socially non-existent school he decided, as he was a year older, to be gracious to me that first evening and teach me grander ways than he presumed I had known.

His mother, a widow, had a house in Chesterfield Street. I bought a bowler-hat and an umbrella, wore a carnation in my button-hole and stayed there with him. His elder brother, Patrick, was in the Irish Guards. Coming home in the early hours of the morning with some fellow-officers he saw my bowler-hat in the hall and fried an egg in it. That was the last hat I wore except in the Army and a top-hat at Ascot and the Derby. My top-hat is hidden in a cupboard in my bedroom so that there may be no temptation for anyone to fry an egg in it.

With Anthony Whitefoord I poured down a lot of drink in my first few weeks: whisky, gin, and tumblerfuls of strange mixtures. I staggered off to my rooms at two or three in the morning, more than once paralytically drunk, to wake fresh and fit, ready for a substantial breakfast. Oh, lost constitution! If I did the same today I should be subhuman for a week.

Tommy Clyde lived out of college from the start. It seemed that Worcester in the end overestimated the numbers it could take that October. He looked like a dashing, fair-haired, made-to-measure musical comedy hero; indeed, his son, Jeremy Clyde, became a very good actor. If you saw a pretty maid leaving Tommy's room he would be sure to be still dabbing lipstick off as you entered. Frances Day, a singing stage beauty, came to Oxford to some function and Tommy was due to be present. We bet him he would not have kissed her properly by the time she left. He won. And it was in the days when ladies were not so quick with their favours.

I read Law as a preliminary to being a barrister. I tried all the lecturers once. They were deadly dull. Why listen to them when they were only spouting what they themselves had written? Why not read their books and cut their lectures? Unfortunately the books turned out too dull for jolly reading as well. My tutor, Mr Parker, was scarcely aware of his pupils. My time to take my weekly essay to him was nine o'clock on Monday morning. As my scout brought in my breakfast his opening remarks, four times out of five, were a welcome: 'A message from Mr Parker, Sir. He can't see you this morning. He's not feeling well.' He did not recover from his heavy drinking as fast as I did.

Mr Parker's indifference to his pupils was so great that even the Provost must have noticed it. At the end of my first year he was replaced by a young Australian lawyer, Alan Brown. However, Law Moderations in the summer of 1937 were easy enough. You merely had to pass them to continue to Finals in summer 1939. A week's solid work seemed about right, though I nearly slipped up. A new pep pill, guaranteed to keep you awake and alert, called benzedrine, had just emerged and could be bought freely at chemists. I took some so that I could stay up all night studying. They put me straight to sleep as if they had been sleeping-pills.

Worcester's academic and sporting record was low. Nor was it the centre of the current jet set. But it had the best food and wine in Oxford.

'What is the point of getting expensive claret and hock from the Buttery if you don't have good food with it?' Mr Johnson, the chef, would demand when you visited his kitchens to order lunch in your rooms. 'I can give you lobster or steak tournedos for half the price you're paying Mr Drake for that wine.'

Mr Johnson did not like Mr Drake, the butler. He diverted money which should have gone to the kitchens. I was happy with both their judgements, and the luncheons brought over by my scout were as good as those in any top restaurant in London.

Balliol had almost as good a kitchen. Julian Amery gave me a fabulous four-course lunch once in his rooms, which I remember mostly for my guilty feeling at the way I treated him. I arrived dressed for tennis, saying that the girl I was playing with at Somerville had booked the court for two o'clock, so there was no time for a long, boozy, political lunch stretching till tea-time. Julian was crestfallen that I could prefer playing tennis with a girl to paying proper respect to his lunch, but I did my best and in time he forgave me. The girl did not for the way I staggered round the tennis-court in front of her friends.

In the cause of providing more university education they cram more undergraduates into Worcester now, five hundred. Despite the hideous new buildings spoiling the fine gardens, there are too many undergraduates for each to have a sitting-room and a bedroom. My stepson at Worcester had a tiny room which could have been in a hostel. Scouts who brought lunch to your rooms belong to the remote past. Today, if you want breakfast, you have to queue up for it in Hall. I never did that once. More is worse. Pleasant, leisured living, so good for the brain, has gone. If your prime object in going to Oxford or Cambridge is to study, you might as well go to a red-brick university where you can get all the textbooks and routine instruction you want. How can you talk educative nonsense and expand your mind through the night in a cramped bed-sitting-room?

My first rooms were in a dark courtyard opposite the Buttery (similar to a large public house's saloon bar and hung with pictures of successful college teams), with the kitchen to the left of the Buttery. Adjacent to my rooms on the right were the well-stocked and chosen cellars. Mr Carey would have thought the location absolutely right for me. Little light came into my rooms, which were at the foot of the building and dingily furnished. But they were mine, absolutely mine, to entertain or do as I liked in, stay in bed half the morning or go to bed at 3 a.m. To invite girls into (they had to be out by ten), to get drunk in – they were freedom.

In the rooms above me lived a tall, gangling half-American whose surname was Henry. He converted freedom into licence. For a year he drifted in an alcoholic haze. In the mornings before lunch I saw him swaying the short distance across to the Buttery to top himself up. He emerged steadier but decidedly drunker with a questioning look. It was difficult to get any sense out of him but he had a wistful charm.

Every night after dinner he clattered up the stairs with his friends, carrying bottles of gin and whisky and great white enamel slop-pails full of beer. The noise was considerable. So were the shrieks of the passers-by (his rooms overlooked the street, the same one I had walked from the station the June before). When the beer was finished the pails were filled with water and emptied with good aim on pedestrians going content-edly home to bed. They may have needed a cold douche to sober them up but they had not expected one.

In the summer of 1937 Henry sailed to America, where his father was a judge who had assumed his son would imbibe culture at Oxford rather than alcohol. On board, the drinks were cheap, cheaper no doubt than in the Worcester Buttery. Henry was not one to miss such an opportunity. On a dark night, after having been seen in his usual stupefied state, he walked off the ship into the sea. He was never seen again. I hope he drowned without realizing what was happening. In his baggage his mother found a diary with typical entries: 'Drunk all week'; 'Drunk again today'; 'Felt gloriously drunk'. The poor woman wrote to the Dean of Worcester, not so much to complain as to suggest that for the sake of other mothers there should be some supervision over their sons' drinking. The Dean considered this with care. By next term a notice had been posted in the Buttery: 'Owing to the abuse of the facilities for obtaining drink, Cherry Brandy and Crème de Menthe will no longer be served in the Buttery after 8.15 p.m.'

Colonel Wilkinson, the Dean, and hence responsible for the discipline of the College, was a remarkable man. After the First World War young soldiers, accustomed to seeing and dealing death *en masse* on the battlefields in a manner not repeated in the Second World War, flooded into the University. They did not accept that they should be subject to petty restrictions after their harrowing experiences. Oxford and Worcester College became temporarily unmanageable. Worcester sent for Colonel Wilkinson, a former Guards officer, to restore order as Dean. He brought his imposing old sergeant-major, Bryant, with him as his assistant in this task and made him College Porter.

Wilkinson, with a Third in English, was limited academically. Specializing in little-known, sixteenth-century English poets he was made Tutor in English. No one from Worcester got a First in English in my time. But with Bryant's help, he did restore and maintain order. He frightened most of the undergraduates. Not dissimilar in build from his giant henchman, he had a heavy military manner. It was unpleasant for an undergraduate to face him if he had broken a college regulation. Actually, Wilkinson was soft inside and was happy when he found an undergraduate who stood up to him without impertinence and to whom he could talk naturally. He had a collection of rare books, with some bound in human skin. He was very proud of these, explaining that the skin was prepared just like leather. It looked paler. He was College Librarian. He kept locked the beautiful Hawksmoor Library, overlooking and running the length of one side of the quadrangle above the entrance to the College; not because he thought, like Carey, that books might damage the morals but because the undergraduates might damage the books. They were too valuable for that risk to be run. I never saw the splendid collection of designs and drawings by James Wyatt, owned by the College, when I was there.

Chapel on Sunday was compulsory. So was eating dinner in Hall four times a week. Each unauthorized absence incurred a fine of half a crown (or 12½p). Not much, on the face of it – but you could get an excellent Havana Henry Clay for sixpence (2½p), which in 1985 would cost at least £3. A half-crown fine was not negligible: it equalled five decent cigars. It was one of Wilkinson's functions to collect the fines.

Dinner in Hall was very early, at 7.30 p.m., and unlike private meals ordered from Mr Johnson not very good. The dons at the top table ate and drank well. It was galling to watch them at it. The undergraduates drank beer and had to wear gowns as they did at lectures. Dinner was dull unless someone was 'sconced'. I forget what prompted this ritual; perhaps extreme obscenity, the breach of a convention or just fun brought a challenge to drink a sconce. A huge silver sconce pot holding two to three pints of beer was ceremonially brought in. If the subject of the sconce could drink the whole pot in a single continuous swallow, he won. The challenger had to pay for his beer. If he could not down it in one go he had to buy beer for his table or immediate group. Spurred on by the financial incentive a surprising number drank the sconce in one gulp to much applause. Frequently the victors, white in the face, left the Hall soon afterwards.

The fifteen-to-one chance of seeing a sconce was not sufficient to prevent those who could afford it eating out far more often than the three permitted evenings. My favourite places for dinner were the Junior Carlton Club and The George, then a restaurant of almost London standards. In The George wine was apt to make the undergraduates lively. Rolls, pieces of smoked salmon and raw meat were thrown from table to table across the restaurant (that is how I discovered how agreeable raw steak can be). We thought these juvenile antics were very funny. Non-undergraduate diners, local or from London, were not annoyed but amused: a free show of how carefree and money-free Oxford undergraduates were reputed to behave.

Towards the end of term the summons came to see the Dean about fines. He lived in pleasant rooms in the new (Georgian) buildings. He was unmarried but not suspiciously so. The half-crowns were collected in a large porcelain wash-bowl. (There was no running water in the rooms. Scouts brought hot water for shaving and washing.) In anticipation of one such visit I learned and practised a trick borrowed from Wall of Death cyclists who horizontally rode round the top of a circular wall without dropping lower or falling into the middle.

'If I can roll a half-crown horizontally round the top of the bowl and keep it going for five minutes, will you let me off my fines?'

The bowl was emptied of its half-crowns into a large heap. I began. The Dean had no knowledge of dynamics. He was amazed. For a laugh-ridden hour I tried to teach him how to throw the half-crown in and hold and move the bowl to keep the half-crown circling in its orbit at the top. It was beyond him but I escaped the fines.

Occasionally the Dean visited me in my rooms. It was something of an honour. One tea-time in my second year he came and found I had sported my oak, the thick outer door shut to secure absolute privacy. Later he looked at me sadly. He did not approve of girls in undergraduates' rooms even during the permitted times. (He would never have admitted women as members of the College if he had still been Dean of Worcester.) He never came to see me again. I was sad about that.

Part of the Christmas vacation of my first year I spent in Munich. The Nazis were on the upsurge. A sinister, thin-faced waiter who snarled at me contemptuously about English swine disclosed that he was an officer in a Nazi paramilitary force. A half-Jewish boy asked me if I could help him to get out of Germany. Pro-Nazis asked why the English press attacked Hitler: 'We have said nothing about your king.' It was the time of Edward VIII's abdication.

I was vaguely aware of something nasty brewing but I had come to enjoy myself. I behaved badly, drinking in night-clubs, arriving back at the staid hotel, the Bayerischer Hof, at four, five, six in the morning. As contemptuous of the Germans as the waiter was of the English, at five one morning I collected all the shoes outside the bedroom doors on the floor below mine and dropped them down the lift-shaft. By the time the owners wanted them back I was sound asleep and never knew what happened.

Another time I was followed out of a night-club, where I had been pirouetting, drunkenly twirling my overcoat, by some Americans. On the pavement the Americans surrounded me and one of them said, 'We're going to teach you a lesson. You're a disgrace to the English-speaking people.'

'That shouldn't worry you,' I replied. 'You can't speak English.'

They went away. Uncle Arthur would have been horrified, but he had made it possible.

In the afternoon I boned up on culture, visiting the Alte Pinakothek and the Neue Pinakothek. At eighteen my head cleared rapidly and I was not too addled to remember them with pleasure. But my real business was to find a girl to go to bed with.

I had visited a Paris brothel: they were legal then. Naked women sat with their floppy breasts dangling on the tables and demanded drink. At the moment a selection could no longer be avoided, I fled in horror. I had some fumbling gropings and physical entanglements with girls who drew back too soon, but I was still a virgin – a dreadfully immature condition which must be remedied and with a 'nice' girl.

There was a night-club where I sat up at the bar several nights running next to a dark, slim, pretty girl. She always wore a white, filmy dress. Looking sideways I could see most of one or other of her lovely milk-white breasts. She wore no bra, or whatever the garment was called then, but was not dressed indecently. We talked animatedly and drank. There was genuine mutual attraction. As the drink did its friendly work we would kiss and she would put her tongue excitingly in my mouth. After a night or two the kiss was accompanied, or followed, by my putting my hand in the top of her dress and playing with her nipples for as long as she thought no one was looking. We both got excited. I began to ask her if she would let me go to bed with her. After another evening's resistance she coyly agreed. I told a friend I was with that I was going off with her.

'Can I come with you and wait outside and have her after you've finished?'

I was shocked and furious at the repellent suggestion.

'But you know she's a tart, don't you? I just thought it would save you money.'

I did not believe him. I left with her alone. We arrived at her small, not luxurious but clean flat. She kissed me again lovingly and lingeringly, held my hand and gently guided me to her bedroom. To my mortification she explained that I was expected to pay. I did so with deflating disappointment. She undressed and lay on her back on the bed. I was so confused that I no longer thought of her as the girl I had spent happy evenings with, I was conscious only of a patch of black pubic hair. I undressed and lay on the bed.

'Oh, you don't know what to do.' Her laugh had changed from girlish to metallic. 'I'll show you.'

When I was in place she bumped up and down, rising quite high in the air until she judged correctly there was no further need of this activity. It was awful. Only once more did I pay for sex. I spent the night in 1949 with a sweet, pretty Siamese taxi dancer in Bangkok who also wore white. She was charming and it was nice.

In my second year at Worcester I had rooms on the top floor in the old cottages near the arch leading to the gardens. The sitting-room had white painted panelling and window-seats which looked on to the garden. I had met an American art teacher in the summer and told him what the room looked like. That was before he had asked me which place I liked to be kissed on most and I had thoughtlessly said the neck and he had tried to implement what he supposed to be my desire. We were on a tour of South Wales and had to share a room in an hotel near Merthyr Tydfil. I was already shocked by the sight of young men aimlessly standing on the street-corners in that town of total unemployment and now I was shocked yet more.

The art teacher persuaded me that El Greco's red, yellow and blue colours would be perfect against white panelling. He painted samples, and I tried to match them with the colours of the dye for the covers of the armchairs and divan which I had bought extravagantly, disdaining the frumpy College furniture. The colours were not like El Greco's but the divan was useful.

Oxford was wonderful. I had joined the English Group and the Experimental Theatre Group which read advanced plays I could not understand. I was a member of the Labour Club, while belonging to the Conservative Junior Carlton Club. At the Labour Club I met Philip Toynbee, who was uncertain whether to be literary or political. For the time being he was a Communist and a fluent debater. I was to have a hand in getting him elected the first Communist President of the Oxford Union. At one Labour Club meeting Philip became very merry and executed a solo singing and dancing act. A Communist present took him aside and gravely told him he was letting down the working-class movement by his frivolity. Philip was so appalled at the enormity of his betrayal that he sat down and stayed quiet for an hour.

Some committee meetings of the Labour Club were held at Somerville. They were popular. It was a way of getting among the girl undergraduates, which might lead to the discussion of more entertaining topics than politics. Girls had to battle mightily for the few places available at Oxford. They tended to prefer male undergraduates who were intelligent, unless they compensated for their stupidity by being rich or good-looking.

My strength lay in a special category: persistence. I would talk all day to any reasonable-looking girl willing to be talked to. I was also a good listener, keen to learn about the female mind, with which I was little acquainted. I have never learned much about it. Nor did I meet success in the conventional sense till I was nearly twenty. I masked my envy of my more competent male friends by loftily indicating I was above all that. I would affect distaste when Herbert Howarth talked about his girl-friend's pubic hairs crackling like dry twigs in a fire. I gave sage advice to Steven Watson, a clever boy with a gammy leg, when he told me of the emotional upheavals involved in his affair with an attractive Burmese girl undergraduate.

But I could not help being fascinated by the exploits of Donald Wise, a Worcester man who became a prisoner of war of the Japanese and subsequently foreign correspondent for the *Daily Mirror* and the *Daily Express*. The rooms below mine in my second year were occupied by P. E. Roberts, the elderly Vice-Provost, who had never been to India but was a great expert on it. He had a home in North Oxford and did not sleep every night in his rooms. It was a reasonable risk after 12 p.m. when the gates were locked to climb over a distant part of the garden wall (the Worcester gardens were vast), over the Vice-Provost's garden wall and thence into his rooms. The windows were always open. Donald Wise, having completed his entry and exit, would come up the staircase to my rooms and tell me what he had been up to.

At one time he made love to an enthusiastic barmaid in a churchyard. 'Make it big again, Sir. Please, Mr Wise, Sir,' she would beg as she lay back on a gravestone. Another local girl enjoyed doing things to him which I had no idea girls enjoyed, opening up exotic prospects. When Donald Wise was a prisoner of war I used sometimes to see his luscious and provocative little wife when I was on leave and sought to console her. I was on the verge more than once of proposing mutual consolation, but was deterred by the thought of poor Donald building railways for the Japanese. I need not have been so squeamish. The marriage, alas, was brief.

As for myself, progress in matters of love continued slowly. I saw a lot of one pleasant girl undergraduate, but though she would let me kiss and fondle her, the halt sign was quickly waved. She was in love with a beautiful, fair-haired undergraduate at Exeter, Michael Pitt-Rivers. I liked him and would have liked him more but for her fixation on him. After Michael tired of her she suddenly decided that it was me she had been in love with all the time, but it was too late. I was hideously embarrassed when she followed me to a train I was catching and thrust flowers at me through the carriage window. When you want them, they don't want you. When they change to wanting you, the desire has faltered. Not always, but too often.

Literary friends suggested that I promote and edit a joint Oxford and Cambridge magazine for 'good writing'. It was called *Light and Dark*. Through it I met two lifelong friends. One was Arthur Schlesinger, Jr, an American with a humorous face and jokes to go with it. He was to write speeches for and advise Adlai Stevenson and John F. Kennedy, and was on the latter's White House staff when he was assassinated; but his real work is writing and teaching history. Playing at politics is his pastime. Foolishly I bet him $50 that Nixon would survive Watergate. The other friend was Charles Wintour, the only Beaverbrook editor to maintain a separate political judgement from Beaverbrook without losing his friendship. His early ambition was to edit the *Evening Standard* and he did it brilliantly for years.

*Light and Dark* was not bad. Some of the poetry was affected and the short stories tended to be plotless, but contemporary comments on University and national events were lively. There was a very good account by Barbara Downs and Bruce Watkin in the Mass Observation style, noting the time of each incident, audience reaction and speaker's mannerisms, of an Oxford University Conservative Association meeting addressed by Lady Astor.

> 8.28. Clapping starts left back at entrance of Lady Astor. Lady Astor in black dress, relieved round collar, with white hat pill box blue peak at front . . . Tall man in front row in heavy overcoat turns about three quarters left, grins largely to friend behind and claps his hands slowly and heavily.
>
> Lady Astor: I've always thought – er – felt (sniggers in Hall) that having all this *culture* (laughter) . . . not that you take much notice if you're anything like my sons (laughter) . . . most important thing in the world today is the English Way of Thinking (two or three Hear! Hear!) I'm a Virginian – that's why I believe in the English Way of Thinking . . . you're Conservatives . . . you might be Bolshevists by the time you're forty (laughter). If you're Bolshevists at the age of nineteen you'll be confirmed Conservatives by the time you're forty. (Louder and longer clapping, clapping five seconds.)

Through editing *Light and Dark* I made interesting friends some of whom I forgot. When Barbara Pym died in January 1980 I wished I had known that remarkable author rightly likened by Lord David Cecil to Jane Austen. In a bookshop in Madison Avenue I browsed through her diaries and found I had known her quite well. How dim of me to lose so great a heroine from my memory: I must have been too preoccupied with myself to recognize genius when I met it.

In the spring term of 1938 I advanced from the monthly *Light and Dark* to a weekly newspaper, *The Oxford Camera*, after the domed Radcliffe Camera Library. It was sold on the streets. It had spirit, too much. The shadow of war touched even light-hearted undergraduates, who became the more light-hearted because of it. Bruce Watkin wrote an unusual gossip column. He also attacked the dons for planning air-raid shelters for themselves and none for the undergraduates: the story had some basis.

The dons were outraged. The Proctor sent for me and *The Oxford Camera* was closed, but not before we ran a successful campaign to get Philip Toynbee elected as the first Communist President of the Union. I was not a Communist but I liked Philip Toynbee and it was fun. Anyway the Communists were more against Hitler than Chamberlain was, until the Hitler–Stalin pact changed all that.

*The Oxford Camera* caused a minor stir. It seemed a pity to let this jolly rival to the respectable *Isis* and *Cherwell* vanish. Some of us decided to go into immediate production again under another name, *The Oxford Comment*. I was the main financier (helped by my brother) and the editor, but the Proctors would not allow another weekly under my avowed editorship. A group was formed and their names printed as publishers: Woodrow Wyatt, Hugh Fraser, Simon Wardell and Oswald Berry.

Oswald Berry was included to provide funds. His father was Lord Kemsley, owner of the *Sunday Times* and *Daily Sketch*. Simon Wardell was in the group because his father, Captain Wardell, worked for Beaverbrook in some high-powered way on the business side of Beaverbrook Newspapers. Simon was therefore presumed to know about newspapers. He put some money in, charm with a slanted smile, and ideas. He had a gift for friendship and making jokes about people without malice. He wrote some astonishing successful plays before dying early. Hugh Fraser was there because he wanted to be President of the Union and hoped *The Oxford Comment* would help his campaign, which it did. He was conspiratorial, but so loudly that his plots were public before he had finished describing them. I enjoyed his jokes from the moment I met him at eighteen until he died in 1984. The summer before, in Italy, he had still seemed immortal as he sat by the swimming-pool laughing loudly as I read him extracts from the early part of this book. Hugh was successful politically, becoming Secretary for Air, but not as successful as all politicians think they deserve to be.

By way of apprenticeship to politics he interviewed for *The Oxford Comment* Harry Pollitt, the miners' leader and prominent Communist. Of more value to the paper were his racing tips. He was not afraid to give confident selections. By the end of the term anyone backing all Hugh's selections for a £1 win would have been £20 up plus profits on numerous placed horses. Hugh's tips were so good that they were copied by the national Press. Enraptured by his success Hugh put it about that he was the editor of *The Oxford Comment*. Mildly irritated, I telephoned from the *Comment*'s office on the lower floor of the

Carlton Club, where I did the editing, layout and much of the writing, to the Club above where I knew Hugh was drinking. I told Robey, the Club Steward, ever ready for a leg-pull, to tell Hugh Fraser that the Senior Proctor wanted to speak to him urgently.

An apprehensive Hugh came to the telephone. 'Hugh Fraser here.'

I disguised my voice by holding my nose. 'The Proctors are rather concerned about *The Oxford Comment*. I understand you are the Editor.'

'Oh no. No, I'm not the Editor. It's Woodrow Wyatt.'

So my editorship was confirmed.

Julian Amery interviewed Oswald Mosley and George Lansbury. David Ormsby-Gore wrote the gramophone notes. Bruce Watkin's gossip column provoked two or three truculent readers a week into calling at the office to demand an apology for themselves or for ladies they were interested in. We ran a straw poll on a far bigger sample than a Gallup poll, proving that a decisive majority of 1938 Union members would overturn the 1932 Union Resolution not 'to fight for King and Country', which was said to have given Hitler misleading comfort.

I wrote mildly outrageous articles. In one I said that the Union was no longer a serious debating society. It was called 'Are you nice enough to be President of the Union?' and pilloried the sheeplike President, Raymond Walton, for claiming that 'niceness' was a more important qualification than oratorical ability.

Another article of mine was headed 'Oxford women are awful'. I compared the town girls who tried to look pretty with the average girl undergraduate: 'The latter is wearing ill-fitting clothes, has a shiny face, untidy hair and a sloppy ungainly walk.' Rousing stuff, which got rousing protests. Underneath the article were photographs of the three girl undergraduates generally acknowledged to be the prettiest. The caption under one photograph was 'Miss Susan Cox'. When I met her as a result of the article she had a tailored navy-blue dress with white horizontal stripes at the top, blue eyes and naturally blonde wavy hair. She was bright and laughed at my jokes. I fell in love with her and for once was not rebuffed.

It was she who was in my rooms when the Dean came over and found my oak sported. She is associated with some of the happiest days of my life. I thought it was for ever. We had dinner in my rooms on the night of the Worcester Commemoration Ball and the late summer evening light caught her beautiful head in a way which made me think, That is how she will look when she's thirty-five. How wonderful.

In the Easter vacation she had made some excuse to her parents about staying with friends in Paris and we spent five days together at an hotel in Fontainebleau. It was cheap but clean and simple, and it seemed like the Ritz. We bicycled in the forest, saw where the Impressionists lived, threw bread to the carp in the Palace lake, many of them alive when Marie Antoinette was. I persuaded Susan to sit on the throne in the Palace when the attendant was out of the room. She was perfect and serene on it. Once when it was chilly I stopped her putting on her cardigan because her bare arms were so lovely.

For a special night out we would have dinner at L'Aigle Noir, Fontainebleau's top in elegance. Whenever I see in France a road sign 'Fontainebleau' I recall those miraculous days and shall until I die. She was a year older than me and left Oxford a year earlier. In my third year, as was the custom, I had lodgings out of College, where she visited me at week-ends. The lodgings were in a pretty cottage at the bottom of Bath Place. They were near New College, where I used to sit mooning in the cloisters looking at the great ilex tree in the middle and seeing nothing outside the cloisters but ancient University buildings.

A member of New College who interested me was Alan Hare. He asked me for a drink in his rooms. At twelve in the morning we drank Château Latour. I was deeply impressed. Château Latour is now owned by Longman Pearson, which owns the *Financial Times*, of which Alan was Chairman. One of his retirement tasks is to supervise Château Latour. He has had long training for it.

Oxford time passed in its idyllic way. I had more friends out of Worcester than in it. That brought about an alarming incident in my second year. One night around 11.25 p.m. Philip Toynbee and Patrick Anderson, a former President of the Union and a fourth year Worcester man, were drinking in my rooms. There was a loud bang on the door. When I opened it four six-foot Worcester rugger-playing, rowing toughs forced their way in. 'We've come to throw you in the lake,' their spokesman announced.

The lake at Worcester was large with rare wild ducks and overhanging trees. It was pleasantly sited, with a view of the Provost's gardens and the fine Georgian façade of his lodgings on the other side as you walked towards the playing-fields beyond. It was a dream setting, with a real boat, for *The Tempest*, a regular production of the College dramatic society. I was fond of the lake but it was a cold night. I had no wish to be plunged into it fully clothed. I hoped other arrangements could be made.

'Why do you want to throw me in the lake?'

'Because you have more friends out of the College than in it. You're not a proper Worcester man. You hardly ever go into the Junior Common Room, and when you do it's twelve in the morning and you're still wearing your black silk pyjamas. You edit beastly newspapers which get the College a bad name. You're a disgrace to the College. That's why we're going to throw you in the lake.'

Then they grabbed me. I fought furiously, thinking of that icy water. They couldn't get me through the narrow doorway. Philip Toynbee valiantly came to my aid. Patrick Anderson, perhaps thinking that as a renowned Worcester man in his fourth year he should be neutral, sat saying nothing. There was a pause in the struggle. I got back into my sitting-room, battered but not yet vanquished, surprised at the strength of my resistance. The four toughs stood panting at the doorway preparing for a fresh assault and considering the best way to get me out. Philip's shrewd blows and tugs had made it more difficult for them than they had expected.

My spirits up I harangued them. I told them they were so full of prejudices and empty of brains that they were not fit for a University education. Anything they didn't immediately understand, they wanted to destroy. Didn't they know Oxford was the home of tolerance? It was not Nazi Germany, where they were busy burning books. And so on for fifteen minutes, inspired by a fear of icy water as strong as when my father pushed me into the Cornish breakers.

'Do you still want to throw me in the lake?'

They shuffled. One of them looked at his watch. 'I'm out of College. I've got to be back in my rooms by twelve.' Another said, 'It's getting late.' Angry and baffled they went down the stairs. They never came back.

At the end of September 1938 Chamberlain returned from Munich with his piece of paper. I joined with all right-minded people in condemning Chamberlain's surrender to Hitler but inside I was relieved, like nearly all the nation. I was a coward. I did not want to be killed, nor did I want my last year at Oxford spoiled. There was already a blemish on it. At some point during it I would have to work if I were to pass my Finals in reasonable order. The new Law Tutor, the Australian enthusiast Alan Brown, said I could get a First if I tried. He was over-optimistic. I had not the brain for it, nor the memory or the wrists.

At dinner at All Souls I once told the Warden and some of the Fellows that they owed their position to their strong wrists. They were half-convinced, though they had not seen themselves as athletes before. Success at examinations is achieved largely by speed of legible writing, by covering the maximum amount of paper in three hours. This requires strong wrists, like a good spin bowler's. Add to them a video tape memory of the printed page, and you can't fail.

My wrists are weak. I write slowly and appallingly. (My mother wrote to me at school: 'You will never get on in life if you don't improve your writing.' It took me an hour to decipher the scrawl containing this message, but she was right.) I could never memorize by rote. I was a non-starter. Give me twenty-four hours and the facility to turn up reference books and I might do as well as anyone. Alan Brown did not believe me. He liked my essays and thought application would do the rest. He had a remedy for the handwriting. Just before Finals he took me to a stationery shop and made me buy a Parker pen of the sort he had used to get his own First.

More realistic than Alan Brown I delayed trying to memorize yards of facts till after the second week of my last term. My lousy memory had a better chance of retaining them for a few weeks than for a few months. During the two weeks' examinations I was so befuddled that I had to ask a co-examinee the next day's subjects. One was the History of Law. I had overlooked the standard book. I sat up all night reading it and may have done better in that than in some other subjects.

There were only six Firsts out of 146 examinees in Jurisprudence in 1939. One of them went to the earnest Sir Keith Joseph, Bt. Well it would, wouldn't it? I was sent for to have a viva voce. It was faintly possible that it was to see if I were worthy of a First. More likely it was that the examiners wanted to see if they could square their consciences with upgrading me from a Third. I think Alan Brown had been at them. I got a Second.

Thus concluded my life at Oxford. I wished it could have gone on for ever. It was all I had hoped. I made lasting friends. My mind was opened to new ideas and new vistas. I had talked to and enjoyed every sort of person. My understanding of the variety of life was greater. Oxford had been excitingly new against a background ages old. Worcester had been a happy base from which to explore it.

Unfortunately, Alan Brown had told Uncle Arthur that he expected me to get a First if I worked hard enough. My unwelcome Second was assumed by him to be due to my laziness. This was partly true, but I doubt if it would have made any difference if I had studied twelve hours a day. A little earlier I had been obliged to make a fearful confession to him in his office. I had overspent his generous allowance by £500 in my three Oxford years. I had never been able to resist overspending in the first part of the year, leaving nothing for the last. I had bills I could not pay. To a man punctilious in money matters and unaware of the habits of undergraduates this was a dreadful crime.

He drew out his cheque-book. 'That's a very large sum. I'll give it to you this time but not again. I am very disappointed.' There was no smile.

My Second, plus my overspending, at first determined him to cut me off entirely. I heard afterwards that my mother was very angry with him: 'It's your fault. You shouldn't have given him so much money in such large amounts at a time.' Alternative propositions were put. Either I must live with my mother at her house in Oxshott near Esher and he would give me £3 a week until I finished my Bar Finals and got started at the Bar. Or he would give me £150 as a final pay-off and have nothing more to do with me. Go back to the Esher I had escaped from and live as a pauper? The discipline my uncle proposed made sense to him. To me it brought a vision of intolerable imprisonment. I chose the lump sum and did not see him again until after the war.

We were reconciled briefly. He thought I had done well in the Army and was mildly impressed by my being an MP though still abhorring the Labour Party. Contact was finally severed when I voted for a reduction in the proposed Civil List allowance for Princess Elizabeth before she was married in 1947. It was a foolish and trendy-Left thing to do, which I regret as I had met Prince Philip with Tom Driberg and liked him, and because it prevented me restoring the old terms with Uncle Arthur which would have made him happy. He died rich in February 1956. I was not mentioned in his Will, though I believe I had once been fairly prominent in it.

In July 1939 I went to live in rooms in a council-house in Cambridge with Susan – I don't remember why she was there. It was very agreeable. I read for my Bar Finals in the Cambridge University Library, when I was not reading in the library at the Temple which could be used by Inner Temple members. There, fickle in mind, I would gaze speculatively at the beautiful Rose Heilbron, also reading for the Bar. The perfect Portia, she became a judge in 1974. Maybe being sentenced by a beautiful judge is better than being sent down by an ugly one.

Ever optimistic, I relied on something happening before my money was gone. Perhaps it would be the war looming closer in June, July and August. When in mournful mood, I said to myself, 'Born in one war, killed in the next. So to Hell with it all.' As the war got closer Susan and I decided to get married in Cambridge. At least we would have done that much before the war obliterated us, or me. I was just twenty-one. Ten days before war was declared on Sunday, 3 September, I joined up, signing on with the Suffolk Regiment, the regiment closest to Cambridge. It was another of my major blunders. I could easily have got exemption from call-up until after the Bar Finals in March 1940, but in a fit of romanticism I felt that, as I had been saying to everyone 'Hitler must be stopped', I was bound to take the earliest possible hand in doing so.

The last week-end of August we stayed in an hotel at King's Lynn. On the Saturday night we went to a seaside concert party on the Hunstanton Pier. The audience and the cast were in a shaky state: Poland had been invaded the day before. I remember a joke which one pierrot made: 'I only know two words of Spanish. One is *mañana*, which means tomorrow. The other is pyjama, which means tonight.'

# CHAPTER IV

—————⚏—————

# An Improbable Soldier

I ARRIVED AT THE OCTU (Officer Cadet Training Unit) at Colchester in October 1939. The Certificate A I had unconventionally gained at Eastbourne must have persuaded the authorities that I was just what they were looking for to stop Hitler. A turn-up for the book. Our rank was private soldier. If we failed the course, that was the rank in which we would be dispatched to other units. Life had become earnest.

The majority of us were from public schools and/or the universities. A number were old friends. Charles Wintour was there, resplendent with the hitherto unrevealed aura of being the son of a major-general. At a TEWT (Tactical Exercise Without Troops) the officer in charge depicted on the model table a Cumbrian farmhouse threatened with attack from several directions. 'How would you deal with it?'

We mumbled forlornly until Charles called out in a clear, clipped voice, 'All-round defence, Sir.' It was the magic, meaningless formula.

'Excellent, the only one of you with any military sense.'

Charles preened himself.

Peter Cranmer, an English rugger player and well-known county cricketer I had met with my cousin, was in the next bed. He sang bawdy songs in a raucous voice and was fond of one attached to the tune of 'Steam Boat Bill': 'Craven A, Craven A,/ Never heard of fornication,/Quite content with masturbation.' It had many verses which at one time I could not avoid knowing by heart.

Colchester Barracks were bleak. They were built in early Victorian times with the manifest intention of indicating to private soldiers that they would not be cosseted. Even public school boys accustomed to rough living were shattered. The iron frames under the palliasses were not made for easy slumber. There was no hot water for washing or shaving. There were no baths. There was no heating. The lavatories were in outdoor rows exposed to wind and snow.

It was exceptionally cold that winter on the Essex coast. The water in the lavatory-bowls froze; not that it mattered, it was impossible to pull the chain because the water in the cistern was frozen, too. The food was so horrible that many skipped breakfast and bought bottles of frozen milk from the milk-cart eccentrically allowed in at 6.30 a.m. on the barrack square. We huddled under the bedclothes and broke the milk into swallowable pieces with a penknife.

It was not unbearable, but it was an abrupt contrast to the lazy luxury of the Oxford I had left a few months previously. I wallowed in self-pity, bewailing my lost career. Each month in the Army was a month out of life. It was an unproductive state of mind.

Colchester had its lighter side. There were friends who turned it all into a joke. There was the martinet Colonel, who believed fervently that unthinking discipline alone could win wars. He told a story from the 1914 war. A German machine-gun post was overrun. All the gunners were found dead, chained to their posts so that they could not run away. 'If they had had better discipline – of the kind I am giving you – that wouldn't have been necessary.' He assumed instant obedience to his orders. One day he shouted to his driver 'Stop'. He opened the door and got out, without noticing that the car was still going at 15 mph. He broke his leg and we got a new CO.

The War Office was disturbed that young officers in France could not deal with or supervise instant repairs to broken-down vehicles. A civilian instructor was hired to teach us about the mysteries of something called the Otto cycle and the workings of the internal combustion engine. A section was added to the passing-out examination, practical and written. Totally without mechanical sense or awareness of sparking-plugs, carburettors, distributors or the like, I was baffled and bemused. When this part of the examination came I despaired. If I could not say what this or that tube was, and why, I would be condemned to the ranks for the rest of the war. And I could not say. I looked at the young sergeant in charge. Did I dare? Would I be court-martialled and sent to the gruesome glass-house? I slipped him a ten shilling note, a lot of money then. He grinned and I passed. For the rest of my time in the Army no one asked me so much as to open a bonnet.

As we approached our commissioning we were told to state our religions. 'It's to wear on your identification discs so they'll know what kind of burial you need.' I had been confirmed in my loss of religion by church parades. If you said you were a non-believer you could not be more than marched to the church door. There was a risk of being detailed for cookhouse fatigues, but the move usually paid. But now, like other agnostics and atheists, I wrote 'C of E'. They might as well bury me the way golf-playing Mr Gibson would have done it.

One cadet wrote 'Atheist'. 'You can't have that on your identity disc', he was told. 'All officers have to have a religion. There's never been one who hasn't. It's War Office regulations.' Stubbornly he refused. The War Office was consulted. Why on earth was he making such a fuss about a trifle? The cadet explained. It was a matter of strong conviction. 'My father is Bishop of London. So I have to make a stand.' The War Office gave in to Harry Fisher. His father became Archbishop of Canterbury and he became a judge.

As a second lieutenant I did not look, walk or drill in a way creditable to the Army. My uniform was made by a decent tailor but it was permanently rumpled. Before the war there was a famous advertisement for recruiting Boy Scouts, showing two youths. One was slumped against a lamppost, a cigarette drooping from his mouth, eyes down, hands in pockets of dirty, ill-fitting trousers, uncut hair. The caption was: 'Before joining the Boy Scouts'. The other was upright, smart, neat, without a cigarette, looking keenly ahead and captioned: 'After joining the Boy Scouts'. I was like the first one.

I was posted to a unit where a senior officer threw his energies into changing me into the second. He was short, trim, with a mean and bitter expression. He had been a regular officer. Army cuts had forced him into a civilian job and on I think the Reserve. Now he was back, ready for revenge on the society which had done him wrong. He seized on me, a pampered

Oxford undergraduate, as its handily available representative. He hated me on sight. I was in his power and helpless while he marshalled all his resources of spite to provoke or break me.

'You can't salute properly. The other ranks are laughing at you. It's the longest way up and the shortest way down. Practise outside my window.'

After half an hour: 'I said, it's the longest way up and the shortest way down. Another half an hour.'

This went on for a fortnight.

'Get a new hat. That's disgusting.'

He threw away my brand-new hat. I had to buy another exactly the same.

'Your drilling is a disgrace. You can't march. Extra drilling by the CSM for three weeks until you get it right.'

'You're only on probation. I shall report you as not fit to be an officer. I'll get you reduced to the ranks.'

He never removed that alarming threat. His peak of viciousness was reached when he ordered me to report for inspection in full marching kit at 6 a.m. every morning for ten days at the house where he lived. Preparing the heavy pack, properly filled and clean, and putting it on at the correct angle made me sleepless, as I thought all night about it. As I marched unhappily to the house he would be waiting at the window, watch in hand, wearing a dressing-gown. Gloating, he would first inspect me, then take everything out of the pack to check that all that should be there was there and throw the articles on the ground.

'Put them all back again correctly. And stand up straight. You must be the most sloppy officer in the Army. Same time tomorrow.'

Sometimes he would say darkly, 'You think you are ill-used.' And misquoting Swift, 'Big fleas have small fleas on their backs to bite 'em. Small fleas have smaller fleas and so on *ad infinitum*.' He did not say which category of flea he put me in. It must have been minute. Perhaps he was thinking of some senior officer biting him. He could not have been thinking of me. I was too cowed to bite anyone by this time.

His persecution pushed me in my misery into a cowardly act. I asked for a Medical Board, to see if I could get out of the Army by playing on my bad eyesight. By the time the results came through I was quite happy with another unit. I was posted away from it because I had been regraded as unfit for a fighting unit. It took me a long time to get myself graded up again and to rejoin the unit I had come to like.

In August 1940 I was sent to Dover. I commanded a platoon which doubled with another platoon on two tasks designed to halt the German invasion. On some days we had to blow up a railway bridge; on others we operated from a fortified cottage. We had to put railway sleepers across a sunken lane to stop German tanks coming up it. The German tanks were to be destroyed by our Lewis guns, rifles from the last war and one Bren gun in poor repair. On 15 September the supposedly genuine alert of an invasion was given. It was our turn to blow up the railway bridge. The Company Commander visited us on his rounds.

'Is it true, Wyatt, that you sent back your batman for your tea-pot and kettle after you had taken up position?'

'Certainly, Sir. We had forgotten them. You can't fight the Germans without a cup of tea.'

He was satisfied with this sensible explanation.

In the other position we were visited by high-ranking US military officers and officials from the US Embassy. Gravely they examined our pitiful armoury. We demonstrated the speed with which we could erect the roadblock.

'Do you really think you could hold up German tanks here?'

'Yes,' I said with the utmost confidence.

A young US naval officer winked at me.

My platoon enjoyed the late summer and early autumn days. German bombers and fighters were over daily, often battling with Spitfires. We rushed across the sunny fields towards pilots floating down from abandoned aircraft. If we brought in a German, the friendly young Londoners would immediately offer the frightened man a cup of tea. They felt no individual animosity. We fired our antique weapons joyously at any aeroplane that looked German, bringing several requests from the RAF that we should learn to recognize Spitfires. We laughed when one of the cooks was blown unhurt out of the cookhouse door by a German shell from Calais. The German long-range shelling was persistent: I was not subject to German gunfire again until

84

June 1944. Some of the soldiers actually waved to a low-flying German pilot and he waved back at them after shooting down a barrage-balloon. It was more a fun circus than a war.

France had fallen. Inadequately armed Britain was alone. Some of the Cabinet were in panic. Secret arrangements were made to take the King and Government to Canada. Not once did we who knew nothing think there was the slightest possibility of a German victory. We had not been conquered since 1066. Why should we be now? That was the uninformed but correct view of the ordinary soldiers and their families. Their unreasoning faith was a better shield than that provided by some of the highest and most intelligent in the land, who thought it time to ask Hitler for negotiations. It is the clever people who want to negotiate with aggressors, not the mass of the population. They are sturdy.

Around the time I left Oxford I met Edward J. O'Brien. He published yearly his selection from magazines of the best American and British short stories, and sometimes a combined volume of both. He was an American living in a pleasant house on the green at Gerrard's Cross, choosing novels and books for filming by Hollywood film companies. By way of encouraging me into a literary career he included a short story, 'Iron on Iron', which I had written when I was twenty, in his *The Best Short Stories, British and American* for 1940. My name was in the contents list with those of H. E. Bates, G. F. Green, V. S. Pritchett, H. H. Richardson, Erskine Caldwell, William Faulkner, Ernest Hemingway, William Saroyan and Irwin Shaw. I was full of pride.

I still aimed at being a writer as well as a barrister and an MP. I went to see the Managing Editor of Collins, F. T. Smith, in a poky book-and-paper cluttered room at the top of their offices at St James's Place. He lived at Sutton and was neither literary nor smart. I do not think Collins, which tended to be snobbish, appreciated how good a man they had. He was agreeable and sympathetic, gleams of youth flickering behind a staid exterior which might have been that of a local bank manager. He saw a possibility of enticing promising new writers on to Collins list. He liked my enthusiasm and gravely weighed me up as a possible editor for an unusual publication. Thus, *English Story* was founded.

It lasted ten years, from 1940 to 1950. It more than paid for itself. In the war years its sales were high. Paper rationing restricted the number of books which could be published and dear, reliable F. T. Smith was kind to *English Story* with paper. Short stories had a wartime vogue with ARP workers, servicemen and others who had no time to read a long book. *English Story* had an interesting list of contributors – Alun Lewis, William Sansom, J. Maclaren-Ross, Alex Comfort, Denton Welch, Angus Wilson, besides already well-known writers such as Osbert Sitwell, Elizabeth Bowen and Stephen Spender. It declined after the war, till the sales no longer justified publication. Today the Arts Council would give a subsidy to a similar publication which, being under no commercial pressure, would idle along losing thousands while being written and read by an esoteric handful. F. T. Smith took the place of the Arts Council as patron of *English Story* and got his money's worth.

*English Story* was edited from strange places: Army huts, tents, barracks. Bundles of manuscripts were sent to me in Normandy and India. They travelled in Army vehicles. They were often read by candlelight. They were nearly hit by shells. But not one was lost. The rejected manuscripts returned safely to their disappointed owners. The accepted, proofs corrected, got into print. At the beginning Susan sorted the manuscripts and sent on to me any with the vaguest promise. Still swimming in romantic sentimentality, I asked Mr Smith if the volumes could be described as edited by Woodrow and Susan Wyatt. 'Do you think that fair or wise?' he asked. 'You are the editor making the decisions.' But he agreed.

Before two volumes appeared under the joint editorship Susan had gone. I was away in the Army. She was very attractive and I was an inexpert and selfish lover. She was a clear target for older, experienced men who had not been called up in the Services. She worked as a temporary civil servant at the Board of Trade. An older man, another civil servant, saw his chance. There was not much feeling about husbands away on service. Two or three years later I was in bed with a girl whose husband was abroad in the Army. She told me she had just had a letter from him: 'I think of all your loveliness and what a waste it is for it not to be in someone's arms, or perhaps it is.' She momentarily made me dislike Arthur Koestler, the great womanizer and writer, by whose brain and charm I had been attracted. She deserted me for him. Her husband was killed in Italy.

Susan told me early in 1941 that she was in love with her civil servant and wanted to marry him. He was pleasant but not remarkable and forty-two.

'I would have carried you to the stars. By his age, if I were at the Board of Trade, I would be President of it, not a civil servant. Don't you want to come to the stars with me?'

She didn't. She was probably right. I never got to the stars and she has long been contentedly married to the man from the Board of Trade.

My unit was stationed at Acrise Place in Kent, an attractive country-house that had a large old bath with a wooden surround and was in working order. I cried in it night after night. This was far the worst disaster I had met.

As I no longer had a home I joined the Reform Club. Members of the Forces paid no entrance fee and only half the subscription. If you were stationed out of London, it was half again; a good bargain. There were brown, early Victorian bedrooms at the top for five or ten shillings a night (no restaurant in London was supposed to charge more than five shillings for a meal in the war, apart from permitted small supplements). There was a valet to look after you. You could get drinks into the small hours. Barry's architecture was splendid. The breakfast was of pre-war standard.

I stayed there often on leave and ate many breakfasts with Hubert Henderson, father of Nico, Ambassador to the USA during the Falklands War. Sir Hubert was a distinguished economist seconded to the Treasury. He was immensely kind and gave me a high-level but simple course in economics over our kippers or bacon and eggs. A delightful old journalist, George Edinger, talked to me about journalism and politics in the evenings. I think it was through him that I met Guy Burgess. He would crouch by one's chair, knees bent and body gently bouncing. He drank a lot and chain-smoked nervously: the nicotine stains on his fingers were unsightly. His shirt collar was dirty. His hair and appearance were untidy. He was scruffy. But he was engaging, with a round and boyish face. He was full of jolly jokes and anecdotes and irreverence for the great. I was always pleased to see him. I was as amazed as Hector McNeil was when it turned out in May 1951 that he was a Russian spy. Hector had been a Minister of State at the Foreign Office where Guy Burgess was his Private Secretary. He had said nothing to Hector or me to give a glimmer of a suggestion that he was a traitor. He seemed thoroughly English, if self-consciously eccentric. I do not believe he meant to be a traitor – he must have drifted into treachery as an amusing adventure and got trapped.

*English Story* and my literary hopes moved me to talk to people connected with writing when I was on leave in London. Cyril Connolly, who edited the marvellous *Horizon*, assisted by the likeable Stephen Spender with the perpetually worried face, was a mentor. I had meals at his Bedford Square flat and listened to him pontificate with awe and profit. He should have been a great writer. When I urged him to fulfil his promise he said, 'I can't. I am too frightened. I criticize others so much that any new book that I wrote would have to be superb or I would be sneered at. I couldn't face that. And I couldn't write a superb book.' The real reason was that he was too lazy. The spirit was willing but the flesh loved the best food and wine, idle, sophisticated chatter, a variety of pretty mistresses, and sitting in a comfortable chair. When we landed in Normandy I sent him some Camembert, the first in England since 1940. Hopeless at keeping letters, I was delighted to find recently half of a long one he wrote back – the other half must have got torn off and is lost to literature. Here is a little of what is left:

> When the tin arrived my first thought from the smell was *Quelle mauvaise plaisanterie* as Madame du Deffand said when she felt Gibbon's face and thought it was his behind. Finding it was from you reassured me and I opened it to find two *bien coulant* [how he loved French phrases] and quite wonderful Camembert . . . and they are nostalgic, delicious and nourishing and already the talk of Bloomsbury!
>
> I was interested in your letter. What I wanted to say and didn't that argumentative evening was that I am a determined

'life for Art's-saker' – I don't believe that it is possible to live and write, one must live *to* write – by all means *immerse* yourself in the Army. Since you are a writer your faculties of reflection and creation will return in time . . .

I nearly told Tom [Driberg] . . . I didn't press him for articles because I detested the horrible brand of journalese which he had now appropriated to himself, 'vased flowers' and such expressions . . .

A few wasted years won't matter and they will provide you with such wonderful material. On the other hand I have all the right feelings but can't get at the material. . . .

Cyril Connolly published in *Horizon* 'A Letter from France', which I wrote while under threat of court-martial. He included it in his *Golden Horizon* compiled after *Horizon*'s death, for which his inertia was the principal reason. He said my piece got in because it was the only first-hand account of a battle area by a serviceman that *Horizon* had received. When I had been an MP a few years he said to Tom Driberg, 'Oh, Woodrow Wyatt. Failed Literature.' He had withdrawn 'Since you are a writer your faculties of reflection and creation will return in time', which had once encouraged me.

Cyril with his podgy face tried hard to be a sage but his manner and looks were against him. His quick, sharp comments were those of a clever schoolboy drawing attention to himself. He affected rudeness to give himself an air of toughness and cover his insecurity. He got in first with attacks as a pre-emptive strike. But *Horizon* was good, particularly during the war. Possibly it was the best high-quality journal of all time, better than *The Yellow Book*. It lasted from 1939 to 1950. I was elated when I appeared in it: it was the ambition of all young writers to be published alongside the most distinguished writers of the epoch.

Helpers formed a court round Cyril. Sonia Brownell was one of them, to whom Cyril dedicated *Golden Horizon*. She was a blonde with a fair and inviting face of great prettiness, given to using French instead of English whenever she thought she could make a literary effect, and to impress Cyril (successfully). I found it trying if I took her out when on leave. 'Sonia, please say it in English. You know I can't understand French.'

Bang went my chance of making a pass at her. I consoled

myself by thinking of her legs. They were enormous, quite inappropriate for what was on top. She would have been happier if she had not strained herself by perpetually putting on a cultural show, fearful of being caught out as not being all that bright.

Somehow she snuggled up to poor George Orwell (only a friendly voice on the telephone to me) before he died and got him to marry her. Why he did is a mystery. The marriage could never have been consummated. However, it worked out well for Sonia financially. I hope the poor man did not die to a barrage of French phrases. Orwell was not keen on foreigners. He took the Attlee line. Dangerous foreigners begin at Calais and don't stop until you get to Bombay, where they speak English and play cricket.

A contributor to *English Story* was Julian Maclaren-Ross. Tall, gaunt and sprawling, utterly unable to manage his own life, he was a Scott Fitzgerald figure. He wrote excellent stories in minute and precise lettering. Once I found him wandering round a barracks dressed as a private soldier but not acting as one. He was morbid and pessimistic, Army life twisting the screws of his depression several notches down. Understanding what he felt, I did what I could. Improperly I invited him frequently to my quarters and we drank and talked, his sharp, long, narrow face intermittently lighting up as humour strayed into his bitterness. He wrote an account of our meetings in *Memoirs of the Forties* which is passably accurate, though he exaggerates my skill at getting soldiers off at courts-martial, likening me to 'Perry Mason. His clients were always acquitted, he'd succeeded in getting off a chap who'd burned down his tent and had even secured an acquittal in a case of what sounded uncommonly like murder.' There was a touch of impressive talent in Maclaren-Ross which never quite got out to spread its wings. He is due for a revival.

Another underestimated writer for *English Story* was William Sansom, though he won more recognition. He was cheerful by nature and got amusement and material to write about from being in the London Fire Service. He lived somewhere towards Hampstead with a charming and intelligent girlfriend. He had a high-handed approach to women. One day when I was on leave he rang me at the Reform: 'Come to dinner tonight. We'll have an entertainment. I've got a girl for you.'

The dinner was cooked by his girlfriend. It was very good. The other girl was a half-Hawaiian nurse, redolent with sensual Pacific beauty.

After dinner as we lolled pleasantly on the edge of drunkenness Bill said, 'The girls must give us a dance.' To the sound of the gramophone the dancing began with swaying hips. 'That won't do. You have to dance bare-breasted for a tired soldier from the front.'

After slight formal reluctance the girls obeyed. They were both gorgeous. The half-Hawaiian girl would have improved any Gauguin. The contrast of her sun-touched skin with the faint dawn rosiness of Bill's blonde girlfriend was triumphantly erotic.

When the entertainment had lasted an hour or so Bill pointed to a divan-style bed and said to the half-Hawaiian girl, 'You and Woodrow can sleep here.'

We didn't sleep.

Some two or three months later I was on leave again. She rang me at the Reform: 'I'm pregnant. I know it must be you. My fiancé won't like it. I must have an abortion.'

I sent her the £50 she needed for the abortion which, as a nurse, she said she could easily arrange. That was the last I heard from her. If by chance she is still alive and should see these words: Thank you. I hope she had a happy life and that the pleasure she knew how to give with the whole of her glorious being was appreciated and justly rewarded.

The war moved on without my seeing any active service. I was reconciled to the Army and almost enjoyed it. I was impressed by its efficiency and the care it took of private soldiers. There was none of the arrogance with which Italian officers were said to behave, carried in vehicles behind their tired, marching troops. At the end of a twenty-mile route-march officers had to see that their men were comfortable and fed before they could look after themselves. Platoon commanders must understand their men, listen to their troubles, help them if they could. It was a kind of welfare state with discipline.

I was shocked by stories of mothers who had died because

they could not afford a doctor or a hospital; of intelligent boys with their education cut off at fourteen because their families were so poor they had to go to work; of squalid homes where there was not enough to eat; of unemployed fathers. My thoughts veered to socialism. If the Army could function so well without the stimulus of personal gain, why could not Britain after the war?

Life under the Tories had been cruel and directed unfeelingly. Life might by its nature be unfair, but it did not have to be that unfair. There must be scope to relieve the worst poverty, to give decent medical care and housing, to provide equal opportunity in education. The Tories would obviously do nothing about it. Capitalism had done nothing about it. And the Tories had been useless in their supposedly strongest area: defence and managing foreign policy to prevent war.

Many young officers were feeling the same. The Army Bureau of Current Affairs was set up to give soldiers education in the workings of the society for which they were fighting. It was a noble gesture, worthy of Periclean Athens fighting the Persians. 'Neutral' background material was supplied for the young officers who conducted such sessions with the troops. Neutral in this context inevitably emerged as anti-Tory. Whoever dreamed up ABCA at the War Office was in part responsible for Labour's landslide victory in 1945. The great educational exercise flooded the other ranks with ideas that were novel to them. They came with the authority of the Army. The soldiers transmitted the general concept to their families. Churchill was splendid but the Conservatives were a shower, with the possible exception of Eden, and Butler with his Education Act. Beveridge was fine, but only Labour could be trusted to implement his scheme. The Liberal Party he espoused had not a hope.

I was not a smart regimental officer good at crawling in the mud or leading patrols. Whenever I thought of leading a patrol behind enemy lines at night I panicked with cowardice. It was terrifying to the limit when on an exercise I had to take a detachment up a water-tower. It was 200 feet high. The narrow iron ladder with no rails tilted backwards. My horror of heights paralyzes me to inanity. I would rather give up and fall off than go on. Somehow I got to the top of that water-tower. Somehow

I got down again. Somehow I controlled my shaking. The soldiers who climbed up and down like monkeys had not noticed it, but I had.

It was a relief when an order came for me to go to the Junior Staff College at Brasenose, Oxford. The Staff sounded much less dangerous than the situations I imagined. I worked far harder at Oxford this time than before. Fear is a great incentive.

I was sent as Staff Captain to the 185th Infantry Brigade, then part of the 79th Armoured Division. The Brigade was unusual at this stage of the war; its three battalions were made up of regulars who had yet done no fighting. They had been brought back from garrison duties in distant outposts of the Empire to prepare for the Second Front. When the time came they fought magnificently. They were not battle-shy or weary, like those who had gone through the Desert Wars. They were fresh, keen and perfectly disciplined. They were commanded by a jolly, red-faced brigadier called Bruce who had served a long time in Asia. It was difficult to get him into dinner before 11 p.m.

'Always had my dinner later than that in Malaya.'

'What about the Mess servants, Brigadier?'

'That's what they're for.'

We got on well. When he was promoted to Major-General of a West African Division due to go to Burma he asked me to go with him as his Deputy Assistant Adjutant and Quartermaster-General (DAA and QMG). Though it meant promotion to Major I declined. I would not get my dinner before 2 a.m. once he was back in Asia.

I became a major when I was made an increment DAAG, a kind of supplementary, at the headquarters of the 3rd British Infantry (Assault) Division. In the autumn of 1943 and the subsequent winter we were in Scotland, planning and training for the great invasion. The training took place in much more unpleasant conditions than we found in Normandy the following June. We had to climb out of landing-craft shoulder-high into a sea so cold that it froze as it reached the top of the beach, then spend a night or two in our sodden clothes. The beaches were chosen as being most like those on which the landings would be made in France.

93

In a remote country house the staff worked late into the night planning the detail of the invasion. My sphere was arranging the loading and unloading of the assault craft, so that men, weapons, ammunition and supplies would be fast out in the right order, the troops fully accoutred and equipped when they sprang from the beaches as Jason's armed men once sprang from the teeth of a dragon he had sown in the ground. To keep awake I became a chain-smoker, hitting fifty to sixty cigarettes a day until amoebic hepatitis, which I caught in Burma in 1949, made smoking cigarettes so foul that I was able to give it up entirely in favour of cigars and pipes.

To enable us to do our work accurately we were issued with many top secret documents, some carrying the most secret franking known to the Army. One of these showed the code names, with the real names alongside, of all the beaches in Normandy where the landings were to be made. The rule with such documents, personally numbered to the recipient, was that they should be returned to the register or a certificate supplied, signed by the officer who had received them, that they had been burned or otherwise destroyed. The time came when I must account for the list of beaches, which I had scarcely needed to look at. I searched in my trays, drawers of my desk, everywhere. I could not find it. Absent-minded from birth, I could not remember whether I had burned it in the fireplace where I often disposed of such documents. I was sure I had. Then I was not sure. I asked other staff officers to let me look through their papers. My personally numbered copy was not there.

What was I to do? To admit I had lost it would bring the whole disciplinary machinery of the Army on my head plus potential disgrace. Yet if I had lost it and said nothing, what if it had fallen into a German agent's hands? As the 3rd British Infantry Division landed it would be slaughtered. The thought was unbearable.

I went to the General. He was stern but less angry than I expected. The War Office was informed. Intelligence and counter-intelligence agents descended on us. One of them was Kenneth Younger, later a Labour Minister of State at the Foreign Office. We became friendly but never discussed the incident. A court of inquiry was convened. Several HQ officers told me I was mad. 'You don't think you're the first person to lose one of those things, do you? You should have shut up and said you had destroyed it.'

The court of inquiry ordered me to be reprimanded and that the reprimand be entered on my records, where it still is. If I had been a regular the lost seniority would have meant lost promotion. To a temporary officer it meant nothing.

I had supposed that the invasion plans would be changed, but we carried on as before. The ways of counter-intelligence were obscure but effective. Maybe they fed the information to the Germans in such a manner that, if they had in fact secured the original document, it would make them think it a bluff. Maybe they concluded I was just a silly clot who had forgotten he had destroyed it, so there was no need to do anything. I stayed anxious until D-day. Heavenly relief. The defences on our beaches were no stronger than had been anticipated.

In the days before D-day I assembled the Division. Despite my carelessness the Commander of the Division, then Major-General T. G. Rennie, wrote to Lt-General J. T. Crocker, Commander 1 Corps, on 25 May 1944:

> I am particularly anxious that two officers on the increment staff of this HQ should join my Headquarters overseas as early as possible. They are Major W. L. Wyatt, now D.A.A. and Q.M.G. and . . .
> Major Wyatt was, for over a year, Staff Captain to 185 Infantry Brigade, and was pulled out as the best Staff Captain available to be D.A.A.G. of the Division . . . He was, in fact, responsible for concentrating the Division in the South, of which he made a first class job, and also for making the present marshalling plan which gives all appearance of going smoothly . . .
> Wyatt is completely au fait with the build up of the Division and will be invaluable in sorting out any difficulties.

I quote from General Rennie's letter because I am rather proud of it and because, despite the early attempt to remove my commission, it showed I was not a liability.

Some of us knew the date of D-day, though it was subject to last minute variation for weather. Less than a week before it Tom Harrisson, of Mass Observation and other fame, gave a party at his house in Ladbroke Gardens. He was just off to be dropped behind the lines in Borneo to organize the savages against the Japanese. The party was full of intellectuals, writers, jolly girls and fast-flowing and fast-consumed drink. J. B. Priestley was loudly and ever more drunkenly explaining that some broadcasts he had made were the reason why we were winning the war; the Government did not understand the nature of the British people; only he, the blunt Yorkshireman, did.

'Utter balls. You're just a windbag,' I shouted at him. That was not my complete view when sober, but it did well for a party, rousing Priestley into furious volubility to the general pleasure. After midnight I said to Tom, 'I must be getting back to Portsmouth.'

'You must drop Priestley first. We can't get a taxi. He's absolutely out.'

William Empson, a charming poet I was friendly with, and I dragged a reluctant, staggering Priestley into my Army jeep. He said he lived in Albany. The three of us set off. Dreadfully drunk I could not remember where Albany was, save that it was somewhere in the area of Piccadilly. For a quarter of an hour I drove round and round Eros in Piccadilly Circus at 30 mph on the wrong side of the road.

Priestley waved desperately for help and screamed in fright: 'You're going to kill me. Let me out. Take me home.'

'How can I if you don't know how to get there?'

I tried another approach, which I thought would work, down Jermyn Street. The terrified Priestley had several times been prevented by William Empson from jumping out on to the road. Once in Jermyn Street, almost at Albany, he managed it. He fell into the gutter. William Empson and I got out and looked at his motionless but heavily breathing body.

'We'd better get him back into the jeep. You can't leave a distinguished man like that lying in the gutter,' William said.

I prodded him with my foot. 'He's only a silly old dramatist.'

We left him there. He must have got home. He went on writing, talking and complaining for years afterwards.

I got home by singing. Whenever I drowsed off in a drunken stupor I awoke myself by bellowing out 'Craven A' and other uplifting songs. I lost the new road to Portsmouth. An atavistic instinct took me on the old route past Haslemere, where the highwayman who murdered a sailor returning home from one of the ships of the Napoleonic Wars was hanged, and down roads no longer the main road. I was in my tent by 2.30 a.m. and up fresh and alcohol-free by 6.30. Oh, constitution of forty years ago, won't you come back to me?

On D-day plus one I was sent to Normandy. I was wrong about it being safer on the staff. In the crammed bridgehead the HQ was sited in front of the artillery. The Divisional HQ had a strength of about 120. The casualty rate was so high that 130 were killed or wounded before we broke out of the bridgehead. It was a much higher turnover than in the front-line battalions.

I surprised myself by not being scared all the time. An hour or more might pass without shells landing close, either aimed at us or dropping just short of the artillery they were meant for.

The anti-personnel bombs were spine-chillers. They spattered shrapnel from nought to ten feet. At night it was fairly safe in a slit trench, but the Germans dropped the anti-personnel bombs in such close clusters that one would occasionally fall straight into a slit trench, obliterating the inhabitant. They knew where our HQ was.

It was disconcerting to pass a military policeman controlling traffic at a crossroads as you drove to the front line and find on the way back that he had been blown to bits. Moving about behind the front lines was more dangerous than being in them in a slit trench.

None of us thought we would be killed. Those of us who survived were right. When the body is young and lusty, death seems an impossibility. As it begins to creak and you can hardly run, remembering vaingloriously as I do that at sixteen you could do the hundred yards in 10.2/5th seconds, death seems more probable. That is why insurance companies do not like drivers under twenty-five and many old men crawl along cautiously in cars or on the ground. I quickly recovered from terror whenever shells or bombs ceased landing nearby and trusted in my destiny. For the hell of it I would drive at normal speed past signs reading 'Drive slowly – dust causes shells' and 'You are in sight of the enemy now'; and once, as I was reminded after the war by the junior officer who was with me, was nearly shot or captured or both as a result.

Sometimes friends like Michael Pitt-Rivers and Michael Astor would turn up, looking grand in scout-cars on missions reporting direct to Army HQ. That was amusing. Sometimes friends would be killed. That was sharp sadness. But tragedy was not always through death. There was the pitiful face of K. P. Smith sitting in the back of his car on the way to the beachhead and a bitter journey home. He was the Brigadier commanding 185th Infantry Brigade and a regular soldier. The Brigade was planned to take Lebissey Wood in the first few hours and to advance much farther than it did. Its failure was a major reason for our being pinned so long into our tiny bridgehead. K. P. Smith was held responsible and sacked, his career broken. I had been his staff captain and he had pleaded with me to stay with him and not go to Divisional HQ. His desolate face haunted me. Would it have made any difference if I had been at his side? Would it have given him that minute piece of extra confidence he might have needed to take risks at a moment when perhaps he fatally hesitated?

Battle scenes, so strange to me then, are now so familiar from television and films that I shall not pile my impressions on the heap. After about twelve weeks we were out of the bridge-head and the Germans were beginning their brave retreat which, despite their determined and courageous counter-offensives, was to take them back into Germany itself.

The Division was given a rest. From the start the German plan had been to roll the British and Canadians back into the sea. The far larger American forces in the Cherbourg area, easily contained by light German forces, could then be rapidly dispatched. The weight of the German armour, their best troops, Rommel, the lot, were hurled at us. It was a compliment we could have done without. All the British and Canadian troops fought with a heroism and efficiency which, if it had been present in Malaya, would have repelled the Japanese. The 3rd Division deserved its rest.

Early during that rest period, some officers of brigadier rank called on me at the command vehicle I worked in.

'You've got to do something about Fearless Fred. He's absol-

98

utely useless. We all know that you and the DAAG kept the Division going in the bridgehead. Fearless Fred is a wobbling muddler. It's far too dangerous to go into action again with him as A/Q. He's got to go before he wrecks the Division.'

'Why don't you do something about it? You're much more senior than me.'

'We're regular soldiers. We can't risk our futures in the Army. You'll be out of it as soon as the war ends.'

They were right. Lt-Colonel F. C. Rea (Fearless Fred), A/Q and my immediate superior, was a disagreeable disaster. A solicitor from the Territorials, he had a large, fleshy face stamped with indecision and a shambling, heavy walk. When shells came near he was quicker even than me into a slit trench and often could not be persuaded out until long after the danger had gone. Much of my work was undoing his mistakes and stopping him making new ones. While he cowered in comparative safety, I was up half or all the night doing what he should, but could not, do. It had been very tiring.

Fred was a compound of cowardice and incompetence, foully insulting to his inferiors, blustering with his equals, and syco-phantic with his superiors. I was prepared to carry him again when the Division once more went into action but agreed with the brigadiers that it might not be possible to pick up all his blunders in time to avoid calamity. Battles did not stop when I slept, and Fearless Fred might be awake and out of his slit trench long enough to give contradictory orders. Curiously, though he loathed me, he was fearful of my going, and a few days previously had in a maudlin, rambling speech told me that everything I did was first class and that he would not allow me to be released for regimental duty knowing he needed me to carry him.

I looked up King's Regulations to get the procedure right for complaining about one's superior officer. You had to tell him you wanted to see his superior, who was no longer General Rennie but General Whistler. The DAAG and I went to Fred's tent.

'We would like an interview with the General, Sir,' I said formally after one of my best salutes.

'What for?'

'To tell him you're no good, Sir.'

99

His heavy face sagged. He rushed off to the General to get his case in first. He had supervised the luxurious fitting out of a scout-car for the General, was obsequious in attending to his comfort, took unjustified credit for everything which went right and put equally unjustified blame for anything which went wrong on someone else. The General saw a different side of him.

In half an hour he returned. 'The General will see you now.'

'You're not allowed to complain about your superior officer,' the General began.

'It's in King's Regulations, Sir,' I said. There was a look of distaste at this barrack-room lawyer approach. I ploughed on. Colonel Rea was bad for the administration of the Division, whose respect he had lost. His inefficiency was made worse by his cowardice. I gave instances.

'I shall have to think about it.' The General's tone was nasty.

Soon after, he sent for me as the ringleader. 'You can't stay in 3 Division. You will have to get a posting somewhere else.'

'There's no need for me to go. I'm all right. It's Colonel Rea who must leave for the good of the Division, Sir.'

'That's ridiculous.'

A couple of days later he sent for me again. 'If you won't go voluntarily, how do I get rid of you?'

I was ready for this. 'You put in an adverse report on me – a 194E – saying I'm inefficient and incompetent.'

'But you're not.'

'It's the only way it can be done, Sir.'

And it was what I wanted. An adverse report had to be shown to the officer reported on, who was allowed to add his comments before it was sent to higher authority. Fearless Fred and the General concocted the 194E together. It was anodyne. It actually said: 'He is a capable second grade officer. . . . He is not inefficient. . . .' They had to say that because they had previously sent in a now cancelled recommendation for me to be given an MBE. The 194E recommended me for a reduction in rank. The worst they could find to support their adverse report was: 'He is casual about routine matters that do not interest him . . .' and 'When in certain moods is resentful of criticism. . . .' The former was rubbish. The latter had some truth. Fearless Fred put everyone in a resentful mood and I have never been grateful for criticism.

I wrote my reply. Fearless Fred was the centre-piece. I excoriated him, leaving out only the cowardice. The Regulations said I must give him my comments for onward transmission. He was sitting in a canvas seat at a table in his tent when I handed them to him. His great head sagged and was nearly on the table when he finished reading.

'This is terrible.'

Once more I was in front of the General. He was in a rage. 'In thirty years in the Army I have never known such insubordination. Here you are, with an adverse report on you, and what do you do? You write a disgraceful attack on your superior officer. It's mutiny. I am asking Corps HQ to convene a court-martial. In the meanwhile you are under open arrest and suspended from duty.'

What luck! I found a sloping field with rich green grass warm in the autumn sunshine sheltered by thick hedges and pitched my tent. My batman worked in peacetime in the kitchens of the Savoy as a trainee chef. He supplemented the Army rations with fresh provisions and herbs from the local farms and got bottles of what wine was left in the Normandy area. I sat in my comfortable canvas chair reading and choosing stories sent in to *English Story* and writing 'Letter from France', which Cyril Connolly published in the October issue of *Horizon*.

Open arrest dragged on a few weeks. The Division, with me travelling separately in cheerful disgrace, had got to Brussels before I heard whether I was to be court-martialled. I ought to have been worried but I was not. I trusted optimistically in the fairness of the Army. The senior officers I had dealt with at Corps HQ knew the truth. When they wanted to be certain that something was done properly they always asked me, not Fearless Fred. And the brigadiers had been circumspectly active on my behalf.

When my papers came back there was written on the bottom: 'This officer is right. But it would be bad for discipline if he were to continue to serve in 21 Army Group. He may keep his rank and choose any other theatre of war in which he wishes to serve. B. L. Montgomery.'

The General was furious I had won. (When I was Under-Secretary of State for War six and a half years later I was tempted to send for his papers and to recommend a posting for him to somewhere like Tristan da Cunha but I refrained.) Fearless Fred was sent to a beach battalion, the lowest form of Army life. The Division got a new A/Q, DAQMG and DAAG and I went back to England. My active service under gunfire was over. It had often been alarming but with intervals of bliss. One came when I was over at Argentan on 26 August 1944. I had finished my business and was turning back when I saw the signpost, 'Paris, 160 km'. The BBC that morning said Paris had just been liberated by General Leclerc and the Free French Forces. I had promised a French girl I was friendly with in Normandy that if I got to Paris I would call on her relations living near the Place de l'Etoile and tell them that their family were safe. I turned my jeep, without authorization, towards beloved Paris. The BBC was not quite right. Germans were still shooting from windows and the rooftops but the tanks of the 2nd French Armoured Division were parked in the Avenue Kléber.

I must have been about the first English or American soldier in Paris. Girls smothered me with flowers, embraces and kisses; bartenders poured champagne for me. Apologies were profuse when I was mistaken for an American. 'Oh, but we *knew* the *English* would return,' a policeman said, who had been ecstatic on greeting his 'first American soldier', and added '*Vive l'Angleterre!*' An old man by the Arc de Triomphe grabbed me: 'Look, I have kept this since the last war.' He waved a huge handkerchief with a Union Jack printed in the middle. The Normandy girl's family were astonished and elated, despite guns going off in the street and the windows of their apartment splintering from a stray shot. Paris was in a riot of joy. My five years in the Army had not been wasted.

On the way out of Paris I gave a lift to two country girls who were on their way home, thrilled by their pilgrimage to see their adored de Gaulle in Paris, freed at last. 'And the French tanks were the first into Paris,' I said. 'They gave us that honour,' one of them replied, and both burst into tears. I nearly did, too. The chivalrous Allied gesture had been beautifully acknowledged.

When I see Parisians in the Paris streets now I think, wistfully, that some of them still like us but they all loved us that 26th day of August. Then they would happily have taken the Union with Britain that Churchill offered the collapsing French Government in 1940. The love-affair between Britain and France has usually been one-sided. Sometimes the elegant, sophisticated lady smiles on the clumsy British suitor; more often she spurns him with a prod from her dainty shoe.

In London I called at the War Office. I was treated gingerly as a unique specimen who had defied authority and got away with it.

'Where would you like to go?'

'India.' My political life was about to start. I was fascinated by India. Something had to be done about it after the war.

'By air or sea?'

I chose the sea voyage. I could read about India and have a jolly holiday. The war was nearly over. What did it matter?

But first I had some leave. The Army was becoming a very pleasant organization to be in.

Raymond Blackburn was a captain and a young solicitor who had a full head of striking white hair, a Heathcliffe handsome face and dark eyes alight with enthusiam. He talked persuasively and was good at defending soldiers at courtsmartial. I had had to arrange the court-martial of a captain who, as D-day approached, concluded that his young wife needed him more than the Army did and announced his sudden conversion to pacifism. Raymond defended him and got him a light sentence. During the preliminaries to the trial I met and talked to Raymond several times. He had been put on the list of official Labour candidates by the agency of Captain F. J. Bellenger, who had served throughout the First World War (wounded twice) and became a captain in 1940 before leaving the Army to sit in the Commons full time. Fred Bellenger was a kindly man, a prosperous estate agent who dressed accordingly – not at all my idea of a Labour MP from a mining area. He wrote a column for servicemen in the *Daily Mirror* and hoped to be something at the War Office if Labour won. He became Financial Secretary there from 1945 to 1946 and Secretary of State for War from 1946 to 1947.

Then Attlee sent for him. Fred described the interview to me.

'Bellenger, I want your resignation.'

Poor Fred was aghast. He was not brilliant but there were worse ministers.

'I am very sorry to hear that, Prime Minister. I thought I'd been doing rather well. Could you give me any reason?'

'No good. That's all. No good.'

End of interview.

Raymond Blackburn's career was sadder. He made an exceptionally brilliant maiden speech about the looming shadow of nuclear warfare which enthralled the House. A new parliamentary figure had arrived. Attlee, then Prime Minister, sent him a warm congratulatory note. So did Churchill, whom he visited several times at Chartwell where he was given too much praise and drink. He lost his balance. Drinking far more than he could manage he became frequently aggressive. John Freeman – who had also known him in the Army – and I had to persuade him out of the Chamber on one turbulent occasion.

We urged him to be more sensible so that he could secure the glittering future to which his oratorical and mental gifts entitled him, but he was lost to reason. He stopped answering letters, which lay in heaps on the floor of his flat. He insulted his local constituency party. He left Parliament in 1951 and the promise of his life was wasted. Something went wrong in his highly strung head, for which I partly blame Churchill, who enjoyed and returned the flattery of this scintillating young man.

I shall always be grateful to Raymond Blackburn. Apart from introducing me to Fred Bellenger, who put me on Labour's list of candidates, he got me the chance to be adopted at Aston, Birmingham. Himself already the candidate at King's Norton, Birmingham, Raymond lobbied for me to be put on the short-list at a selection conference which was to be held in the period between my leaving France and departing for India. The local party was worried that the quality of those on offer was not good enough to dislodge a large Tory majority. They wanted a serviceman who might appeal to working-class patriotism, always much stronger than intellectuals suppose.

As it happened, they had two servicemen to choose from: Roy Jenkins, a captain in the Intelligence Corps with the bonus of having a father who was a well-known miners' MP, and myself. It was the only time I ever did anything better politically than Roy and it was by chance. Jim Meadows, the local agent, lived in a tiny back-to-back house, 81 Mansfield Road. He asked us both, separately, whether we would like to stay the night with him. He explained that the lavatory was down the garden path, that washing and shaving was in the kitchen sink, that comfort was minimal. Roy said he would prefer to stay in an hotel. I thought it could not be worse than slit-trenches and was anyway agog, after my Bolton experiences with Tom Harrisson, to see more deeply how the working classes lived and get among them. I asked to stay with Jim. He was delighted and immediately became my advocate. He also remained a close and loyal friend, despite my leaving the Labour Party.

We had to speak for fifteen minutes and answer questions at the selection conference. I had never made a political speech and learned mine by heart. It was terrible and my hesitant, embarrassed delivery was punctuated by long blanks, the selection committee thinking anxiously that I was so stuck I would not be able to go on. My answers to questions were nervous and naïve. But they chose me. It was my staying at 81 Mansfield Road that did it.

The chances of winning Aston were slim, but I had made a start. I knew that as soon as the election was announced all service candidates overseas would be flown back and demobbed if successful. That prospect was better than carrying a field-marshal's baton in my knapsack to India.

# CHAPTER V

---◧◩◨---

# An Ecstatic MP

AT FIRST I WAS APPALLED. The coolies who unloaded the ship at Bombay seemed, with their beanpole thin legs, half starved and incapable of carrying their burdens. The poverty, the over-crowding, screeched at you. Like everyone else, Indian and British, I soon got used to it. The beauty of most of the people and of the buildings, the exotic sights and smells, the romantic past all around, overwhelmed me. It was as exciting as going to Oxford, and educated Indians were natural Oxford under-graduates in their willingness to talk into the night. I have never fallen out of love with India or Indians.

I was posted to Movements, GHQ, Delhi. That was on the left-hand side of the Secretariat built by Baker on both sides of the approach to Lutyens's Viceroy's House. They were the last great architectural fling of the British Raj: pink, with touches of white, like the New Delhi Lutyens also built. Indians tended to emphasize the white. Perhaps that was because of an ancient prophecy which K. M. Panikkar, Dewan, or Prime Minister, of Bikaner, told me about. There would be thirteen Delhis and the last would be white. This was the thirteenth, so it had to be white as an omen of the end of the British Raj.

The corridors in the Secretariat were high and wide. It was December when I arrived, the so-called cold season which was like an English summer. Skinny men in dhotis crouched over braziers in the corridors. They were the *chaprasis* or messengers. 'They're no good in the winter because it's too cold for them, and they're no good in the summer because it's too hot for them,' one of the staff remarked. English visitors tended to confuse the word *chaprasi* with *chapati*, the large round and flat pancake of unleavened bread served with every meal. Mrs Naidu, the poetess and Congress leader, told me that Mrs Nichol, a

Labour member of the Parliamentary Delegation which went out in 1946, said to her, 'I do love Indian food but, oh, those *chaprasis* do lie so heavily on me after lunch.' Maybe, but I think the same joke may have been told of others.

The first serious matter to be discussed was the annual month's leave. As the last arrival I would have to take mine in the next few weeks, still in the cold season, the scorching hot weather slots, when everyone wanted to be out of Delhi, already being filled. I was delighted. With the Germans on the run the war in Europe would be over and an election called soon after my leave finished. I could find out a lot about India with the help of a month's tour. The first impact of a country often leaves the clearest and truest impressions. After a few months, qualifications, contradictions and the ifs and buts set in.

I plunged headlong into Indian politics. Nehru was in gaol. His cousin, R. K. Nehru, was near the top of the Indian Civil Service. He had an elegant, vivacious wife, Raja, who was openly active on behalf of Indian prisoners of war of the Japanese who had deserted to Subhas Bhose's Indian National Army to fight the British. Husband and wife wanted Independence and found no inconsistency in one of them working to keep the British Raj going and the other working to destroy it. They were both pro-British and steeped in British ways, as was Nehru himself. Sri Prakasa, a leading member of Congress, said to me, 'Nehru's not really Indian. He's English. He approaches Independence not as a passionate nationalist but as an English liberal who thinks it is unreasonable for India not to govern herself.'

Nehru's cousins entertained and instructed me. I bathed in their warmth and sophisticated hospitality. Being of aristocratic Brahmin background, they were natural supporters of Congress. They saw life through cultured, liberal Indian eyes tinted with Hinduism. They could not understand the Muslim demand for Pakistan and thought it arose from a perverse megalomania of Mr Jinnah. They were certain that when Jawaharlal Nehru and other Congress leaders were able to circulate freely again, the Muslim League would evaporate.

Tarsi Shah Nawaz from the Punjab taught me otherwise. She was my age, not beautiful but with a compelling energy which made her lively face attractive as it lit to her enthusiasm. Of old

Mogul aristocratic descent, she felt it painful that those who had ruled India and were the last to hold out against the British should be made subordinate to the Hindus they had conquered. She was convinced that this was what would happen to the minority Muslims in a unified India. The Hindus were cleverer at commerce and politics. The Muslims would be the peasants, manipulated by smart Hindus. The Muslims might have the simple martial virtues but the Hindus had the brains, and the post-war world would not be propitious for another imposition of military rule by the Muslims over the Hindus. So Tarsi and her friends concluded that Pakistan it must be. Tarsi had been a Communist, perhaps still was when I first met her: Pakistan to her was not a pawn in an imperialist plot, as many in Congress alleged.

I met the Communists. They were young and persuasively idealistic, contemptuous of the corrupt politicians in the other parties, sceptical of British willingness to hand over power unless forced to. As Russia was in the war they, unlike Congress, supported the war effort. They were full of facts about Indian conditions, and they were sincere. Those who had money – and some came from prosperous backgrounds – gave it to the Communist Party. But early on I realized that their chance of persuading the Indian masses to accept Marxism was zero. The Muslims were too religious. The Hindus were religious too and stuck in the caste system. Only a full-scale war of independence with the Communists in the vanguard could win them the converts they needed, and the British were not going to let them have that opportunity.

One morning I had a visitor in my office at the Secretariat. He was some kind of intelligence officer. 'We have been watching you,' he said. 'You keep seeing Indians and visiting their homes. There are plenty of British here to talk to. Why do you want to see Indians? No one else does.'

It took me an hour and a half to convince him that I was not engaged in a conspiracy to overthrow the British Raj and that my innocent desire was to find out all I could about India before returning to England for the General Election. To do that it was necessary for me to see Indians who, though he might find it surprising, were among the overwhelming majority of the population in India.

'It's most unusual. Be careful.'

But I met many British, too. One of them I shall call Jane, whose husband was attached to an international research organisation at Coonoor in southern India. I fell in love with her. She had fair hair, blue eyes and considerable intelligence. She was small and graceful, with lovely legs, and was like the fairy on top of a Christmas tree. In India crops and love-affairs grow fast and die quickly. The nights are soft and warm and the moon is hardly ever obscured by clouds. Before she introduced us Freda Wint said, 'She is the most attractive girl in India and you are attractive, too. There is bound to be an explosion.' Freda Wint was a close friend of Susan's out in India in Old Delhi, with her husband Guy Wint. I do not know what she said to Jane about me but her forecast was correct.

Jane knew a lot about India, both from the Indian angle and the British. Governors, senior ICS officials and Indians alike opened their hearts and minds to this enchanting creature. I stayed with her and her husband during my month's leave. The hills around Coonoor were like the Sussex Downs on a perfect English summer's day. We lay on them reading poetry and feeling young and happy. She gave me on 2 April 1945 a little black, leather-bound New Testament, though our behaviour was not in precise accordance with its principles. I have it still. She had a gift for love which was irresistible. After the war I would motor after the House rose to spend a few hours with her at a house she had in Hertfordshire. Then, I would travel many miles to see a mistress, however briefly.

It was pleasant travelling in India if you could afford a first-class compartment. In my month's tour I went to Lahore, Amritsar, Calcutta, Madras, Bikaner (a native state) and other centres, equipped with a copy of Murray's *Handbook of India* given me by Cyril Connolly. The train stopped at stations for meals at the platform restaurant. The food was horrible, but unusually I did not mind about that. I fed on the sights and sounds. The hordes of beggars on the platform were heavily outnumbered by the thousands getting off and on the trains or waiting patiently as they did for days for the right connection. The filthy wooden-seated and wooden backed third-class carriages had no fans. They carried five or six times their quotas, some standing on the running-boards clinging on to anything they could get hold of, some sitting on the ledges of open windows with their bottoms protruding, some on the roof, others standing in the compartments and the corridors. No travellers accepted that a train was too full to get on and no officials tried to prevent them. Stations and the train were a focal point of Indian life.

My candidature for the forthcoming General Election was a passport to see anyone not in gaol. In Madras I visited C. Rajagopalacharya. He was Prime Minister of Madras until Congress withdrew from governing the provinces in 1939. He was sad at not being in government but he had not long to wait. He was in the Interim Government of India in 1946 until Independence and succeeded Mountbatten as Governor-General of India before going back to run Madras again. He was sixty-six when I met him.

'How old are you?'

'Twenty-six.'

He was highly amused. 'But old enough to rule India.'

C. Rajagopalacharya adored the British, while wanting self-government. He was in from the beginning with Gandhi in his non co-operation movement in 1919. He did his regulation stints of imprisonment but felt civil disobedience was pointless after the Cripps mission of 1942. He thought Gandhi was silly to make Congress reject Cripps's offer of immediate *de jure* self-government after the war and *de facto* self-government in 1942 in return for co-operation in the war effort. If Gandhi had accepted the offer there would probably have been a unified India today.

C.R. was equivocal about Gandhi. They pretended to like each other but did not. Gandhi was jealous of C.R., who had a better brain. He resented his huge popularity in Madras where Brahmins count more than Banyas, the merchant, money-lending caste to which Gandhi belonged. C.R. hinted that there was something phoney about Gandhi and was cynical about his methods of ensuring a mass following but he did not dare say so publicly or his chances of office after Independence would be gone.

C.R. gave me quantities of coconut-milk to drink. It was

delicious. In Calcutta, in a great dark house built by some East India Company merchant in the eighteenth century, H. S. Suhrawardy showed me how to slice mangoes. We must have eaten twenty apiece. Though William Hickey says Rose Aylmer, of Landor's 'form divine', was destroyed when she was eighteen by her eating pineapples, Suhrawardy and I thought it must have been mangoes. (I went to pay my respects at her grave in Calcutta at the South Park Street Cemetery and silently lamented the early loss of such beauty.) The water in the swamps where the mango trees stood in the eighteenth century was frequently polluted and the fruit, delicious to eat, delicate in colour and innocent in appearance, carried killer diseases like typhoid. Ours must have stood in pure water.

Suhrawardy was plump and sleek, dressed in an immaculate white tunic. He spoke Oxford English with better elocution than Professor Higgins and far more polished phrases. He was Food Minister in the Bengal Government which, not being Congress, had continued in office. His enemies said he had made much money out of food hoarding in the great Bengal famine. They may have said so because Bengali politicians were notoriously corrupt and Suhrawardy was noted for dishonesty and intrigue. He was sympathetic to the Muslim League but unostentatiously so, waiting to see how things developed before committing himself. Jinnah once told me he did not trust him. Nor did I. But he was charming, civilized and free with valuable information, particularly about his enemies. He became Prime Minister of Pakistan in 1956, eight years after Jinnah was dead. He did not last long. As Jinnah feared, he was not the type of politician on which to found a young state.

During my month's tour I let India wash over me. Impressions fell in haystacks. I resisted none, and out of the jumble patterns emerged. The Muslim League had become too solid to vanish for the convenience of the Congress leaders. Jinnah was certain to get a Muslim area more or less autonomous. It was not practicable for dear, muddled Master Tara Singh, to whom I talked in Amritsar, to get a separate state for his Sikhs, scattered as they were round the Punjab, despite their loyalty as soldiers of the British Raj. Nor could Panikkar with all his guile and erudition save the Princely States (he had been Secretary to the Indian States delegation to the pre-war Round Table Conference).

But Panikkar did not have to worry about his future. The librarian to the Maharaja of Bikaner, K. P. Sharma, was also the court astrologer. He was excellent at casting horoscopes. He had to be. Whenever he made a mistake about the Maharaja's immediate future he was put in the local gaol to encourage him to do better next time. He was careful with Prime Minister Panikkar, too. Panikkar's charted path was prosperous. He was puzzled by one of the predictions, however. It was that in a few years Panikkar would have a post of great responsibility and influence hundreds of miles to the north-east of Delhi. The stars presumably knew that Mao Tse-tung would conquer China and that Panikkar would be Indian Ambassador in Peking from 1948 to 1952; that he would be trusted by Peking as a representative of a country which in Communist Chinese eyes had just defeated imperialism; by America because he was pro-Oxford (where he got a scholarship and a First), pro-British and pro-Western; and thus would be able to persuade both parties into beginning the negotiations which ended the war in Korea. It must have been the days that the astrologer spent in the local gaol brushing up the stars which inspired him.

The Bikaner court astrologer cast my horoscope in early 1945. I had never met him. He knew I was a major, and possibly Panikkar had told him that I was a parliamentary candidate, though he said he had not done so, but he could not have told him that I would win Aston with its huge Tory majority. The horoscope is awry in places. Some things have happened at different times to the forecast. But allowing for Indian hyperbole and flattery, and an understandable ignorance of the British political and social system, the horoscope has always maintained a rough reliability in direction. I look at it in my bleakest moments. There is a comforting all's well that ends well touch to it that fuels my optimism. I seem to keep going in reasonable order till I am seventy-four, at which point Mr Sharma becomes silent or enigmatic. I hope it is merely that the clouds hid the stars from his futuristic telescope at that point. For those interested in such matters I include the horoscope in an appendix at the end of the book, with my annotations. Logically it should all be nonsense, but somehow it is not entirely so.

Unfortunately Mr Sharma also cast Guy Wint's horoscope. It foretold early success, to be followed quickly by a tailing off. Guy's father was a West Country postmaster. Guy won a scholarship to Oxford. He did not get the Fellowship he strove for. He started with good jobs but they declined in significance compared with his intellectual abilities. After many years he became a member of the Senior Common Room at St Antony's, Oxford; it was not the kind of academic post he had hoped for as an undergraduate. He had a stroke on a train standing at Paddington Station in September, 1961 and died in 1969. He wrote a moving book, *The Third Killer*, recording his sensations during his long speechlessness and immobility. Otherwise there was nothing. I am sure the horoscope was always heavy in his mind.

A few months after my return to Delhi there came a call for parliamentary candidates in the Services to return to England. I left India and the Army and this time I travelled by air. The Labour Party held a Conference in Blackpool from 21 May to 25 May 1945. I hurried down there, bursting with my news about India. Krishna Menon addressed a meeting. Politely and hesitantly I explained with facts and figures that he had got it wrong about the Muslim League, which had not been invented by the British as he suggested. India could not be handed over to Congress to run as one unit without the consent of Jinnah. The gloomy Krishna Menon, Secretary of the India League since 1927 and a St Pancras Labour councillor since 1934, scowled at me with his long, malevolent face. How, he demanded, could a novice like me claim to know more about India than he did? I said I didn't, but I had just been there and he hadn't since long before the war, so he was out of touch. He never forgave me. When he was High Commissioner for India in London he tried to prevent me seeing Nehru whenever he visited the city. Despite Attlee's refusal to communicate with Delhi through Krishna Menon because so much was leaked to the Russians, Nehru continued to think him wonderful and made him Minister of Defence, which was a strange post for someone who wanted the Communists to win.

Fervent that the Labour Party should understand the urgent need for Indian Independence, I sought out Aneurin Bevan. I had winkles and cockles with him on the front. I succumbed immediately to his charm but was amazed at his reaction. He was amused: 'Congress are gutless. They haven't even been able to get rid of a mere 30,000 British troops all these years. Why should they expect us to do it for them? We have more important things to do.'

I had better luck with Stafford Cripps. He wanted Indian Independence quickly. He listened courteously and, despite his weakness for Congress, recognized that the Muslim League must be taken seriously. He talked to me as an equal. It was a talent he had with the young and it drew them to him. At that meeting at the Imperial Hotel in Blackpool my permanent admiration of him began.

From Blackpool it was off to the hustings. I learned a speech by heart, adding a few variations when I dared to, so that the ardent helpers who went to all the meetings might have some alleviation of the monotony. The meetings were better attended than in television days and there was excitement in the air. Not six years but sixty might have divided 1939 and 1945. It was a new world.

I covered every alley, courtyard and set of back-to-back houses in Aston. Ugly, cramped, wretched in their disrepair, there were not two hundred bathrooms among the lot; they were more like stables than dwellings for humans. Jim Meadow's house was two up, two down. In my bedroom we put pails and a strategically placed towel on the bed to catch the water dripping through the roof, yet his was one of the best houses. But Jim and his wife, Edna, were very cosy in that house. Jugs of beer from the local pub, roast beef, cabbage and roast potatoes: Edna cooked well and the political talk with the many who dropped in made us contented on a Sunday afternoon.

The outrage felt by an outsider at atrocious conditions is not always shared by those who live in them. Edna kept her little house so well that, despite the holes in it, I looked forward to staying there and much preferred it to the idea of a bedroom at an impersonal hotel. So it was with others in much worse straits. Miserable houses do not automatically make miserable people. That explains why in Aston many stayed Tory despite rotten landlords and housing.

On my vote-soliciting rounds I approached a house with boards in place of half the windows, holes in the bulging walls, slates off the roof, the front-door lintels lop-sided. I knocked on the front door, from which most of the paint had fallen, and the door almost fell down. An old, unshaven man tugged its remains open, wearing a torn and dirty shirt, torn trousers, and boots with the soles coming away from the uppers. 'I'm the Labour candidate. Can we count on your vote?' I asked confidently. He glared at me. 'Go on with you. You don't even believe in the Union Jack,' and he quickly slammed the door.

As the campaign went on, signs of hope began to appear. Canvass returns in Lozells, the posher part where there were lace curtains in the windows and kippers for tea, were showing more support than expected. A few days before polling day reports came in of Labour stickers going up where they had never been seen before, not even when John Strachey narrowly won Aston for Labour in 1929. The unimaginable started to be imaginable: the Tory majority of 12,000 might not be invulnerable. Polling day was 5 July, the day after my twenty-seventh birthday.

To give time for the counting of servicemen's votes coming in from all over the world, the results were not to be announced until 26 July. We spent the intervening period on endless calculations of how the vote had gone, alternating between pessimism and optimism, the latter gradually gaining the upper hand, though we could not forget the huge crowds which cheered Churchill in the streets when he came to Birmingham. I was among them, seeing Churchill for the first time, and cheering him too, without intending to vote Tory. So maybe others had done the same. Just before the count Mr Lovesey, the wily Tory agent, said he thought we might have done it by two thousand. He was wrong. We had done it by six.

The celebrations lasted all day, and half the night Jim played 'Strephon's a Member of Parliament' from *Iolanthe* on the gramophone again and again, shouting Woodrow instead of Strephon. I was not the youngest MP but the second youngest; Ned Carson, son of the great Lord Carson, elected Tory MP for Thanet, was twenty-five.

The next great event was the meeting of the 390 Labour MPs

at Beaver Hall on 28 July, where Attlee was acclaimed as Prime Minister and Leader of the Party. In my innocence I knew nothing of the intrigues that Herbert Morrison had been busy with in the hope of becoming Prime Minister himself. I still thought all was sweetness and friendship at the top of the Labour Party. But poor Morrison, who seemed so cheerful with his one eye, quiff in the front of his hair, easy speaking style and spontaneous quips, had a grievance which could never go away. When he lost his seat in 1931, the handful of Labour MPs left after the slaughter had made Attlee Deputy Leader. In 1935 Morrison was back in the House again. He thought his succession to the now departed leader, George Lansbury, would be automatic, but the Labour MPs chose the quiet, mousy Attlee he despised.

'It was the Freemasons who did it,' Morrison told me when I got to know him better. 'There were about forty of them. They had a meeting and decided to keep me out by voting for Attlee. That was enough. That's why I hate Freemasons.'

The post-election meeting at Beaver Hall was Morrison's last chance. Technically the Parliamentary Labour Party chose its leader at the beginning of each session and had not yet done so in 1945. There were hundreds of new Labour MPs who had taken no part in choosing Attlee. Morrison did not want Attlee to go to the Palace as prospective Prime Minister until the meeting at Beaver Hall had decided who was Labour's leader. He and Harold Laski, Chairman of the Labour Party, wrote to Attlee to that effect, Morrison saying he would be a candidate for the leadership. Morrison enlisted the support of Cripps (who had been his protégé when he first joined the Labour Party) and a few others but came unstuck with Ernest Bevin, who told him 'to stop mucking about or you won't be in the Government at all.'

No one suggested a leadership election at Beaver Hall. And Attlee left his resignation from the Labour Party leadership until 1955, when Morrison was nearly sixty-eight and out of the running, as Attlee knew he would be. Many disliked Morrison besides Attlee; Bevin for one, who made the famous reply to someone remarking that Morrison was his own worst enemy, 'not while I'm alive'. Churchill, in whose War Cabinet he was, detested Morrison as a low-level party manoeuvrer. I found him engagingly friendly, and in the frankness of his ambition more honest than most politicians. The Labour Party owed him much for his organizational ability and the good advertisement it got from the efficient way he ran the London County Council from 1930 to 1940.

Two days after the Beaver Hall meeting Hugh Dalton, the new Chancellor of the Exchequer, gave a dinner for twelve new Members he considered might prove to be bright sparks. Eight, including myself, became ministers within six years, two of these becoming Leaders of the Labour Party. A seventh, Dick Crossman, had to wait nearly twenty-one years for office. It was the first time I met Hugh Gaitskell and Harold Wilson. Hugh Dalton asked us all in turn to say what the Government's problems would be and how they should be tackled. In this weighty company I was terrified. Nearly all were twice as clever and knowledgeable as I was, but Dalton was kind to me as he always was to the young.

On 1 August the House met in the House of Lords, the Commons Chamber not yet having been rebuilt. The first business was to choose a Speaker. When Winston Churchill came in to take his place the Tories stood up and sang 'For He's a Jolly Good Fellow'. There was no Speaker and no Rules of Order to stop them. He was moved and I felt sorry for this great man, rejected for the sins of his associates.

The response to 'For He's a Jolly Good Fellow' was instant. A Labour MP leaped up and began 'The Red Flag' and the ranks of Labour, overflowing on to the Opposition benches, joined in. That was the first and last time that bloodthirsty and ridiculous anthem was sung in the Chamber of the House of Lords, where previously the only thing red had been the colour of the benches (it is red for the Lords and green for the Commons). All very exhilarating.

Walking down Westminster Hall and through St Stephen's Hall I was conscious of Britain's glorious past, which I mistakenly thought extended to her present and future. It seemed a proud privilege to be an MP in 1945, to mix with the world famous and to believe that Britain would continue to have a decisive voice in how the world developed. What was said at Westminster was then listened to with respect in distant capitals.

When you asked the Prime Minister about India or Germany, it was not merely a few newspapers in Britain which took the answer seriously.

I was standing by the ticker-tape outside the Members' Smoking Room when Attlee first spoke to me. To me he was a great man, so far above me that he was nearly out of sight. I made some footling answer, ending with 'Sir'. 'Don't call me Sir,' he said brusquely. 'We're both members of the same party. Call me Clem.' In his curt way he was trying to put me at ease. But he could never do that with me or anyone else. When Stafford Cripps resigned in October 1950 before his last long illness he told me how surprised he had been at his final meeting with Attlee. 'We talked for more than an hour. It was the first real conversation I ever had with him.' They had known each other since Stafford became Solicitor-General in the same Labour Government as Attlee in 1930.

When Attlee tried small-talk it was agonizing. His jokes were laughed at in the wrong places. The toughest politicians uttered nervous idiocies to him. He must have thought he was surrounded by lunatics. At a party in the garden of No. 10 I asked him where he was going for his holiday. He said it was somewhere around Norway, where he was also making an official visit and the Navy was going to drop him off.

'That's very kind of them,' I said nervously, reaching for an adequate continuation of the conversation.

'Why? I should jolly well hope they would.'

Petrified I could not think of any way to progress from there.

He shunned any form of intimacy, probably feeling it would lead to entanglements. Someone very senior dared to suggest to him that, when he fired a minister, he might be a little gentler. That registered. There was a pleasant but ineffectual Under-Secretary whom I shall call George Smith, who was getting nowhere. When Smith was still just short of sixty Attlee sent for him.

'Well, George, some of us have given long and loyal service to the Party.'

'Yes, Clem,' George said.

'And there comes a time when we must think of handing on to younger spirits.'

'You're not thinking of resigning are you, Clem?' Smith asked anxiously.

Attlee was happier with his normal style. Frank Owen was Editor of the *Daily Express* before becoming Editor of the *Evening Standard* from 1937 to 1941. Attlee understandably disliked both these Beaverbrook papers. Owen joined up in 1941 and in South-East Asia conducted some newspapers for servicemen in a lively but non-political manner. After leaving the Army he became Editor of the strongly anti-Labour *Daily Mail*. At a reception in the Commons I was talking to him when Attlee passed by. 'Do you know Frank Owen?' I asked him. Attlee stopped and stared at Owen. 'Yes, I know him. He's returned like a dog to his own vomit.' Then he walked on.

Maurice Edelman was an accomplished journalist and novelist and a Labour MP. He was at a private dinner party where Princess Margaret was also present. He used the occasion and what he heard in an article in an American magazine. The Palace was annoyed and said so to Attlee, now Leader of the Opposition. Edelman told me that Attlee asked to see him and rebuked him for his bad behaviour. Edelman defended himself and asked what he had done wrong. 'It wasn't the behaviour of a gentleman,' Attlee said. 'I don't know what you mean,' the flustered Edelman answered. 'Exactly,' Attlee replied. The interview was over.

Some were surprised that Attlee took the earldom to which ex-prime ministers are entitled. To him it was consistent with his belief in the monarchy and the Victorian virtues. He never wanted to turn society upside-down or extinguish its rewards for service. He wanted to improve it. Fairness and moderation were his guides both in public and personal dealings.

Four days after the King's Speech which opened the proceedings of the 1945 Parliament on 16 August, I decided to make my maiden speech. There were rows of new Labour MPs waiting to take the plunge. John Freeman had led the way as the Mover of the Address in Reply to the Gracious Speech. Dressed in the uniform of a Rifle Brigade major, young and handsome, he spoke impressively: 'Today we go into action. Today may rightly be regarded as the "D-day" in the battle of the new Britain.' We all felt the same on the Labour side. We were about to change Britain.

On the day I made my maiden speech I sat next to Jim Callaghan. He was called before me and spoke with ease and fluency. His accomplished performance made me more nervous. I was miles out of my class. After three more speakers, it was my turn. I stumbled for thirteen minutes through a speech about India, the only subject I dared talk about. I spoke of starvation and self-government and despotism in the Princely States. It was boring and banal, slightly relieved by Quintin Hogg's breach of the convention that maiden speakers should not be interrupted. I said I had asked the Prime Minister of a native state what he would do if I were a subject of his state and demanded constitutional government. His reply had been: 'I would offer you a good job to keep you quiet.' At which point Quintin Hogg shouted; 'That's what they do here!'

It was the sole joke in my earnest speech. It shot a hole in my story which led up to the gaoling of any such subjects who refused the job and persisted in asking for democracy. But it did not matter. No one was listening, apart from those waiting to make their own speeches, or the odd old Member dropping in to look briefly at the new intake.

I followed up my speech with numerous questions on India and other subjects, particularly the Army. I scurried about enthusiastically, attending committees, talking endlessly to other MPs late into the night. It was a dream-world turned real. In the Members' Smoking Room I sat happily in the circle round Nye Bevan. He was a clubbable man who liked to drink, gossip and pour out his comments among a group of admirers. Michael Foot, John Strachey, Tom Driberg and Geoffrey Bing, descendant of a Chinese sea captain, were among them. The conversation was brisk and funny, the jokes frequently provided by Nye Bevan. There was a veteran Labour MP called Seymour Cocks. Once when his name came up on the indicator as speaking in the Chamber Nye looked up and said, 'Oh yes, Seymour Cocks and hear more balls.'

I had no money other than my parliamentary salary of £600 a year. There was no secretarial allowance, and although £6 to £7 a week or thereabouts was the going rate for a secretary it was over half my £600, from which tax and contributions to an unfunded pension were also deducted. I had to pay, too, for a two-roomed flat I had taken at Chatsworth Court just off the Earls Court Road. 'A good address,' remarked my Uncle Arthur, with whom I was temporarily reconciled. I was still getting a little from *English Story* but my income was far below what I needed for constituency expenses, clothes, food and wine at a time when I drank something like a bottle and three-quarters of wine a day and liked to eat well. So I began to write for newspapers and magazines. It is a convenient but tiring way of making money. Writing is the hardest form of work for the naturally lazy. Some do it easily. For me the concentration required is painful. It is fine when you have finished but hell while you are doing it.

Tom Driberg introduced me to Bill Richardson, the Editor of *Reynolds News*, the Co-operative Sunday newspaper supporting the Labour Party. Bill Richardson was sturdy, ruddy and friendly and allowed me to write some articles. *Reynolds News* was somewhat to the Left, but so was I in an untutored, unthought-out way. The root-and-branch changing of the world for the better has a simplistic attraction at twenty-seven.

I could not write for *Reynolds News* unless I was a member of the National Union of Journalists. I applied to join. What have you written in the Press? I was asked. 'Almost nothing,' was the answer. 'Then you can't be a member of the NUJ.' 'How can I show you what I have written in the Press if you won't let me write in *Reynolds News*?' I asked. After persuasion from Bill Richardson I was allowed in. I have been a member of that myopic organization ever since. By its success in preventing non-members from making regular contributions to the Press, and its support of union chapels refusing to print criticisms of the print and other unions, it has done what it can to restrict freedom of expression, which is strange for a body representing journalists.

My articles were stilted, full of facts, and very dull. Tom Driberg showed me how to put some lightness into them and a modicum of good English and punctuation. He also made me giggle for many days by pointing out that the Speaker's announcement at the end of Questions, 'The Clerk will now proceed to read the Orders of the Day', fits the tune of the 'Battle Hymn of the Republic', which we hummed to the Speaker's words. Tom encouraged me to experiment with the procedures of the Commons, to extract from them the maximum available to a backbencher trying to get himself heard. Immediately after the war not everyone wanted to put down questions and make speeches, as they do now. The Speaker would allow two supplementaries from the same Member at Question Time and ministers were subject to a mild cross-examination, which they now avoid with the one-off brush-off.

My interest in India brought me a place on the Parliamentary Delegation which went to India in the Christmas recess, landing there on 3 January 1946. En route we stopped at Shepheard's Hotel in Cairo, where I ordered three dozen fried eggs after arriving in the middle of the night. Arthur Bottomley, one of the delegates, was very amused and ordered six for himself. Eggs were still rationed in England and a feast of them, though only half the size of English eggs, could not be missed. Arthur was a former official of the National Union of Public Employees, eleven years older than I, solid and sensible, the kind of man who used to be the bulwark of the Labour Party. He had tolerance and no vindictiveness. He was underrated when Commonwealth Secretary in Wilson's 1964 government. He had not a clue about India but he got hold of the essentials, quickly outstripping Reg Sorensen, who was also in the Delegation, a colleague of Krishna Menon in the India League and an uncritical devotee of Gandhi and Congress.

The Parliamentary Delegation went to spy out the land and to convince India that Britain genuinely intended to hand over power. The immediate reaction of the ever-suspicious Nehru and other Congress leaders was that they would not see us. All Britain had to do was to quit India, and Nehru saw the Parliamentary Delegation as a device for further delay. But Gandhi was curious to see the strange ragbag of British MPs, and Congress changed its attitude.

The ten of us set off to Madras by air to meet Gandhi. The RAF lost my luggage, which momentous event is recorded for posterity in *Transfer of Power*, the official history of the run-up to Independence. It was the second time I lost my luggage in India. When I left in May 1945 by air to take part in the election I arranged for a tin box, beautifully secured, to be sent on by sea. It contained books precious to me, including a proof copy of *The Unquiet Grave*, profusely amended and annotated by Cyril Connolly. The box never arrived. If that copy of *The Unquiet Grave* is still circulating in the bazaars, I hope they are getting the price for it that it would now fetch at Christie's. Or maybe somebody burned it.

The meeting with Gandhi was comical. I recognized him at once as a great humourist. It is a pity P. G. Wodehouse never met him: he would have developed him lovingly into a notable literary character. We were taken late in the evening to the large encampment which always assembled wherever Gandhi halted. The paths were neat and well swept, the bungalows fresh and clean. A band of Gandhi youths bearing flaming torches accompanied us through the camp, which was not luxurious but agreeable in the simplicity enforced by Gandhi. As Mrs Naidu said, it cost a great deal of money to keep Gandhi in poverty.

Later that year, when he was finally persuaded to talk to the Cabinet Mission in Delhi, Gandhi announced that he would stay in the sweepers' quarters among the Untouchables. As they lived in swarming, unhygienic squalor, there was considerable alarm for Gandhi's safety and health, but I guessed what would happen. Gandhi's multimillionaire friend, G.D. Birla, bought a chunk of the sweepers' quarters, turned the inhabitants out, and cleansed, disinfected and decorated the little buildings with lavish quantities of whitewash. In forty-eight hours Gandhi's Delhi camp looked as spruce and agreeable as the one we saw him in at Madras.

Gandhi was waiting for us upstairs and we were led to a veranda, where a semicircle of chairs was arranged so that Gandhi, squatting on the floor, could see us all. His nearly naked body shone like a polished betel-nut or well-groomed horse, and gleamed with health. There were no hairs on it and it reflected what light there was. Ben Kingsley's face in the film *Gandhi* has some resemblance to its hero's, but Gandhi would have been horrified by the mass of furry hair on his chest. This was one of the many inaccuracies, distortions and omissions of that film concocted by Goldcrest and Sir Richard Attenborough, who denigrated the British in the style of the trendy Left and gave a halo to Gandhi on the assumption that he was not only a saint but had accelerated Independence, whereas his main political contribution was to delay it.

The preliminaries to the meeting were polite trivialities. Gandhi asked how old I was. The answer, twenty-seven, provoked one of his high-pitched giggles.

'Hee, hee, hee. Younger than my grandsons but old enough to be one of the rulers of India.' (It was much what Rajagopalacharya had said to me in Madras the year before.)

Whereupon Mrs Muriel Nichol asked him how many sons he had and, in a supplementary, how many daughters.

'I have a million daughters. Are you satisfied?'

'Yes, but are you, Mr Gandhi?' Mrs Nichol replied. She didn't realize, with Gandhi's fondness for close contact with women, what a good point she had made.

The ten MPs began to ask serious questions. Gandhi gave no serious answers. He was amused by our bewilderment. When asked about the method and machinery for handing over power he repeated again and again: 'Get off our backs. We can't walk. Get off our backs.'

It was quiet and the hum of the camp was soothing in the warm night air on the veranda. After two and a half hours of meaningless exchanges Bob Richards, the Welsh leader of the Delegation and Under-Secretary for India in the 1924 Labour Government, fell asleep. Something disturbed him and he woke up with a jerk and stared at Gandhi. 'Well, Mr Jinnah,' he began. Gandhi was momentarily startled by what he may have thought a joke. Then the high-pitched 'Hee, hee, hee' started again. 'You flatter me,' he said. 'Hee, hee, hee,' laughing for several minutes.

But it had all been a joke. Gandhi intended to make fools of us. Afterwards I asked Agatha Harrison, an English Quaker member of his court, why all his replies to sensible questions had been nonsense. The answer was that Gandhi had been testing our sincerity. (Gandhi was always testing other people's sincerity but keenly resented anyone trying to test his.) It seemed he thought it possible we might be sincere but that we would have to give much more evidence before he would believe it, thus implying that the ten MPs drawn from three parties were lying when they repeatedly asserted that Britain was determined on Independence and India would get it as soon as it could be established to whom power should be handed over.

I was invited to a separate interview with Gandhi. At 6.30 a.m. in the cool new air we walked up and down on a flat rooftop. He made more sense this time. He was against further discussions and conferences: the time for them was over. It was too late for Dominion status with full self-government to succeed. Congress and he had been in favour of Dominion status but then his great friend, Charlie Andrews, had persuaded him it was not suitable for countries without English racial origins. Only complete separation and full Independence with no special links would do.

What Britain had to do now was simple. India had become accustomed to British rule. 'The slave clings to his chains and he must have them struck from him.' We must quit India forthwith and not bother about what happened afterwards. If we did not want to hand over to Congress, we must hand over to Mr Jinnah and the Muslim League. He would tell Congress to serve under Mr Jinnah and we would see what would happen. 'I have some favourite lines from a Moody and Sankey hymnal, which I am sorry are not sung so often nowadays: "Keep Thou my feet; I do not ask to see/The distant scene, – one step enough for me."' On no account was Britain to divide India. It must be handed over intact. If Britain had no thoughts of self-interest, she would gain from Indian freedom. Her trade with India would increase because there was so much goodwill towards her.

That interview with Gandhi was the first of several private conversations I had with him. I felt no awe of him as did the Congress leaders, particularly Nehru, and as I did of Attlee and sometimes Cripps. I liked Gandhi enormously and I think he liked me, once sending a message complaining that I had not been to see him and was neglecting him: 'Perhaps you saw enough of me last time.' He laughed at my jokes and I laughed at his, which were subtler and better than mine.

He was bored by much of the reverence he was smothered in by his humourless disciples. The physically unattractive white females, speaking humbly like nuns in the presence of a saint, were the worst, though some of the Indians were creepy too. I was with him when he was told who was to come in his immediate entourage on a trip with him. 'Oh dear, must they come?' he asked pleadingly. 'They are so solemn.' There was no escape unless he were to hurt their feelings, and he was too kind for that.

Psychologically Gandhi was deep in the caste system, knowing much of it was evil but not able to disown it within himself. Publicly he was a champion of the Untouchables, but he could never persuade Dr Ambedkar, their leader, that he meant it. As a Gujerati Bania, the son of a Princely State Prime Minister, it had been instilled in Gandhi from infancy that he was of a superior caste. 'While at school I often happened to touch the Untouchables, and as I could never conceal the fact from my parents my mother would tell me that the shortest cut to purification after the unholy touch was to cancel the touch by touching any Muslim passing by. And simply out of reverence and regard for my mother I often did so. . . .' No wonder the Muslims made so many converts among low non-caste Hindus, especially in the North where Muslim power was at its greatest.

Gandhi undertook over twenty fasts for various political objects. Not one of them was aimed at removing from the Untouchables the curse they were born with. Yet a threat to 'fast unto death' unless the Hindus abolished Untouchability would have destroyed it as a concept. It would have given speedy release to the Untouchables from their pitiful degradation, for which many millions of them are still waiting.

Not that 'fasting unto death' was ever on Gandhi's programme. I asked him what would have happened if the British Government on some occasion had kept its nerve and had not made the concession which he could use to justify the end of a fast: 'Oh, there was never any risk of my dying,' he replied. 'I always drink fruit juice when I am fasting. I can keep going for months. Fasting is very good for the health. I do it often.' He glanced at my tummy, already larger than it should have been, and smiled impishly: 'Hee, hee, hee, you look as though you could do with a fast.' His perfectly balanced body testified to his vegetarian diet and his fasts. I have tried fasting three times. Disaster. The lost weight returns in three weeks.

Gandhi was not so fixed on non-violence as was generally

supposed. After one of his bouts of saying that, if it were God's will that there would be a civil war there would be one, and on the whole he thought it was God's will, I said to him, 'Of course, if there is a civil war, the Muslims will win it hands down.'

'Why?' he asked suspiciously.

'Because you will tell Congress to adopt non-violence. The Muslims won't take any notice. They'll sweep through India with fire and the sword.'

'Yes,' he said slowly, 'I would certainly tell Congress to adopt non-violence.' Then he quickened sharply: 'But I wouldn't expect them to. What I would expect them to do is to take one eye for one eye and one tooth for one tooth. Not like the British, who take one hundred eyes for one eye and one hundred teeth for one tooth.'

Another time when the atmosphere was tricky I said to him, 'I hope Congress won't think of starting a rising. We could easily put it down. There are quite enough British troops and the Indian Army is still very loyal.' That was true. Wavell told me he had enough troops to deal with any insurrection. As an expert in mopping up large Italian armies in North Africa he was a reliable guide. The unwarlike Congress was neither well organized nor as well armed as the Italian troops, and the Muslims would be on our side.

He looked solemn. 'I should hate to think the British had become so weak that they could not put down any rebellion. If there were to be an uprising it would be their duty to put it down. I hope they would.' He grimaced at the uncomfortable thought that the British he admired so much might not be able to. After all, he had led an Indian Ambulance Corps in South Africa alongside our troops during the Boer War, and during a Zulu uprising in 1906, and had raised another in 1914.

It was impossible not to be charmed by Gandhi and to enjoy his jokes. One of his best arose during the stay of the Cabinet Mission. There was a period when he refused to see the three ministers, and negotiations were halted. He recommended them to go away and let events evolve as they might. Finally he relented and said he would call on them at six o'clock on a Thursday morning. It did not matter to Stafford, who managed on four or five hours sleep, but it was hard on seventy-five-year-old Pethick-Lawrence, and on A. V. Alexander, accustomed to sleeping off the previous night's alcoholic intake at that time in the morning.

In the English drawing-room of the large house where the Cabinet ministers were staying Gandhi perched on the sofa in his loin-cloth. The three important ministers who had come six thousand miles began to talk. No answer. Baffled, the three became quiet. Gandhi smiled and handed Cripps a piece of paper on which he had scribbled: 'This is my day of silence but please go on talking.'

They did, somewhat bewildered. From time to time Gandhi passed them little notes containing some of his favourite aphorisms, such as: 'He who gives quickly gives twice.' And that was all they got.

It was exciting to visit Gandhi. He lived in an ambiance of power and revelled in it. Perhaps King Solomon's court was like his, thronged with worshippers who bathed in his wisdom and attended to his whims. Gandhi lived in magnificent style despite the simplicity of his surroundings: any discomforts were self-imposed when he was following some temporary fad. He lived as though money did not exist. Others – principally the industrialist G. D. Birla, who thought cottage industries were barmy – paid the cost of his staff (mostly volunteers but they had to be fed), his lodgings and all the expenses which went with his great establishment. It is easier to contemplate and meditate on the world calmly if you are not harassed by bills and the tax collector or any details pertaining thereto. It was right that Gandhi should not have to bother about earthly things but it nullified his personal identification with the Depressed Classes and the other poor among the masses.

It was on this trip that I met Nehru – on 10 January 1946. Then fifty-six, he was handsome, sharp, full of life, argument and strength, not remotely like the pallid version of him in the film *Gandhi*. He was also irascible. I made a bad start with him. He was explaining that the Muslim League was a chimera, that its recent successes in the provincial elections meant nothing. When Congress got into gear again, which would be soon now that the Congress leaders were out of gaol, support for the Muslim League would melt away. I disagreed. I explained that while he had been in gaol the previous year I had travelled in the Punjab and Bengal and other areas with large Muslim populations. I had talked not merely to the League's leaders but to young and enthusiastic Muslim Leaguers down the line. Muslim League support was solid and he would have to talk to them about Pakistan.

I expected him to be irritated. I did not expect him to jump away from the chimney-piece he had been leaning on and shout at me, furious in the face. I was frightened but I held my ground. Gradually he became more rational and we talked sensibly for four hours. By the end he had conceded that the British might have to agree to Pakistan, but that must be after a plebiscite to confirm the wish for it among Muslims in contiguous districts. The recent election results were not sufficient evidence: the Muslims did not know what they had been voting for. If the plebiscite showed a genuine demand for Pakistan, he would accept it provided there were territorial adjustments to exclude solid blocks of Hindu territory. This was considerable progress, particularly as he had just said publicly that he would not sit at the same table with the Muslim League: a remark he waved airily away to me as not serious.

I passed on the gist of Nehru's conversation to Wavell, the Viceroy, who reported it to London as the first indication that Congress knew its claim to represent the Muslims was fading.

Nehru was both needled and amused by the British. He, like other educated Indians, had come to resent middle-class British residents, whom he understandably regarded as his social inferiors, running clubs from which he and other Indians, however eminent, were excluded. He could not understand why we called ourselves white. 'We always think of British Tommies as having horrid red hands and faces. I remember how frightened of them we were when we were children.' He hated self-important officials treating him insolently as an unimportant member of a subject race, though he could be funny about them.

Educated Indians saw the British not as cruel but insensitive, secure in their power. They were no worse than rulers of Native States, rather better indeed, but the latter were of similar colour or race, which made all the difference. Yet Nehru was pleased that he had been at Harrow and was certain he had received good treatment in and out of prison during the war because Churchill was an Old Harrovian.

I stayed with Nehru in his family house at Allahabad. Hundreds came to stand outside the gate and look at the house for a while before drifting away, to be replaced by others. It was called Darshan: respectful, silent salutation for a great man which, it was evident, Nehru loved. We went down to the Ganges, the holy river, its banks thronged by many thousands. As soon as they saw Nehru coming, the crowds parted before us. The homage was noisier than at the house. You could see a sense of power running through Nehru which exhilarated him. I was affected by it too, and I was not the object of the adulation. Men may be sincere, perhaps selfless, but there is nothing like a large dose of power for uplifting the spirit and injecting energy.

Back at his house Nehru explained he had no power base in Congress. Sardar Patel was the machine politician who had absolute control. Nehru's support came from the kind of spontaneous feelings of the ordinary Hindus I had just seen, most of whom were not members of the Congress Party; or from the younger intellectuals, like the ones who gathered at his house in the evenings for long discussions. These were very jolly. We talked of everything: the future of India, the nature of Indians, the British, the philosophy of government, democracy. Nehru, who presided like a don at a large tutorial, was an English democrat to his finger-tips. He inclined vaguely to an unworked-out socialism but he shunned Communism or any form of absolutism. Sitting on the floor, listening attentively to Nehru, was a young woman with a strong face. She said little, apparently agreeing with his outlook. It was his daughter, Mrs Indira Gandhi. (No relation of Mahatma Gandhi: I never met her husband, who vanished from view early on.) She was forbidding and acid and I did not like her, nor she me. What would her father have said during those conversations at Allahabad if he had known that one day this girl would rule India, imprison her critics without trial, clamp strict censorship on the Press, govern with emergency powers and behave in a way that was anathema to his whole being? I think he would have been sad but also proud that democracy in India was so strong that first it overthrew her and then made her defer to it before it restored her.

During the tour I met Mr Jinnah several times, usually at his Lutyens English-style house in New Delhi. I became Jinnah's friend so far as it was possible to be friendly with so austere and uncommunicative a man. He would say that I was the only Englishman he trusted, possibly because I have always been a good listener and thought he talked sense. When I called on him he did not have his whisky and soda removed but offered me one, too. That was a great compliment. The Muslim League were fanatical about Islamic abstinence from alcohol. I spent hours at drinkless Muslim parties, though once in the Punjab the host, a major political leader, whispered to me, 'I can't stand this any more. Come behind this screen.' And there was the whisky and the gin.

If I had exposed Jinnah's drinking habits (there was no alcohol at his luncheons, dinner or other parties) I would have blown him sky-high, as I could have by breaching his confidence on many issues, particularly when he asked, 'Why don't the British drop all this talk of Independence? It's not necessary and it will do no good. If you said you would stay, the Muslims would fight for you and we could rule India together for ever. The Hindus are too feeble to resist and everyone would be happier.'

Mr Jinnah had a gaunt look and did not smile much, but he could put on charm, except possibly to his sister, Fatima, who kept house for him and whom he would round on to my embarrassment and who, though forbidding-looking herself, was plainly terrified of him. He was careful over his appearance, tending to dress in a neat English style while at home and an elegant Muslim outfit in public. English was his natural language and he would use it often at public meetings as an alternative to Urdu which, I was told, he did not speak well. On a platform his tall, erect, slim figure was impressive. There was nothing untidy or casual about him. In private his manners were precise, if aloof. He lacked the instant social sympathy of Gandhi or Nehru and was more intense and single-minded about politics than either of them.

Jinnah was anxious not to be drawn into arguments because the Hindus were cleverer than the Muslims and would snare them into contradictory and intellectually shaky positions. He had been an ardent member of Congress, 'but everything they did or said was expressed in the Hindu way.' He felt stifled. He knew that if the Muslims did not get out of Congress and have their own organization they would be swamped. 'Why do the Hindus resist Pakistan? They would be left governing three-quarters of India which is far more than they have ever had before.'

Naturally Jinnah hated Gandhi. He referred to him as 'that Gandhi fellow who sits behind the scenes and pulls the strings, and never comes out into the open.' There was truth in that. Jinnah felt that Gandhi's evasiveness and double-talk prevented headway being made with him over anything concrete. His ground was always shifting, which impelled Jinnah to stick to the simple demand for Pakistan and ignore the details: this rallied and held steady the Muslims. He also resented the inference he drew from the British treatment of Gandhi that the Hindu leader was considered to be greater and more important than Jinnah. 'I don't get special trains. I wouldn't mind being imprisoned in the Aga Khan's palace like Gandhi for a year or two if it were necessary to get Pakistan.'

A visit to Agra to see the Taj Mahal by moonlight is an item on most tourist trips. I had time only to see the Agra gaol. In it was Jaya Prakash Narayan, the most prominent of the Socialists in Congress advocating violent revolution. He had been imprisoned for organizing the burning of police-stations and the blowing up of trains. Political prisoners lived in reasonable comfort with two rooms, a servant, books, newspapers. Nehru wrote the whole of quite a good book, *Discovery of India*, while he was a political prisoner.

I had a pleasant relaxed conversation with J. P. Narayan lasting for several hours. He began by not believing that the British were willing to hand over power. Our protestations that we were, covered a subtle plan to exploit Indian disagreements so that we could keep power indefinitely. We were too wedded to imperialism to do anything else. I was very passionate. I told him the Labour Government were committed in their hearts to ending British rule. So were the Labour Party, most of whom were as good Socialists as he was. But we needed help to hand over without chaos and to avoid the division of India. I must have convinced him. I asked him towards the end whether he and his friends would guarantee not to begin a fresh campaign of violence if they were released.

'After what you have said, we will be willing to give British sincerity a trial. I give you my word that we would stick to peaceful methods.'

On the basis of that pledge the centrally held political prisoners, officially considered as terrorists, were let out during the Cabinet Mission's stay. They scrupulously kept the promise that had been made to me. J. P. Narayan was not disappointed by the British but he became disillusioned by the corruption in Congress and by its abandonment of Socialist aims. Even Nehru let him down on the latter.

It was a lovely trip. History was being made among delightful people, whatever their politics or religion. I was treated as though I mattered, though I did not take too seriously an official of the Viceroy's staff who solemnly informed me that as an MP I was entitled, like the ruler of the most insignificant Native States, to a one-gun salute. I never got one. It might have been fun but there was plenty without it.

As usual sex was in my thoughts. In Lahore there was a glorious Muslim girl of seventeen. I took her for motor-car rides and taught her the rudiments of driving. She was like a soft, ripe peach pressing to fall from the branch. She was curious about the young MP. Often I was on the verge of kissing her and igniting the flames we both knew would follow. I resisted the temptation, and now wish I had not. I was scared. She came from a noble and powerful Muslim family I was staying with. Her mother was watching us, disapprovingly aware of a crisis in our relations. There would have been a fearsome scandal which could have had political repercussions. Damn and blast, but the memory is still sweet in spite of the regret for what might have been. I can see now her curving figure and lovely Indo-European face, her complexion touched gently and exotically by thousands of years of sun.

As soon as we returned to England the Delegation was summoned to No. 10 by Attlee, who asked us all for our opinions. As I was the youngest mine came last. Official notes of that meeting on 13 February 1946 record that I said that the need for action on Independence and the formation of a Viceroy's Executive Council was urgent. Pakistan in the shape of Muslim majority areas was inevitable. It was not all that Jinnah demanded but the best he could be allowed, and he should be given four weeks or so to decide whether to accept on this basis. The official note goes on: 'He [Mr Wyatt] would suggest sending a strong team of Ministers to negotiate.' It was a good shot. The Cabinet Mission was dispatched on 19 March, arriving on the 24th.

When I got back with the Parliamentary Delegation I had a message from Stafford Cripps. I was not to write or say anything about India until I had seen him. This was a mild blow. I was hoping to write some articles to augment my tiny income and buy a car. I saw him at Whitehall Court, where Bernard Shaw had once had a flat. Would I go with him as his Personal Assistant on the impending Cabinet Mission? He was also taking Major (Billy) Short, an expert on the Sikhs. From messages from India and my own reports he realized that I had got on well with Jinnah. He could not bear to be in the same room as Jinnah. He could cope with Gandhi but he must have some line to Jinnah and his thinking. Would I be it? Wouldn't I just!

# CHAPTER VI

## History in India

THE THREE CABINET MINISTERS who tried to give away an Empire, and found their every suggestion for doing it frustrated by the intended recipients, were the highest level group Britain ever sent to India. They had plenipotentiary power to negotiate, merely submitting final details to London for Cabinet approval which were given without demur.

Sixty-one-year-old A. V. Alexander, First Lord of the Admiralty, was a robust sturdy Co-op Labour MP of the old-fashioned kind and unburdened by ideology. He was short in intellect but long in commonsense. He was emphatically patriotic, loved the Navy, admired Churchill and became an earl, which made him very proud. He found the Hindu leaders of Congress baffling and tricky. He got off to a bad start. On our arrival at the airport we were surrounded by Indian Press reporters. One of them noticing A.V. was hot and sticky, asked him if he would like a drink. 'I certainly should.' He was bustled off to a tent and downed a large quantity of beer. The next morning the Indian papers carried the headlines 'Cabinet Mission arrives. A. V. Alexander asks for a beer.' Stafford Cripps was furious and ticked him off sharply. Didn't he realize that the Indian leaders he would be dealing with were all teetotal and would introduce prohibition when we had gone? Poor Alexander, always scared of Stafford, was as crushed as a frightened schoolboy. Thereafter he kept his serious drinking till Stafford went to bed. One evening there was a great ceremonial dinner at the Viceroy's House with the highest in India present. Stafford had gone to bed early. A.V. was free to drink as he liked and his inhibitions began to go. He thought he would like to play a few tunes on the piano but there wasn't one. Egging him on I said, 'I'll ask them to bring one in. And if you dare to play "The Red

Flag", I'll promise to sing the words.' I spoke to an ADC, who spoke to Wavell. Six splendid Pathans in red uniforms carried a grand piano into the state drawing room. A.V. began with old music hall songs. The audience smiled in pleasure at this relief from the tension and tedium of the formal stately dinner (Viceroys' and Governors' courts were more stiffly royal than any King's. The Prince of Wales remarked that he never knew how royalty really lived until he stayed with Lord Lloyd, Governor of Bombay.) Then out crashed the Tannenbaum music stolen by 'The Red Flag'. In my appalling voice I roared out the verses,

> The People's Flag is deepest red
> It shrouded oft our martyred Dead
> And 'ere their limbs grew stiff and cold
> Their hearts' blood dyed its every fold.
>
> Then raise the scarlet standard high!
> Beneath its shade we'll live and die.
> Tho' Cowards flinch and Traitors jeer,
> We'll keep the Red Flag flying here!

Horror and shock fastened on the faces of the listeners. So this Labour Government really did stand for Red revolution! 'Treachery to the Sovereign,' one voice said. I heard a senior ICS official moan to his colleague, 'Nothing like that can ever have happened in the Viceroy's House before.' Only the Viceroy was amused, apart from me and the jolly A.V. who both knew how preposterous and inappropriate to the then Labour Party the words of Labour's anthem were.

I liked A.V. for his lack of pomposity, his willingness to be earthy, for his reliability, for his sense of fun.

I liked Wavell, too. As Viceroy he was an ex-officio member of the Cabinet Mission. His face was kindly and round, intelligent and honest. He had an attractive stocky way of walking. His fairness and steadiness must have made him a wonderful commander to serve under. Politicians thought him too slow to understand quickly changing political moves and departures from previously agreed approaches. Possibly that was true. Generals, admirals, air marshals, field marshals and other high ranking officers are often devious and skilled at little conspiracies to get their way while pretending disdain for cunning politicians they accuse of twisting to cover their backs or advance their careers. Wavell was not one of those. He played it without dissembling. He was horrified by my hero, Stafford, accepting false interpretations of the Cabinet Mission plan from Congress, eager to claim that Gandhi and his colleagues had adhered to the Cabinet Mission plan when they hadn't. He was appalled by the evident bias of Cripps and to a lesser degree that of Pethick-Lawrence, not shared by A.V., towards Congress. He was shocked by the excessive reverence paid to Gandhi in contrast to the slighting, sometimes hectoring treatment given to Jinnah. But he knew what was going on all right and understood the politics and possibilities of the Indian situation well.

He persuaded the Muslim League, bitter at the wriggling evasions of Congress over the Cabinet Mission's Statement being construed as adherence to it, to join a Coalition government at the centre in October after we had gone. That averted the civil war brewing up through the Muslims' anger at being cheated by the chicanery which had left Congress in possession of the Interim Government hitherto. Wavell probably would have managed some parts of the final transfer of power better than Mountbatten though with less glamour. As a land soldier, accustomed to dealing with people on the ground, he would not have moved the date of transfer of power forward so far, thus causing the partition boundaries to be drawn up so precipitately that the slaughter was greater than it need have been.

As in the war, Wavell was unfairly replaced, a victim of the prejudice of politicians. The first time it was Churchill, the second Attlee, Cripps and Pethick-Lawrence. Wavell used to invite me to dine with him alone in his library/sitting room. He would pull out his maps of the Middle East and trace again the campaign during which he defeated and captured forces several times the size of his: 130,000 prisoners, 800 field guns, 400 tanks, were his haul when he seized the whole of Cyrenaica. He could have taken all North Africa and prevented the Germans making a stronghold in North Africa if Churchill had not been romantically obsessed with helping the Greeks. El Alamein would have been superfluous.

Wavell lost the argument. His forces were fatally depleted

by sending a large contingent to Greece just as the Germans arrived in North Africa. The result was that the newly occupied Cyrenaica was lost, Greece (always a hopeless cause) was lost, Crete, which could have been defended successfully, was lost and the end of the war and the eventual onslaught on the 'soft underbelly' of Europe was unjustifiably delayed. Wavell was a far better General than Churchill. Nor did he wait, like Montgomery, until he had an overwhelming preponderance before engaging the enemy. But Churchill was Prime Minister. Wavell had proved him wrong so he had to be removed. Churchill was not always generous. The Dictionary of National Biography says Wavell never complained about this 'in public or in private'. Well, he did to me more than once and at length. Thirty-seven years later I read some of his friendly comments about me and my suggestions in the Official History of The Transfer of Power and a wave of the affection I always felt for that underrated general and statesman rose again.

Wavell knew India better than anyone in the Cabinet Mission. He had spent his childhood there, had served in the Army in India in his youth, was C-in-C in India in 1941 and Supreme Commander of the South-West Pacific until 1943, when he became Viceroy. His *Other Men's Flowers*, an anthology of poetry, and his writings, showed the humanity and breadth of his reading and knowledge. He was not the intellectual equal of Cripps, but nor was he a simple-minded soldier with a narrow outlook. He was not a politicians' man. They mistook his care before he spoke for foolishness. His main purpose in his talks with me privately over dinner, which surprised the Viceroy's staff and the contents of which I did not reveal to Stafford, was to understand the intentions of the three Cabinet ministers, particularly those of Cripps. Not out of mischievousness but so that he might help them better. I did a lot of explaining of people to other people between the 24 March and the end of June when the Cabinet Mission at last left India.

Curiously when Wavell made his sole complaint against me, he did not do so direct to me but through Cripps when they were out riding in the early morning. Perhaps he thought it was silly and too embarrassing. The Military Secretary had twice asked me to a formal dinner at the Viceroy's House and I had twice refused. Lady Wavell, who was very conscious of her royal role as Vicereine, was much put out. Didn't I realize, Wavell asked Stafford, that I had gravely snubbed her by rejecting what amounted to a royal command? It must have seemed odd to her, knowing how prized were invitations to dine with the Viceroy. I greatly pleased one girl by getting her parents an invitation to lunch at the Viceroy's House on her father's retirement from a senior civil engineering post – in all his service in India he had never been inside the Viceroy's House before. I disliked the self-conscious imitation of a royal court down to ADCs' taking guests to sit after dinner with the Viceroy or Vicereine for a few minutes' stilted conversation before making way for the next on the list. Who, except for snobbish reasons, would have wanted to make conversation to Lady Wavell? Though she tried to make her husband play at being royal he didn't warm to the part, tending to fall asleep. After one formal dinner he asked me the same question and got the same answer three times within five minutes. I much preferred using my evenings to meet Indians and talking through the current political gossip. However, a compromise with honour was finally reached. I was allowed to choose one of a number of dates in consultation with the Military Secretary. Such a trivial matter became so inflated only because of the meticulous respect with which the British Raj treated protocol: it was part of the act.

Pethick-Lawrence, Secretary of State for India, was technically the leader of the Mission. During the war Nye Bevan called him 'a crusted old Tory', which was unkind but he was a foolish old dodderer graduated out of the trendy Left of his youth. His father, a carpenter from Cornwall, founded a successful building firm and sent his son to Eton in 1885. He got two Firsts at Cambridge, two Adam Smith prizes and became a Fellow of Trinity demonstrating that academic cleverness is not all.

Maybe he rebelled against his comfortable *nouveau riche* background. First he became a social worker in the East End like Attlee which was a reasonable expression of a desire to help others. Then he married a Miss Pethick and changed his name to Pethick-Lawrence, which was cranky. Under his wife's influence he devoted himself, to the exclusion of almost all else, to Votes for Women until the First World War. Too old to be called up he became an ostentatious militant pacifist and an exhibitionist conscientious objector. He demanded peace by negotiation not because he was trying to avoid Russia being taken over by the Communists but because he was against self defence. He had some knowledge of India from the Round Table Conference days in 1931 but it was lop-sidedly pro-Congress. On this trip he became disenchanted, not with Congress, but with Gandhi who bewildered him. And Pethick-Lawrence's pernicketiness irritated Wavell.

In the first few days I was worried that the obscurantism of the India Office staff Pethick-Lawrence brought with him might have damaging effects. I spoke to Stafford about it. He broke in sharply, 'Quite frankly it doesn't matter what they say because *I* am running this party. Let them talk away about constitutional and parliamentary control but it won't have any result. *We* are really doing the negotiations and keeping them out of it.'

What he promised came to pass. Cripps towered over the others. He imposed his decisions on them. He was not first among equals but first among inferiors. The piercing eye, the unfolding logic supported by sixteen hours a day of thought and work, the capacity to unravel the complicated in an instant, were invincible. Most were afraid less they provoked his impatience by not understanding a point or an argument as fast as he did. I was lucky never to attract his unspoken, or spoken, scorn. Though my knowledge of India was far less comprehensive than his, it was more recent. I think he felt I had an insight into the weight to be reasonably given to the views of the political parties and their leaders. He told someone on the Cabinet Mission staff that I couldn't help but get into the Cabinet. I wish he had been right.

Stafford had an unjustified reputation for austerity and asceticism. As a young man he was almost as keen on high-spirited amusement as his brother Freddie Cripps, a well-known lotus-eater. One thing I remember about Freddie was a joke he told me in the bar at White's: '"Did you hear what that extraordinary man Carruthers did last weekend?" a man asked a friend in Bombay. "He took a baboon up to Poona to stay with him." "Male or female?" the friend enquired. "Oh female, there's nothing queer about Carruthers."'

Freddie adored his brother which was in itself a tribute coming from a man whose friends and milieu were far from Socialist. It was down those steps of White's that a loutish member kicked Nye Bevan. A double disgrace really. The front of White's was built by James Wyatt.

Stafford's intestines were always in a mess. He tried hard to get into the Army in 1914 when he was twenty-five but was rejected as unfit, so he insisted on driving a lorry in France for the Red Cross. After a year he was ordered back to England to run a munitions factory. He was too brilliant a chemist to be wasted; when twenty-two he was part author of a paper about inert gas read before the Royal Society. Good at administration, he ran the explosives factory remarkably well putting, as usual, all his hours and energy into it. It nearly killed him. By the end of the war the doctors said he would be dead shortly, they could do nothing for him. A friend suggested a nature cure which basically meant a vegetarian diet and no alcohol. All else having failed, Stafford tried it and gained another thirty years of life which otherwise he would have lost. He went to bed very early and woke up around 4 a.m. ready to do what for most would have been a whole day's work before his early (too early for my liking) morning conference. He drafted the whole of the final detailed Cabinet Mission Plan in one morning before breakfast and showed it to me at nine o'clock.

He said I slept too much, but teasingly. He never told me I drank too much, though I drank a lot then: half a bottle of whisky or gin at night to put me to sleep in the 120 degrees of Delhi, the alcohol sweating out of me in the night. He disapproved of A.V.'s drinking because it did not wear well on him. Forced to give up many physical pleasures, he had a slight and natural tendency to wonder why others still indulged in them. When the doctors made him stop smoking he said I ought to too, but merely laughed when I said I wasn't going to do everything his doctors made him do.

He was quite flirtatious, alert to take an interest in a pretty girl if Isobel wasn't around; he found my second wife attractive and displayed a little harmless attention to her. He was neither prudish nor censorious. He would remark how strange it was of God (in whom he unhesitatingly believed) to put the place of supreme emotional and physical satisfaction next to the organs of excretion. He was very tolerant when I was briefly put out by a slim, fair-haired, sexy American correspondent, with a Marilyn Monroe figure, abruptly ending a hectic affair I had been having with her (it was romantic in moonlit Simla, walking beside her as she was carried in a rickshaw up and down the hilly footpaths on our way to the hotel. She would say, 'Tonight I'm going to seduce you', or, 'This time you're going to rape me.') To my distress she tired of me rapidly, finding an Indian Communist more exciting. He probably was, and doubtless well versed in the Kama Sutra.

As his faith in conventional medicine evaporated Stafford Cripps was prey to unorthodox practitioners, not always quacks. He once persuaded me into taking a course conducted by a young man on the Alexander method which he decided momentarily was the way to health for everyone. The basic principle was that not holding the spine properly led to the faulty disposition of other parts of the body, causing manifold and serious ailments. The head must be in the right elongated posture and the spine will follow suit. Much manipulation was required, supplemented by constant thinking, to stretch your neck and to will it erect without violently forcing it. I would watch Stafford discussing matters of state and suppose that his head was as it was because he was simultaneously operating the Alexander method. I wrote an article about it in *Illustrated* which gave pleasure all round, particularly to me. The photographer used a briefly clad dark little model of enchanting shape and prettiness for demonstrations of healthy standing, sitting, lying. Unfortunately she was recently married and that, if there were no other reason, made her immune to my optimistic signals.

It was difficult if not impossible to change Stafford's mind once made up unless you found an intellectual chink. The first draft of a constitutional settlement he wrote for the Cabinet Mission depended on the balance between Congress and Muslim League in a unified India being held by the Princes.

'You can't do that,' I said.

'Why not?'

'It would be impracticable.'

'I don't see why.'

'Anyway the Princes are not elected. It would be undemocratic. Worse than that it would be immoral.'

The appeal to reason failed. The appeal to morality hit a weak spot. He tore the scheme up.

Stafford was not always a good judge of character. Like many of high integrity, including Ernie Bevin, he could be mesmerized by the flashy. There was an Italian film producer, Filippo del Giudice, who made successful films during and after the war – *In Which We Serve*, *The Way Ahead*, *Henry V*, *Hamlet*, among others. He was desperate for government money and argued that trade would follow successful British films abroad. He had an extraordinary, over-lush house with many beams called Sheepcote, in the country not far from London. Adjacent was a barn turned into a luxurious private cinema where Ernie Bevin, Stafford Cripps, their wives and I watched many films while Filippo showered champagne and compliments so outrageous that only simple men like his principal guests, and I fear I was one of them, could be taken in. A heavy scent was sprayed in the drawing-room while we ate, to obliterate the smell of cigarettes and cigars, and in the dining-room when we left it.

Famous film stars, writers and directors, called his 'talents', were paraded to impress Filippo's important guests. I met Peter Ustinov at Sheepcote. He entertained us with mimicry and long, funny stories. He was almost slim, engaging, and on his way to fame but not quite there yet. Anna Magnani, a torrential Italian film star, was staying there once. She was having an affair with an Italian film director, Roberto Rossellini, then working on a film in Stromboli. Miss Magnani heard that he was paying court to a Swedish actress in the film, Ingrid Bergman. Her wails and shrieks of rage as she upbraided Mr Rossellini on the long-distance telephone reverberated around the house.

This atmosphere of artistic emotion intrigued Stafford and Ernie Bevin. 'You can't judge Filippo like normal people,' Stafford said. 'Creative artists are different.' The parties cost a fortune. When Benn Levy, the playwright and Labour MP, asked Filippo how he could afford them, he answered cheerfully, 'Ippity pays.' (Ippity was Filippo's name for Excess Profits Tax, against which the parties were charged.)

One day Stafford sent for me. 'I'm worried about Filippo. He's been trying to become a naturalized British subject for ages. He left Italy to come here before the war because he was anti-Fascist and fell foul of Mussolini. He only just escaped being put in gaol. He's done all these marvellous things for the British film industry and promoted Britain abroad as no one else could. And now the Home Office are holding up his naturalization though Ernie and I are his sponsors. It's too bad. Please go and see the Home Office and make them get a move on.'

They were uneasy at the Home Office. What could they say to such grand sponsors as the Foreign Secretary and the Chancellor of the Exchequer? Their investigations had revealed that Filippo had not been a hero fighting for democracy; he had fled Italy because he was wanted on criminal charges involving embezzlement. Filippo never got naturalized but Stafford went on believing in him.

I was asked to liaise with Harold Wilson, a protégé of Stafford and President of the Board of Trade, to organize government help for the film industry. I warmed to Harold Wilson and especially his wife, Mary. They used to come to dinner when I lived in Eaton Terrace, which made me surprised when Harold announced on becoming Leader of the Parliamentary Labour Party that he had never accepted hospitality from Labour MPs and would continue not to do so. The Film Finance Corporation was set up. Poor Filippo, without whom it would never have been created, got nothing. His financial affairs and reputation were too far gone.

Stafford was determined that Gandhi should be in on the negotiations from the start and stay with them to the end. Gandhi had admitted to him that he had wrecked Stafford's 1942 negotiations, in which he had refused to take a direct part, when they were on the point of success. He had a weird moral ascendancy over Stafford, who could not see through the humbug and vanity mingled with Gandhi's real virtues, just as he could not distinguish between the dross and the gold of Filippo del Giudice.

Gandhi did try to avoid being enmeshed in practical talks about Independence. He said he had no status and would stay in Poona – 'I'm not even a four anna member of Congress.'

Moreover, he could not stand the heat of Delhi. (Only the Viceroy had air-conditioning, and that in a small working area of the Viceroy's House.) Eventually he came to Delhi in a special train of one beautifully spruced-up third-class carriage and an engine. With a flourish he announced his new status: 'I have appointed myself as adviser to the British nation through the Cabinet Mission.'

Gandhi and Patel had not liked my suggestions which I had sent with Sudhir Ghosh, Gandhi's acolyte, for a loose Pakistan, with a federated government controlling defence and foreign affairs. They were determined that there should be no sort of autonomy, however limited, for the Muslim League. That was the basic issue on which the Cabinet Mission and its plan failed. We were soon in trouble.

I kept a diary during the Cabinet Mission. It was the only time in my life, apart from a few weeks when I was arguing with Harold Wilson about the nationalization of steel, that I did so. Sometimes it differs from other accounts but I back my diary, which was written daily as it happened.

On 3 April it records my being woken by Sudhir Ghosh at six-thirty. Gandhi had sent for him in his bedroom at a quarter to four. He could not sleep all night for worrying about the sincerity of the British. 'That makes two of us,' I observed, now that I had been thoroughly roused. Sudhir did not think that funny: 'This is serious.'

Gandhi said we must do three little things for him before he could believe we meant business: we must release all the political prisoners; abolish the Salt Tax so that the people could manufacture their own salt; and promise not to have anything more to do with those whom Gandhi called 'bad men'. High on his list of 'bad men' were Dr Ambedkar, elected leader of the Depressed Classes, or Untouchables, and M.L. Roy, a Bengali politician who had attacked Gandhi as a fraud. Sudhir was rather ashamed of the third condition.

I hurried off to tell Pethick-Lawrence and Stafford Cripps. They were stunned. Stafford was in a panic. 'If Gandhi decides that he doesn't trust us, he'll give the order "Nothing doing" and that'll be the end of the Cabinet Mission, as it was of the Mission in 1942.'

The political prisoner issue was complicated. I had explained to Sudhir that their release was up to the new provincial governments. Gandhi said the Viceroy had power to overrule those governments and had done it in the past, so why not now? Gandhi was autocrat or democrat as suited his objective.

I argued strongly with the Cabinet Mission that at least the two political prisoners held centrally at Agra gaol should be released at once – the Socialist revolutionary leaders Jaya Prakash Narayan and Dr Lohia, who had pledged in Agra during the visit of the Parliamentary Delegation that there would be no incitement to violence if they were set free. Pethick-Lawrence, feeble as ever, said he did not see how he could overrule the Viceroy, but he accepted what the two political prisoners had told me. I did not win that morning but did so shortly after: the steam was taken out of Gandhi's sincerity tests and the two released prisoners were as good as lambs.

The removal of the Salt Tax should have been quick and easy. Gandhi had always been right in saying that it was a monstrous imposition on the poor. But bureaucracy is slow to relinquish old practices. Four days later Sudhir Ghosh was back in my bedroom again. He was upset because when Gandhi woke at 3 a.m. Sudhir could not be found. When he was finally produced, Gandhi was very cross with him for not being immediately available. A conference was held with his disciples about the Salt Tax. Gandhi was in agony (he was frequently a great nuisance to his entourage in the middle of the night: perhaps a girl lying next to him was too pretty for him to sublimate his sexual instincts easily, one of his self-imposed tests).

Again I pressed the point with the Mission. The next day Sir Archibald Rowlands, Finance Member of the Government of India, went to talk with Gandhi. Beforehand he was confident that he could persuade Gandhi how impracticable it would be to abolish the Salt Tax. Within an hour Gandhi had converted him. Promptly he gave instructions for a scheme to be prepared for its abolition. Gandhi was mollified.

Two tests more or less passed and one to go. The third was no real problem. Gandhi was forced to realize how ludicrous he would look if he insisted that the Cabinet Mission should not see political leaders merely because he thought they were 'bad men', while they were seeing hundreds of others of equal or lesser importance. For the time being Gandhi had run out of tricks to sabotage the Mission and was in an amiable mood.

Jinnah had told me that he would be delighted to meet Gandhi when he arrived in Delhi. Sudhir passed this on and Gandhi was pleased. But Pethick-Lawrence foolishly sent a note to say he thought it inadvisable for Gandhi to meet Jinnah yet. Gandhi's reaction was to chuckle: 'I suppose that means I can go tomorrow.' The magic moment was lost. Gandhi and Jinnah, the two principals, never met during the negotiations. Another black mark for Pethick-Lawrence.

On 15 April I put in a paper to the Cabinet Mission. Partly it was a plea for them to treat Jinnah more considerately. Jinnah had claimed to me the night before that no one had been asked to make a case for Pakistan. He was convinced that the negotiations were a farce and that hidden hands (I assumed he meant Gandhi and Stafford Cripps) were directing the Mission to give India to a Congress government. 'Let them finish us off if they want to. I don't care. It would be better than this agony of not knowing where we are. I, and those who are willing to be, will be killed. The only people who can settle this are Gandhi, Nehru, Patel and myself.'

Partly, my paper looked into the future. Britain should not try to impose a solution but instead hand over to an Interim Government of any kind that could be formed. 'But,' I wrote, 'it should also be made clear that British support would only be made available to an Interim Government for a fixed period, say six months or a year. At the end of that period if no agreement was in sight all British troops and authority would be withdrawn.'

I returned again and again to a fixed date for withdrawal in order to force the Indians to agree on their own solution if we could not tempt them to one, though Jinnah was always hoping for a British award (insisting that it was essential), and so were Congress in their hearts. Gandhi could not visualize an India without a final decision from the British Raj, however much he told us that all we had to do was to get off India's back.

I went on pressing for some such solution, but with little success. An entry in my diary for 30 May reads:

147

Our trouble is that we simply will not face up to the fact that we have promised them Independence and we have got to go. We keep clinging on to our sense of responsibility and hoping we can salvage something from the wreckage. It's like a husband trying to make compromise arrangements with a wife who no longer loves him and wants him to leave the house. It's no good him trying to take lodgings in a boarding house in the same street.

After days of time-wasting interviews, mainly with nonentities and representatives of minorities whose views were not germane to the Transfer of Power, the Mission began considering the content of its great plan. There was a respite for an Easter holiday in glorious Kashmir, where I stayed in considerable comfort at the British Resident's house (what a splendid life officials of that kind had). Before we went to Kashmir Stafford asked at the morning conference if anyone knew of an auspicious day on which to announce the Mission's conclusions. I said, half jokingly, that we should apply to the Bengal Government which, I understood, had an excellent official astrologer. Joyce, the Press Officer, was then deputed by Stafford to find out from this astrologer the most auspicious day. That shows what can happen to the most acute European minds in the mystic air of India!

We returned to the appalling heat of Delhi on 24 April to find growing speculation that we were about to make an award concocted in Kashmir. When it transpired we were not, impatience and temper rose along with the heat. Gandhi was especially cross. In the deteriorating atmosphere invitations were sent out to both sides to come to a conference at Simla where the Mission's thinking would be paraded for inspection and a hoped-for agreement. Four representatives from the Muslim League and four from Congress were invited.

Congress included in their four, as well as Nehru and Patel, two Congress Muslims, Maulana Azad and Gaffar Khan, from the North-West Frontier Province, to rub Jinnah's nose in the unpalatable fact that he did not represent all the Muslims. It was childish and spiteful, and a sign that they wanted no compromise with Jinnah and Pakistan. Gandhi played the fool by saying he might come to Simla if he were wanted but his inner voices told him he ought not to. Knowing Gandhi so well by now I never doubted that he would come; his irrepressible exhibitionism would ensure that he remained at the centre of the stage.

Jinnah, slighted by the subservient approach of the Mission to Gandhi, who pleaded with the latter to come to Simla, offering him special trains with elaborate quarters and a magnificent house for his entourage of fifteen, suddenly found that his engagements prevented him from arriving in time for the intended opening of the conference on 2 May. When he did come on the 4th he was in a huff. Without his being consulted, arrangements had been made for photographs to be taken of the opening of the conference the next morning. The two sides were to be shown exchanging greetings and chatting on the lawn of Viceregal Lodge. Jinnah angrily said No. Pethick-Lawrence flapped about, saying the Press had had nothing since we came out, how could we cancel their one newsworthy occasion? As usual when there was something difficult to be done with Jinnah, I was sent to placate him: I found that he was genuinely disturbed.

'The Cabinet Mission won't realize what the dispute is all about. Otherwise they couldn't have insulted me by asking me to be photographed with two people like Maulana Azad and Gaffar Khan. They are both stooges, I won't have anything to do with them. They've only been put up as delegates to sabotage the negotiations. I'll talk to Nehru or to Patel or to that Gandhi fellow who stays behind the scene pulling the strings. But Azad – he's like my bearer. He can understand a few words of English but he can only answer "Yes" or "No". Gaffar Khan's even worse. He's like another bearer who comes with a chit saying he speaks perfect English but when you talk to him he doesn't understand a word. What's the use of discussing important matters with people like that?'

Jinnah decently agreed to compromise. He said it was to help me, whom he liked, but not the Mission whom with good reason he did not like. The Congress party was to arrive at a quarter to ten, be filmed and photographed and then pushed inside the Viceregal Lodge before Jinnah arrived ten minutes later for his bout of photography. As I expected, Congress arrived ten minutes after they had promised, in the hope that they would still be on the lawn when Jinnah and his three colleagues arrived, and thus that some photographs of Congress and the Muslim League leaders going in together would be taken and put Jinnah in a bad mood. Jinnah was too smart for them. He arrived just after ten to make sure Congress would already have gone in before he got there. He then faithfully honoured the arrangements he had made with me to be photographed from every angle.

The conference began with Congress demanding that the agenda be reversed. Pethick-Lawrence as Chairman explained that the Mission thought there should be some form of central Union government, and that the best hope of solving the communal problem would be through a system of grouping of provinces into basically Hindu and Muslim groups. He proposed to discuss the system for the grouping of provinces first, because if that could be broadly agreed, the constitution of, and the subjects reserved to, the Union government would follow naturally, with the discussion leading on to the constitution-making machinery.

Congress said, Oh no, they wanted it the other way round. (They were after a very strong central government which would totally control the provinces, so that the grouping of the Muslim majority provinces together would be meaningless in so far as their having any genuine local autonomy of distinct Muslim identity.) Jinnah saw the trap and argued strongly that the Cabinet Mission agenda (it was really Stafford's) should be followed. Congress stuck out for the order best suited to their sabotage tactics and Jinnah finally said he would leave it to Pethick-Lawrence. The latter, with his customary pro-Congress bias, let Congress have their way. Jinnah told me afterwards that he had given in only because he did not want to spoil the atmosphere.

The Simla Conference illumined the characters and aims of the contestants. Congress never had any intention of compromising or admitting that Jinnah represented the Muslims. Their game was to humiliate Jinnah, with the purpose of goading him into being unreasonable so that the Mission would be forced on to the Congress side. They were determined not to concede Pakistan or anything like it.

On the evening of the second day of the conference Gandhi

came to see Stafford. Stafford spoke to him about a list of 'suggested points of agreement between Congress and the Muslim League'. These modified, while clarifying the Mission's proposals made at the outset of the conference for a high degree of autonomy for three groups of provinces. One group was Hindu majority provinces, and the other two groups consisted of Muslim majority provinces. Stafford read the points to Gandhi, who listened very carefully. Gandhi said, 'You won't expect me to say that I accept them, will you?' Cripps said he would not. Gandhi thought for a moment or two. 'But I will say this. I look on them with favour.'

He then undertook to explain them to the Congress Working Committee 'to the best of my ability' (always an ominous touch, indicating he would find an excuse for changing his mind if it suited him). He suggested that the points be sent to Congress and the Muslim League in the morning and that the conference should be postponed for two days to give everyone time to consider them.

The next day, Wednesday, he began backsliding. He told his intimates that he had not realized that, if Congress agreed to the suggested points of agreement, they would be binding on them. I commented in my diary: 'This is rather like saying that one doesn't realise that if one enters into a contract the terms of the contract have to be honoured whether one subsequently likes them or not.' Gandhi was ever thus.

On Thursday morning I woke with a strong feeling that Jinnah was in need of a visit before the conference met again. I was right. The suggested points of agreement had maddened him. He was quite content with the original formula. Why had it been varied? 'I can see no point in continuing the negotiations. It's quite useless. I would have finished with the conference before now if I wasn't trying to help.'

I began to talk him round. I told him Congress would be delighted if he broke up the conference. They would tell the world, 'Look how unreasonable these people are. They won't even discuss their demands.' The British would be unable to press for concessions for the Muslim League because the Muslim League would not be there to ask for them. I said, 'Stick to your guns. Never mind how many new suggestions are put to you.

Just continue plugging along. If Congress break up the conference they'll look less reasonable than you, and Congress is so sensitive to world opinion they'd hate that.'

He started to thaw. He would go on with the conference if he were allowed to state his points of *dis*agreement with the suggested 'points of agreement'. I said 'Fine', and to my relief he said, 'All right then, I'll follow the line you suggest.' He was prepared to stand by the federated Union government concept. He thought that this was a very big concession, as it involved giving up the claim for the fully sovereign Pakistan for which the Muslim League had fought. He felt the Cabinet Mission had not sufficiently recognized how huge a gesture this was.

'It's my sincere contribution towards getting an amicable settlement, and Congress in return should concede the policy of grouping the provinces with the largest Muslim populations in sections from the outset. Can I rely on the Misson not to let me down?'

'Certainly,' I replied, with a trifle more confidence than I felt.

If the Cabinet Mission had shown the same attention to the views of Jinnah as to those of Congress, and had sought to butter him up as they did Gandhi, the trauma of that Thursday morning would never have arisen. As I was leaving he said, 'I can talk to you because I know where I am. You don't keep shifting the basis of the conversation every fifteen minutes. If we disagree and I can't persuade you, we both know where we have disagreed.' He then promised to come to the conference that afternoon, adding with a smile, 'And I'll keep coming until someone else breaks it up.' Before the Mission left, Wavell and I agreed that Jinnah was the straightest and easiest of all the Indian politicians to deal with.

At the conference that Thursday afternoon there was some excitement. Nehru and Jinnah got so close to agreement on their understanding of the 'points of agreement' that they were left to talk together in the conference-room while the rest walked up and down the lawn, to the fascination of the Press. When they came back it seemed they had agreed on an umpire to arbitrate where their understanding varied. They said they would meet again outside and return to the conference on Saturday to report progress. In my diary for Friday I wrote:

The fundamental issue at present is that Jinnah will agree to a Union government but is not prepared to accept the legislature to go with it that Congress wants. On the other hand Congress are not prepared to agree to the groups having an executive and legislature of their own, which Jinnah regards as vital for his case. How you can arbitrate about this I am not sure.

The Jinnah and Nehru meeting happened on the Saturday and got nowhere. They both went back to square one again. Stafford was disgusted at 'your friend Jinnah', as he described him to me. He unfairly accused Jinnah of going back on everything he had said. Next morning I was sent down to Jinnah with a note he had asked for of the Mission's understanding of his minimum demands. Stafford said, 'As soon as he sees them he will step them up wildly and there will be nothing to pin the Cabinet Mission's Statement on.'

But Jinnah did not do so. He had already prepared a note of the minimum demands of the Muslim League. We compared our note with his. There was little difference. Once again Stafford had misjudged Jinnah. I told Jinnah that in large measure the Mission's final proposals met his points, apart from the proposal for the establishment of Union legislature and a Union executive. He was vehemently opposed to that. I did not tell him that the Mission's statement would contain a preamble with a distorted and unnecessary diatribe against Pakistan (I tried to water down that passage but failed). I thought it better for Jinnah to absorb it when he was alone. I knew I would have to deal with his anger afterwards, as I was the only person who could.

The Simla Conference came to an end with all parties sadly understanding each other's position better. I had what I thought was to be a last look around delicious Simla squatting prettily on its hills, redolent with memories of the British who created it. Kipling spoke through the streets and houses. It must have been impossible for wives allowed to escape from the heat of the plains, where they had left their husbands still toiling, not to have had affairs with young officers in such a place. At lunch with me the day before I left for Delhi, Mrs Naidu, later Governor of Uttar Pradesh, talked of the attractive Muslim culture at Lucknow as very decadent, citing people we both knew.

'The decay has charm like all things in decay.'

'Like the British Empire?'

'Yes, that has the iridescence of decay, particularly with bright young things like you floating around.'

As she intended, I felt pleasantly flattered.

When I called to say goodbye to Jinnah we ran over the course again and he charmingly asked me to thank the Mission for their work.

Before the Mission's Statement was published, Wavell asked me to prepare a draft for the broadcast he would make about it. The gist of the most contentious provision was that provinces would be grouped into three sections. Section A, far the largest, would contain the six great Hindu provinces. Sections B and C would contain the provinces where the Muslims were in a majority. The Sections would proceed to group constitution-making and *after*, but *not before*, the constitutional arrangements came into operation, any province could decide to come out of any group in which it had been placed – such a decision to be made *after* the first general election under the new constitution. The Viceroy would at once seek to form an Interim Government, composed only of political leaders. Later it was laid down that no one could be in the Interim Government who had not accepted the provisions of the Mission's Statement and had agreed to work them.

Gandhi's reactions varied almost daily. Initially he said the Mission had brought forth something 'of which they could be very proud'. Three days after the Statement he dropped his posture of being 'adviser' to the British nation and asserted himself as the dictator of Congress and its working committee. He openly took over negotiations with the Mission, with streams of complaints and queries for clarification.

Four days after the Statement Gandhi succeeded in trapping the Mission into dangerous controversy. He overruled the wiser, moderate heads in the Congress working committee who were prepared for some compromise to preserve the unity of India. Gandhi was the fanatic who all his life had a desire to impose his whole will, paraded as saintly or divine, and nothing but his will, on others. With all he learned and admired from the British, he never imbibed the spirit of compromise which is at the centre of the British approach.

Jinnah understood the Statement and did not like it. He raised no points of interpretation. He stayed on in Simla, brooding unhappily, and told Abell, the Viceroy's secretary, on the telephone that there was no use his coming to Delhi unless the Mission were prepared to change their Statement.

On the Sunday after Thursday's publication of the Statement I told Stafford that I thought I should go to see Jinnah. He was against it. The next day Stafford collapsed with an attack of colitis. His intestines rarely gave him any length of peace – he had already had a minor collapse on 2 May. This one was more serious. Overwork and Gandhi's relentless corkscrew wriggling had worn him down. He was carted off to the Willingdon Hospital saying, 'Whatever happens, don't let the old man come and see me.'

As Stafford was in hospital I talked over my wish to visit Jinnah with Pethick-Lawrence and A.V. They both thought I should go. Though I had started as Stafford's Personal Assistant, the Mission had come to regard me as the agent of them all, able to manoeuvre in situations where they could not. They particularly wanted Jinnah to know, despite the claims of the Hindu Press, that Congress would not be allowed to modify the Statement. That is what we all believed at the time: the betrayal was still to come.

I left Delhi by train for Simla at 5 a.m. on 23 May. I had had only three hours' sleep and I did not feel strong enough to tackle Jinnah that day. I arranged to see him on the Friday morning. Simla was drab and empty. No newspapermen patrolling at the hotel entrance eager for a scrap of news. No Viceregal cars. I had dinner with Sir Firoze Khan, later Prime Minister of Pakistan. Sir Firoze was so out of touch that he thought nothing would alter in India for at least five years, and if there were an Interim Government it would last another twenty years before the British went.

I found Jinnah nervous and edgy, less in command of himself than I had seen him before. He had to make a decision determining the future of the Muslims, aided by few whose advice was worth much. The Congress leadership abounded with men (and women) of stature who could dissect courses of action as skilfully as the top politicians of the world. Jinnah had to think it all out by himself. At the moment, this was frightening him. For the first time he was fearful of meeting the Muslim League working committee and its All India Council.

The second I came into the room he asked what all the comings and goings in Delhi amounted to. I told him the Congress leaders were not being allowed to alter the Statement. He was relieved, but less so when I pointed out that this meant that he could not either. He was bitterly hurt, and so were all the Muslims, at the onslaught on Pakistan in the preamble 'made in order to appease Congress'. It was also inconsistent, he went on, with the rest of the Statement, which put heavy stress on the inadequacy of paper safeguards to meet the communal problem. The Statement was 'impractical'. The machinery could not work with no spirit of co-operation on the other side. What was required was a surgical operation. He had explained to the Viceroy that there should be an entirely separate Constituent Assembly for deciding the structure of the Union. He thought that Wavell had understood, but evidently he had not.

The outlook was bleak. I let him talk on as he might to a sympathetic colleague. After much more of this I suggested he could say that the British had no business to pronounce on the merits of Pakistan or bluntly to turn down what millions of people wanted. Their attack on Pakistan was outrageous. The Muslims never expected the British to give them Pakistan. They knew they would have to get it by their own strong right arm. The scheme outlined in the Mission's Statement was impracticable and could not work. Nevertheless, in order to show that they would give it a trial, they would accept the Statement and would not go out of their way to sabotage the proceedings. They would accept the Statement as a first step on the road to Pakistan.

I had spoken at length. When I finished, his face lit up. He hit the table with his hand. 'That's it. You've got it!' he shouted.

And that's exactly what he made the Muslim League do.

In Delhi Gandhi was still at his tricks. I wrote a paper reiterating the need for a fixed date to be announced for a total British withdrawal after the formation of an Interim Government in 'a year to a year and a half'. But I was getting restless, feeling there was not much more I could do. I was missing out on my parliamentary career. I saw Cripps for the first time after he had been ill on 31 May. He agreed I could go home if I wanted to but gave me a lecture.

'You have to be patient. When I was Ambassador in Moscow during the war nothing happened for weeks on end. I got frustrated and bored, thinking I was wasting my time. Then Hitler attacked Russia and suddenly I had a mass of vital things to do.'

He thought I was being silly and he was right. Here I was in the middle of the most important British undertaking since we first set up shop in Madras in 1639 and I was so impatient that I wanted to go home and make speeches in the Commons no one would listen to. I had not long to wait.

Jinnah, now back in Delhi, was due to see the Viceroy on 3 June. At dinner the night before with Ian Scott, Deputy Private Secretary to the Viceroy, I said I should like to see Wavell before he saw Jinnah and press on him that he must promise the Muslim League that we would back them if they accepted the Mission's plan, as we would back Congress in similar circumstances. At least we must implement the constitution establishing the Muslim areas. I did not see Wavell, but Abell told me that Scott had represented my views and that it had been agreed to take my line.

The next day the Muslim League working committee met. Jinnah was advocating the kind of resolution he and I had discussed at Simla and getting support when Hassan Isphahani raised the question of what would happen if they accepted and Congress did not. The Muslim League would look fools and would be forever nailed as having been willing to accept less than Pakistan if the British let them down. 'Yes,' Jinnah said to Isphahani, 'you've made a most important point. I am not quite satisfied on this myself.' Isphahani said he understood that Jinnah had got an assurance from the Viceroy yesterday. Jinnah nodded and said, 'Mm, but I wanted an assurance in writing and I didn't get it.'

At the Viceroy's House everyone was scared that a written assurance might be published and annoy Congress. I got my way and a letter was drafted assuring Jinnah that if one party accepted and the other did not, we would implement the scheme as far as we could with the assistance of the party which did accept.

Two evenings later the Muslim Council issued a resolution

in the style recommended by me to Jinnah in Simla. At lunchtime the following day I met several Muslim Leaguers in the dining-room of the Imperial Hotel. They asked me, 'Are you happy now?' and congratulated me, saying they knew I had drafted the resolution going before the Council that afternoon. In the evening I saw more Muslim Leaguers. Two newspaper correspondents asked Iftikar Udin, a member of the Muslim League working committee, what was in the resolution. He pointed to me: 'Ask him – he drafted it. I only hope he drafts the Congress one, too.'

It was the only genuine acceptance of the Cabinet Mission Statement. Congress never accepted it. Their claim to have done so was based on a dishonest assurance from Stafford and Pethick-Lawrence that delegates to the Constituent Assembly were not obliged to meet in their three groups to evolve group constitutions if they did not want to. The opposite was the nub of the scheme, as Jinnah had been assured and as the Cabinet Mission and Congress both knew. However, Stafford and Pethick-Lawrence were so anxious not to leave India without some show of an acceptance from Congress that they accepted a bogus one on 25 June. It was the Congress insistence on their interpretation, designed to prevent the group constitutions ever coming into existence (thus destroying the embryo of Pakistan before it could be born), which forced Jinnah eventually to withdraw his acceptance. Congress were thus left pretending to have accepted, and to have fought against Jinnah for the unity of India. The truth was that Congress had smashed it and had made a sovereign Pakistan inevitable.

Congress coupled their 'acceptance' of the Mission's Statement with the rejection of the Interim Government. Agreement had almost been reached, with Jinnah removing his original demand for parity with Congress, when Gandhi ordered Congress to back off. I complained angrily to Agatha Harrison and Penderel Moon about the latest development: 'The little fellow has bitched everything once again, as in 1942.'

I had been to see Gandhi on the afternoon of 9 June at his urgent insistence. 'I have been examining the Mission's Statement with a lawyer's mind,' he said, then pointing to his head, 'although a very aged one. Now the Cabinet Mission have put out their document, they no longer have the right to interpret it. That is for others. The lawgiver cannot interpret his own laws.' He moved on to what he called 'the bugbear of parity': 'If the British insist on Congress accepting parity with the Muslim League in the Interim Government, I will say to them, "You had better run your own government yourselves." I will tell Congress to take no part in it.' But he told them that even after Jinnah dropped his insistence on parity.

I protested that it was unimportant how many representatives each side had in the government so long as they were the best men.

'When you make a remark like that you are not in the skin of India.'

It was quite clear that Gandhi intended that the British plan should get nowhere and all was ended. I said, 'I agree with you about one thing. We should get off your backs, as you have always said to me. The Mission are now wasting their time here. We should go home and announce a British withdrawal. Then you would all have to make your own minds up.'

He told his entourage what I had said. One of them, the sly Rajkumari Amrit Kaur, repeated it to Stafford Cripps. She disliked me, as I her. She hoped to get me into trouble. She did. Stafford said my remarks to Gandhi were appalling disloyalty to the Mission and I must tell Attlee what I had done when we got home. That was to be a painful interview. From behind the Speaker's Chair Attlee walked with me down the corridor to his office, chatting about Stafford's health: 'These passionate spirits are apt to burn themselves out from time to time.' When I had gulped out my confession he said, 'You should never be disloyal to your team even if you disagree with them.' I could not stop a tear falling from my eye. I was deeply ashamed. At this distance I think that perhaps Stafford was a trifle unfair. The records show that he engaged in considerable duplicity himself, especially when intriguing with Gandhi and Congress behind the Viceroy's back. I do not think Attlee could have taken so severe a view of me as I thought he did at the time. Otherwise he would hardly have made me Under-Secretary of State for War in 1951, remarking as he did, 'That's a very good place to start.' That is where *he* had started in the 1924 Labour Government.

I am sure Gandhi never meant to harm me. He would have supposed Rajkumari Amrit Kaur could be trusted to keep a confidence. He used to say to me, 'I'd rather trust someone and be deceived than not trust them at all.' Unfortunately his dictum was not helpful to me in this incident. Without it I might have been a minister much earlier.

We left India on 29 June. Not all was black. We had extinguished any doubts that Independence was on the way. The Mission's scheme became and remained the ground rules for discussion. The embryo of the Pakistan the Mission had lambasted in order to murder it was sufficiently outlined for it to be born.

A personal postscript: On 12 and 13 December 1945 there was a two-day Commons debate on India. I made a long speech on the first day. After describing the growing collapse of the British administration I said there were two courses open:

> One is to reimpose in its old and most vigorous form the British Raj. . . . That would take anything from fifteen to twenty years to get into its stride because we should have to rehabilitate the prestige of the British before we could do it. In the meantime no advance would be made with the Constitution and that would be a complete denial of all our pledges to India. It would require heavy reinforcements of British troops and it would also be completely impossible in the face of world opinion. It is a course which the government obviously cannot contemplate and I mention it because it is the only thing which could be done apart from the course which I should now like to suggest.
>
> That course is that . . . we should say that we cannot support the existing state of affairs any longer. We must say clearly and unequivocally to India that on a certain fixed day we are going to leave India with our troops and our officials . . . and we must do that before the administrative machinery has completely crumbled in our hands. The date of the withdrawal should certainly be not more than twelve months ahead. If it is . . . circumstances may have run on so fast that we should not be able to take any such step.

The next day R.A. Butler wound up for the Conservatives. He had a strong family connection with India and understood something of its nature, unlike Winston Churchill whose experience of India was that of a subaltern. I was thrilled when Rab got to this passage:

> I turn my attention to the remarkable speech of the Honourable Member for Aston [Mr Wyatt] in the debate yesterday. The Honourable Member has had the opportunity which, alas I have not had . . . to go to India and to acquaint himself almost hourly with the situation. We must, therefore, pay full respect to what he has said in such a clear and definite manner.

He then quoted my proposition that we must announce that we would leave India on a certain fixed day. He went on:

> The Honourable gentleman developed his case very fully. I take it that honourable members have studied all his arguments and the reasons he gave in support of them. I can only say that such a policy does not recommend itself either to me or to my honourable and right honourable friends on this side. I, personally, could not reconcile my conscience – nor could we on this side of the House – to such a policy whereby we should fade away in the night and plunge in one moment from the culmination of our years of service, to the depths of indifference to what is to happen next.

I learned afterwards that my speech requesting the announcement of a fixed date of withdrawal finally tipped the balance in favour of what I had been advocating for so long. The India and Burma Committee of the Cabinet had before it on 20 December a draft statement in a Cabinet paper which had been gestating since the debate. Wavell's extraordinary plan for gradually removing what remained of the British presence to the Muslim majority provinces was discarded. Clause 5 of the draft statement read: 'H.M.G. therefore believe that it is their duty both to their own countrymen and to the Indian people to state now their definite intentions as to the future. It is their intention to recommend Parliament to hand over power in India by March 31st 1948. . . .'

That was three months later than I had proposed. The statement that the Government eventually issued on 20 February 1947 extended it another three months to June 1948 and beyond what I thought sensible, though to get the date exactly right was hard. Mountbatten's principal contribution in India was to advance that date by some nine months. That was a mistake:

there was not enough time left to organize the inevitable partition so as to minimize the bloodshed.

Strangely, admirers of Mountbatten have claimed that it was he who conceived the idea of announcing a date for withdrawal. This is untrue. I had pressed it since the spring of 1946. Attlee did not invite Mountbatten to be Viceroy until 18 December 1946. Mountbatten went on holiday to Switzerland for Christmas to think about it and did not accept the post until after he got back. On 3 January he wrote to Attlee that it was of fundamental importance that the policy statement should announce a date for the termination of the Raj. Yes, indeed, but that had already been decided before Mountbatten came on the scene. Perhaps Mountbatten, a boastful man who always exaggerated his own achievements, came to persuade himself that he had really invented the fixed date of withdrawal. He had plenty of other, real, achievements, so I shall not let him take this one away from me.

I saw Mountbatten before he left. He was chiefly concerned with what he should wear on arrival. 'They're all a bit left wing, aren't they? Hadn't I better land in ordinary day clothes?' He was delighted when I said, 'No, you are the last Viceroy. You are royal. You must wear your grandest uniform and all your decorations and be met in full panoply and with all the works. Otherwise they will feel slighted.' And that is what he did, to everyone's pleasure.

I met that flashing lady, Edwina Mountbatten, several times and was a slave to her charm. She was avidly interested in the politics of India, anxious to learn everything. She was quicker and more intelligent than her husband and understood politics better. I was glad to help her, against Tory opposition, to get a Bill through Parliament which enabled her to get full use of her money, hitherto tied up in trusts. Unfortunately, she became bewitched by Nehru, and, tutored by Cripps, the Mountbattens adopted an absurdly over-deferential approach to Gandhi. They were acutely biased in favour of Congress, which immensely increased their difficulties with Jinnah. Mountbatten foolishly thought Pakistan 'sheer madness' and Jinnah 'a psychopathic case'. But Jinnah was the best politician of them all.

Mountbatten had a nice panache as the last Viceroy, but he

did not write his own instructions as some have claimed. His instructions from Attlee were clear and precise. He was controlled from London, though less fussily than Wavell. He did a good job, handicapped by not being able to cope with detail. Lord Ismay, his Chief of Staff in India and Churchill's wartime Chief of Defence Staff, wrote to Lady Ismay on 23 April 1947:

'We have made innumerable drafts . . . but it is impossible to get Dickie to go through them methodically. He is a grand chap in a thousand ways, but clarity of thought and writing is not his strong suit.' Who should know better than Ismay?

So ends the account of how I saw the months leading to the hand-over of power. I had been an active and not wholly insignificant participant in the voluntary surrender of the greatest empire in history; greater than that of the Greeks, the Romans or Alexander the Great. Whatever I did in the future would never be on so grand a scale as that. It was a splendid feeling.

# CHAPTER VII

———— ❈❈❈ ————

# Sparkling Friends

TRAVELLERS WHO HAVE HAD exotic adventures in distant lands return confident that their friends and acquaintances will be fascinated by them. They are not. They are as absorbed as they ever were with local gossip, the stable centre of their universe. The traveller must soon stop being a bore with his tales, and catch up on what was going on while he was away, or be stranded on an unfashionable beach. It was July when I got back, nearly time for the long summer recess.

I found the livelier elements on the Labour back benches, to whom I was attracted, amusing themselves by devising irritants for the Government: they had not much else to do. Apparently our foreign policy was all wrong and we were too slow in pushing through socialism at home. The Government was pusillanimous because it had not got its heart in socialism. Clearly my friends were cleverer than I. It was flattering that they thought me worth talking to and plotting with.

By the time Parliament met again some of us were ready to challenge the Government's foreign policy with an amendment to the King's Speech in November 1946. It was tantamount to a motion of no confidence, something customarily left to the Opposition. Our action evoked the painful cry from Ernie Bevin that he had been 'stabbed in the back'. What fools we were, sparkling as some of the group may have been. When we met to draw up the amendment the question was asked, who was to move it? Immediately I proposed Dick Crossman. He did it brilliantly. The amendment collected fifty-seven Labour signatures, from which we became known as Heinz's 57 Varieties.

Despite our many differences which grew with the years I remained friendly with Dick until his death. I was always happy with him. Before the war he worked with the Workers' Education Association. He was a supreme teacher, who never talked down but who tried to encourage his hearers to understand as he did. He loved bringing out the intelligence of his listeners, like Socrates, on whom he was an expert. He was one of the two or three best speakers in the Commons. With pungency and precision he would build up an inexorably logical case, to which there seemed no answer. It took me a long time to realize that the elegant structure depended on the acceptance of his premise, and that was frequently flawed. When his premise was unsound, what followed became no more than arresting nonsense. He saw situations in startling black and white. There was always a precipice ahead, in front of which he considerately placed a danger signal.

It never bothered him that the Government walked straight past the notice and came to no harm.

Dick was a glorious conversationalist. Propositions, para-doxes, contradictions, theories, cascaded from him like a fountain. His idea of the moment was his enthusiasm. When another charged irresistibly into his brain, his previous stance was abandoned. Some put this down to dishonesty and called him Dick Double Crossman. That was unfair. He believed in his latest creation, untroubled by its going in the opposite direction to the one formerly announced as the sole correct one. He was a purveyor of changing notions, not of plans for practical action. His schemes as a minister for reforms of the Commons and of pensions were disastrous.

He longed to be Editor of the *New Statesman*. Kingsley Martin, not an unshakeable rock himself, did not trust him. He made him Assistant Editor and dangled the hope that one day Dick might succeed him if he became more consistent, but Kingsley was determined he would not. It was when I worked on the *New Statesman* that I came to know Dick really well. There was a tram we took to the Commons from the *New Statesman* office that swooped excitingly underground for part of the journey and then re-emerged on the Embankment. We would sit in front, on the top, pleasurably awaiting the daily drama while Dick did most of the talking, giving me an education in socialism. We also talked about Kingsley Martin.

Dick, outwardly so sure that his was the best brain in Britain, was hobbled by unexpected chains of deference to authority. Perhaps he acquired them at that strange pre-war Winchester where the pride of the boys in their own intellectual superiority was tempered by an atmosphere of deliberate physical brutality. It affected even Stafford, who told me how hurt he was when George VI, the highest in the land, did not give him one word of thanks for what he had done for the country when he handed over his seals of office before going away to die. Stafford forgot, no doubt, that before the war he had fervently advocated that the first Act of Parliament of a Labour Government should be one to abolish the Monarchy. Cripps, Gaitskell, D. N. Pritt, Douglas Jay, Mosley and many other notabilities never lost the imprint of Winchester, which was far more damaging than that of softly snobbish Eton.

Dick was like a latently dangerous Alsatian with Kingsley, sometimes alarming him by the ferocity of his attacks but grovelling affectionately on the floor when called to heel. At that time (1947) I was paid some £15 a week for two and a half days' work and Dick about £25 for four days' work. Dick thought this sweated labour. I agreed. When Kingsley, with Dick and I plus the Communist Aylmer Vallance, ran the front end of the paper the *New Statesman* was highly prosperous, with a rising circulation approaching 100,000. We decided to ask for more money.

Kingsley, his abundant up-ended white hair making him look more vividly patriarchal than ever, listened impatiently: 'I'm surprised at you both. When I was your age [actually there was a gap between Dick and myself of eleven years] I worked the whole week for the *Manchester Guardian* for £3 a week. I never complained about the money [implying that good Socialists did not do that]. I knew it was an honour to work for the *Guardian*. I only had a bicycle. You've both got cars. You should be proud to work for the *New Statesman*.'

No pay rise. I waited for Dick, as the senior, to put up a fight. Instead, betrayed by his deferential streak, he said, 'I see, Kingsley. I suppose you're right.' And we slunk out.

When Harold Wilson was plotting with the Bevanites to become Leader of the Labour Party they used to meet frequently and secretly at Dick's house in Vincent Square. Dick made him his hero. Once as we talked at Vincent Square Dick was telling me about the meetings (Dick could never keep a secret) and praising Wilson's miraculous abilities. Dick suddenly stopped. He pointed at a chair. 'That,' he said reverently, 'is the very chair *he* sits on.'

'Why don't you put a plaque on it?' I asked. Dick did not think it funny.

Dick had violent dislikes. He could be intemperately malicious about people, sometimes, if he were not in awe of them, to their face. He hated Attlee, an old friend of his family. Once he told me how annoyed he was at the reception of the report of the Anglo-American Commission on Palestine, on which he had sat:

'No one was interested in our report [that was not true, actually]. Ernie Bevin wouldn't see me. In the end I asked to see Attlee, who gave me an interview. He let me talk for half an hour while he sat saying nothing, doodling on a piece of paper. When I had finished, do you know what he said? He looked up and asked "How's your mother?" And that was the end of it. Why did he never give me a job? He gave you one.'

'Because he thinks you're irresponsible.'

'Of course I'm irresponsible. He never gave me any responsibility. I hate that man.'

When Dick finally entered Wilson's Cabinet at the age of nearly fifty-seven his colleagues must have felt the same as Attlee. There he sat taking copious notes for his diaries, intended for publication, breaking every convention of confidentiality, inhibiting frank discussion. He played the same trick on his civil servants without their knowing it.

I rarely roused his venom, though I did so in 1951. Dick wanted to visit the Army and its commanders in Germany and asked for War Office permission. The officials thought it sounded harmless. I was Under-Secretary of State for War and said, 'On no account. He'll charm them into telling him all he wants to know, thinking that as an MP he'll keep the confidential bits confidential. Then he'll use the material to attack the Government over rearmament. He'll add his own distortions and get trusting officers into trouble for telling him too much. Why should we help him? Anyway he's a bad security risk.'

Dick rang me in a fury: 'You're preventing me doing my duty

as an MP. I'll raise it in the House. I'll go to the Minister of Defence. You've no right to stop me.' But he never went to Germany that time and he calmed down, surprised I was so tough. There were several occasions when servicemen and diplomats overseas must have wished their ministers had acted similarly.

A great hate Dick had was for Hugh Gaitskell. They had been at school and at Oxford together but Dick was much the cleverer of the two of them. Dick could never reconcile himself to the bitter injustice of his intellectual inferior streaking ahead of him in politics. He jealously screamed when Hugh became Chancellor of the Exchequer while he was still a backbencher. He was a devoted plotter with the other Bevanites trying to bring Hugh down.

Dick was lucky with his last two wives. They gave him a loving background which did something to steady him, particularly when he was at his successive houses in the country, where Dick talked long and entertainingly. Not that he was ever dull when I used to visit him in Horton General Hospital at Banbury. The indiscretions were unstemmed by illness. He was mischievous but he had a good heart.

Dick was the animating force behind 'Keep Left'. There were fifteen of us in the group, which met weekly and published a pamphlet in May 1947. It was the forerunner of the dissident cliques which were to plague the Labour Party and still do. These are to the Labour Party as the Levellers were to Cromwell, a persistent strain in English life among those who would change society, suspicious of their leaders in the conviction that lust for power has made them betrayers of the true faith. A flavour of Marxism added to the outlook of Levellers is an unpleasant brew. It is a recipe for permanent discontent, for refusal to compromise and for dissatisfaction with society whatever shape it may be and however much the people may like it in that shape. Marxist-Levellers feed on destruction; they can never have enough of it. Cromwell stamped on them: Labour leaders since Gaitskell have been stamped on by them.

We were not all so bad as Marxist-Levellers in the Keep Left group but we were smugly satisfied with our superiority, knowing better than our leaders. I felt honoured to be included in so grand a gathering. I was allowed to write the section of our pamphlet dealing with the failure of the Government to demobilize the wartime Armed Services faster and got a terse ticking-off by Attlee at a Party meeting. 'I'm surprised a former major wrote that. He ought to have known better.' Much of the writing was good, coming from the expert pamphleteer Michael Foot, renowned for his part in the early wartime 'Guilty Men', which won many votes for Labour.

Michael was, and is, a sea-green incorruptible, despite a lapse from his principles as a champion of free speech when he permitted, as Secretary for Employment in the mid-seventies, that dangerous avenue to Press censorship, the closed shop for journalists. His relationship with Beaverbrook never corrupted him; if anything it corrupted Beaverbrook. Beaverbrook loved Michael as a son preferable to his own, whose lack of brains disappointed him and whom embarrassingly he treated abominably in front of others until my heart bled for the decent, kindly man, an RAF hero.

Michael's was the voice of puritan conscience to Beaverbrook. Certainly Beaverbrook's hospitality was lavish, but that is nothing between genuine friends, one of whom is rich and generous. It would have been boorish of Michael if he had rejected it. There was no possibility of Beaverbrook's buying his opinions, any more than there was of his buying those of Nye Bevan, down whose throat he poured champagne, nicknaming him 'The Bollinger Bolshevik'. Too much has been made of Beaverbrook's alleged corruption of innocent young men by accustoming them to luxurious living which they could keep up thereafter only by selling their souls to him.

Beaverbrook had extraordinary prejudices, pursued silly vendettas and adored making mischief, but he was far from evil. I experienced much generosity from him and argued with him to the point of making him red with brief anger. He never minded. He lived on verbal fisticuffs and was happy talking to those who exercised his considerable wits. He would hit you when you were up, but never when you were down. The first person to ring me when I was out of Parliament after the election of 1955 was Beaverbrook. 'Now what can I do to help you?' he growled. And he did help me.

I do not see Michael now. He regards me as a traitor to

socialism or the Labour Party, the same thing in his reckoning. He is not without faults. For a start he is vain, like some of the rest of us. At a party given by Hugh Cudlipp, Jill Craigie, Michael's wife who has kept much of the prettiness she had when I first met her, said to my present wife whom I was just about to marry, 'Do you know what you are doing? Every politician is like an actor on the stage.'

Vanity in politicians is an occupational sin. I had it badly. Perhaps Michael had it more than most. The role of the great orator of the Left was a drug to him. He needed the cheers of the faithful at Party Conferences. They are not the handmaidens to useful thought. Damning denunciations were his speciality. Everyone delighted in them, including his opponents in the Commons, but he did not, or could not, go beyond them to serious, practical solutions. They would have been too boring for the gallery and might have marred the run-up to the peroration.

Michael is a scholarly man, full of general knowledge and admirably soaked in books. He has been torn between being a Montaigne in his library and making a splash in the world. He spurned Attlee's offer of a job in the 1945 Parliament because he did not want to be sullied by power. Yet like a moth he has been doomed to hover round its flame, sitting on the Labour National Executive Committee until finally tempted into entering the Government in 1974.

In the election campaign of 1983 the Tories began by depicting him as a doddery old man who had lost his grip. In my column in the *Sunday Mirror* I urged them to drop this ugly smear: I am glad they listened to me. Apart from his evidently being in full vigour as he tramped round the country I was thinking of the gay, generous man full of wit and passion, whom I used to know and could not bear to see mocked.

I think Michael was once fond of me. He would affectionately tell a story about an incident in a speech I was making in the Commons which amused him for, what he thought, was its audacity. I was explaining from what might be considered a right-wing point of view what the working people really felt when an ultra-left-wing trade union MP interrupted me in disgust: 'Don't be ridiculous. You don't know anything about the working classes.'

'Of course I do,' Michael would gleefully report me as replying. 'I employ them.'

Michael's political strength lay in his true love of the Labour Party, right or wrong. The Labour Party needed him as its leader. Denis Healey would have been more suitable for the task of Prime Minister, but the Labour Party would have been battered more badly at the polls under Healey than it was under Michael. The Marxist-Levellers, with whom I subsume crypto-Communists, the Militant Tendency, Trotskyists, International Revolutionary Socialists and the rest of the fanatical 'Broad Left' rag-bag, would have exploded against Healey. Their fury against Healey's public disapproval of the official Labour policy for abolishing all British and US nuclear weapons in Britain would have been uncontainable. The election would have been dominated by open civil war in the Labour Party, leaving them trailing way behind the Lib-SDP Alliance. The claws of the lunatics were showing but were not dug into Michael. At least they offered superficial support to him as Leader. They would not have for anyone else.

After I left the *New Statesman* at the end of 1948 I worked for some time on *Tribune*, of which Michael was in charge, and I saw much of him. I wrote a number of their editorials, including one praising Nye Bevan's speech in the Commons on 28 February 1951 in favour of Labour's post-Korean War rearmament. It was withdrawn before it could be printed because Nye's resignation over Gaitskell's charges on teeth and spectacles was imminent and he was being urged to dress it up with a good coating of anti-rearmament populism. But at the time I wrote for *Tribune* it was more moderate than the *New Statesman* and quite often backed the Labour Government (after all Nye, worshipped by Michael, was in it), while the *New Statesman* sniped away at it as though it were the government of an enemy country.

The Keep Left pamphlet was manna to Kingsley Martin. He was neurotically convinced that the Labour Cabinet were a bunch of liars, a kind of Fifth Column for capitalism and imperialism of the ilk of Ramsay MacDonald and those of his Labour colleagues who had joined the National Government in 1931. When I began to write for the *New Statesman* Kingsley assured me that Attlee would never give India Independence. When I said, 'But Kingsley, I was on the Cabinet Mission. We were desperately trying to find a way of giving them Independence – the Government are absolutely sincere about it,' he smiled pityingly. 'That's just clever camouflage to hide their using Indian disagreements to hold up Independence indefinitely.'

His judgement was never strong, nor was his courage. He wrote about Czechoslovakia on the front page of the *New Statesman* on 27 August 1938: 'The question of frontier revision, difficult though it is, should at once be tackled. The strategical value of the Bohemian frontier should not be made the occasion of a world war. We should not guarantee the status quo. It should be remembered that Czechoslovakia is now almost surrounded by enemies. . . .'

Kingsley was a front-runner for appeasement. He beat Neville Chamberlain to it by over a month. The Munich meeting with Hitler, at which the Nazis were given a large chunk of Czechoslovakia, did not take place until 29 September. When Kingsley hoped his editorial had been forgotten he began to attack Chamberlain for giving in to Hitler. At the time of the Berlin Blockade Kingsley again wanted to cut and run. The *New Statesman* proposed that, to appease the Russians, they should be offered permanent control of Vienna in return for our being allowed to stay in West Berlin. If he had been Foreign Secretary the Russians would have got both. Fortunately, Ernie Bevin was Foreign Secretary and they got neither. Often Kingsley told me that the Communists were the heirs to the future, certain to take us over in the long run, so why risk annoying them by resisting them? Kingsley was not a Communist, merely a coward like so many who back CND and tell us that if only we were nice to the Russians they would leave us and the West alone.

As a journalist, Kingsley had genius. His weekly Diary was humorous, well constructed, idiosyncratic and right on the pulse of those of the middle classes aspiring to be trendy intellectuals without pain. I supplied a lot of the material, including some good stuff about Princess Elizabeth's wedding, which I watched perched somewhere in the roof of Westminster Abbey. But what I gave Kingsley was never quite suitable. After expert touches he made it unmistakably his and much more readable. I enjoyed my year and a half or so at the *New Statesman* and went on writing for it when I was no longer on the staff.

Kingsley lived with a fat, bright, jolly woman called Dorothy Woodman who was fascinated by Burma. They both considered me left wing about South-East Asia and the colonies, because I have always believed in people and countries running their own affairs, however much of a mess they may make of them. On home issues they thought I inclined to being reactionary. Already I was not invited to meetings of the Keep Left group when it started up again, and was querying its whole approach.

Kingsley was convinced I would end up in the Conservative Party (Harold Macmillan told me that, too). By the end of 1948 I was beginning to think Attlee's programme for the 1945/50 Parliament would take us about far enough in socialism, a view I found I shared with Bertrand Russell despite his subsequent dottiness about the Bomb. However, I never became a Tory, though I supported Mrs Thatcher when she became Leader of the Conservative Party as the person most likely to lessen the British decline. So far I have seen no reason to stop supporting her.

One evening, when staying with Randolph Churchill at East Bergholt, I had a furious row with him. That was not difficult: this one was sparked off by my referring to his father, Winston, as a Tory. Randolph thumped the table, shouting in a rage, 'We were never Tories and never will be. We just make use of the Tory Party.' Quite. Mrs Thatcher is not a Tory either. Nor am I.

Life at the *New Statesman* was deliciously chaotic. The editorials which seemed so assured and authoritative were born of fierce arguments. I remembered the war when I was unable to get my *New Statesman* regularly because of paper rationing and, as a last shot, wrote to the paper asking (successfully) if they would let me jump the queue for a postal subscription, 'otherwise I shall be in danger of forming my own opinions'. I thought then that the *New Statesman* was compiled by gods, calmly, easily and steadily pouring out clear sentences in an untroubled stream. I felt the honour, as Kingsley thought I should, of being among these gods but had not expected them to be so disordered. Perhaps they are more ordered now, and maybe that is one of the reasons why the circulation has fallen to a third of what it used to be.

Under Kingsley the back end of the paper was exceptionally distinguished, with writers like V. S. Pritchett, Leonard Woolf and Raymond Mortimer. They were charming to me, willing to give me a free course in literature, for which they should have charged hundreds of pounds. Leonard Woolf was not merely interesting about Virginia Woolf and the Bloomsbury set, but about how and why he had turned away from his original belief in the Russian Communists, long before the bulk of those intellectuals who were later to do so. Kingsley never did.

Aylmer Vallance was also charming, though dubious about my politics. At the printing works where we put the *New Statesman* to bed he patiently showed me how to cut out lines while leaving the sense the same, and how dropping a word or so could save a line. Aylmer was a first-class journalist who had been Editor of the *News Chronicle*. He was sacked not because he was a Communist but because one night a member of the Cadbury family, who owned the *News Chronicle*, found him making love to a secretary on the top of his office desk, which was much more shocking.

Kingsley was a great editor. He was also considerate, kindly and entertaining. A very good chess player, he tried to teach me without avail. But he did teach me something about journalism.

During this period I got to know Roy Jenkins, who won the by-election at Southwark in 1948. He was unsure of his footing. The miners and other trade-union MPs expected him to be on warm terms with them. His father, a highly respected miners' MP and PPS to Attlee, had been one of them. Why not his son? But Roy had seen another world at Oxford and in the Army. His mother, healthily ambitious, encouraged her talented son to soar high, as good mothers properly do. He had become at ease with people of broader culture, finer intellect and more cosmopolitan than those he had known in provincial Wales: he appreciated their way of living and conversing and found it suited him. He had not yet broken through to being natural and to understanding what was happening within himself, so he could be embarrassed with those of similar origins, and that made him seem affected. They thought he was being snobbish, considering himself too good for them. It was not that at all. Temporarily he was caught between two worlds. It is easy to talk with perfect poise to poor relations in Ireland if you are a Kennedy, but you have to be a Kennedy first. Ernest Bevin was comfortably at the same level with everyone all his life and unconcernedly ate peas off his knife at Buckingham Palace, but Bevin had not been complicated by going to Oxford.

Roy was aware that he had not got his human relations right and that his awkwardness gave him a superior air. I watched him with admiration as he examined and improved himself. For someone to do that is rare. Roy developed a generous and sympathetic spirit. The better he became as an individual, the easier it was for him to straddle several worlds and make solid friendships in all of them. And all the while his brain and knowledge of human beings and politics expanded. At the beginning he was inclined to trim to where power was if his mind told his head it was to his advantage though his heart might be hinting something different. He became big enough to be his own man. It is an achievement to be saluted.

Roy's ambition was large, larger than mine if that were possible. I was amused at the time we were both Birmingham Labour MPs when Roy said to me, 'You're playing for the big stakes, aren't you? Do you mind if I stand for the chairmanship of the Birmingham group of Labour MPs? I think it is more important to me than to you.' I think he saw himself as doing a Joe Chamberlain with Birmingham, but its Labour MPs were a hopeless lot.

Roy was more prudent than I. He has strong convictions but he did not parade them as vigorously or as provocatively as I did. He was just as certain as Hugh Gaitskell and I that Nye Bevan was bogus in presenting his resignation in 1951 as a protest against rearmament but he did not join us, lone voices, in the public counter-attack before and after the 1951 election, which cemented our unpopularity with the Left. He knew nationalization of steel would be disastrous, as did most of the Labour Cabinet, but he let it pass as not being worth loss of office. He did not support Barbara Castle in 1969 when the crunch came in her brave battle to get some sense into the unions with her White Paper, *In Place of Strife*. But Roy drew on his courage to resign from the Deputy Leadership of the Labour Party in 1972 over Labour's decision to hold a referendum over the Common Market. Roy was more confident of his stature by then.

Curiously, if he had asked my advice, which he often did but not on this occasion, probably guessing he would not like it, I should have urged him not to resign. Holding the referendum which Wedgwood Benn had foisted on the Labour Party did not matter, since the country, as could have been foreseen, were two to one in favour of staying in the Common Market when a referendum was held in June 1975. The Deputy Leadership was a key position. Surrendering it raised doubts about Roy's basic loyalty to the Labour Party. It probably cost him the chance to be Harold Wilson's successor, which Mary Wilson, not a bad judge, once firmly believed he would be. The history of the Labour Party and the country would have been changed. Still, after that, no one could accuse Roy of being unwilling to suffer for his principles.

As Home Secretary Roy was not soft but wisely tolerant. He was extremely tough on terrorists and would not be swerved by hunger strikes or threats thereof. He was tough, too, as Chancellor of the Exchequer; the last Chancellor to balance the Budget, control inflation and effectively prune public expenditure while keeping unemployment in check. He was as honourable as Stafford, possibly more so. Before his last Budget he asked me to see him at the Treasury, which strictly he ought not to have done, but I think no harm can be done by revealing it now. He had two possible courses: to have a give-away Budget, which would make election victory surer but do severe damage to the economy; or to carry on with unpopular restraint, which would make prosperity more likely in the future but carried the risk of damaging Labour's electoral prospects.

'You must follow the right and patriotic course. You'll be ashamed of yourself otherwise.'

He was hoping I would say that. It fortified him in his decision to do what few politicians do: put country before party and their own careers. Sadly when Heath won the 1970 election his first Chancellor of the Exchequer, Iain Macleod, soon died.

Neither his successor, Anthony Barber, nor Heath, had the sense to build on Roy's legacy of careful husbandry.

With the exception of Stafford Cripps, who held down prices and wages not by law but by his moral authority, Roy was the best post-war Chancellor; Geoffrey Howe a tolerable third. I think Mrs Thatcher would have been glad to have Roy as her Chancellor when she became Prime Minister. It might have been arranged but Roy, President of the EEC, had other and fresh fish to fry.

Through Roy I met Tony Crosland, an Oxford friend of his. For some years the three of us were very close, until Tony's jealousy of Roy had a disruptive effect. Roy was oddly respectful to Tony, letting him overwhelm him in arguments. He thought Tony the most brilliant man he knew, much above himself intellectually. I had to say, 'Don't be silly, Roy. He's just more bullying, bombastic and abusive than you are. You're much cleverer than he is,' which was true.

Tony had an exaggeratedly arrogant manner. He had a constant need to assert himself, to be the centre of attention, to demonstrate that whoever he was with was inferior to him – unless they were obviously inferior, or of the working classes, when he would treat them with great politeness. I am not sure what he was trying to prove; perhaps it had something to do with his irritation at the unselfconscious assurance of the upper classes, whom he privately admired but outwardly excoriated, resenting that Highgate School – where he went – was not Eton. Tony was attracted by aristocrats, or the genuine upper classes, having affairs with their daughters whenever he could. That was to reassure himself that he was as good as they were. His apparent disdain for those he recognized as grand was affectation; he distinguished exactly between those whose grandness was recent and those upon whom it had sat for generations.

Whatever the reasons for his churlish behaviour, it could be very tiresome. A couple of instances:

My third wife and I gave him dinner at a restaurant. He grabbed the wine-list out of my hand shouting, 'You can't choose the wine. You know nothing about wine. I'm going to choose it', and proceeded to do so. I was annoyed, rather fancying my knowledge of wine, but I let it pass.

One night when he came to dinner he was put out because

the nine other guests, and possibly his host, were not letting him dominate the conversation. Suddenly he announced, 'This is terribly boring' and put his feet up on a sofa, pretending to go to sleep for an hour. This time I was angry and would not speak to him for a week. Hugh Gaitskell, noticing the mutual hostility, said as the three of us were standing in the lobby outside the Commons Chamber, 'What are you two having a row about? Is it over some girl?', which seemed the most likely explanation to him, knowing our weakness. 'No', I said, 'it's because I can't stand Tony's loutish manners any more.'

In his conceit, and he was very conceited, he took to asking disdainfully who else would be there before deciding whether to agree to come to dinner, after commenting 'Oh, they're too boring', meaning they would give him as good as they got. His arrogance frequently pushed him into childishness. One evening in his flat in The Boltons there was a party. Kingsley Amis came with some jazz gramophone records. After a while Tony started taking them off the gramophone, putting another one on arbitrarily, taking it off a quarter of the way through and reaching for another.

Kingsley protested vehemently: 'Leave them alone. They're my records.'

'I don't give a fuck. It's my gramophone. I'm putting them on, not you.'

The distinguished novelist and the distinguished economist, both drunk, then fought over their toys as if they were children in a nursery, punching and rolling on the floor.

Roy, Tony and I played tennis at Ladbroke Square, opposite where Roy and Jennifer Jenkins lived. Jennifer was the model wife for a rising politician. The highly intelligent daughter of a town clerk, she knew something of public affairs before they were married. Her sensible advice, her steady loyalty, her hard work in doubling housewifely with public duties, her ready friendliness, have given Roy an immovable base, and a better wife in some ways than he deserved. Jennifer is a considerable person, competent and valuable. Sometimes she would play tennis with us. Sometimes there would be one of Tony's ever-changing string of girlfriends, in front of whom he disliked being beaten. He did not like losing anyway.

Tony had a peculiar service. He wound himself up and circled his arms stiffly like a windmill. When I was playing against him I would laugh to put him off as the grotesque motions began. 'I can't see what's funny,' he would mutter as he hit the ball furiously into the net. They were happy, laughing afternoons, none of us men playing as well as he thought he did.

Tony's girls were a wonderment to me: nearly always very pretty and frequently fair and blue eyed, occasionally with brains as well. I wished I could have had one or two of them as girlfriends myself. Tony was tall and handsome with an engaging smile, ready to amuse and make laugh any girl he was interested in. My advice to young male wooers, however physically unattractive, is to remember that a man who can make a girl laugh is halfway there. Laughter is a potent aphrodisiac, rivalling money and power.

Tony also suggested the potentiality of power and fame to come. He hardly ever loved the numerous girls he went to bed with. He did it to convince himself that he had triumphed over his homosexual side, which had been in the ascendant at Oxford. He remained attractive to homosexuals. Hugh Dalton, whose fondness for young men occasionally went over the top, was in love with Tony and as his literary executor Tony had the odd task of dealing with the emotional letters Dalton wrote him.

Part of Tony's attraction to women came from the pronounced homosexual aspect of his nature, which made him sympathetic to and understanding of them. When he cared he could exert a powerful boyish charm on them. He would take a month's holiday apart from his second wife in the summer when she visited her family in America. On one of his solo rambles through Europe he stayed with us in Italy. My present wife, Verushka, went through his luggage and found it full of dirty underwear, socks and shirts. Averse to any housework, she washed and ironed the lot, something she has never done for me or for any other man. 'But you know,' she said afterwards, 'though Tony pretends not to care about clothes and dresses, his shirts are very expensive, not at all what the working class wear.'

Clothes were one of Tony's acquired poses to demonstrate his solidarity with ordinary Labour supporters. When Tony was still a don at Trinity College, Oxford, there was a great gaudy. Lord Chief Justice Goddard, another Trinity man, was to be the principal guest. Tony invited Roy and me to come as his personal guests. 'You know you have to wear white ties and tails. Have you got them? You can't let me down.' He rang me three times to make sure I would be properly dressed. I was amused when later he priggishly refused to wear even a dinner-jacket at formal dinners at Buckingham Palace, or when accompanying the Queen on the royal yacht and at banquets in the USA when he was Foreign Secretary. It was a pretentious way to display Socialist principles: an attempt to identify himself with Nye Bevan, who performed the same anti-ritual. But at least Nye Bevan could claim working-class origins, which Tony decidedly could not. Public school, Oxford, father a senior civil servant, comfortable middle-class background, all precluded that.

Tony was openly an intellectual snob. When he was writing *The Future of Socialism*, he was interested in a series of articles I had written for *Illustrated*, a popular magazine now defunct, and borrowed some of their ideas for his book. 'I hope you understand. I can't acknowledge anything from such a low-level magazine, not even in a footnote, in a book like mine. If you had written the articles in a better sort of magazine like *Encounter* I could have.'

When Tony was writing, sobriety and seclusion were his rules. His dedication was impressive. Being honest he was compelled to admit that capitalism and profits, which he understood well, were more useful than Labour Party Clause 4 socialism. He was driven back on schemes for the equitable distribution of wealth, or egalitarianism, setting the upper limits for incomes somewhere in the region of his own. His *Future of Socialism* was an effort to persuade the Labour Party to recognize reality, which does not seem to have worked.

Tony had a rampant ambition, which he overreached. He saw himself as Leader of the Labour Party and Prime Minister. He would have been no good at it. He lacked the wiles of a Harold Wilson and had insufficient robustness. His ambition diminished him, leading him to avoid making a clear stand on important issues. He would account for his wavering by declaring controversial and difficult subjects 'irrelevant'. Whether

Britain went into the Common Market was a matter of substance. Anxious not to offend the pro- and anti-Marketeers in the Labour Party, Tony described it as 'an irrelevance' which, right or wrong, it hardly was.

Tony saw Roy as his chief rival and was jealous when in 1967 Roy became Chancellor of the Exchequer: a job which Tony coveted and thought he would be much better at. Tony's envy soured the old friendship and to some extent affected mine with Tony, who knew I rated Roy his superior as a politician. It was sad. If only Tony had been able to admit to himself that his chance of being Labour's leader was much less than Roy's, and had backed Roy instead of undermining him, the Labour Party might not have deteriorated so badly. As it was, the forces of reason were divided. Tony backed Callaghan, who made him Foreign Secretary (one in the eye for Roy, who would have liked the post).

I tried occasionally to reconcile Roy and Tony. Once, at the peak of their enmity, I asked them both to dinner with the object of reviving past, easy friendship. The dinner went well and all seemed pleased except Arthur Koestler who was also there. He kept muttering in Hungarian to my wife, 'These two [Roy and Tony] are far too left wing. What a lot of rubbish they are talking.' He was puzzled, too, that such intelligent men should be so concerned about their health and what they should eat, or not eat, to maintain it.

Why was I so fond of Tony? Because all that boorishness and jealousy was not the fundamental him. He cared vehemently what happened to England. He was funny and immensely agreeable to be with when he was not sulking. His rudeness was the pose of a pleasant man wanting to seem a tough Al Capone politician. He had a clear, unusual brain which put complex issues into perspective and invested the obvious with originality by treating it as a new phenomenon. Tony with his supercilious mask off was kind and could be sensitively considerate. He was a good friend and a jolly joker who never lost his youth. His most satisfactory personal action was marrying his second wife, Susan, who, reminiscent in looks of the young Julie Christie, gave him the uncritical adulation of a beautiful and clever woman.

# CHAPTER VIII

## America and the American Girl

IN 1948 I GOT MARRIED for the second time. I had been romantic about my first marriage. I was more in love with Susan than she with me. It is unusual for love to be in equal proportions on both sides save in the first flush of sexual excitement. When that wears off, one young partner will be more apt to look elsewhere than the other, who may be badly hurt at the crashing of a dream. Many marriages survive such wanderings. The partners regroup under more solid conditions of affection. What they liked about each other, apart from sex, may come to seem the most important factor. They may grow to overlook each other's infidelities, if their pride is not too badly wounded, for the sake of stronger and more permanent ties. This is more difficult the younger you are. Burning passions burn out through frequent slaking in four to eight years, possibly less for some and a little more for others. Anyone who says he approaches a wife, or vice versa, after three years with the same excitement as in the first two years of love-making is a liar, or more politely, is deluding himself or herself. The longest runs for sustained physical passion are for those not married, who can meet alone but secretly and rarely. They do not have the daily domestic details to dull their desire, or unhindered enjoyment of it, to make it more a routine than a celebration. Couples who wish to delay the ending of the first fine careless rapture should ration themselves to once a month. They may not believe me, but I write from experience.

My first marriage, founded I had thought on all aspects of love, had been a failure. I decided that my second would have more staying power if I did not enter it in a state of bemused rhapsody but with calm appreciation, and that this would lead to a steady association. I had been reading too many novels in which couples not much attracted to each other gradually became intertwined. I also had it in my head that arranged Victorian marriages had a high success rate. Why did I want to be married? It was not too difficult to get a supply of sex, but brief affairs with unattached or married girls did not create a home.

Those born under the sign of Cancer are known to be home-loving. My little flat in Chatsworth Court was more like an apartment in an hotel than a home. I am uneasy living alone. There must be someone to talk to, with whom I can exchange the daily gossip, discuss problems with. I have not the power over myself to sit contentedly reading in empty rooms; I become restless, searching for human contact. I telephone friends frequently when alone, but that is not the same. I have always preferred the company of women, liking their gentleness and perceptiveness. Luckily I am unable to understand women completely. It is better that way: they keep their mystery longer. A woman about the house with whom I am in general sympathy is essential for someone of my gregarious and affectionate nature.

I did not search for a wife but waited for one to turn up. I had a young secretary with dash and style. Her mother, a Communist Jewess from Russia, had a brother who in his teens had fought in Trotsky's army. By this time he had renounced Communism and become a successful businessman in Paris. He was very lively, keen on good French food and wine and all the joys of capitalism, though his sister stayed faithful to the Bolsheviks. I never met her husband, who seemed to have disappeared into oblivion. My secretary, Nora (Alix) Robbins, was strikingly handsome, with a beautiful figure. She sang Russian songs with intensity and verve. She had never had an affair in the full sense. We mainly worked in the sitting-room of my little flat with the bedroom next door.

One day the inevitable happened; inevitable because if two people of the opposite sex who feel any mutual physical attraction work closely together, and have the opportunity, it *is* inevitable. My present wife is attached to a Hungarian proverb: 'Opportunity makes the thief.' Wives have every reason to be careful of presentable secretaries or female personal assistants under the age of forty. It is almost impossible to avoid some form of emotional involvement with them. The relationship is too like that of Heloise and Abelard without the obstacles. MPs and ministers, working uncheckable hours, and with many girls thinking their occupation glamorous, are particularly prone. Their wives should vet their secretaries and insist on their being ugly, middle-aged or older, and deficient in feminine charm, unless they have decided they do not mind losing their husbands or having another woman in their lives.

There was no impediment to my asking Alix to marry me. I felt she had committed herself, and that committed me. I did not feel devouring love as I had known for others but I liked her in and out of bed. She was quick and amusing and had a good intelligence. (She was once a protégé of Geoffrey Crowther, the famous Editor of *The Economist*, who had taken an interest in her education, wanting it to go further to match her attainments.) In my then mood I thought being overboard in love was not important as a foundation to a happy marriage, silly ass that I was. I proposed to her on top of a bus. It would have been kinder and braver if I had not. The moment I did I thought, My God, this is a disaster. At nights I woke up in a panic but in the morning I, the rational man, put aside my fears.

We went to live at 80 Eaton Terrace where I had a cat, named Mr Hodge after Dr Johnson's cat. I was fond of Mr Hodge and nursed him for days when he caught an illness from which he died. When we moved to 16 Tregunter Road we had another cat. Our neighbour was Sir Charles Petrie, the historian. His wife was a frightening lady who became Mayor of Kensington and looked at me haughtily as if wondering what the cat had brought in.

One Sunday I was sitting in the garden at Tregunter Road and noticed the maid next door bring in the Sunday joint of roast beef for the Petries' lunch. She went out, presumably to announce that luncheon was ready, leaving the dining-room empty and the window slightly open at the bottom. A few minutes later my cat leaped over the garden wall carrying a joint of roast beef by the string with which it had been tied, dumped it in a flower-bed and set to on the best meal of its life, out of sight of the Petries. I fled indoors. I still wonder what Sir Charles and Lady Petrie said when Sir Charles advanced to the sideboard, carving-knife poised, and found nothing there. How did they explain to each other the mystery of the vanishing beef? I felt

Lady Petrie looked at me still more as if I were something the cat had brought in, without referring to what the cat had brought out. I was too scared to own up.

At 80 Eaton Terrace we had an agreeable lodger, Paul Capon, a novelist. His novels did not earn him much but he bolstered his income by selling books, about which he had some knowledge. He had an ingenious system of buying a book in one department of Foyles and selling it at a higher price to another. While he was at Eaton Terrace, Cousin Molly died and her books and my father's were sent up from Cornwall. The house was too small to hold them all and Paul sold a number for me, including some rare early New Zealand books, and some now much sought after illustrated bird books of my father's. I wish I had been able to keep them, if only as reminders of my father and Cousin Molly.

Tregunter Road was a pleasant house with, for London, a largish garden. We could not afford proper curtains in the bedrooms, but the rest of the house was more or less furnished. It had a drawing-room the length of the house, with windows at both ends. If you sat on the street side you could see nothing but a long vista of trees in the summer as if it were the country, something I can do in my sitting-room upstairs in Cavendish Avenue in London, where I live now. Turning London into a peaceful countryside or sleepy country town calms me down.

Alix and I were happy for a while but soon began to quarrel violently. I have a temper which dies rapidly but when flaming is very nasty. She had a strong character and her Slav blood could erupt in furious defence of her independence. The storms had thunder as well as lightning and the noise was accentuated by falling objects. I would make resolutions to control myself, but in vain. I was a rotten husband. Then the sex gave out, to make everything worse. Alix sensibly decided to go. After she had packed she sat at the bottom of the stairs and looked up at me sadly with a little smile of hope: 'Couldn't we give it one more try?' I said No and felt a heel, which I was.

It was not her fault. It was mine for not trying harder. We had been married five years and had another three years' waiting for the divorce on the grounds of her desertion. She asked nothing from me save one of the chairs from the Coronation at

Westminster Abbey, 'in remembrance of times past'. We had sat next to Richard Wood and his wife, and during the long wait before the service began he remarked that he and his wife had sworn never to be unfaithful to each other and never to end their marriage. He is a man with a sweet and steadfast nature, an old-fashioned Tory who lived his political life as he thought Christ would have liked him to. That day his goodness made me feel more guilty. I had been in love with an American girl for some time.

She was also Jewish and entrancingly beautiful. Her round face was reminiscent of Ingrid Bergman's or Queen Soraya's. Her smile pulled at everything inside me. She and her husband came to have a drink at Tregunter Road and innocently she smiled at me across the drawing-room, her glass held under her chin as she leaned back in an armchair. I was done for. Her husband was an American correspondent in London. She was twenty-seven and had been married before. She had been married the second time for around two years and was not looking at anyone, or so she thought. It must have been a year before she let me make love to her.

She lived in a little mews house in Regent's Park somewhere behind Clarence Terrace (it is now demolished). I followed Robert Kee's maxim: any reasonably intelligent man not repellent to her can persuade almost any girl to go to bed with him if he is persistent, but it may take time. Knowing that women fall in love through their ears and men through their eyes (I had already done so), I talked to her by the hour on the telephone, thinking beforehand of things to make her laugh and then to interest her. She followed English politics closely, veering towards Nye Bevan rather than Hugh Gaitskell, to whom I had become close. I explained his hopes and aims and mine too. She listened like an indulgent mother and began to share my outlook. I told her the political gossip of the day. We talked about books and plays. I read her my favourite love poems, including, of course, 'This coyness, lady, were no crime'. I advanced to having tea with her in her mews house. We walked in Queen Mary's Rose Garden and over the little bridges in Regent's Park. We saw films together. It was ages before I made any physical advance to her. We were sitting on the floor having tea. She evaded me, saying I had more arms than an octopus, but she did not stop seeing me.

In the late summer of 1952 I had a Smith-Mundt Fellowship, travelling for three and a half months in America. Just before my departure I went on what was to have been a last walk with her in Regent's Park and she promised that next day I could make love to her. I said, 'Don't be disappointed if it doesn't go so well the first time. It often doesn't.' 'Oh, I know what that means,' she replied, and smiled the smile that had first enslaved me, but I had not meant what she was thinking.

I did not sleep for excitement. The first sight of all her beauty is still in my head. She had long, slim, but not thin, legs, perfectly shaped, firm, round breasts. To my delight the long waiting had affected her too. She dug her nails deep into my thighs. On the sea journey across the Atlantic I looked at the marks, thinking of her with joy. It was weeks before they faded.

I thought of her as I toured her country, going to Los Angeles where she came from, and where she said geraniums grew like weeds and covered the rubbish-tips. Fanatically patriotic, I was shocked by the low regard for Britain. Or is patriotism an extension of one's own vanity? I am me and very special; I am British so Britain must be the best and most important country, influencing all the others. On a large fairground at Seattle, Washington, I looked one night at the stars and wept: this vast country thought my darling England was not worth bothering about, equating her to a poor old aunt out of the mainstream. My tour, intended by the State Department to encourage a love of America, made me resentful and scornful. I was a long way from adjusting to Britain's loss of status, and hence mine, and it hurt.

Michael Straight planned my itinerary. He owned *The New Republic*, for which I wrote some articles. I wrote for *The New York Times Sunday Magazine* and gave a few lectures to swell the meagre travelling allowance: we were still not allowed to take money out of Britain in 1952. I stayed with friends or strangers to whom I had introductions and in cheap, nasty hotels. Michael Straight knew everyone of consequence. He flew me in his aeroplane to New England, to stay with his mother who had married a Republican Senator, Senator Tobey. He was a splendid old boy, who rounded sharply on a Republican who attacked Dean Acheson while he was watching us play tennis. One of the players was sometimes Mr Justice Black of the Supreme Court who played an effectively cunning game. I thought if I could play tennis like that when I was sixty-five I should be well pleased; in the event I could not.

Mr Justice Black came from the Deep South. He had an enchanting southern belle for a daughter, who told me that when she first came North aged fifteen she was taken to a drive-in, open-air cinema. She lay on the floor in the back of the car throughout the film, terrified that the Yankees would come and get her. Carpetbaggers still haunted imaginations in the South. I felt more at home there than elsewhere.

In Natchez, Mississippi, 95 per cent of the whites were of British extraction, making it a tropical Cheltenham. They loved their Negro nurses and servants and could not see the inconsistency of their disdain for the rest of the Negroes. I shocked the whites by addressing a meeting of Negroes, urging them not to be afraid to use their vote to advance themselves, but the Natchez whites forgave me my English eccentricity. One Natchez lady pointed to two little Negro children playing in a road. 'You couldn't pick them up, could you?' she asked, screwing her face. 'I don't know, they look rather cuddly,' I replied. She laughed at my absurdity.

Natchez was theoretically dry. The Mayor met me at the airport. 'We must go to my house outside town and have a drink. I daren't have one in Natchez.' But Natchez was awash with parties and drinks and drunks. Some of the girls were lovely. I was instantly attracted by a young married one and she by me, doubtless because she saw me as a dashing visitor from Cosmopolitania. She let me kiss her dewy lips and stroke her strong young breasts but did not dare go further. The ladies of Natchez noticed our disappearances on the veranda and her husband was suspicious. I was unfaithful to my American girl in England only once, out of extreme loneliness, with a tedious, unattractive girl who complained about what her husband would not do to her and invited me to.

I liked Michael Straight and talked by the hour with him and his then wife who wanted to be a doctor. I did not know

Michael had been one of those appalling Apostles at Cambridge and close to Guy Burgess, sympathizing with his views. He was liberal rather than left wing in conversation, praising the American system. I thought I knew him well. Obviously I did not. Burgess and Maclean had fled to Russia just over a year before and the subject must have been in his mind but he gave no sign of being troubled by his omission to tell the authorities the considerable amount he always knew of Burgess's activities in time to prevent his escape and to save the lives of numerous Western agents.

My tour was widespread: down the Western coast across the South and through the middle into the North, Boston and parts of the Eastern coast. I recognized the goodness of the Americans, but in my shallow superiority looked down on them as dull, earnest talkers into the night. It was ridiculous but I was like that. They should have punched me on the nose, but they were too hospitable. I hated New York, where I went several times. I had a cheap room in a barracks of an hotel and felt acutely the evenings and days I had to spend alone. Yet people were kinder to me than I deserved. Even Henry and Claire Luce gave me dinner alone (perhaps thinking I was not acceptable for general consumption) and listened patiently to my nonsense about America.

Ben Sonnenberg, a famous contact man, was kind to me without the slightest hope of my being able to do anything for him. He had an effective system. He would ring, say, a high official of the Treasury and tell him that a visiting potentate of some distant state greatly admired him and would like to meet him. Highly flattered, the official would suggest a date or two for lunch or dinner. Ben would then ring the potentate and tell him that the official concerned greatly admired him, had heard a lot about him and would like to meet him. The meeting, presided over by Ben at his luxurious house, would take place and if a loan emerged Ben collected a large commission. He was also helpful with tickets for booked-out theatres, which was how I got to see *Guys and Dolls*.

In Springfield, capital of Illinois, I met the Governor, Adlai Stevenson. He was running for the Presidency against Eisenhower, whom I had met several times. Eisenhower was a decent, simple man, nowhere near as bright or knowledgeable as Wavell. I did not see how America could choose him in preference to the civilized, intelligent, politically experienced Adlai Stevenson. Anyway, I did not approve of soldiers in politics. My interview with Stevenson was arranged by my old friend Arthur Schlesinger, Jr, who was writing speeches for Adlai Stevenson. I informed Stevenson with all the brash superficiality I could assemble that he could not help but win, and proved it to him state by state. He was fairly pleased but did not seem wholly convinced.

I also met Kenneth Galbraith at Springfield and was dazzled by him. He had not yet written *The Affluent Society* but his fame was mounting. In New York he gave me lunch in a club at the top of a tall building. As we got into the elevator to go down I was saying that I could not understand why any Briton would want to exchange British citizenship for American but that my greatest contempt was for Canadians who became citizens of the USA though they were already in the same continent. 'I was born and brought up in Canada and became a naturalized US citizen,' he said. The elevator seemed to take a long time to get to the bottom.

Beaverbrook was staying in New York in an apartment at the Waldorf-Astoria. Feminine underwear belonging to his current mistress was hung out to dry in the bathroom. When he realized I had seen it he was embarrassed. 'She's not staying here. She just asked if she could wash a few things.' He gave a dinner and announced proudly, 'Now you've each got twelve of the largest and finest oysters in the world. I have had them flown down this morning from Canada specially for you all.' They gazed at me horribly, the size of small saucers. I hate raw oysters and their slimy texture. I covered them with pepper and rammed them down my throat, but I could still taste them. I tasted nothing so awful again until I ate sheep's eyes near the Khyber Pass so as not to offend another great chieftain. As one oyster stuck in my throat and I was nearly sick Beaverbrook asked anxiously, 'Aren't you enjoying them?' 'Yes, they're marvellous,' I gulped, and the small boy that was in Beaverbrook looked happy again at his treat being appreciated.

I walked on the streets of New York with him, his car

following a few yards behind in case he got bored. His walks were not as other people's. Randolph Churchill rang to speak to him one morning in London. His manservant, Charles, said in a voice of awe, 'The Lord is out walking.' 'On the water, I suppose,' Randolph replied.

Beaverbrook read the articles I was writing from America for the *Evening Standard*. I showed him the last one I wrote ahead of polling day before I sent it. State by state I had totted up how the vote would go to put Adlai Stevenson in. 'I wouldn't dare be so certain,' he said, 'but let it go. We're all wrong sometimes.' He told me he had learned his journalism from Rudyard Kipling. 'He taught me the first lesson, that the human being is more important than the thing. I didn't understand that before. If you do a story about a factory, it is not how the factory works that matters. It is the man who runs the factory. Rudyard Kipling used to correct everything I wrote. He took enormous trouble over it.'

It was his intense curiosity and strong feelings about people which made him a good journalist. Gossip about rows in his own kitchen and among his servants fascinated him. He fought causes because he believed in them, which made them exhilarating reading, however absurd. When he was fighting for Empire Free Trade and for duties on foreign food he had an alarm-clock made which went off each minute, signalling that another £1000 had just been spent importing food from outside the Empire. When he told a Royal Commission on the Press that he ran his newspapers solely for the purpose of propaganda, it was almost the truth.

Power came into it and the search for power led him from Canada, where he was a millionaire before he was thirty, to Britain in 1910 when Britain was still at the centre of world affairs. During the Second World War he dreamed fleetingly of becoming Prime Minister, when Churchill's stock was low after the fall of Singapore and his as the bustling Minister of Aircraft Production was high. That was the only time he toyed with treachery to Churchill, to whom he was otherwise devoted. He would bewail to me that he had been a failure: 'I was never Prime Minister.' After Eden's resignation I said, 'Look at what's happened to him. He has no more influence.

You still have your newspapers. You are playing a big part in keeping Britain out of the Common Market. Which of you is the more important?'

Money was a factor, too. He did not intend to let his newspapers make him lose his fortune, though initially they were worrying loss-makers. He died very rich. Through his newspapers he had consistent power, not in and out of it, like most politicians who have it for a brief spell before they are ousted altogether. It is a great thing to own successful newspapers if you are capable of controlling their contents and have a puckish nature, enjoying teasing your enemies and bestowing favours on your friends.

Beaverbrook had a house, Cherkley, in Surrey. It was handsome and well placed to look out over the hills. Inside, it was like a second-rate seaside hotel, brown and dreary; he told me when he wanted furniture he sent his secretary out to buy some. He had no taste of his own. He founded an art gallery in New Brunswick but had no judgement of pictures. In his flat in Arlington Street he showed me a set of sketches and preliminary half-paintings Graham Sutherland had done for the famous portrait of Churchill which Churchill hated and Lady Churchill burned. He had bought them for New Brunswick. 'Are they good?' he asked repeatedly.

I thought several of them better than the final edition, for which Sutherland had seized on one of Winston's unusually unattractive moods in place of a benevolent and more representative one. It had been a sorry thing for the Commons to give him on his eightieth birthday, I felt, as one of the contributors. The choice had been much influenced by Nye Bevan, not out of malice but from a zeal for modern portraiture as distinct from the conventional Sargent type of picture. Winston would have preferred the latter, but he was only the recipient of the gift.

Beaverbrook summoned guests to lunch or dinner rather than invited them. Employees were expected to drop everything for his short-notice invitations. Merely an intermittent contributor to his newspapers, I jumped too. If the dinner were at Cherkley he would send a car and chaffeur to London to take you both ways. Usually there were amusing guests. Occasionally he wanted help with strange gatherings of Canadian provincial prime ministers, or the like, who were dreadfully boring. At such a dinner one of my neighbours was an elderly Canadian. He talked to me about punctuality.

'I like to be called at seven minutes to eight every morning. It's very difficult in hotels. At the Château Frontenac in Quebec [then the best hotel in Canada] I couldn't make them understand that it should be seven minutes to eight, not nine minutes or four minutes. Very annoying.'

'What did you do about it?'

'I bought the hotel and put in new management.'

After dinner, in disbelief, I told Beaverbrook the story and asked if my neighbour were mad.

'No, he's not mad. He's Sir James Dunn. He's got £30 million.'

Sir James owned a vast aluminium plant in Canada. His son, Sir Philip Dunn, became a close friend of mine. His father disliked him and did little or nothing to help him financially. On a visit to London he told Philip, as he was getting into the hotel lift, to get hold of all the money he could and buy a certain share which Sir James knew was about to take off. Philip rushed away, raised whatever he could, then panicked. Suppose his father knew the share was due to collapse, not soar, and thought it amusing to ruin his son, a joke he was quite capable of. The share did go up. It was the only time Sir James helped his heir, except when he died and left him a sizeable sum. However, the great bulk of his fortune went to Lady Dunn, his second wife, who had been his secretary-nurse. (The widow married Beaverbrook in 1963, the year before he died and soon collected another very large fortune.) He was lonely and dying of cancer and she looked after him.

A few weeks before he died my third wife and I had dinner with them *à quatre* at Cherkley. I had not long introduced the first non-heat set web-offset colour newspaper printing press into England, something Fleet Street had still not got around to by 1985. Lady Beaverbrook asked me how web-offset newspaper printing worked and I began to explain. Soon her eyes glazed. 'You asked the question. Now you listen to the answer,' Beaverbrook barked. There was a furious glare and I ploughed on. Web-offset printing cannot be explained in under eight minutes. It was not surprising that Sir James Dunn's second wife was chilly for the rest of the evening.

One of James Dunn's granddaughters by his first wife, Serena Dunn, married Jacob Rothschild. I was the sole witness at their wedding, which I had encouraged. Jacob has the flair of the original Nathan Mayer Rothschild and the looks of the French Baron James de Rothschild who amazed Napoleon III with hospitality of a lavishness beyond the Emperor's means. When I first knew Jacob I thought he was poor as well as young and did not cash the cheque (though it was drawn on Rothschilds) he gave me for his losses playing croquet. Serena and Jacob have been lifelong friends and Jacob a great help over financial matters. Now that we no longer have a house in Wiltshire I miss seeing them as much as I used to with Sunday lunch in the kitchen and jolly games.

In the summer Beaverbrook would sometimes gaze out of the window and say in a mournful voice, 'There lies goodness.' He was referring to his first wife, a beautiful girl he married when she was nineteen, whom he treated badly and who was buried in the garden. As death came closer Beaverbrook became more apprehensive as to what awaited him. He thought there might be a Hell to the specifications of the old Presbyterian preachers, of whom his father had been one. When I asked him what he believed in he said, 'I'll send a telegram to the Moderator of the General Assembly of the Presbyterian Church of Canada, and whatever he says he believes in, that's what I believe in.'

During his last year he was at pains to cement old friendships. Whatever happened to him in the next world, he wanted to be spoken of well in this one, and hoped his friends would see to it. I am glad to. He gave me much good advice, too little of which I heeded. If he liked you he cared. Almost the first time I met him soon after the war he said, 'Brendan Bracken tells me you're a shit.' The last letter he wrote me ended: '. . . in the sure and certain knowledge you will live to do great things in the world'. I am sad I let him down.

I saw another newspaper magnate in the USA, Colonel Robert McCormick, seventy-two-year-old owner of the *Chicago Daily Tribune*. For years he had been passionately anti-British, protesting that George III might never have been defeated because the State Department still obeyed the instructions of the Court of St James's, and once offering personally to punch George V on the nose. If he had still thought us worth attacking, I should have been happier. He compounded my gloom about our declining state. 'Britain's all through, finished. Doesn't matter to the world. Doesn't count any more. Had an influence on our foreign policy once.' The Colonel had turned his attention to the annexation of Canada; we no longer merited his anger.

It took me a long time to recover a sane attitude towards America after my three-and-a-half months' tour. Mortification and jealousy made me anti-American emotionally but not politically. I gnawed at my anguish that America did not see us as equals, belittling our work on the atom bomb as negligible, ignoring the British achievement on radar, downgrading our contribution to winning the war to which America had come so late.

Soon after Eden became Prime Minister he went on a much-advertised trip to see Eisenhower. The forthcoming visit was front-page news for days, the British imagining that it was similarly important in America. Working for BBC TV's *Panorama* I decided that we could do with some cold water on our illusions. I took an aeroplane to New York, arriving about 9 a.m. local time and left at 5 p.m. the same day. I set up television shop at Times Square, Wall Street and Rockefeller Plaza, asking passers-by if they had heard of Eden. The few who vaguely had, could not say who he was. None knew that he was just about to have talks with Eisenhower. When I had explained who Eden was and that he was going to see the President, I asked what they thought was the object of his meeting with Eisenhower. The answer was almost unanimous: 'To get some money off us. That's what they mostly come for.'

I went back to America to cover the presidential election in 1956 for *Panorama*, mainly in the Philadelphia area. It coincided with the Suez campaign, which attracted a pitying and horrified attention in the US. I went to Chicago in 1961 to buy a printing-press but not to America again until 1983. My mind at last adjusted to Britain's diminished role, I loved it. Pleasingly Britain's stock had risen (Mrs Thatcher?) and our value as an ally was more appreciated. I was able to put aside my prejudices and understand why my twenty-year-old son, Pericles, wanted to prolong his two-year stay there indefinitely, and my fifteen-year-old daughter, Petronella, was enthralled. If I were eighteen I think I would leave constricted, restraining, envious England for the still bursting, growing, enthusiastic America, where the reaction to someone who makes money is not to try to take it away from him but to emulate him.

When I returned from my first American trip my American girl had not deserted me. We threw ourselves into the deepest love-making I had known. She was of the age, just entering the thirties, when the sexuality in many women is at its highest and most generous. In a little restaurant off Baker Street called The Bay Tree, or in a teashop where Baker Street changes its name as it starts the approach to St John's Wood Church, if her knee touched mine I understood what romantic lady novelists meant by 'swooning away'. I felt the same when she sang down the telephone to me 'If I were a gate I'd be swinging./If I were a bell I'd be ringing' from *Guys and Dolls*, which I had just seen in America.

I was friendly with some of the Sieffs who owned covered tennis courts in Hall Road. We made up parties for tennis and afterwards she would come to the bathroom I was changing in and we would make love, the risk heightening the excitement. The tennis courts have now given way to respectable housing. When I pass their site I remember. I once asked her if she would like to go to a dance. 'I don't like dancing,' she said. 'Dancing is what I call a dry fuck.'

On Thursdays in the summer we would take a train to the neighbourhood of Box Hill with a picnic. To make love in a field hidden by trees is what Milton must have meant by 'to sport with Amaryllis in the shade'. Returning one Thursday I made love to her in the train (there was no corridor), something I have never done before or since. When I went to her house she would put a milk bottle out by the front door if the coast were not clear and I would go away dispirited. When my second wife left, she came often to Tregunter Road and played 'Greensleeves' on her recorder in the garden. It was sweetly sentimental but not mawkish.

We would probably have married if she had not become

pregnant by her husband. Around that time I met my third wife and we broke it off, though it had been the apogee in the fusion of mind and body. Our meetings being impossible in the evenings had some effect. She emphasized that lonely evenings and weekends were not suited to someone of my character and that I must have a more accessible girlfriend. With someone new in my life, callously I agreed. She treated me as the spoiling mother that I wished I had had. I last heard from her when Gaitskell died in January 1963: she knew how upset I would be. I hope she has had a happy life. For me she remains the ideal American woman: a glorious, understanding, encouraging, wound-healing, gracefully moving Statue of Liberty.

# CHAPTER IX

━━━━◖◗◖◗◖◗━━━━

# A Split Brings
# Office

THE COMMONS SEEMED to me more significant than it was because Churchill was in it. He had the magic of immortality. When he came in to take his seat, visitors at the back of the Gallery stood up and those in front peered over the railings to get a better look. Members murmured to each other, 'Here comes the old man', and visibly sharpened up, trying to anticipate from their reading of that huge baby face what he would do to the quality of the proceedings. His was not a poker face; it was used deliberately to project his emotions, of which he was never ashamed.

Sometimes he would scowl in a bad temper or glare balefully at a Member who had said something unusually obnoxious. He would sulk like a child if the Speaker prevented him turning a question into a speech. If he were about to make a joke, his eye would twinkle to warn everyone to get ready for it. If he discomfited his opponents, there would be a vast schoolboy grin of triumph. When he was amused, his face was convulsed with laughter; when tired, there was no mistaking it. His eyes were ready to shed a tear and sometimes did. Sometimes there would be a look of mock penitence. His face proclaimed it when he was disbelieving, contemptuous or bored. No one else was bored so long as he was in the chamber.

To be in the same assembly, theoretically his equal, was balm to my ego, as it was to that of most others, whether they admitted it to themselves or not. Nye Bevan (whom Churchill had called 'a squalid nuisance in time of war') made his name by challenging him. Others, including myself, tried to do the same.

My first opportunity came in November 1947. Churchill opened for the Opposition against the proposal to give Independence to Burma. He was against it with vigour and venom:

198

We stand on the threshold of another scene of misery and ruin, marking and illustrating the fearful retrogression of civilization which the abandonment by Great Britain of her responsibilities in the East have brought, and are bringing, upon Asia and the world. I say this to the government . . . we shall have no part or lot in it.

When he sat down I jumped up, with many others. It is all a matter of luck for the backbencher whether the Speaker calls him or not. Sometimes a year can go by after one has spoken in an important debate before one catches the Speaker's eye in another. I willed Colonel Clifton-Brown, the Speaker, to understand that I was bursting with a good speech and to call me. With a smile he recognized my desperation and did so. I threw away my laboriously prepared speech, which I would have delivered in my still dreary, prosaic style, and went wham, wham against each of Churchill's arguments. Because it is the custom at least to listen to the speech following your own he sat patiently till I had finished.

What got home to him most was my saying that when his own father, Lord Randolph Churchill, as Secretary for India, annexed Burma in 1886, the first Governor he sent there said annexation was unnecessary, 'a protectorate would have sufficed just as well, or a treaty arrangement of the kind we had with Nepal'. In Burma we had been imperialist for the fun of it and Burma had never lost her nationhood. One by one I demolished Churchill's points. And where, I asked, was R.A. Butler, the Tory expert on India and Burma? He was absent because 'he does not agree with a single word of what the Right Honourable gentleman has just said.'

Butler, Chairman of the Conservative Party and architect of its victory in 1951, told me next day with disloyal glee that I was right, and congratulated me on exposing Churchill's outdated imperialism. When I sat down I heard Chuter Ede, the kindly Home Secretary, describe my speech in cricketing terms: 'Four after four and the last one fairly broke the pavilion clock. That fellow ought to be in the Government.' He did not know I had blotted my copybook with Gandhi, but I felt as elated as a batsman who had just scored a century in his first Test against Australia at Lord's.

Later I met Churchill in the corridor outside the Members' Smoking Room. He stopped me. 'That was a very good debating speech,' he growled in that slow voice to which the world had thrilled in the war and which was now thrilling me. I mumbled something about hoping that I had not been too rude. 'I ask for no quarter.' He paused. 'And I bear no malice.' How could one not love such a man?

He was always friendly to me, occasionally giving me advice, as when I had disparagingly referred to the Chiefs of Staff as 'brass hats'. 'You shouldn't do that. You will have to deal with these people as time goes on and they won't like it.'

He would often talk to me in the Smoking Room. I asked him what Stalin was like. 'Amiable enough in a rough sort of way. When I asked him what really happened to the Kulaks, he answered, "They just disappeared, just disappeared"', and Churchill waved his hands in his expressive way.

I heard he was touched when he was Prime Minister, after illness had kept him away from the Commons and I chanced to ask him the first question on his return: 'Is the Right Honourable gentleman aware that when he is away the magic goes out of the House?' I began. When he was Prime Minister I plagued him with questions, not in thirst for information but because it was exhilarating. When he made a joke against me I was as delighted as he was. There were ways of getting under his skin. He could be goaded into annoyance if accused of failing to assert some British interest which he would have liked to have done but for our weakness in the world.

I ran a campaign against him about the choice of the Belgian F.N. rifle over the British-invented E.M.2 rifle as the replacement for the old bolt-operated rifle which had been in use for fifty years. When I was Under-Secretary of State at the War Office I had got to know the inventors and attended trials. The experts agreed that the British rifle was the best semi-automatic one, convertible to automatic by pressing a button, in the world, almost a personal machine-gun with a bayonet and a pound lighter than the previous rifle. Before we left office in 1951 the decision had been made to manufacture this brilliant British product, with its pleasing prospects of exports. It was hoped that NATO, including the USA, would standardize on it, though that was not essential provided that the same ammunition could be used in all NATO rifles, and that was no problem.

I kept in touch with the inventors, meeting them in different roadside hotels or bars, usually in the Heathrow area. We were all covered by the Official Secrets Act, but their superiors might have been unpleasant to the British rifle team if it had been learned that they were giving a member of the Opposition information with which he could attack the Government. The inventors were in misery. There was no doubt that our rifle was the best, but anti-British jealousy in America, which often arises in such matters, was pushing the powerful US influence against it in favour of the inferior Belgian rifle. Our government was giving in for political, not technical, reasons.

Not getting anywhere with the Service ministers I began to harry the Prime Minister. He could have dodged my questions by passing them back for answer to Antony Head, the Secretary of State for War, but he was interested and enjoyed our little clashes. Before the election there was some uncertainty whether Antony Head would be made Minister of Defence or Secretary of State for War. He waited anxiously by the telephone. The call came for overwrought Antony to speak to the Prime Minister. 'Antony, I've decided on war.' 'Yes sir,' the panic-ridden Antony replied. 'Against whom, sir?'

Eventually I provoked Winston into taking part in a debate, a rare action for a Prime Minister, who is usually remote from detailed technical argument. But Churchill, an old soldier, also recognized that the serviceman's personal weapon was a policy matter of central importance.

I was still in good standing with Attlee and the Parliamentary Labour Party who rather admired my willingness to maul Churchill without always getting the worst of the exchange. I was asked to move the official Opposition motion deploring the Government's decision 'to adopt the Belgian F.N. rifle for use by the British Army in place of the new British E.M.2 rifle' on 1 February 1954. I think it was the last time I spoke from the Dispatch Box in the Commons, certainly on a big occasion: I would have been distressed if I had known that.

I was better briefed by my unofficial expert advice than Churchill was by his. I made a good speech, establishing that the Prime Minister and Secretary of State for War had both said that the British rifle was the best in the world and that nothing had happened since to change their opinion, save that the Americans had said they would not standardize on it. ('I couldn't persuade President Truman to accept our rifle,' Churchill had said.) As the Americans were not going to standardize on the Belgian rifle (they never did), why did that matter, since the ammunition was interchangeable? I went quite far in accusing Churchill of dilatoriness in not pressing ahead with the production of the British rifle, in not understanding the issues, and in falling short of his normal patriotism. I riled him, particularly when I teased him with falsifying the facts to rationalize his decision. He had fallen back on footling arguments that the Belgian rifle looked more like the old British Lee-Enfield, that it would be smarter for ceremonial purposes and that its butt would be more effective in hand-to-hand fighting (this last was not true). 'The Prime Minister wants to meet the new jet age with the butt end of a rifle,' I taunted.

When he replied, he was really roused. He referred darkly to the information with which I was armed, forgetting that his attacks before the war on Britain's failure to rearm had been based on information from high serving officers. He knew that he had made the wrong decision and was part indignant, part ashamed as a result. But his humour did not leave him entirely. That morning he had arranged for a party of MPs to fire the British and Belgian rifles on a range. 'I must admit that the Honourable Member for Aston did not allow his prejudices or malice against the Belgian rifle to prevent him from making a most remarkable score with it this morning. I hope he will live up to that principle, being a faithful seeker after truth, whatever use he makes of information he is able to obtain.'

It must have been the only time Churchill congratulated an MP on his marksmanship, the more remarkable because I am usually a rotten shot but that morning had scored an uninterrupted series of bulls. Or had someone rigged the target to make it look as though I had? Perish the thought.

George Wigg, who followed Churchill, also referred to my making 'a good score this morning. He certainly made a good score this afternoon because never has the Prime Minister made a worse speech in answer.' A compliment from Wigg, who believed he was the ultimate if not sole expert on military matters, was unique. Even the *New Statesman* to which I was fast becoming a reactionary, referred to 'Mr Wyatt's triumph over a tired Prime Minister', characteristically adding in reproof to the Opposition leadership: 'It is a measure of the absence of real controversy in the present Parliament that this compara- tively trivial matter should have struck the Press as a first-class political issue.' The Press were right: the British solider getting an inferior weapon was not a trivial matter. But anxious to make sure I succeeded on my great occasion, I had been too aggressive in my onslaught on Churchill. 'Good, but you shouldn't have over-egged it,' Attlee said tersely when I sat down. The following year both Attlee and Churchill were gone, one to his earldom and the other to his mute, listening role with a lollipop hearing-aid in the Commons he loved. 'I am child of the House of Commons,' he once said.

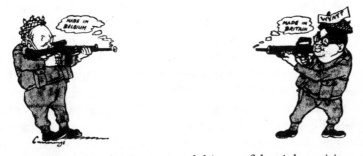

The awful Lord Moran used his confidential position as physician to write a sensational account of Churchill's unfitness to be Prime Minister in his last years of office. Instead of concentrating on his job as a doctor he was making copious notes of Churchill's grumbles and irritability on days when he was regretting, as old men do, his fading physical vigour. The doctor had the effrontery also to retail confidential conversations Churchill had with others on matters of state and gave his opinion in his book *Winston Churchill: The Struggle for Survival 1940–1965* on Winston's thoughts on plans he was maturing. Moran knew nothing of politics, but he was swollen-headed enough to push forward his naïve views and publish his tittle-tattle – the year after Churchill's death, when it would make more money than if he had waited a decent interval. What the silly doctor did not realize was that Churchill sent for him when he was feeling ill and low, not when he felt on top of the world, as was more often the case.

Right to the last in the Commons Churchill was in command of himself and the House. His energies were still great, though not so great as they had been in the war. He was forced to refrain from constant interference with his ministers, which made him a better Prime Minister in peacetime than he otherwise would have been. He was too soft with the union leaders, but that was not because his powers were failing but because he had never stopped wanting to remove the unjustified slur that he was anti-working class, which arose from the Tonypandy affair when he was Home Secretary in 1910 and had to deal toughly with the striking miners, as did his successor in 1984. Churchill did not retire too late, but too soon, by sixteen months. There was no need for an election in 1955. He should have held it in October 1956 and resigned just before it. Then Britain would have been spared the calamity of the Suez campaign.

To have had ten years in the House of Commons with Churchill is a treasured privilege. I can see him now and hear his voice and recall little incidents. Sydney Silverman was a five-foot Labour MP of quick intelligence and physical agility. He specialized in drawing attention to himself by interrupting Churchill. One day Harold Macmillan was being praised by Churchill for 'a very restrained and carefully phrased speech' about German generals accused of war crimes. Sydney Silverman shouted an interruption without, as is the custom, standing up. Churchill slowly turned his head towards where Silverman sat on the front bench below the gangway, his little legs not quite touching the floor. 'The Honourable gentleman is always intervening. On this occasion he didn't even hop off his perch.' The laughter lasted several minutes.

Naturally I tried preparing speeches the Churchill way, but they did not work. I did not have his gift of language, of delivery or of theatre, or the dedication to rehearse words and gestures, to memorize the text, making it safe to look away from it so as to suggest that one was not reading. There were a few who could draw members from their drinks, chess, letters, or sleep in the

Library, when their name came up on the tape. Bob Boothby, Nye Bevan, Dick Crossman, Enoch Powell, Michael Foot, Nigel Birch, Iain Macleod could, but none could compare with the magnificent pull of Churchill. I went out of Parliament in 1955 and when I returned in 1959 I found the glamour had gone.

It is difficult for great men to emerge without a great background. Churchill had started with one and his fame kept the illusion of it going after the reality had vanished. When the outside world cares little for the Commons it is important merely as an assembly of a second-ranking nation. It becomes provincial and its members sound provincial, too: history is not interested. Harold Macmillan tried to act the great figure. He was not a success. The performance was too mannered, the role of the Edwardian beau too music-hall, and neither words nor content were remarkable. The temptation to knock the imaginary top-hat off the old trouper was almost irresistible. Eden had partaken in great events but had no language for them. He put his speeches lucidly but they were without flair.

Eden was thoroughly decent and sincere. His charm arose from a genuine interest in the opinions of others. 'I put that bit in because of you,' he said once to me about a foreign policy speech when I was quite a new Member. 'Did you agree with it?' It was difficult to believe that this agreeable man had a temper on a short fuse, inherited from his nearly mad father, Sir Timothy Eden.

I used to meet the attractive white-and-gold Clarissa Churchill at various parties. She put me through a detailed examination about the life of an MP's wife, but it turned out that it was not me she was interested in but Anthony Eden, whom she married in 1952. He was lucky and she made him happy, having intelligence; a literary sort of girl, as well as being beautiful. She is fiercely loyal to his memory, so it is impossible to have a conversation with her about the Suez fiasco, though she is a joy on every other subject. It was bad luck on her that her life at 10 Downing Street lasted less than two years, but that was still something. Hugh Gaitskell said to me he would give anything just for one day there as Prime Minister.

My own political ambitions did not fare badly in the 1945–55 Parliaments. My speeches were getting better. I was active on committees. I was becoming more in sympathy with the Labour leadership, less impressed with Dick Crossman. I was also aware that trouble was lurking from the Broad Left for the Labour Party.

Time drifted on pleasantly until the General Election of February 1950. I had been on a tour of Burma, Malaya and Indonesia in 1949. I adored Burma. Though plagued by internal Communist and other rebellions, the Burmans were contented. I sat on the banks of the Irrawaddy watching the fish queue up to be taken on the fishermen's rods. Food was plentiful and cheap, an agreeable warm-weather hut could be built quickly out of branches and palm-leaves, lovely girls swinging along in their sarongs, smiles everywhere. Just the place to be a carefree remittance man. They are still poor in Burma, still coping with rebellion, but still happy. Kipling wrote:

By the old Moulmein Pagoda, lookin' eastward to the sea,
There's a Burma girl a-settin', and I know she thinks o' me;
For the wind is in the palm-trees, an' the temple-bells they say:
'Come you back, you British soldier; come you back to Manda-
lay!'
Come you back to Mandalay,
Where the old Flotilla lay:
Can't you 'ear their paddles chunkin' from Rangoon to Manda-
lay?
On the road to Mandalay,
Where the flyin'-fishes play,
An' the dawn comes up like thunder outer China 'crost the Bay!

Kipling never went to Burma. I asked the whereabouts of the old Moulmein Pagoda in Moulmein and they said, 'Which one, there are more than a thousand?' In Moulmein you must look westward if you want to see the sea. There are no flying fishes on the road to Mandalay, and if the dawn came out of China across the bay the sun would have to start rising from the north. But Kipling got the spirit of the place.

There was a depressing moment in Burma. A Buddhist hermit who lived on a lonely hill was renowned for his gift of prophecy. He was thin and grey. I asked him what the future was for Britain. 'Bad', he said. 'I see her sinking lower and lower among the nations for the next fifty years.' I had a feeling he was right.

In Malaya I stayed with Malcolm MacDonald. He was Commissioner-General for the United Kingdom in South-East Asia. His job was co-ordinating the British governors of Malaya, Singapore, North Borneo and Sarawak. Below the highest level he was unpopular with the British officials, who were far more colonially minded than those in India. MacDonald treated Chinese, Malays and others in his governance with easy naturalness as equals. He was active in promoting their speedy independence, which displeased old hands who had been looking forward to a comfortable pre-Japanese Somerset Maugham life ordering natives about.

MacDonald came to the region as Governor-General of Malaya in 1946. He had a beautiful blonde and elegant Canadian wife who was with him infrequently, so he continued relations with his Chinese mistress, to the horror of the unthinking British down the line. MacDonald was first rate. It was mainly due to him that the Chinese Communists lost the battle for the body and mind of Malaya. He was a modern pro-consul worthy of the end of a great empire, receptive to the history and culture of the peoples he governed: on their side and not the administrators'. He collected their artefacts and knew their significance.

His heart yearned for English politics, and he talked eagerly to me about them, his appealing, boyish face quick and animated. He would have loved to have been in Attlee's government, but the call could never come: Attlee admired him but could not risk the furore of putting the son of Ramsay MacDonald into a Labour government. But he had a good life, despite its being unexpectedly in distant lands.

When I returned from my South-East Asia tour I went next day to the Commons, where I collapsed. I had a virulent attack of amoebic hepatitis, which the School of Tropical Medicine deduced from the dates I must have caught in Burma, probably from drinking the waters of the Irrawaddy which looked so delicious but can be lethal. The doctors wanted to take me to hospital and told me I must do nothing for at least four weeks and not expect to recover for six to nine months. I refused. I would be destitute unless I wrote immediately a series of commissioned articles for the *New Statesman* and *Picture Post*.

I moved my bed to the drawing-room of 80 Eaton Terrace and sat up in it, dictating for three weeks, to the amazement of the doctors and myself, proving that mind can conquer defective matter. Cigarettes, to which I had been a slave, tasted so foul that I gave them up, as I mentioned earlier. When the urge to smoke returned, I stuck to cigars or a pipe, abandoning cigarettes and, I hope, lung cancer, for ever. The chief casualty was my liver. Once able to drink several bottles of wine and glasses of port a day, since the early 1970s I have been gradually driven back to drinking two or three glasses of wine in the evening and for days at a time nothing at all. The articles turned out well. I began that year to write a weekly column for *Reynolds News*, which I continued to do for twelve years, and also to work part-time for *Tribune*, though neither journal could have thought me a left-wing firebrand.

For the February election in 1950 I tried an experiment. I held indoor meetings only on seven days. I did very little calling door-to-door. A common reaction is, 'He only comes to see you when he wants your vote', so why bother? I believed that the candidate, or what he did in a general election, had little or no bearing on the result. Candidates who are ill in bed during a general election campaign do neither worse nor better than those who are up and about. It is the national mood affected by regional variations which is decisive, and now we are in the television era local candidates are even more carried in or out by the popular tide.

My deliberately low or lazy profile was successful. My share of the vote went up more than that of any of the other Birmingham Labour candidates. The rushing round of a candidate is demanded by party workers because they do not understand ordinary voters who, in a general election, though not a by-election, find the lambasting they get from local party workers insupportable when added to the bombardment they receive from the Press, television and radio.

In my election address I made no mention of socialism or future nationalization. With the possible exception of steel, which I was already having doubts about, I could not see why we needed to nationalize anything else. I concentrated on the

My father, 1915　　　My mother, 1915

Sharp shooting at six　　　An earnest captain

Bonython. Where dreams were made

My first wife, Susan Cox,
featured in the *Oxford Comment*

My second wife, Alix Robbins,
in 1950

Before I wore a bow tie. With Councillor Jim Meadows,
my agent at Aston

My third wife, Moorea Hastings

With Gandhi in January 1946 just before he made fools of the Parliamentary delegation. I am second from the right

Absorbing Buddhism in the Shwe Dagon Pagoda, Burma in 1949

The evening Hugh Gaitskell blew me up at the Bosworth Labour Party dinner in Coalville. Moorea is on the right

Making a thirteen part television series on philosophy with Bertrand Russell in 1959

National Health Service and the Welfare State and the improvement of the general standard of living. Ordinary people were better off than before the war and opportunity more widely available. Attlee's government had been very good. It set the pattern for the thirteen years of Conservative government which began in 1951 and, thanks to R.A. Butler, wisely did not tamper with Attlee's moderate revolution. In 1950 I assumed that the structure of the fair state had been completed and that the Labour Party would want to embellish rather than continually reshape it. Stafford Cripps, still Chancellor of the Exchequer, contemplated no dramatic upheavals, nor did Morrison, Bevin, Bevan, Dalton, Gaitskell or Wilson.

Labour's total votes cast in 1950 went up beyond the 1945 level to a record number. In votes cast Labour was over 600,000 ahead of the Conservatives. But the great majority of nearly 200 was cut to eight over all others. That was because honest Chuter Ede as Home Secretary had gone too far in boundary adjustment. More votes were needed to elect a Labour than a Conservative government. That Labour could govern with a majority of three, as in 1964, and only on Liberal sufferance, as in 1974, was as yet unthinkable. Attlee felt insecure with his small majority, though it was as safe as a larger one. Labour militants, however bitter in their accusations that true socialism has been betrayed, would never be responsible for the downfall of a Labour government. But trouble was ahead.

In the summer Stafford became seriously ill again. It was soon clear he would have to resign, which he finally did in October. One day in the Members' Smoking Room Nye Bevan asked me if I knew whom Stafford had recommended as next chancellor of the Exchequer. Without thinking of the consequences, and assuming that Nye knew anyway, I replied, 'Hugh Gaitskell, of course.' Gaitskell was Stafford's deputy, as Minister of State for Economic Affairs, and acted for him when illness kept him away. He understood economics and was the obvious choice.

Nye went red with anger. I thought he would have apoplexy. 'I should be Chancellor,' he spluttered. 'They've no business to jump Gaitskell over my head. I am much more senior. It's disgraceful.' And he jumped out of his chair and rushed into the corridor.

That was the beginning of the Bevanite split. It was not ideological. It sprang from personal vanity and ambition. Nye despised Hugh and was determined to keep him away from the succession to the leadership, which he burned to have himself. At that time I should have been happy for Nye to be leader. Though he was lazy, he would have been a good Prime Minister, with a rolling sweep of history and a deep love of his country. Unlike Wedgwood Benn, sometimes ridiculously compared to him, he was sensible and willing to make compromises, as he did with the doctors and dentists to get their co-operation in the National Health Service. Nye talked hot air about seizing 'the commanding heights of the economy', of which he said steel was one, but he was too pragmatic to be a keen nationalizer. If he had lived till the Labour Government of 1964 he might well have warned against the folly of a hundred per cent nationalization of steel. He could persuade the Labour Party, as their acknowledged Socialist prophet, of many things they would not swallow from anyone else.

By the time Stafford went, the Korean War had started. Attlee and the Labour Government were firm in backing the USA in implementation of the United Nations resolution calling on the United Nations to defend South Korea against North Korean aggression. The West was jolted out of its happy hope that Russia was not interested in more expansion, and rearmament programmes began. When the Chinese poured by the hundred thousands into South Korea the Labour Government planned to increase its rearmament programme by nearly one-third over three years. Attlee announced the new programme on 29 January 1951. On 15 February, Nye, now Minister of Labour, endorsed this new rearmament programme, speaking for the Government at his own request: 'So we do beg . . . that we should not have all these jeers about the rearmament we are putting under way. We shall carry it out, we shall fulfil our obligations to our friends and allies.'

But it had to be paid for. To decide how was the job of Hugh Gaitskell, at forty-one one of the youngest ever Chancellors of the Exchequer. One of his proposals involved putting a small charge on teeth and spectacles. He had no reason to expect a violent reaction from Nye. When Stafford was Chancellor a Bill was introduced for a shilling prescription charge. Nye, still Minister of Health, commended it to a Parliamentary Labour Party meeting in October 1949 with one of his vivid phrases which stuck in my mind: 'Something has to be done about the cascades of medicine pouring down British throats, and they are not even bringing the bottles back!'

The Bill was eventually thought to be too tiresome administratively to be implemented. But the principle that a wholly free National Health Service was not sacrosanct had been established by its architect.

As the time came nearer for the Budget, Nye's jealousy of Hugh consumed him. He took the proposed charges on teeth and spectacles, already agreed by the Cabinet, as a personal challenge to his pride and petulantly threatened Gaitskell and the Cabinet. A week before Budget Day he said in a speech at Bermondsey that he would not remain in a government which put charges on National Health Service patients. He hoped his resignation threat would force Gaitskell to drop the charges on teeth and spectacles, thus proving that though he might not be Chancellor of the Exchequer, he could dominate him. He was not concerned with reducing the size of the rearmament programme which he had so recently and vigorously defended, though like others he wondered whether it would be practicable in the time allotted to it.

Nye's public threat made it impossible for the Cabinet to surrender to him, as he would have realized if his irrational jealousy of Hugh Gaitskell had not disturbed his balance. Gaitskell properly said he would resign and let someone else present an altered Budget if that was what the Prime Minister and the Cabinet wanted, but the details of his Budget were part of a measured whole (including a substantial increase in old-age pensions which would have to be dropped if the charges on teeth and spectacles were omitted). He could not change the plan of his Budget if he stayed Chancellor. Naturally the Cabinet and Attlee, who was in hospital, backed Hugh.

Working for *Tribune* I knew what Nye's envy was driving him to and was appalled. Jennie Lee, his wife, could have calmed him, but the female of the species was deadlier than the male and, whenever his resolve to resign wobbled, she strengthened him in it. I knew Hugh Gaitskell a little and liked him but my emotional allegiance had been more to Nye. I was so shocked by what I knew to be a campaign to destroy the Chancellor, not because he was a bad minister but because Nye could not control his animosity, that I wrote to Hugh. I told him I knew that the attack on the construction of his Budget was not genuine but a vendetta designed to destroy him. I told him that he was right, should stick to the Budget he had made, and I would support him whatever the outcome. It was the start of a long friendship.

If Attlee had not been away ill it is faintly possible that he could have talked Nye round. Hugh's Budget speech, and his reasons for what he had done, were received well in the House and Labour backbenchers were not alarmed. The passage about charges on teeth and spectacles caused no opposition or heightened attention, save one quiet murmur of 'Shame' from Jennie Lee, looking like a tragic heroine out of Shakespeare, and no one took any notice, so little did the Parliamentary Labour Party think that any issue of importance or of principle had been raised.

Hopes grew that Nye, seeing nobody cared about his trivial teeth and spectacles, would reconsider his on-off resignation and finally plump for off. If he resigned on such an issue he would look ridiculous, as his friends saw. But the malcontents were trying to crown him as the leader of the Left, who would sweep away Attlee's gentle approach and gallop towards true socialism. With the persuasive extremist Ian Mikardo prominent in advice, they urged him to widen the issue and to pretend that his resignation was over the menace the rearmament programme represented for socialism's forward march. His blood racing, Nye fell for the flattery, ignoring his own speech in February when he had extolled the rearmament programme for its reasonableness and restraint.

Harold Wilson had told me a few days previously in the Lobby of the House of Commons that he was worried about the effect on him as President of the Board of Trade of the adverse balance of trade he saw arising from the Korean War. He feared he would be blamed for it, to the detriment of his political career. He thought a resignation at this stage of his life would do his long-term career good. It would win him backing from the rank and file of the Labour Party activistis, among whom he would be able to work and with whom, as a civil servant in the war and as a minister ever since, he had had no contact. He, too, was jealous because he had not been made Chancellor of the Exchequer, thinking his earlier arrival in the Cabinet gave him a prior claim to Hugh's. If Nye were going he would go with him, under his protection (Hugh Dalton dubbed him somewhat unkindly 'Nye's little running dog').

I admired Wilson and thought him sincere. Now his attitude shocked and disappointed me greatly. It was the last time I spoke to him for nearly eight years, when I was asked by Hugh Gaitskell to teach him how to look trustworthy on television during the election campaign of 1959. I was convinced he was cultivating the rising Left as his best hope of one day becoming Leader. Naturally he knew why I dropped him and did not like it.

On 22 April, pushed into it by his wife and friends (ambition, human relations and emotional impulses are nearly always more decisive in politics than grave consideration of the interests of the state), Nye resigned. Wilson followed the next day. Nye made the customary personal statement on 23 April. It was pathetic. Nobody was convinced by his sudden discovery that the rearmament programme he had so strongly supported now imperilled the safety of socialism and the realm. The more Nye felt the House slipping away from him, the more bitter he became against Hugh, whom he had thought to destroy but had instead elevated above him.

Attlee did not blame Hugh. He knew that Nye was impossible in the angry mood he had worked himself up to. His concern was for the unity of the party and how to limit the damage Nye had done and was doing. I was moved by the way he tried to take the personal nastiness out of the dispute, and by his patent loyalty to the party he had served so long. I wrote and told him so. He replied in his own handwriting on 29 April, thanking me and saying he hoped to be in the House again on Monday, information to which I attached no significance. The reason for it soon became clear, however. He intended to offer me the job of Under-Secretary of State for War to replace Michael Stewart who had moved to the Ministry of Supply to take John Freeman's place. I was surprised, thinking that the Gandhi incident was still a black against me, but delighted. Nye's resignation had dismayed me but I got an unexpected bonus from it.

So began the only time I had office out of twenty-one years in Parliament. It lasted six months, until we lost the election on 25 October. Attlee had a system by which he tended to appoint junior ministers to redress the weaknesses of their seniors. John Strachey was Secretary of State for War and lukewarm about the rearmament programme. Celia, his wife, was later to tell Dora Gaitskell, herself a mother of three, 'We would so like to support Hugh over nuclear weapons, but you see we have our children to think about.' Attlee thought I was more robust on defence. He was not put off by my saying the previous Saturday in Birmingham: 'I am sorry to have to say it, but Nye Bevan and his friends did not think of the reasons for their resignation until after the resignations had been decided on ... the issue was largely personal ... the question of rearmament and raw materials had to be dragged in to justify their resignations.' Attlee agreed with me.

I knew John Strachey well and was fond of him. Our mild political differences never stopped us being on intimate terms. Once Bob Boothby, John and I went to the *Folies Bergère* in Paris. During the evening we asked each other what we thought was the experience which gave us the most pleasure. John said, 'having an orgasm at the same moment as a girl you are in love with'. My answer was not nearly so entertaining and I cannot remember Bob Boothby's. On a much later occasion John and I were sitting side by side in the Commons looking up at a pretty girl sitting in the Gallery facing us.

'Would you like to go to bed with her?' he asked.

'Yes, of course.'

'So would I. I thought when I was over sixty I would stop thinking about girls that way. I'm madly in love with a girl I'm having an affair with now. Do you think it's silly of me?'

Thinking of Goethe chasing teenage girls when he was eighty, I said, 'Certainly not. Good luck to you.'

John was engagingly romantic. Every morning he came to the War Office with a fresh rose in his button-hole which he had picked in his garden before leaving his house at Theydon Bois in Essex. Being romantic he was susceptible to Nye, but he did not think it worth resigning over teeth and spectacles. Politically he was ambitious. He had an excellent technique for dealing with Attlee. Whenever he thought he might be heading for trouble he would tell Attlee at once and ask his advice. Attlee would be delighted. He hated to have political disasters sprung on him or hear about them second-hand. Attlee never interfered with ministers, but woe betide them if they were too frightened to own up to their blunders in time.

When John became Minister of Food in 1946 he was persuaded by an old Socialist friend, Leslie Plummer, who worked for Beaverbrook and was supposed to know about commerce, to grow ground nuts in Tanganyika on a scale large enough to feed Britain and the world. As a result, £30 million (equivalent to about £500 million in 1985) was spent on this Utopian project. Drought and other calamities came upon it like an Old Testament scourge and all the money was lost. The Tory Press had a glorious time reporting the dismal failure of this crazy 'Socialist' scheme (though it might have succeeded to universal benefit if the years in which it was tried had been normal for rain).

Everyone expected John to be sacked, as any other minister would have been. What they did not know was that John had forewarned Attlee well in advance of the collapse of the scheme and asked his advice. Attlee was so pleased that he had had the courage to do this that he saw him through, though after the 1950 election he moved him to the War Office where he was fairly confident that John would be too pacific to do anything dangerous.

John was an intellectual; that is to say he wrote difficult books which appealed to intellectuals, especially those who considered themselves of the thinking Left. His most famous, *The Coming Struggle for Power*, was published in 1932 when he was close to, but not quite in, the Communist Party, which he publicly abjured in April 1940. As he was stronger in thought than in decisive stands, the unkind dubbed the book 'The Coming Struggle for Strachey'.

John liked to maintain his reputation as an intellectual and do himself good politically by making thoughtful speeches to be delivered on a Saturday when the papers were short of news for Sunday. Nearly always the *Observer* gave his speeches front-page treatment and printed wads of them. John spent days preparing them and ensured that the Sunday papers got them no later than Friday, to give them time to prepare the most newsworthy bits for publication. But he always sent them first for approval and advice to Attlee, who was flattered by this courtesy and would sometimes make suggestions. Attlee's approval removed any chance that John might be at risk for not conforming to government policy.

When I joined him at the War Office he showed me his speeches before processing them. I usually thought them harmless but a trifle insipid. However, after reading one I said, 'This is very good, but you can't make it and stay Secretary of State for War. You should make your mind up what you want to do most.'

'Why, what's the matter with it?'

'Well, you can't be Secretary of State for War and say that the rearmament programme is very much open to question and you're not sure about it yourself. What do you suppose the generals you're telling to carry it out will think, let alone Clem?'

He was disappointed. He looked again at the ambivalent speech which had taken him many hours. 'Oh dear, I suppose you're right.'

That was one speech he neither sent to Attlee nor delivered.

John was MP for my seat, Aston, in 1929. He became PPS to Mosley, Chancellor of the Duchy of Lancaster in the Labour Government, and was fascinated by him. When Mosley flounced off to start the New Party in 1931, John went with him. Others like Nye Bevan were tempted by this glamorous man with his radically attractive notions for ending unemployment and ushering in a new deal. When I met him at lunch at Annie Fleming's not long before he died I could see why, despite his faded energy. On realizing he was one of the guests, priggishly I nearly left but, still priggishly, I decided to stay and be rude to him. This was not easy. His wife Diana and he were charming. But I gave him a drubbing about his arrogance and being the most conceited man in England, which had brought his ambitions to nought when he could have been Prime Minister. In his stupendous vanity, I told him, he thought he was so marvellous that he could bypass the normal route to the political top. Mosley argued back but not very well; however, he did not seem much offended and invited my wife and me to visit them in Paris which, again priggishly, we never did. I think he was more of a pretend-monster than a real one, making silly attacks on the Jews, which he could not have believed in but which he hoped would win him easy popularity with the nasty and unthinking.

When John saw the direction Mosley was going he soon shook away, bouncing from Fascist totalitarianism towards Communist totalitarianism. But as the Bevanite split developed he sailed a middle course, voted for Hugh Gaitskell as Leader when Attlee retired, and for George Brown when Hugh died.

John was kind to me. He gave me my own sphere of authority and never questioned what I did. My predecessor, Michael Stewart, one day to be an effective pro-American Foreign Secretary, hardly went out of his office. Sir George Turner, Permanent Under-Secretary, had said to me, 'We're very sorry Michael is going. We've come to think of him as one of us.' I was determined that the civil servants would not think me one of them. Hugh Dalton had said to me, 'You must show the civil servants immediately that you are not going to agree with everything they put in front of you. The first things they give you to sign you must say you won't, they've got it wrong. If you don't they'll have you where they want you.'

One of my jobs was to write, which meant sign, letters to the many MPs who had written to ask for constituents to be exempt from the reservist call-up caused by the Korean War. I overturned the Civil Service decisions in about six of the first batch of letters prepared for my signature. Then I said I would sign nothing more in the office. I would do all that kind of work at home in the evening, to give me more time to find out what was going on in the Army and the War Office. The civil servants looked glum at their lost hope of keeping me stuck to my desk as a dutiful signing machine, leaving them undisturbed to do as they pleased.

I was in raptures. I was the youngest member of the Government. I was on my way to real power. I sat proudly in my official car as it drove into Horse Guards Parade between the sentries – a privilege I exercised as Vice-President of the Army Council.

Nothing could go wrong. I was going to work like a demon at my job to show how good I was and also because, after nearly six years in the Army, I cared strongly about it. I went everywhere and looked into everything. I visited our troops in Germany, Austria and Trieste. The Commander in Vienna was a young, jolly general, Mike West, decorated three times for bravery. He had a pretty, fair-haired wife, Christine, and we all played tennis and went to the heuriger cafés, drinking the new wine and talking happily into the night. The generals I had known in the war were neither so uninhibited nor so eclectic in their interests.

One night I was watching that dreary fraud of a play, *Waiting for Godot*, when I heard someone chortling in the row behind. It was General West. 'Isn't it marvellous,' he said in the interval. He was a dashing general and a great success when he commanded the Commonwealth Division in Korea. If we had still had an empire, he would have become Governor of Madras or somewhere like that when he left the Army instead of mouldering in a business job which he hated.

In Trieste I was received by a guard of honour of helmeted and ceremonially white uniformed Italian soldiers. That was overdoing it for an Under-Secretary but I enjoyed it hugely. Trieste was being argued over by the Italians and the Yugoslavs. We were holding the ring. It was sad, as it always is, when people have to be forced to live under rulers of a different nationality, as some were bound to in Trieste. But the saddest thing in Trieste was the Castle of Miramar, built by the sea in 1856 for the unlucky Archduke Maximilian. He and his beautiful bride lived there briefly in the enchantment of youth, high position and glittering prospects, until the French lured him into being the Emperor of Mexico and deserted him. He was shot by a firing squad in 1867. His twenty-seven-year-old widow lived on for sixty years, sent mad with grief for her lost husband and happiness. Their pretty possessions, speaking of the tragedy which befell their owners, are still at Miramar. Vanity of vanities, saith the preacher: all is vanity.

Montgomery was Deputy Supreme Allied Commander in Europe. I talked to him often. The first time was at the edge of a muddy field where deck-chairs had been arranged for us. I had a mongrel bitch from the Battersea Dogs' Home that loved rolling in mud. I told my secretary to keep her well away but he let her go. She came bounding through the mud towards me and leaped perversely not on to my lap but Montgomery's. 'What's this? Whatever's this?' the great general cried, as his handkerchief competed inadequately with the mud all over his trousers.

Montgomery had the conventional general's view of politicians. They were all dishonest time-servers and intriguers (not like Montgomery, innocently calumniating Eisenhower and Bradley behind their backs!). We got on pretty well, all the same. His brain was clear and decisive. If Montgomery had been able to persuade the Western Allied powers, particularly the Americans, to let the Allied armies continue their advance when Germany was collapsing, much of East Germany and Eastern Europe would not now be enslaved by Russia.

Some five years after our meetings Richard Dimbleby was talking to Montgomery about me and deprecating my being a socialist. 'Never mind about his politics,' Montgomery snapped. 'He was a first-rate Under-Secretary of War.' But I do not think he remembered how he once saved me from being court-martialled.

I took War Office questions in the House early on when John was away. As noted amusedly by an editorial in the *Evening Standard*, I had improved my usually untidy appearance by carefully brushing my hair and putting on a new suit and tie. Attlee sat beside me. When I sat down his clipped voice said, 'Very good. You kept the answers short. That's the way to do it.' His praise was like nectar.

But he was not so pleased when I sent him a paper urging that we should join the European Defence Community. This was meant to be a unified army of all the Western European countries. If we had taken it up we should have been the greatest influence in it, we should have been able to shape the eventual Common Market to our needs, avoiding all the rows about the CAP and British overpayments to the Community still unresolved in the eighties. The delightful Bill Slim, CIGS, was dead against me. 'What would happen to the cap badges of the Royal Warwickshire Regiment?' he demanded. It was his old regiment. 'Nothing,' I said. 'All regiments would keep their identity as they did when they served under non-British Allied commanders in the war.' What actually happened to the Royal Warwickshire cap badges was that they disappeared when the Royal Warwickshire Regiment was disbanded as surplus to requirements a few years afterwards.

Attlee curtly remarked that it was not the sort of policy matter with which an Under-Secretary should concern himself. His belief in world government excluded close relations with smaller groups of foreigners down the line, especially Europeans. Anthony Eden said to me in the 1960s that, if he were as young as I, he would probably have felt similarly enthusiastic about the Common Market, but at his age he could not contemplate it. There was a generation gap. Its effect on the senior members of the two major parties harmfully delayed our accession to the Treaty of Rome for years.

In John's absence I attended the occasional Cabinet Defence Committee at No. 10 and felt very grand sitting at the Cabinet table. I remember one meeting. The Defence Chiefs wanted to accept an invitation for British warships to visit a Spanish naval base. There were to be regattas and jollifications with Franco's sailors. Herbert Morrison, the Foreign Secretary, was cheerily keen. He thought the Spanish sailors would see the beauty of democracy if they consorted with ours. When my turn came, I mumbled that the War Office had no view on the matter. 'Well, I have,' Attlee barked. 'The less we have to do with these people, the better. Visit not approved.' Attlee enjoyed squashing Morrison.

I had a mild brush with Attlee. Lynn Ungoed-Thomas, who had been made Solicitor-General at the same time as I went to the War Office, and I piloted a complicated Bill through the Commons. The Opposition kept pressing for an amendment to it which we knew would be inimical to ordinary servicemen's interests. Armed with departmental briefs we vigorously explained, with the Government's full backing, why the Government could not change its mind and told the Opposition to get stuffed – or words to that effect. The Bill went to the Lords, where the Tory peers, at the behest of their friends in the Commons, promptly put into the Bill the provisions we had said it was impossible to accept.

Lord Jowitt was the Lord Chancellor. He was an oily but

magnificent-looking man who did not mind what he said so long as he stayed Lord Chancellor. In 1929 he had been elected as a Liberal. Ramsay MacDonald had no Labour MP fit for the post of Attorney-General, so he offered it to Jowitt, provided that he left the Liberal Party to join Labour. Jowitt jumped at it. In 1931 he left Labour for the National Government to keep the job. In 1939 he became a Labour MP again in time to become Solicitor-General in Churchill's 1940 government, in which he stayed for the rest of the war. Then he was made Labour's Lord Chancellor and ended up an earl. The last time I met him he was cadging free transport on cargo ships for his foreign travels, and pleading poverty, but he left a fair sum. Though he was bogus, and his splendid presence was better suited to Gilbert and Sullivan than to real life, I did not dislike him.

Jowitt asked Lynn and me to see him. It would be a great convenience to him if, when the Bill got back to the Commons, we would accept the Lords' amendments. It never occurred to him that we had meant what we said and might object now to saying the opposite. Right and wrong were of no interest to him. We said we could not oblige him and thought that was the end of the matter. It was not. Jowitt went to Attlee and persuaded him that we were young fools who talked rot about principles. It was Attlee's turn to see us.

'How can we eat our words?' we asked him. 'We would look ridiculous.'

Attlee took his pipe out of his mouth. 'Have to get used to that when you're a minister. Jowitt has a difficult time getting our legislation through the Lords. They don't like it. Go away and don't be silly.'

We left meekly. I recited with a wooden face the new departmental brief, explaining why Lynn and I now disagreed with what we had said before, and accepted the Lords' amendments, to the happy jeers of the Opposition.

I enjoyed working with the Civil Service. Their behaviour was proper. If I disagreed with what they wanted me to do, they put a clear case and I put mine. If they were convinced I was right, they willingly co-operated. If they were unconvinced, they still co-operated but with less enthusiasm. If they convinced me

I was wrong, there was no problem. It was almost an intellectual game, in which the civil servants played fair.

It is only unintelligent or weak ministers who lose the final decision-making to the civil servants, who understandably take it over if they can. Civil servants run a department only if a minister is too lazy or too incompetent to find out what they are doing or is too feeble to assert himself. The complaint of many in the Labour Party that civil servants set out to frustrate Labour's manifestos is unjustified, but they like implementation of them to make sense with minimal damage. Nye Bevan had genuine co-operation from the civil servants in creating the Health Service, with much discussion on the best way to deal with the details.

An illustration will show what I mean. British troops in the Korean War were mainly drawn from peaceful stations abroad, where they had been getting overseas allowances to compensate them for having to buy things which would be provided free or cheaply in a home posting. These allowances were regarded as a pleasant little perk to add to the basic pay. On being hurled into the Korean War theatre they lost them; troops in a battle area get their basic necessities free and do not use luxuries. Our soldiers were fighting alongside far better paid, but not noticeably braver or more efficient, US servicemen, as E.J. Kahn wrote in 'No one But the Glosters' in the *New Yorker* in May 1951; I went out to Westchester, New York in 1952 to thank him for his tribute. The loss of the overseas allowance made the gap much worse. First I argued that they should get an overseas allowance just the same. The civil servants riposted as above. Then I said they should have a hard-living allowance. No good: servicemen must expect rough conditions. What about battle pay? Servicemen are enlisted to fight, so why should they be paid more when they do? That would be an unfortunate precedent. Precedent? I thought. I dug up some precedents of campaign gratuities paid in the past. After a spirited argument the civil servants began to come round to my side, but they maintained that the gratuity would have to be paid also to sailors and airmen. Well, why not? We started putting the proposals through an inter-Service committee.

'The First Lord of the Admiralty wants to speak to you,' my

secretary said one morning. It was Frank Pakenham in a temper: 'I'm told you are trying to pay a bonus to my sailors. How dare you? I am going to complain to the Prime Minister.'

'All right. You tell the Navy you don't want them to have the gratuity and see how they like it. I am sure the Army won't mind.'

There were no further protests from the Admiralty. The War Office, pleased we had taken the initiative, persuaded the civil servants in the other departments including the Treasury that it was a good and just idea. It did not give much to our servicemen resisting the Chinese in Korea, but it was a token recognition of their bravery and fighting skills. The plan was agreed before the October election. Later I heard it caused some administrative difficulties and was known, pleasurably to me, as 'Mr Wyatt's gratuity', but it got paid.

There was a system in the War Office by which members of the Army Council took turns to review the more serious courts-martial in which heavy sentences had been given. Like John Mortimer's Mr Rumpole, I have always been squeamish about harsh sentences, either because I shrink from man's inhumanity to man, or because of a touch of 'there, but for the grace of God, go I'. I have always been against capital punishment, even for traitors, mutineers or cowardice in the face of the enemy. Guardsmen and troopers featured in some of the cases, convicted of homosexuality offences committed in exchange for gifts from civilians. One case concerned a civilian who supplied hampers from Fortnum and Mason's in return for being ridden around by troopers wearing breastplates and the upper part of their uniforms. More infantile than shocking, I felt. I was for clemency and reducing the sentences. The generals took the opposite view, which surprised me, since most regular officers had been to public schools. 'Could it be,' I innocently asked a couple of generals, 'that you are afraid you may be suppressed homosexuals yourselves and want to prove you are not?' There was no resentment: leniency in such cases became more common.

It was an unhappy day when election defeat ripped my short glory away but I had had a crash course in how Whitehall works which I never forgot.

# CHAPTER X

❦

# The Bevanites' Revenge

GAITSKELL AND I were the principal defenders of Labour's rearmament programme. Most of Labour's leaders ducked it. The Bevanite stance was popular in the constituency parties. Three weeks before the October election the Bevanites captured four out of the seven seats on the National Executive from the constituency party section at the Scarborough Conference. Denis Healey, still Secretary of Labour's International Department and not yet an MP, belaboured Hugh and me on the seafront for not being more vigorous in putting our case. We were slightly pained, thinking we were going to the limit in exciting venom from the Left. The split in the once solid Labour Party had come, and it was not easy to predict who would win.

In subsequent years the still stout-hearted Denis Healey was to say to me, 'Why do you keep making speeches which annoy people so much? All you have to do is keep quiet and wait for another Labour government. It's bound to happen some time and you could be a minister again automatically.' Sound advice which I never followed.

Nye called Hugh 'a desiccated calculating machine', thinking him cold and unemotional. It was a serious misjudgement, which proved Nye's undoing. Hugh was passionate in the cause of reason. He loved the Labour Party and wanted to make it something like the German Social Democratic Party was then: free of ideological bitterness and hatred, strong for prosperity and justice and equality, the determined but moderate natural party of government which Harold Wilson foolishly thought he had achieved while actually destroying it.

Hugh tried and failed to get rid of Labour's constitutional curse, Clause 4, which officially condemned it to aspire to nationalize everything. Hugh knew that the British, like himself, were against such Marxist thinking, which would injure, not benefit, the ordinary people. He was asked why he made such an issue of Clause 4 after the 1959 election. Why not let it die away into desuetude? He could not. Clause 4 was a symbol, like the mark of Cain. Wearing it was an affront to the public and bad for the wearer.

Hugh loved dancing and parties. He was annoyed with me when my dancing did not meet the standards he expected at a little dance he gave at Frognal Gardens. He said I was there under false pretences, but he asked me to other dances in the hope I would remain seated at the side. He was a boisterous dancer in the twenties' manner. He worked and played hard, drinking but not getting drunk. Roy Jenkins, Tony Crosland and I went with him to a dull political conference in Paris. In the evening we wanted to go to a two- or three-star restaurant and afterwards to bed. Hugh insisted on going to a Russian restaurant where he knew the proprietor. The food was ghastly but Hugh loved the Russian orchestra and demanded more and louder music long after everyone else had left and when our heads were dropping on to the table with sleep. What could we do? He was our leader.

For years the four of us were very close. His favourite was Tony Crosland. There was a scintilla of platonic homosexuality in his affection for Tony, which Socrates would have understood. Hugh loved his mind but also his looks and the eternal undergraduate youthfulness of his raffish parties in The Boltons. Roy once told me he asked Hugh what things had moved him most. There were two. One was something about Tony. The other, to my pride, was 'seeing Woodrow standing up and making a speech at a Party meeting'. They were usually speeches putting a case which the majority believed in, but did not wish to risk unpopularity with the Left by saying so publicly.

At one of Hugh's parties I met Ian and Annie Fleming. He was just beginning his James Bond series, having despaired of scoring as the great literary figure he had hoped to be. He was sardonic and often morose, with a smile like a swift flash of sun through a storm-cloud. He had the appearance of an underfed stray cat, claws practised in scratching, inducing nervousness in new and sometimes old acquaintances. He would thaw if stroked gently. At one of Solly Zuckerman's evening functions at the Zoo we talked for an hour or more. He told me how ashamed he was at being such a failure as a writer of distinction. I explained to him that he had not understood that in James Bond he had created one of the greatest characters in English fiction, who would live as long as anyone in Dickens (he would have thought a reference to someone out of Conan Doyle or John Buchan derogatory). The more I spoke, the longer the sun stayed out and the cat began to purr. And when I finished, 'What is more, your book suggests you have a fascinating sex life', his delight shone. A pity I never asked him for a signed copy of the first edition of *Casino Royale*. It would be worth thousands now.

He married Annie on several conditions. She was not to go with him in the winter to Goldeneye in Jamaica when he wrote his books. She was not to accompany him on his annual outing to Sandwich to play golf. He would not attend her smart lunch and dinner parties, because he thought the guests were awful, though they thought themselves distinguished and frequently were. I confess to having enjoyed them, meeting people like Noël Coward and hearing Roy Thomson complain that he did not like being given presents because he might be expected to give one back. She had a pretty little house in Victoria Square, built by Sir Matthew Wyatt. Ian hardly ever stayed in the handsome country-house that they remodelled.

Annie's previous marriage to the good-looking Esmond Rothermere, nearly invited as a young man to be King of Hungary, collapsed. 'He said he couldn't make love to me any more. It made his hair fall out,' she told me, but I think there were other reasons: Esmond with his next wife, the delicious Mary Rothermere, produced a handsome son about the same age as my daughter whose looks and manner remind me of Esmond. Annie and Ian were well suited. She could be sharp, but she was a splendid woman, funny to and about her friends and enemies, but a warm and true friend. She liked to be at the centre of events. Hugh Gaitskell was very fond of her, but never to the diminution of his marriage to the loyal, protective, lioness Dora which lasted securely and happily for twenty-six years.

Apart from knowing Ian Fleming, not yet and perhaps still

not accepted as literary, I was not much in the literary world in those days. Through my friend Robin Maugham, a fair writer himself, I met his uncle Somerset Maugham and was appropriately impressed. Occasionally I met Evelyn Waugh, who alarmed me, as he intended, by holding a long white ivory trumpet to his ear and asking me to repeat everything I said, though he had obviously heard it the first time.

Evelyn Waugh and I shared a barber, the elderly Mr Banks, at Trumper's in Curzon Street. One day Mr Banks asked, 'What does Mr Waugh do?'

'He's a writer.'

On my next visit the question was, 'What kind of a writer is Mr Waugh?'

'A funny writer.'

This evidently interested Mr Banks. When I went to have my hair cut again he asked, 'Do you think Mr Waugh would let me have one of his books?'

'I'm sure he would.'

Some time passed before my next haircut. As he advanced towards me with his scissors, Mr Banks looked reproachful.

'Mr Waugh gave me a book. We took it to Margate on holiday. The wife read it: she didn't think it was funny. My daughter and the son-in-law read it: they didn't think it was funny. I read it: I didn't think it was funny. I thought you said he was a funny writer.'

The book was *Helena*, a tedious novel about a third-century Roman saint for whom Waugh chose Colchester as her birthplace. Did Evelyn Waugh give Mr Banks the book because he was annoyed with me for saying he was a funny writer or because he was annoyed with Mr Banks for his temerity in asking for a book? Either way my reputation as a literary critic was blasted.

At George Weidenfeld's parties writers mingled with ambassadors and habitués of the gossip columns. I met George at the end of the war when we were both protégés of Elsa Knight Thompson, an intense and very left-wing American lady who organized BBC broadcasts and helped us both. I liked George instantly. He left Austria in 1938 to escape the Nazis when he was nineteen. With the aid of a few introductions to people in

London he raised himself higher and higher through his skill with people, particularly women, with whom he has had much more success than I though physically he is not noticeably more attractive. Flicking through a manuscript he can judge almost by touch whether it will sell; he has a gift for suggesting subjects to authors and persuading them to turn them into books for him. One of his earliest authors was Harold Wilson, who wrote a ghastly book about coal and later arranged for George to have first a knighthood and then a life peerage. Not bad going for the boy from Austria who built a distinguished publishing business on nothing but an instinct for books and a talent for mesmerizing people. He has injected colour into London's literary life.

But I was more concerned during the 1950s with politics and helping Hugh all I could. I gave lunches at my house for him to meet the trade-union leaders in secret to avoid newspaper talk of conspiracies. He needed to build friendships with them. The more they grew to know him, the more staunch they became. That was to be of great value to him when he needed their block votes to resist hare-brained left-wing policies and to overturn the famous one-sided nuclear disarmament resolution passed at the Scarborough Conference of 1960. Union friends he made, many of them through me, saw him through many internal Labour Party arguments when Hugh's judgement was queried, sometimes plausibly. As he said to me, 'Anyone can support me when I am right. What I need is people who will support me when I am wrong.'

When he became Leader of the Party in October 1955 Hugh remarked to me, 'I am not going to be a chairman just collecting the voices. I don't intend to be a leader like Attlee, leading from behind.' He charged into battle, principles proudly flying. When he was unsaddled he got up again and fought on. He would never give in. His determination was fortified by the conviction that he must win or the Labour Party would be doomed. He was the opposite of a 'desiccated calculating machine', often taking chances with his political career which alarmed Roy, Tony and me.

Six months before he became Leader in October 1955 the three of us wrote Hugh an anxious letter. It was a trifle pompous and silly, showing we had lost our nerve while he kept his. We told him we had only supported the platform on the motion to take the Whip away from Nye Bevan, after he had voted against the Party in a defence debate, 'out of loyalty and regardless of our personal views'. It took us hours to draft that letter. It finished: '. . . please do not think you have to write a reply to this – if one comes we shall all be too frightened to open the envelope!'

Hugh was mildly irritated, mostly with me. 'You should have known better. You have been in government and know the difficulties. Tony and Roy are much less experienced.' In retrospect the suggestion that I led astray these two innocents, who were to soar high above me politically, has a comical ring. Hugh's annoyance did not stop me publicly demanding that Labour's National Executive should not add expulsion from the Party to Nye's loss of the Whip. This prompted George Brown to tell me that I was not a person to go tiger-hunting with. Actually Hugh was not the main instigator of the move either to withdraw the Whip from or to expel Nye. The Chief Whip, Willie Whiteley, Jim Callaghan and the usually placid Chuter Ede were much keener on it, and Hugh went along with the majority of the Shadow Cabinet.

Previously Nye had made a commotion over the Parliamentary Party's reluctant agreement to support German rearmament. I did not like the Germans and still shiver at them but Adenauer, the greatest European statesman of the century, who made as much impression on me at our one meeting as Churchill had, had persuaded them to accept democracy and repent of their sins without losing their will to achieve. It was hypocritical to claim that the reformed West Germany was not as entitled to have a defence force as East Germany or Stalin's totalitarian Russia.

My support of German rearmament and of Labour's rearmament programme brought me increasing political difficulties. In the constituency parties the Bevanites were rising. The boundary commissioners split up my old Aston division. Each of its three wards went to a new constituency, though the mutilated Aston kept its old name. In the new constituencies my old friends were outnumbered by two to one. I would have survived if they

229

had not been scattered, but in selection conferences in the three new constituencies familiar faces were outnumbered two to one by new faces who were strongly Bevanite. Dear Jim Meadows, still my agent at Aston, and later to be Lord Mayor of Birmingham, struggled valiantly for me, canvassing night and day the delegates to the selection conferences of the new constituencies. He believed in me and loved me, as I loved him with his chubby face and his passion for every detail of political interest. It was no use. My support for Hugh and opposition to Nye had labelled me too right wing. The tide towards the dotty Left was gathering power and pace.

One new constituency went to Birmingham-born Vic Yates, a talkative nonentity and pacifist who unctuously uttered the current slogans against Labour's official policy on German rearmament and against defence generally. The one still called Aston went to Julius Silverman, one of the best chess players in the Commons and on the very left. The third adopted Denis Howell, a young Birmingham city councillor with no embarrassing political baggage in his knapsack and with whom I was friendly. I had not expected him to oppose me. He has had various minor posts in Labour governments, including that of Minister of Sport, which he has filled well. I was cross with him at the time, commenting unsportingly to the Press that there was no loyalty in politics. Denis told me that after he had been unobtrusively attending the Commons for some months he was introduced to Nye as the person who had defeated me at a selection conference in Birmingham and Nye, looking at him without favour, remarked, 'Well, at least you knew Woodrow was here.'

Even more than Stafford, Hugh attracted the young. He was not a great orator, but the intensity of his beliefs gave his logically composed speeches a gallantry which raised them from the ordinary. It was an honour to fight alongside him. The loyalty he was given he returned in greater measure. Attlee said that to become leader of a party the most important ingredient was to have a few devoted friends. Hugh had them and deserved them. I was glad at times to say things for him which would have been unwisely risky for him to have said himself.

When Frank Cousins was General Secretary of the Transport

and General Workers' Union, using their great card vote as his private property, Hugh suggested I should make a speech criticizing him. I went further than he expected, calling Cousins 'the bully with the block vote', a phrase which caught on. But Hugh did not mind when I pointed out that a minnow like me had to say something striking to get reported. Most of the speeches I made when I was close to him were extensions of his feelings. He was my hero and I cared nothing for the consequences to myself.

At the election in May 1955 I stood at Grantham, not yet famous for being the birthplace of Margaret Thatcher. It was, and is, a safe Conservative seat. In my optimism I thought as the campaign went on that I might win it. Meetings were good, but often they are when you are losing – some paranormal forewarning communicates itself to your supporters and they rally round. So did the cows when I stopped at hamlets or farm buildings and blared my views over the loudspeaker. Cows love loudspeakers and their votes were mine for the shouting; but not the votes of those on the electoral roll. Nevertheless, the Labour vote was the highest yet recorded and the Conservative majority of 2375 the lowest.

The Ed Murrow CBS current affairs programme chose Grantham as one of the constituencies they covered in the British election campaign. It was no help to me, as no one in England saw the programme in time. But Mrs Grace Wyndham Goldie, in charge of Current Affairs television at Lime Grove, saw it. That was better for me than if I had won. I was out of Parliament with almost no resources but my journalism. MPs then had no lavish pay or redundancy money and I was uncertain what to do next. Mrs Wyndham Goldie liked what she saw and I was soon to hear from her.

I was living in Limerston Street, sharing a house with Moorea Hastings who lived in the bottom part. I had met her at the tail-end of my affair with my American girl. We were both staying at Buscot Park with Gavin Faringdon, an unusual Labour peer, very left wing abroad but not so much at home. He was rich. He had Bevanite friends, including the sinister-looking Ian Mikardo who was pleasant to talk to. Nye wrote much of his disappointing *In Place of Fear* at Buscot. I had known Gavin since 1945 and he did not discard me when I became a Gaitskellite.

Gavin was not attracted to women physically. His mother persuaded him to marry in hope of an heir, but the bride found out that he did not provide what she had expected from marriage and the marriage ended abruptly. In 1934, aged thirty-two, Gavin succeeded to his grandfather's title and much of his money (he had been something to do with railways). He was very generous in a secretive way. Several times I heard, but never from him, of people he had rescued. He had steady boyfriends, the reigning one acting as a kind of major domo as well. His choices were excellent and the household had a cosy marital atmosphere. As many of his visitors were poor, guests were forbidden to tip the servants on pain of never being asked again. That was pleasant for the guests, and the servants were amply compensated by Gavin.

Gavin had one stinginess: wine. It never arrived until late in the meal and was usually plonk. The table was resplendent with silver and gold ornaments and plates. The servants were plentiful, prompt and correct in serving the usually indifferently cooked courses which needed the non-existent wine to wash them down. A remoteness in Gavin discouraged the thirsty from asking for it. One day Roy was at the far end from Gavin at a table around which eighteen were sitting impatiently waiting for wine towards the end of the second course. A great cry came from Roy: 'Gavin, can I have some water?' There were astonished stares as in an H.M. Bateman cartoon, but it precipitated two decanters of acid white wine which had been standing on a side-table. However, Gavin had some excellent claret, including pre-Phylloxera, which he brought out when there were only one or two of us.

The week-end I met Moorea at Buscot we played squash in Gavin's squash-court. She was plumply pretty and laughed a lot. She turned into a much thinner, strikingly handsome woman with considerable style and elegance, reminiscent of her celebrated grandmother, the Marchesa Casati (Malu), as seen in a picture painted by Augustus John and a bust by Epstein. Moorea's grandmother had been a close friend of D'Annunzio, the Italian poet and First World War hero; probably they were lovers, but Malu was generally more interested in making a show than making love. She gave a great dinner party in her house in Venice, now the Guggenheim Museum, and had a wax model, *à la* Madame Tussaud, made of herself and dressed identically. She sat at one end of the table, the model at the other. Neither Marchesa moved to acknowledge or speak to the guests, uncertain whether to laugh or to be insulted. She had a cheetah which she took on a lead and sometimes wore a live snake. At one of her balls she had pages painted gold. Unkind friends spread a rumour that one died through having no outlets for the skin to breathe through. This was untrue but seemed plausible at a party given by someone with the attitude of a Roman empress.

She was not much connected to the real world, bravely defying it and in some degree conquering it. When I saw the dead body of this beautiful woman in her seventies it was that of a girl of eighteen. It is possible to argue that Malu's life was worthlessly profligate, but we take nothing out of the world and while she was in it she shone like a resplendent dragonfly. That is worth much in a generally dull world. She died almost in poverty, dependent on the good nature of her friends and her granddaughter, but she gave more than she took.

In 1925 her only child, Cristina, married Jack Hastings, later Earl of Huntingdon. His mother, daughter of an Australian sheep magnate, opposed the marriage. She thought Cristina beneath her son socially, presumably taking the insular English view that all foreign aristocracy is bogus. This seemed unduly snobbish, given that her daughter-in-law came from one of the two or three families which had dominated Milan and its environs for eight hundred years. Quite good enough, even for her son, who would be the senior surviving legitimate male Plantagenet with the best genealogical claim to the throne: a majority of the Protestant nobles wanted the Earl of Huntingdon, not James I, to succeed Elizabeth but, like Moorea's father, to whom in his portrait he looks remarkably similar, he was not of an aggressive disposition, preferring peacefulness to power and trouble.

Cristina, who became a Communist, had a touch of her mother. On her return from a visit to Italy a friend asked her why her arm was in a sling. 'I was angry with a servant and hit

233

him so hard that it broke something in my arm,' the unabashed Communist replied.

After her divorce from Jack, she married the charming and good-looking Wogan Philipps, once the idol of the Bloomsbury set. He had been married to Rosamond Lehmann with whom John Strachey, as he told me wistfully, had been unsuccessfully in love and whose face I admired, and whose words I awaited with awe, when I sat across the table from her on the Committee of the Society of Authors. Wogan became the first and so far only Communist in the House of Lords. He was dedicated to Communism by persuasion and emotion rather than intellect. When Cristina died in 1953, he married Tamara Rust, Russian international athlete and widow of the editor of the *Daily Worker*. Wogan and Cristina had guilt feelings about having money but sensibly did not give it all away, though they created an agricultural co-operative in Italy.

Moorea was thus exposed to hefty Communist and left-wing influence as she grew up, but it had no lasting effect. Jack in his youth was very Left, a talented painter, especially of murals, and a pupil of the Communist Diego Rivera, the Mexican painter. He was also a good polo player. It was through his influence that Cristina joined the Communist Party, Jack holding back to become a respectable, far from rabid junior Agriculture Minister for five years in Attlee's government. Jack was another reason for regretting the passing of Empire. He would have been just right for governing a tranquil province or colony, and all would have enjoyed it including himself.

Moorea was named after the Pacific island on which she was conceived during her parents' honeymoon. She was (I assume still is) very intelligent. Her formal education was disrupted by frequent changes of school, sometimes at the behest of her English grandmother who paid the bills, but she made up for that by wide reading. Her ambition was to be an actress and I spent many hours listening to her go over her parts. I thought her rather accomplished in the repertory theatres she played in, but there were too many girls wanting to be actresses at the time.

Moorea had good taste, leaning towards the dramatic and strong colours and lines. She made Tower House, Park Village

West, into what a Russian diplomat I gave lunch to called 'a little palace'. Our time together was always a trifle turbulent. I take most of the blame. Her Italian strain was fierce but my temper as ever was short and nasty. I am too easily provoked, and though I quickly forget the hurtful things I say, the recipients cannot be expected to have the same facility. I have, too, a tendency to nag, to which I attach little significance once I have discharged my complaints and am unreasonably surprised they should rankle after their instant passing from my mind. Almost daily I make a new resolution not to lose my temper and not to complain about trivial household matters. I am wearying to live with, and the majority of my rows are about nothing at all.

Despite my defects, I thought I had a marriage which would last. I interested Moorea and made her laugh. She enjoyed my summaries of what was happening in the world and liked giving parties, for which she had a talent. But the sex gave out early, doubtless my fault, and she, as her Italian grandmother would have done, correctly thought me not good-looking, not a person to be proud of being seen with on entering a room or restaurant. Eventually she found a better-looking and more amiable man to go off with, though I tried hard to stop her. I believe she has been much happier than she would have been if she had stayed with me.

I was not strictly faithful to her physically, but I thought we had a marriage sufficiently civilized and free of humbug for odd infidelities on either side not to destroy it. There are many such marriages which stay the course comfortably and healthily. It would be biologically impossible for husbands and wives never to feel attracted outside their marriage after their mutual sexual excitement has calmed, and sometimes before.

This marriage was the first in which I had a child, Pericles. Childless marriages should be readily dissolvable; they are merely two-party contracts which ought to be ended easily if one or both of the parties are dissatisfied. Children introduce other parties to the contract, who can be presumed not to wish the contract to be ended until they have reached the age when they are no longer affected by a broken home. A father is a father and a mother is a mother, and to give a feeling of security when the infant most needs it they ought to be in the same house. They may shout at each other, but the presence of a child may help them to learn to tone down their furies and, if they have external romantic concerns, there may be less friction. Stepfathers and stepmothers, try as they may, are usually a poor substitute for the real thing. It is unsettling and unnatural for a child to be torn between two households, or to be tempted to play off one parent against the other.

Moorea and I were married in 1956. We had lived together for a year or so beforehand. I enjoyed being with her. She was never dull, and emerged to ever better looks as though from a chrysalis. Through her Italian connections I came to see and love Italy. She had money, which was helpful. I do not regret my time with her, it was full of incident and variety, opening new vistas. The family house in Milan in which Moorea had a share had a beautiful tower outside the huge picture-window of the apartment Moorea's mother had made for herself at the top.

Cristina's half-brother Camillo, much younger than she, was the current and last Marchese Casati. He was Moorea's half-uncle, son of the old Marchese and his second wife, daughter of an American senator from the South. Camillo was brought up without discipline and without any work ethic, either for service to his country or to himself. He was a classic case of a person who has a great deal of money but who does not know how to use it. Yet he was agreeable, kind and intelligent. In Rome he had the most comprehensive and valuable collection ever assembled of birds which land in Italy. He had shot or collected them himself, including those which landed on an island which he owned, and knew his subject well. His first wife, Lydia, was a beautiful cabaret singer. When he tired of her he bought a divorce from the Vatican, which declared his marriage void on the grounds that he never genuinely intended to marry her. My question, 'What does that make the daughter of the marriage?' was not popular. Camillo then married a lovely girl, Anna, the wife of a doctor, the Vatican obliging with another expensive divorce.

I found Anna exceedingly attractive and flirtatious. I played a lot of table-tennis with her. My relations with Camillo and Anna were friendly but a shade dull. I think Camillo thought that, as I was a Labour MP, I must be very respectable and would find even a night-club cabaret shocking. In turn I thought him conventional, not liable to throw his hat in the air. He never asked us to any of the wild parties which, after his death, it emerged he was fond of giving. He progressed through them to more exotic entertainment. He would get his wife to pick up students and young men on the beach, not difficult for her, and bring them back to their apartment in Rome, where he would watch and photograph them making love. Anna, it seemed, warned him of the danger that she might fall in love with one of them. This happened. Instead of photographing Anna and the student she had fallen in love with during the next session of love-making, Camillo shot the student dead, then shot Anna whom he truly loved, and finally himself.

There was much good in Camillo. It was a pitiable end to a great family, brought about by an enquiring mind having no sense of purpose and no desire for one.

# CHAPTER XI

———— ◑◐ ————

# TV and Communists
# in the Unions

IN THE SUMMER OF 1955 Grace Wyndham Goldie asked me to
see her. ITV was to be launched shortly. The BBC was worried
that most of its captive audience would disappear if BBC programmes were not improved. *Panorama* was to be elevated from
the trivial to the substantial, though remaining simple enough
to hold the interest of a large audience. Richard Dimbleby was
to be the static anchor man. Would I be his partner, the roving
reporter often abroad? From what she had seen of me election-
eering at Grantham in the Ed Murrow CBS film, Grace was
certain I would come out well on the TV screen.

I was more doubtful. A film test was arranged on a piece of
wasteland at Shepherd's Bush. Brian Connell and I were tested
for different roles. I had to ask him questions about Germany.
When the rushes were shown, I was horrified. I looked and
sounded like a stuffed pig and recoiled from this revelation of
myself as someone I should hate to see or hear. Why should an
audience feel differently?

I said no to television. Grace, because it was too late to get
someone else, pleaded with me. *Panorama* in its new form was
due to start on 18 September 1955; the tickets for Malta had
been arranged. Wouldn't I just try it? If the result was too awful,
they would scrap it and put in a discussion or some film.
Fearfully, I agreed.

I was my own producer, director, arranger. There was a
cameraman and a sound recordist with his box of tricks. The
camera, a Mitchell 35″, was heavy. I helped hump the camera
and other equipment around, as well as organizing the interviews
with notables and ordinary people, the locations and background film of the surroundings. I was entitled to first-class
travel but, save once when I had an overnight flight with filming

to begin in the morning, never claimed it, thinking it a waste of public money. The programmes I made for *Panorama* were highly cost effective. The three of us in our team mucked in merrily together, except that the other two were usually prejudiced against foreign food.

No one at the BBC told me what to do when I got to Malta. There was talk of a new status for the island and there was an evenly balanced contest between Dom Mintoff, the Labour Prime Minister, and his Nationalist Party opponent, Borg Olivier. At that stage a possible development was for Malta to have MPs at Westminster, as the French had contrived for some of their outlying territories not big enough for complete independence. If we had done this, as I urged, for Malta, Gibraltar, the Seychelles and the smaller West Indian islands, much trouble would have been avoided, including the clash with the United States over Grenada.

Ignorant of television I decided on a direct approach to attract viewers' attention. I stood on a promontory with the sea behind me. 'To my right,' I yelled, 'are Africa and Egypt. On my left are Sicily and Italy. In front of me is Cyprus. Behind me is Gibraltar. That is why for centuries Malta has been of strategic importance to anyone who wants to control the Mediterranean.' It was not polished but I had to start somehow. At one time I believe the BBC showed my Malta programme to recruits to television as an example of how much TV reporting had advanced since I began.

I wrapped up Malta in an item lasting about twenty minutes. It was considered a success. Previously the BBC had thought it impossible to deal seriously with a country or important subject in under half to three-quarters of an hour. Accustomed as a journalist and politician to getting all the main points into a short space, I developed new techniques for television reports which were later much copied. I introduced, too, a different type of questioning to the hitherto deferential 'Yes, Sir/No, Sir' approach to the important by the BBC interviewer. None of the people I interviewed seemed to me more awesome than many I had been used to dealing with on level terms for eleven years. I asked firm questions, central to the issues, and would not let the interviewee dodge them, which was a surprise to some in Britain who expected exaggerated respect from the BBC, as did foreign potentates who had never seen television.

My interviewing set a new style, making the viewer feel that the interviewees were fallible like the rest of us. But I was never rude, nor did I interrupt the answers. I am not responsible for the modern trend by which reasonable questioning becomes hostile and browbeating. I was determined that everyone's case should be put properly. When someone significant to the story in Cyprus reneged on an interview I pointed to the seat where he would have sat, asked the questions I would have asked him and gave the answers I thought he would have given, possibly better than he would have. It caused a mild stir.

I was the first person to interview King Hussein for television. He was twenty and had been on the throne of Jordan for three years. His kingdom was shaky and I wrote that he would be lucky to last another three years. He is still there nearly thirty years later, surviving assassination attempts and the efforts of Palestinians, Nasser, the Syrians and others ill-disposed to him to destroy him. I should have known better. His bravery was joined to commonsense and instinctive political judgement.

Shortly after I met him he more or less broke off the alliance with Britain and threw out General Glubb, Commander of the famous Arab Legion. I was stoned entering Jordan from Israel and supposed something was up, but the British Ambassador in Amman told me my queasiness was due to my inexperience of the Middle East and that Britain's and Glubb's influence were rock solid – so much for the man on the spot. King Hussein realized that Britain was a failing power in the Middle East and that to be associated closely with us, fond of Israel as we were, would not be protection but suicide. His grandfather, King Abdullah, was murdered because he tried to get peace with Israel and peace was not a marketable commodity among nationalist Arabs and frenzied Palestinians, of whom he had acquired more than he wanted.

His hunch was vindicated when the pro-British King Faisal of Iraq and most of his government, who looked very happy in their reliance on the British connection when I interviewed them for television on well-watered lawns, were murdered in July 1958. Nasser was partly behind that. I met Nasser several times before and after Suez, usually but not always for television. When I was going back and forth between Egypt and Israel I nearly managed to arrange a secret meeting between Ben Gurion and Nasser. Ben Gurion, as I told Nasser, was keen, and Nasser was tempted. It was left to his successor, Sadat, however, bravely to establish a rapport with, improbably, the fiercely nationalist Begin.

Nasser was agreeable and sincere. He lived simply and tried to improve life for the fellahîn who had suffered under corrupt governments. He wanted to be friendly to Britain and told me his version of how the break came. It began with a stop-over visit to Cairo by Anthony Eden, still Foreign Secretary, on his way to a meeting of the South-East Asia Treaty Organization. Nasser received a message that Eden would like him to call at six in the evening at the British Embassy. Nasser thought this peculiar, assuming it would have been more polite for Eden to call on him as the head of Egypt's government. He swallowed the affront, however, and went to see Eden at the British Embassy. He was put in a drawing-room to wait for him.

Eden entered and called him Colonel Nasser, which he hated. He walked up and down in front of the seated Nasser and lectured him on British policy in the Middle East and where Egypt fitted into it. He invited no comment or discussion, and when his near-monologue was over looked at his watch: 'I am afraid I must go now. I have to change for dinner. I thought you would like to know what our policy is. It's been very nice meeting you, Colonel Nasser.'

Nasser said to me, 'I know I'm not very important and Egypt is not very important, but I was hurt. The Russians sent me copies of secret correspondence with Washington. When I asked why, they said it was because Egypt is a very important country. I know it is only flattery, but at least they take the trouble to pretend to treat us as equals.'

Then came Nasser's request for arms from the West. He told me he had to get more arms or his own Army officers would have staged a coup against him. He asked the British, who said they were satisfied that the balance of arms between Israel and the Arab countries was about right: to give Egypt more would be unfair to Israel. He asked the Americans, who said, 'You know what the British have said and we agree.' He went to the Russians, who arranged for him to be supplied by Czechoslovakia.

America and Britain made a hullabaloo. To punish Nasser for dealing with Moscow, the clumsy Foster Dulles withdrew United States' aid for the Aswan Dam, the basis for Nasser's great plan for the revival of Egyptian agriculture. Britain did the same. 'They went back on their word. They were trying to destroy me. I thought to myself,' Nasser said, 'What is the thing I can do which will most annoy them? I came up with the answer – nationalize the Suez Canal.'

My TV appearances catapulted me into fame. *Panorama* was the best and most popular current affairs programme on BBC or ITV. We had an audience of between 9 and 14 million. When I walked in the street or went into any public place I was recognized and my autograph sought. It was a pleasant feeling, not diluted by the meretriciousness of my prominence. My erstwhile companions in Parliament were amazed. Michael Stewart, at the end of a speech I made at a Fabian conference, said, 'Woodrow will now return to being a television star, while I return to the humble obscurity of the House of Commons.' Edna Healey was overheard by someone talking to me on the telephone. 'Do you actually *know* him?' the wife of Labour's future Chancellor of the Exchequer was asked. She said her prestige soared. All jolly stuff and not usually dangerous, though it was once in Algiers.

The French settlers were angrily suspicious of their government's promise that Algiers would stay part of France and furious at the failure to end the murders and bombings by Algerian nationalists. They were raging, too, at the US Government, which was giving large donations to the Algerian trade unions. A great rally to pacify the settlers had been arranged, to be addressed by the French Prime Minister. I thought Algeria would make a good item for *Panorama*.

On the day of the rally there was a funeral procession for the burial of a French farmer shot by an Arab terrorist. The cameraman, the sound recordist and I went to film the scene as background to the story. As the huge procession of white settlers marched by, some saw our camera and were inflamed. The shouts and threatening gestures mounted. The procession halted. Large groups left it and moved towards us. In a moment we were surrounded by a sea of hatred. Burly farmers smashed the camera and destroyed the film. They hurled us to the ground, kicking and pummelling us with murder in their eyes and animal noises in their throats. In my schoolboy French I shouted, '*Nous sommes Anglais. Nous sommes BBC. Nous sommes amis!*' That enraged them the more. I was grabbed by the throat and my head banged on the ground. I thought that this must be what a Negro felt when being lynched in the Deep South, uselessly protesting his innocence to men who will not listen, do not care, possessed by a mad determination to kill. We were done for. Then two men in civilian clothes waving revolvers forced their way through. Menacingly pointing their guns, they ordered the mob away. Like snarling lions reluctantly relinquishing their prey, the crowd gradually dropped back. Our rescuers, who had had a rough time, were special police and I vowed never to think ill of their kind in future.

Next morning a deputation headed by the French Mayor of Algiers, accompanied by some of the French settlers who had nearly killed us, called at our hotel. Wild beasts had been transformed overnight into smiling, friendly humans, looking as though they would never harm anyone. 'You see, we thought you were Americans.' Relieved to be alive, I said I quite understood. But I did not. The incident got publicity in England. The producer of *Panorama* wanted me to explain to the viewers that the smashed camera and lost film had prevented the item being as complete as I should have liked. I said No. Audiences are bored by programme makers' problems. They always demand effortless miracles.

The overseas trips were amusing. In Ghana, still the cheerful prosperous Gold Coast, the sinister but companionable crypto-Communist, Geoffrey Bing, was Prime Minister Nkrumah's Constitutional Adviser. He was devising laws on the best British precedents to enable Nkrumah to put his opponents in gaol as soon as the British left. This, with Geoffrey as his Attorney-General, Nkrumah promptly did, growing madder all the time and proclaiming himself divine. One of the early victims was a lawyer, Joe Appiah, a bearded Othello whom I admired when I watched him eloquently captivating a large meeting. Joe was Stafford Cripps's son-in-law, happily married to his daughter Peggy, but that did not deter Nkrumah from imprisoning him, aided by Geoffrey with his Chinese eyes and grin.

Knowing that Nkrumah would extinguish democracy, I interviewed the Opposition leaders. When Nkrumah heard of this he was furious. He cancelled my promised interview with him. Geoffrey persuaded him that, whatever he might be about to do in Ghana, it remained customary in Britain to hear both sides of the case. The interview in the lovely old castle overlooking the sea was in chill contrast to the sun outside. When the programme was shown in England, Nkrumah began libel proceedings against me and the BBC, but his English lawyers must have told him he would not win and we heard nothing more. Poor Gold Coast, rich (for Africa) and free under the law with the British in charge, reduced to poverty and the arbitrary tyranny of the gun and the gaoler by Nkrumah and his successors.

Another African country where the old order has been destroyed was Liberia. Before going I was asked by the Liberian Embassy in London to take full evening dress and decorations. I was to attend the annual ball celebrating the setting up of the state in 1847 by freed American slaves. The dances were the dances of the plantation-owners at the time of the slaves' departure. Their descendants gracefully danced the stately waltz, minuet, the gavotte, the men's tail-coats swirling, their chests covered in decorations, and many of their partners wearing pretty sashes of various orders. It may have been comical but it was touching. The slaves were proudly the equals of their masters. Queen Victoria, first head of state to recognize the sovereignty of Liberia, would have enjoyed the scene.

The aristocracy were those who claimed descent from the slaves and lived mainly on the coast. The lower classes were those whose ancestors had always been free. William Tubman was the President who governed firmly but not oppressively, permitting mild corruption in which he shared but not outrageously so. He allowed latitude of choice to his easy-going people, especially in religion. Churches of esoteric sects were everywhere: Swedenborgians, Jehovah's Witnesses, Seventh Day Adventists, Rosicrucians, as well as more conventional churches. When I saw President Tubman at his house in the interior I asked him why he permitted such a copious variety of religions, the creeds of some of which seemed likely to unsettle simple people. He was amused: 'We can't afford a proper police force to keep the people in order. The ministers of the churches do it for us. Everyone loves going to church and choosing which one to go to. When the ministers tell them to behave, they do so.' A practical answer.

The shipowners in Britain were alarmed at the rapid growth of the Liberian flag-of-convenience fleet, attracting shipowners world-wide by the ease and cheapness of registration, to the detriment of British merchant shipping. They told me that President Tubman would be embarrassed if I put it to him that he could entice shipowners to fly the Liberian flag only because the standards of seaworthiness and living conditions were far below those of Britain. 'Naturally,' he said, smiling and undisturbed. 'No one would register with us if we insisted on the same expensive standards as you. That's the whole idea.'

President Tubman ruled for twenty-seven years and died in 1971. I am glad he did not live to see his old friends and the mild ruling class murdered by the sergeants in 1980, and the brutal People's Redemption Council established in their place.

I became *persona non grata* in Bahrain as well as Ghana. The *de facto* Prime Minister, Sir Charles Belgrave, had got the job, which he did excellently for thirty-one years, by answering an advertisement placed in the old *Morning Post* by the Amir, as good as most other ways of securing a prime minister. Neither Sir Charles nor the Amir thought democracy suitable for Bahrain, even at the municipal level of drains and gutters. There had recently been some disturbances, promoted by a few who demurred at the total blackout of expression. Sir Charles was reluctant to let me in with my television team, and was horrified when he learned I was down in the town asking people's opinions, particularly about the illicit signs proclaiming 'Sir Charles Belgrave must go', displayed all over the island. A detachment of the local Army was dispatched to make me desist. Fortunately we were tipped off, rapidly changed location, and got all the interviews I wanted before the soldiers arrived.

Sir Charles, whom I had already interviewed, courteously but firmly suggested I should pack up and leave on the next aeroplane. He was anxious, no doubt, to prepare to put down the revolution which would ensue when my little film was shown in England. But none came, though Sir Charles did go the following year. My filming had its repercussions soon after when my visa for a television tour of Saudi Arabia was cancelled at the instance of the King, who had heard about my adventures in Bahrain.

Bahrain was a pretty and civilized place. Other Gulf States, just becoming oil-rich, were dreadful to look at: nasty deserts made worse with concrete and shacks, and huge American cars parked alongside. Saudi Arabia, which I visited twice in the 1970s, is much the same, save that more of the desert is covered with concrete, new office blocks and brash Americanized hotels. Understandably the rich from these parts prefer to spend more time abroad than in their own hideous, religion-tormented countries. When I was in Kuwait nearly thirty years ago I asked what they lived on in barren Abu Dhabi where oil had not yet been developed. 'Oh, some on whisky and the ruler's son on methylated spirits.' They had my sympathy. In Abu Dhabi's new prosperity the puritan Muslims have prohibited even that consolation.

My best friend in the Middle East was Emile Bustani, a Lebanese Maronite Christian. He had built up a huge contracting business, employing only Arabs, of whom many were Palestinian. (I use the term Arab as it is generally understood: most outside Arabia who are described as Arabs are of other origins, though speaking Arabic.) Emile Bustani proved that Arabs could be as good at business as Jews or Westerners. He bubbled with energy and intelligence, his big, round face at the top of his short, plump, fast-moving body always smiling; he was ready to make a joke and quick to respond. He knew all the kings and leaders from Damascus to Riyadh. When anyone hesitated to be interviewed by me, he arranged it. Cars, aeroplanes, hotels, were always at hand. However important the business he might be working on, he would drop it if I needed help quickly.

Emile was a true friend. He never tried to influence me with Arab propaganda against Israel, relying on me to be fair between the two. He was not hostile to Israel and wanted peace with her, which made him suspect occasionally among Arab leaders though he was a close friend of Nasser. Emile was immersed in politics, a Lebanese MP, and incorruptible. If he had not been killed when he impetuously ordered his pilot to fly into a storm off Beirut in March 1963 and the aeroplane crashed into the sea, he would have become President of Lebanon. Few would have been more likely to reconcile the apparently irreconcilable. His charm, honesty, good nature and gift for friendship made him an irresistible negotiator. For years I looked forward to seeing his face crinkled with laughter coming towards me across an airfield and to hearing his enthusiastic voice launching into his latest political solution. He was one of those for whom I wept when he died. I wish I could see him again, sitting in a chair opposite me playing with his worry beads. He had a happy life, a delightful, elegant wife, a wine-cellar of which any Frenchman would have been proud. He was so pleased with it that he constructed an anteroom bar adjoining it for quicker access to the temperature-controlled racks.

In June 1957 I went to South Africa. As a playground for middle-class whites it was superb: sun and scenery, swimming-pools and tennis, attractive girls, plentiful servants, excellent home-grown wine, large houses and gardens. Perfect, except that I have never been able to feel superior or averse to people because they are of a different race or colour. Towards stupid or nasty people, yes, but they can be of any colour.

You cannot be happy as a white in South Africa unless you are convinced you belong to a master race and that the others are subhumans who ought to be content to serve you. I know that when the Boers and the British developed South Africa there were not many blacks, and that the blacks there have a higher standard of living than in neighbouring African countries. But as a Cypriot in the crowd said when I asked him on my television programme whether he was not afraid of his standard of living falling if the British left, 'The spirit of freedom has nothing to do with the standard of living.'

I found the Africans pleasing and their treatment worse than that of slaves in Ancient Athens or Rome, who had some access to the best education and could rise to the highest positions. In Africa I learned that education for the blacks was limited to the rudimentary, and that the only possibility of serious education was in illegal schools. So I filmed the illegal schools. I interviewed black leaders. I filmed Soweto. But the white apartheid arguments were fairly shown.

The Prime Minister, Strijdom, told me he would not be interviewed with Opposition or black leaders, and so I interviewed him alone in the house Cecil Rhodes had lived in. I did not suppose that he meant the programme was to exclude any coloured speakers, but that is just what he did mean. My piece took the whole of a *Panorama* programme. It was the first time that millions in Britain got a glimpse of what life was really like in South Africa: paradise under a live volcano. The South African Government – the Prime Minister in particular being incensed by appearing in the same programme as blacks – officially protested to the British Government and the BBC. I was pleased about that; it meant they had been hit where it hurt.

I was pleased, too, about another programme. It was a discussion with Arthur Miller who had a new play in London. I was not much interested in his views but wanted to meet his wife, Marilyn Monroe. I did. She was as gorgeous as they say she was, with the charm of an innocent child.

Television was exciting but exhausting. For weeks at a stretch I would sum up to the camera in the studio at the end of my item on Monday and then catch an aeroplane to a distant part where I was to make my film for the following week. In conjunction with the cutting editor I chose the silent film to be used, and wrote and delivered the commentary to fit. The interviews had to be carefully edited and I would not let any of the items be shaped without my concurrence: they had my name on them. The process took most of the week-end and Mondays. The bits said straight to the camera had to be rehearsed and learned. Neither Richard Dimbleby nor I would read from a teleprompter, which we thought unprofessional and unnatural. You will see what I mean if you watch the newsreaders' eyes moving from side to side as they read the words from a teleprompter while pretending not to.

Richard was brilliant at appearing natural. He had sets of little cards which he memorized. He was unflappable: a boom could fall on his head without ruffling his precise performance

248

or his control of the programme. He rarely devised an item of his own, being thought not quite up to it and more valuable as a calm presenter and link man. This hurt him. He was ecstatic when he was able to tell me one Monday that he had his very own item that night. It was an enquiry into why audiences no longer stood when 'God Save the Queen' was played at the end of the day's showings at a cinema, a subject he took very seriously.

I became fond of Richard Dimbleby, a simple, generous man considerate to everyone and helpful to newcomers. Not an intellectual, he had an instinctive feel of what appealed to ordinary people. Mrs Wyndham Goldie's determination to have clear and fair expositions of current affairs, and Richard's comforting mantle suggesting that anyone with commonsense would enjoy and understand them, were the major reasons for *Panorama*'s vast audiences. It has shrunk to a vestige of its former self, because left-wing, often very left-wing, producers, presenters, directors, reporters and editors and researchers were allowed to take over and slant it in line with their political bias.

Grace Wyndham Goldie should have been made Director-General of the BBC. She would have been another Reith, gentler and more tolerant but firm on quality and impartiality. She was the last senior official of the BBC who cared deeply about impartiality and insisted on having it. No one was allowed to slant, right, left or liberal, in the programmes she controlled, though they could have what politics they liked provided they did not show. She had a talent for developing the promising – Michael Peacock, Alasdair Milne, Donald Baverstock, Chris Chataway, Aidan Crawley, Christopher Mayhew, John Freeman, Robert Kee; and for devising new programmes which were not trash yet had a wide popular appeal. She could have run the BBC far better than any of Reith's successors, and would have left a modern ethos behind her. The highest she reached was Head of Talks and Current Affairs TV. The prejudice against women was, and is, nearly insurmountable.

In April 1956 Bill Carron, a member of the AEU Executive whom I knew well, told me an alarming story. The Communists were about to take over the million-strong engineers' union through the apathy of the members, who did not bother to vote at branch meetings, and aided by Communist and far Left officials who falsified the votes. In the Division No. 5 (Sheffield and East Midlands) election for the Executive in 1953, Bill at first appeared to have lost to his Communist opponent. It was then discovered that, in the Communist-influenced branches, many of the signatures on the register and ballot-papers were forged and the members concerned were not present at their branches on voting night. When the false votes were disqualified Bill just scraped in.

Bill was now standing for the Presidency, which entailed another election in Division No. 5. There was also an election for General Secretary. The Communists already had two out of seven on the Executive, and a third, a fellow-traveller, voting with them. They were confident of winning all three of the posts now up for election, through manipulation of the votes by local officials and the lack of interest among members in getting to their branches to vote. This would give them a majority. The threat to the economy and to the Labour Party of a huge AEU block vote supporting extremist policies at Labour conferences, was obvious. What, Bill asked, was I going to do about it?

I discussed it with Grace Wyndham Goldie. The BBC could not take sides but it had a duty to inform and to uphold democracy. Grace was game if the Director-General, Sir Ian Jacob, agreed. I went to see that sensible man. I said the theme would be democracy. AEU members had the right to have Communists or Fascists controlling their union if that was what they wished, but they should do it consciously, not from being unaware that their failure to vote would bring that about. Sir Ian gave me the go-ahead. None of his successors would have. They would have been too scared of the left-wing producers whom they allowed to infiltrate the BBC.

I filmed branch meetings deserted by nearly all but the dedicated extremists. The ordinary members were driven away by the calculated tedium of the meetings, where long and unimportant correspondence was read, fanciful resolutions debated, and the important business left to the end. I interviewed AEU factory workers and learned that most did not know the politics of the candidates or even that there were to be elections. They were surprised to hear that their union was about to fall to the Communists unless they acted.

'Tonight I'm going to do something that I've never done before on television,' I began my broadcast on 14 May 1956. 'I'm going to talk to just one group of the community only – the members of the Amalgamated Engineering Union, or the AEU for short, and I'm going to ask you to take part in your own elections, the elections which decide who should be the full-time officials who run your union. I'm going to do that because your union is not only the second largest, with nearly one million members, it is almost perhaps the most important in the entire country. You're the backbone of the British engineering industry, you're at the heart of the British export trade, and at this very moment your union is on the verge of coming under the control of the Communists. If it does, your union will become more than just an organization which deals with wage disputes and conditions of work. It will become an instrument of the Communist Party. This is a democratic country and you've the right to vote in as many Communist officials as you like. But do you really want to have your union run by the Communists?'

At the end of the programme I said, 'And that, AEU members, is the story of how the affairs of your great union are on the verge of becoming controlled by a tiny minority . . . it is just as important to vote in these elections as it is to vote in a parliamentary election . . . if the Communists get one more seat, then they will have complete control of the Executive Council . . . and if that should happen, then the AEU will be the largest and most important union in the whole of the free world to come under Communist control. It's your decision.'

My broadcast lasted twenty minutes and shook the union world. The voting went up by 40 per cent. It was still a turn-out of less than 11 per cent, but it was enough to defeat the Communist candidates for all three posts. The AEU was saved. There were long struggles ahead, in which I took a considerable part, before the AEU (now the AUEW) reformed its voting system to give everyone a secret home postal vote. If that had been done earlier, Hugh Scanlon would not have been elected the union's President in 1967. There was considerable manipulation of votes at branch meetings, particularly in the Manchester area. Scanlon, during most of his ten-year Presidency, was very Left indeed, undermining Wilson's feeble Labour governments, blocking Labour's proposed union reform of 1969 and doing immense damage to the country.

But the Communists never got complete control of the AUEW and are now unlikely to, because members no longer have to go to boring branch meetings but can vote from their own armchairs. I let them know in my weekly column in the *News of the World* (previously in my column in the *Daily Mirror* and the *Sunday Mirror*) which are the candidates to support if they do not want left-wing extremists to take over. As important elections approach, anxious AUEW members write to remind me that I have not yet published my list of names – hurry up, please. So do other union members, if they are in one of the exceptional unions which give individual members proper facilities to vote.

After my AEU triumph I had a letter from Mr Jock Byrne in Scotland, the last full-time non-Communist official left in the ETU. Would I meet him secretly in Glasgow? We met in an hotel. Jock brought with him masses of confidential documents and Executive Council minutes detailing how branches were recorded as voting in union elections. He was risking his job but he had decided to trust me. The documents proved beyond doubt that since the war the Communists had controlled the ETU by falsifying election returns. Branches with local Communist officials running the elections added or deducted any figures needed to get a Communist candidate elected.

Jock himself, to the surprise of the Communists, and despite their manipulations, had come top in the June 1948 election for Assistant General Secretary, even of a rigged poll, out of three candidates. He was shown as having 2500 votes more than the Communist candidate, Haxell, but as having missed getting an overall majority by 229 votes out of some 55,000, itself an unbelievable total for 216,000 members in union elections conducted through branches. Of course, Jock had really won.

ETU rules required a run-off between the two top candidates and it was held in September. The alarmed Communists made a thorough job of it this time. Blackpool recorded 5 votes for Byrne and 695 for Haxell, the Communist, yet only 559 members at Blackpool were up to date with their union dues and entitled to vote. In the first ballot in June the Leyland ETU branch had voted 3 for Byrne and 28 for the Communist Haxell. In the run-off ballot Byrne got 7 and Haxell 146. The Dorking branch had 206 members entitled to vote. In the second ballot Byrne was accorded 20 and Haxell 189, making a total of votes cast in excess of the electorate. So it had gone on in thirty-two Communist-controlled branches which between them, in connivance with the Communist-controlled head office, rigged their ballots sufficiently to give an additional 8000 votes on paper to Haxell. Eleven of those thirty-two branches recorded votes in excess of their membership. Haxell was declared the winner by nearly 5000 votes.

Jock, alone against the vilification of the Communist-led Left, bravely went on trying. In March 1955 he stood for the General Secretaryship, with his opponent again Haxell, the Communist. Jock was cheated out of his win. He came back to fight again for the now vacant Assistant General Secretary post in September 1955 against another Communist opponent, McLennan. In the March election for the General Secretaryship Dewsbury had voted 43 for Byrne and 227 for the Communist. Now it was 13 for Byrne and 345 for the Communist. Bradford increased the Communist vote from 95 to 424; in London Station Engineers No. 11 the Communist vote went up from 277 to 622. Once more Jock Byrne was swindled out of his victory.

For months I studied the documents Jock had given me, had more meetings, asked innumerable questions. I approached Les Cannon, then an ETU education officer running the ETU school at Esher. I had been told that, though a Communist, he was not entirely lost to honesty. He refused to speak to me.

I prepared a dossier several thousand words long, with tables detailing how the ETU branches had cooked the votes in important elections for officers of the union. I sent it to the General Council of the TUC. I saw Sir Vincent Tewson, its General Secretary. He brushed me off. I saw George Woodcock, the supercilious and weak Assistant General Secretary of the TUC, whose character was enfeebled by his being under the influence of Dick Crossman who was a Fellow at New College

253

when George Woodcock won a scholarship there in the thirties. He too brushed me off. I saw Vic Feather, the Assistant Secretary of the TUC. He was horrified. He secretly encouraged me to continue my campaign; secretly because the officials senior to him were cowards, who wanted to avoid the agony of declaring themselves against evil for fear they would get hurt in the ensuing fracas.

Stalwart, sturdy Vic, who believed in democracy for union members and opposed with all his heart its corruption by Communists and the far Left, suggested I should send my dossier to all the members of the General Council individually. I expected them to rise in wrath against the crooked Communist President, General Secretary, Assistant General Secretary and others fraudulently running the ETU. They shrank away with excuses. The horror of most of them was at me, washing their dirty linen in public, muddying the internal affairs of unions, disturbing their amiable relations with the Communist rulers of the ETU, who were popular with the bulk of the TUC leaders. The General Council had the power to investigate my evidence and require the ETU to leave the TUC unless electoral corruption were ended. That they chose not to was an early sign of the new malaise infecting the leaders of the unions and the Labour Party: the courage to fight the Communists and militant Left was fading. The staunch in the General Council were increasingly outnumbered.

I plugged on. I wrote a series of articles in *Illustrated* in September 1956 about the threat to the unions, and consequently to the Labour Party, whose policies were largely determined by their block votes, of infiltration by the Communists and their allies. In December 1956 I turned the articles into a booklet, *The Peril in Our Midst*. It was well reviewed and widely circulated and caused interest where I hoped it would.

Les Cannon rang. Disenchantment with the Communist Party, accumulating for some time in his head, had turned to active enmity when the Russian tanks suppressed the government set up by the ordinary people of Hungary. He said he was now on my side. He could help me with inside knowledge of how the Communist conspiracy worked, as he had been one of the principal conspirators. I could help him in his fight to destroy the Communists in the ETU. Frank Chapple stayed officially in the Communist Party a little longer, waiting to secure the nominations he needed for an ETU Executive election. I did not meet him until a year after I had started working with Les. Frank was suspicious of my motives, supposing that my concern for democracy must be a cover for a capitalist plot to destroy the unions. It was some time before the Marxist nonsense he had imbibed in his brain was purged out of it.

In late 1957 I got permission from Ian Jacob to do another *Panorama* programme about union democracy, this time in the ETU. Helped by my new friends, I organized a devastating exposure of how the Communists had just defrauded Les Cannon, now their ex-colleague and chief enemy, of his victory in an election for a seat on the Executive. It was difficult to persuade ETU members to come out in the open. It was against the rules for members to say anything about union affairs to an outsider: to speak to the media was a major crime. Any member who did so was likely to be, and often was, expelled, losing his union card as a result. The least punishments were suspension and heavy fines. The rules were turned against any opponent of the Communists. The Communists themselves broke the rules as they pleased: the power to prosecute was theirs alone. For those with genuine complaints but no alternative trade, it was a reign of terror to be defied only by the very brave.

I do not like gimmicks on TV, but in my *Panorama* item on 9 December 1957 I had no alternative but to talk to a number of witnesses from the ETU, with their faces hidden from the cameras. The fear in their voices made the more convincing their description of how they had watched Communist officials falsifying the election returns and disqualifying votes for Les Cannon. I did not dare put on Cannon himself: he would have been expelled and unable to carry on the fight. I invited the ETU Communist leaders Foulkes and Haxell to come to answer the charges. They refused. My piece on the ETU was a national sensation. The following Monday Foulkes and Haxell were again asked to appear on *Panorama*. Foulkes said he would if he were allowed to make a twenty-minute statement and be asked no questions. In those days the BBC was not willing to be intimidated by Communists or the extreme Left. Richard

Dimbleby on *Panorama* robustly commented: 'The BBC couldn't accept these conditions so he is not here tonight.'

I followed Richard by dealing with some of the facts in the programme I had showed the previous Monday which were contested by the ETU executive. More witnesses demonstrated how spurious votes for the Communists were included and those for Les Cannon improperly disqualified. It was clear to everyone that Cannon had really won but would be barred from taking his seat on the Executive. I pointed out that the rules allowed for a fresh election in the case of dispute and suggested that this was the fair and honourable course. Some hope with the Communists in command!

In January 1958 I wrote a long article in the *New Statesman*, with masses of detailed statistics supplied by Jock Byrne and Les Cannon, updating the material in the TV programme and what I had been writing for a year and a half in various journals. I wanted impeccable left-wing sponsorship for my attack on the Communists, disarming those who might think I was engaged in some Labour right-wing witch hunt. My article in the *New Statesman* became the source material in the campaign to get rid of the Communists in the ETU. The evidence was irrefutable, though the ETU Executive vainly tried to refute it in a feeble pamphlet. Foulkes, Haxell and the whole corrupt Communist lot were on the run. And there was a new dimension. It was becoming increasingly obvious that the fraudulent take-over of the ETU was not the work of a few wayward Communists acting on their own initiative, as the Communist Party was later to pretend. It was a conspiracy organized from the headquarters of the Communist Party, as Mr Justice Winn confirmed and enunciated in his High Court judgement in 1961.

Just before my *New Statesman* article appeared I was in trouble with my local Labour Party, Holborn and St Pancras South. I was out of Parliament and longing to get back. I thought my activities were strengthening the Labour Party by weakening Communist influence in it. The members of the management committee of the Holborn and St Pancras South Labour Party thought otherwise, as the resolution before it on the 16 January 1958 shows:

Emergency Resolution held over from last meeting to give Mr.
Woodrow Wyatt the opportunity of being present.

Holborn and St. Pancras South Labour Party disassociates
itself from the anti-working class activities of one of its
members, Mr. Woodrow Wyatt, who has sought to villify
[sic] and bring into disrepute the Electrical Trades Union
by an unscrupulous use of Television.

Mr. Wyatt has previously sold himself to press and radio
for the purpose of witch-hunting good trade unionists in
Briggs Motor Bodies at a time when those workers were
engaged in a fight with the Ford Motor Company against
unemployment and short-time working.

For this activity Mr. Wyatt has been well-praised by the
capitalists but we, the members of his own Party, condemn
him for it. We ask the N.E.C. to remove Mr. Wyatt's
name from the list of Prospective Parliamentary Labour
Candidates.

Note: This resolution has now been endorsed by Ward 6
and stands in their name.

The resolution was carried by a large majority. It was sent
to the National Executive Committee of the Labour Party for
action and debated there. Harold Wilson sat silent, doubtless
hoping I would be removed from the list of candidates, as he
knew that, back in the Parliamentary Labour Party, I would
never vote for him to be Leader. Hugh, now Leader of the Party,
made the NEC throw the resolution out. But the fact that it had
arrived at the NEC at all was a clear sign that the old Labour
Party was beginning to disappear, taking on a hue I had not
anticipated when I joined it. It was also a sign that I had no
future in the Labour Party if Hugh were not Leader. If I had
known how short Hugh's life was to be, I might have accepted
the offer he made me in 1958 of one of the four life peerages
Harold Macmillan allotted him under his new life peerage
scheme. That would have given me a permanent base in Parliament but I thought, correctly, I could get back to the Commons
and, foolishly, that my political prospects were bright.

Les Cannon and I continued working together. When he came
to see me at Tower House he would tell me to play loud music, as
Communist engineers might have hidden microphones there. He
rebuked me when I laughed for not understanding the seriousness
of what we were up against. It made me feel daringly like an

257

undercover agent. Frank Chapple had overcome his distrust of my motives and I met him more often. Les and he were whole-time campaigners, late into the night, throughout the week-ends, touring and speaking at branches all over Britain, collecting support and evidence of Communist malpractices. They and their helpers badly needed secretarial help, living and travelling expenses, cars and the like. I gave them money from friends, well-wishers and myself to keep them going.

Though the facts were overwhelming, the Communists went on perverting the rules and blocking justice, precisely as they always do wherever they are in power in an institution or a country. In February 1959 Les and I decided to give Sir Vincent Tewson one more chance to stir the General Council of the TUC into action. We sent a long letter, written by Les in consultation with me, to Tewson and every member of the General Council, appealing to them to intervene: 'Having tried to use the constitutional machinery of the ETU and found it wrongfully blocked at every turn, the only course left to me seems to be to appeal to the General Council of the TUC, which I now do.'

Nothing happened. There was nothing left but to go to law. I asked Hartley Shawcross where to get the best legal advice. He recommended a young solicitor, Ben Hooberman of Lawford and Co., whose methodical work in a recent case had impressed him. Hartley suggested briefing Gerald Gardiner as Counsel. I was doubtful, knowing Gardiner, later Lord Chancellor, to be on the woolly Left in politics, but Hartley convinced me that he would be excellent at this kind of case. At our first meeting Gardiner seemed incredulous and half-hearted, which worried me, but when he satisfied himself of the facts he was shocked and magnificent.

The writ, citing examples of fraud against the Communists and demanding a rerun or Declaration of the true result of the December 1959 election for General Secretary, of which Haxell was falsely named the winner and the dogged Jock Byrne was once more falsely named the loser, was issued on the 10 May 1960. Jock Byrne and Frank Chapple were the plaintiffs. Frank had become an Executive Councillor in January 1958 and had been an immense help from within the citadel, enraging his old Communist colleagues. There was still much work and expense in collecting and preparing evidence. The ETU Executive repeatedly asked for more time to prepare their defence. It was June 1961, at the end of a forty-two day trial, before Mr Justice Winn was able to deliver his 40,000-word judgement in the High Court which overthrew Haxell. It was five years after Jock Byrne had asked me to meet him in Glasgow. Justice had been procured at great cost in effort and money and through the courage and determination of a few members of the ETU who would not be silenced.

The naïve, particularly Tory secretaries for employment, who have no real comprehension of what happens in unions, always assume it easy for ordinary members to get redress over electoral malpractices. It has been almost impossible. That is why the only certain way of ensuring fair union elections is through postal ballots sent direct to members' homes by an independent body and returned to that body for counting. That was the practice instituted in 1962 by Jock Byrne, declared General Secretary at last by the judge, Les Cannon, Frank Chapple and their supporters. Since then elections in the ETU (now the Electrical, Electronic, Telecommunications and Plumbing Trades Union) have been without a taint of corruption, and have returned commonsense moderate executives who represent their members accurately.

The General Council of the TUC was comically shamed into action by the trial. An ultimatum was sent to the Executive of the ETU demanding the resignation of Foulkes from the Presidency, a new election for the post and the barring from office for five years of all the ETU members found guilty by the judge of conspiracy to rig the ballot in the Byrne–Haxell General Secretary election of December 1959. The still Communist dominated ETU Executive rejected the ultimatum, and the ETU were solemnly and pointlessly expelled by the autumn TUC Congress, to be reinstated a few months later when the new, properly elected Executive took over. The belated action of the TUC General Council was a clear admission by the craven Vincent Tewson and George Woodcock, about to succeed him as General Secretary, and the cowardly majority on the General Council, that they had had ample powers to deal with corruption in the ETU all along.

Les Cannon died of cancer on 19 December 1970 at the age of fifty-one. He smoked too much, but the appalling strain of the years in which he fought the Communists must have shortened his life by several years. I visited him often in his last few months and we talked about the future we both knew he would never see. He had plans for increasing productivity as the best means of improving the standard of living for ordinary trade unionists, some of which he and Frank, now General Secretary of the ETU, had already implemented and others which were carried forward by Frank after Les died.

I knew Les craved some recognition from the State for his valiant battle for union democracy. I approached Ted Heath, an old friend, who was Prime Minister and asked him if he could arrange a knighthood for Les in the 1971 New Year's Honours and, if he could, to let Les know immediately because he would be dead before the New Year. Ted, whose heart is full of kindness, saw to it at once. The sadness of Les's last days was made less grievous by his pride that he had got a knighthood.

Jock Byrne was the hero who fought for decades against the corrupt Communists, the last man they could not break. He was staunch when Les and Frank were on the other side. He had nothing but what he earned as an official of the ETU. His standing out against his tough, unscrupulous masters was the greatest bravery I encountered during my forays in the murky world of Communist intrigue and manipulation in the unions. He was helped a little in his resistance by being in Scotland, remote from the centre, but he could not have survived without immense courage and through skilful use of his knowledge of the voluminous rule book which blocked Communist openings against him.

By the time Jock Byrne became General Secretary he was already ill from worry and overwork. His reward was the defeat of evil, but he did not enjoy it long. In 1965 he was too exhausted to carry on in his new post; in 1966 he resigned and in February 1970 he died. Understandably he had had initial reservations about Les and Frank, but he overcame them and appointed them his assistants on becoming General Secretary. The three made a good team in polishing off the remaining redoubts of corrupt Communist power.

Frank Chapple succeeded Jock as General Secretary and held the job for eighteen years. We became close friends. Frank shed his Marxism. The constraints of Communism had never suited his cheerful, ranging nature. Discovering from his own experience that Communism in practice did not remove poverty and injustice and added loss of freedom and corruption to other ills, he was already drifting away from the Communist Party before Hungary. His realism, commonsense and honesty, obliging him to speak out when others dissembled, gave him an exciting career in trade unionism. When I see his stocky figure and hear his uninhibited comments, my spirits get a lift as they did whenever I saw Jim Meadows, my agent at Aston, a similar character.

Perhaps the best thing I ever did was stopping the Communists capturing the engineers' union and fuelling, and in part initiating, the long campaign to prise the Communists and their allies out of the ETU. My success was acknowledged by the Communists and their associates, who poured hatred on me by the bucket and still do. Bert Ramelson, long the Industrial Organizer of the Communist Party, told me in 1973 when I was making a TV programme about Communists in the unions, 'We have never forgiven you and never will for what you did to us in the AEU and the ETU. We have never forgotten.' It was said with chilling amiability. It was horribly true. As I went round selection conferences looking for a route back to Parliament, the Communists had already been there, feeding poison into the minds of their friends and of the gullible who liked to be called 'good Socialists'. Frank Chapple warned me that King Street (then the headquarters of the Communist Party) would probably try to damage the business I started in Banbury in 1961. Certainly there was Communist influence behind the fomenting of strikes and go-slows to cripple the business, and the union rejection of the plan which might have saved it in 1982. Perhaps this was coincidental. I think it was not.

I never stopped campaigning for compulsory secret home ballots for union elections. I was determined to make a reluctant government include them in the Trade Union Act which became law in September 1984. I bombarded ministers, with help from Frank Chapple, argued for compulsory postal ballots continu-

261

ously in the *Sunday Mirror*, and intensified the campaign with articles in the *News of the World* and *The Times* in 1984. In the summer the Lords passed an amendment demanding postal ballots and I helped some of those responsible for the amendment. I did not get all I wanted, but the new Act states that secret home postal ballots should be the normal practice and outlaws branch meeting votes. Work-place ballots are allowed, but union members who feel these have been improperly conducted may complain to the Certification Officer for Trade Unions. If he finds reason in their complaints, he will undertake the long and costly legal processes to force the union concerned to hold a secret home postal ballot.

The 1984 Act makes it very much harder, almost impossible, to get away with rigging union elections. Tom King, Secretary for Employment, after the necessary amendments had been made to the Bill, generously told me, 'This is your victory and you should say so.' I dedicate it to Jock Byrne, Les Cannon and all those unionists who laboured long, resisting vilification, to win democratic rights for union members. If the new system of voting works as it should, most unions should by 1990 have more sensible executives than today, making industrial advance easier and modifying Labour's East European style policies.

# CHAPTER XII

——————— ❦❦ ———————

# A Rift with Gaitskell

THE YEAR 1959 started as though it would be an *annus mirabilis* for me. The summer was hot and dry. I had a little horse bought for £400 by the trainer David Hastings, a cousin of my wife, and heir, till David died, to her father's earldom. He was an eccentric trainer at Seven Barrows, Lambourn. He disliked most of his owners, who were usually allowed to ring him only at a fixed time on Sundays, when he was curt with them if they irritated him. Rich owners and valuable horses seldom came to his yard. Luckily he was friendly to me and we had happy dream-hours poring over pedigrees, tracing the lineage of the very cheap horses he bought for me back to the inevitable Derby and classic winners (the ancestry of all racehorses has the same illustrious beginnings), with my asking why my current horse should not be a throw-back and win fabulous races.

David had a sharp eye for potentially good horses, blemished in some way and going cheaply in the sale ring, but which he believed he could make sound. The horse I had in training in 1959 was a two-year-old. The big buyers thought him too small to race well. In 1959 few courses were watered and the going became very hard, which troubled many bigger horses but never Godiva's Pink Flower. (I had wanted to call him Vote Labour but the Jockey Club haughtily rejected the name as political propaganda, so I settled for a combination of his dam, Lady Godiva, and his sire, Pink Flower.) Godiva's Pink Flower would have run happily on tarmac and loved racing, which in racing terms means he was genuine or, in my terms, probably unintelligent. Clever horses are apt to resent being ridden to exhaustion and, after early promise, may refuse the extra ounce of effort demanded by the jockey in a cause which means a lot to its connections but is obscure to the horse.

Godiva's Pink Flower never jibbed. After he had won a race at Nottingham I said to David, 'Let's run him at the Royal Ascot meeting. I've never been there and it would be fun to go and see one's own horse running.' David was horrified. 'You can't run a £400 horse there. All the others will be worth £5000 or more. We'd be tailed off last and be a laughing-stock.'

He had another objection. Looking somewhat like Lord Emsworth and with a similar love of old clothes and reclusive habits, he hated having to put on a top-hat and morning-coat and being thrust among crowds of smart people, the sight of whom made him curl up. The thought that he might actually have to speak to some he knew was to him a nightmare. It was the only time I overruled him. Groaning, he entered it for the great two-year-old sprint race, the New Stakes. Godiva's Pink Flower had no chance, but I was more confident than David that he would not disgrace us; he was too sweet a horse to do that. I asked a bookmaker for a bet that he would come in fourth. The bookmaker refused me, saying that there was no demand for such bets. 'But I'm making a demand now.' Bored with arguing, the bookmaker gave in.

The race was on Thursday, Ladies' Day, which has the largest attendance of the four-day royal meeting. In the paddock I told our elderly jockey, Bill Elliott, that the only bet I had was on Godiva's Pink Flower to be fourth. 'I'll do my best for you, Sir,' he said gravely, like a college servant humouring a foolish undergraduate.

David and I climbed to the owners' and trainers' stand to watch. David, dispiritedly wearing an antique and crumpled morning-suit, was gloomy and apprehensive. To trail sixty yards in a five-furlong race would be humiliation. David was expecting a gap that size, which would label him the stupidest trainer to enter a horse at Royal Ascot. The Duke of Norfolk had a star performer in the race, the best two-year-old of the year, called Sound Track. When the starter got the horses off, Sound Track went into a comfortable lead. David, who could read a race perfectly through his binoculars, had focused on Godiva's Pink Flower and shook his head mournfully. Halfway through the race the commentator's voice boomed, 'Godiva's Pink Flower coming up fast.' As the horses approached the stands the voice kept repeating, 'Sound Track followed by Godiva's Pink Flower'. How astonished the spectators in the Royal Enclosure would have been if, instead of Godiva's Pink Flower, they had heard the amazing advice 'Vote Labour', as I had intended.

As Godiva's Pink Flower finished a respectable second I turned in glee to Jakie Astor, who had also had a runner in the race. 'How marvellous, Jakie. We were terrified of looking idiots by our horse being tailed off last.'

'Mine was,' he replied stoically.

Down in the unsaddling enclosure Elliott, as he got off Godiva's Pink Flower, said, still gravely but with nearly a concession to a smile, 'Sorry I lost you your bet, Sir.' The second prize was nearly as much as I had paid for the horse. My irrational joy at the small success was near uncontainable. I had contributed nothing to it. I could not have selected the horse at the sales, ridden or trained it. The credit was all David's. Godiva's Pink Flower ran ten times that summer. He was first twice, second twice, third three times, and never out of the first four except in his last race when he had too much weight in a nursery handicap. We sold the brave little animal for ten times what we paid for him.

I had horses with David for thirteen years, starting with one given to me by Moorea. The training bills were then £8 a week. When I gave up racing they had reached £15 a week. One horse, Coventry Express, won its first race at fifty to one. I had a mere £5 each way as insurance against disbursing tips and so on in the unlikely event of its winning.

In the mid-sixties racing began to be less successful and my present wife, Verushka, disliked travelling to small and distant racecourses to watch our horse finishing way down the field. It seemed a good time to stop. David was so skilful with the horses he bought me that I finished racing with a mild but distinct gain, mainly through David's selling the successful horses for much more than we had paid. The most I spent on a horse was £600, and that was the only one which never got into the frame. Beloved David, I am grateful for the hours of magic happiness you gave me, as we dreamed of improbable victories, then went into your office and realistically entered our current horse in an undistinguished handicap at Newmarket, where it came in third.

While Godiva's Pink Flower was busy running at Goodwood, we went for a holiday to Venice, staying with Arthur Jeffries, a picture-dealer of American origin and rich, though not through his art gallery. That was another delight of 1959. Arthur had a pretty house with a garden just off one of the canals and lived in great style. He had his own gondola and gondoliers who propelled us, with a magnificent lunch, to the Lido where Arthur had a hut on the beach in what he said was the smartest part. He had beavered away for years to get himself promoted to it. Arthur was a man of some taste and had beautiful antique furniture in London. Graham Sutherland painted one of his best portraits of him, showing the sadness behind the eyes of this kindly, moody man. He did not like being a homosexual but he could not help it. As with Oscar Wilde and Tom Driberg, he was frequently attracted by the low and disreputable. He was warned several times to desist by the Italian police, who disapprove of foreigners corrupting local morals, and he tried. But the fatal attraction always drew him back again. At last the Italian police told him he must leave Venice or be prosecuted. The unhappy and good man committed suicide. He felt himself caught in a tragedy he could not avert.

In 1959 this was some way ahead. The sun, the lagoon, the islands, the Lido (where I first drank Bellini, a delicious combination of peach juice and champagne), the splendour of Venice and jolly occasions were paramount, and so were the mosquitoes and gnats. Peggy Guggenheim gave a dinner in the garden of her house (now the Guggenheim Museum) where Malu once shone with D'Annunzio at her side. The butter, melting in the dishes, had interesting black specks, which I assumed were nutmeg or some other spice until I ate it and got a mouthful of insects. Peggy had generally a good eye but could be taken in by indifferent young artists who thought her an easy touch, giving her famous collection a patchy look, like her butter.

One late afternoon, wandering in the back squares of Venice, I saw a tall, beautiful girl peering into shop windows. I followed her for a while because she was enchanting to watch, but did not dare speak to her. That evening we went to dinner at a house on the Grand Canal. There was the girl of the shop windows,

Caroline, and her husband, David Somerset, both immortalized by Ian Fleming who put them into his James Bond film *From Russia with Love* as having sleeper reservations on a train. A long friendship began.

Caroline knew and, mysteriously, liked Paul Getty. Once he invited her to lunch at an hotel in Guildford near where he lived. Caroline arrived early and ordered herself a drink. When Paul Getty came, he waited for her to finish her drink. When the waiter brought the bill for it he offered it to Getty, who said, to Caroline's astonishment, 'No, it's for the lady.'

One of the two or three richest men in the world, he was also one of the meanest, fearful of being done out of a ha'penny. His mistresses got such tiny allowances that it was amazing they stayed. It could not have been because he was amusing: whenever I sat next to him I found him miserable, despite trying my utmost by flattery and jokes to get some animation from him. It is a truism that enormous riches are no passport to happiness but, like most truisms, it is a fact. One Christmas, when I was staying at lovely Luggala in County Wicklow with the ravishing, fair-haired Oonagh Oranmore, a Guinness heiress, she told me how unhappy she was. When I said that, with all her vast possessions and the fascinating pursuits and friends they made available to her, she ought not to be, she snapped at me, 'How silly of you to think that money can make you happy.' Maybe not, but it helps if you are lonely and have been jilted to sit in a luxurious bath in a beautiful bathroom with a glass of champagne near your hand and servants at call. The rich who cannot enjoy life are fools.

John Strachey said to me during my string of rejections at selection conferences, 'You'll find a constituency right wing enough to take you in the end.' I was handicapped because I had fought conspicuously against Communist influence in the unions. If I had supported their activities or said nothing I should have passed as centre or left wing and easily got another seat. That is how the marking goes. The nearer you are to promoting a dictatorship, providing it is Marxist, the more left wing you are. Defending democracy is right wing. In the constituencies I had so far attempted I was known to have Hugh Gaitskell's backing.

Seventy-two-year-old Arthur Allen had been on the National Executive of the National Union of Boot and Shoe Operatives, strong in Leicestershire. He had been Hugh's PPS when he was Chancellor of the Exchequer, and was his PPS as Leader of the Opposition. He found the journey and the work were getting too tiring for him to go on as MP for Bosworth in Leicestershire, which he had held since 1945. He was a delightful man, sensible and calm, unmoved by the Bevanite tirades. He worked hard in his constituency and was liked by the local party. He suggested I should be his successor. We made no mention of Hugh's hope that I would be. Even so, it was close run at the 1959 selection conference. There were strong contenders with local associations. My past as the scourge of the Communists was against me again. For instance, under the front-page heading, 'Communists Smear Woodrow Wyatt', the local newspaper in North Islington for 14 March 1958 wrote about the Labour selection conference for the by-election (caused by the death in a car crash of the brilliant young MP, Wilfred Fienburgh, author of *No Love for Johnny*, who wrote popular political articles as good as or better than mine, and thought much the same):

> Communists are said to have prompted the condemnation of Mr. Woodrow Wyatt's nomination: last weekend North Woolwich AEU passed a resolution calling on the North Islington Labour Party 'to refuse to accept such a discredited member of the Labour Party as a prospective representative of their electorate'. At the Hackney Trades Council meeting on Thursday a resolution moved by the AEU Stoke Newington protested against the BBC's TV Panorama programme and Mr. Wyatt in particular referring to 'the cockeyed presentation by Wyatt of our unions and their problems'.

The newspaper added: '. . . it is understood that Mr. Woodrow Wyatt's nomination by Labour's national executive had the blessing of Mr. Gaitskell. Mr. Woodrow Wyatt was also nominated by North Islington Labour Party's executive committee'. The blessing sank me completely. So we had decided on a different tactic.

I think I won because of my answer to the question 'Why do you want to represent Bosworth?' The textbook answer was blah about its being a microcosm of England, miners at Coalville in the north, industrial workers living in the Hinckley area in the south of the thirty-five-mile-long constituency, farms in between and all around, marvellous people, backbone of the country and so forth. Instead I replied, 'Because it's the only constituency party left with a safe Labour majority which is likely to take me.' The laughter at this brazen honesty was considerable, and so was the appreciation.

I had no difficulty when I answered the next question: 'Would you be willing to live in the constituency?'

'Certainly not. But I will promise to come up once a month on a Saturday morning, except during August and Christmas, to talk to constituents about their problems.'

I chose Saturdays because I could combine my visits with attending the monthly party meetings on Saturday afternoons. MPs who voluntarily spend time in their constituencies are idiots: they are bothered by petty local problems, preventing them from thinking about national issues. London MPs cannot help it. Douglas Jay, sitting for a Battersea seat, was plagued by constituents calling on him at the House and by having to attend constituency functions across the river, which could not be evaded by pleading time and distance.

Bosworth with its flowing acres and villages was the opposite of Aston. Everywhere there were pretty rural scenes and churches. The mines had not spoiled the Charnwood Forest nearby, where I often picnicked on a Saturday before the afternoon party meeting. The miners, six or seven thousand, were dwindling in numbers and significance as uneconomic pits closed, but they were still important in the local constituency party. I loved the element of comradely brigandry in their small communities from which they sometimes defied the nation. At the first miners' dinner I went to, my face must have shown surprise at the champagne, smoked salmon, roast duck, everything more lavish than at large gatherings in most London hotels. 'Nothing is too good for the miners,' Frank Smith, Secretary/Agent of the local miners, said to me. The miners always expected Moorea, and later Verushka, to put on her best jewellery and most glamorous dresses when she attended their dinners and dances. To do less would have been an insult, as though we thought we were going slumming.

Being a miner was like being in the Army, with less discipline and better pay. Danger in the pits was always in the air. Crawling along a two-and-a-half foot high coalface, which I tried once or twice, needed peak physical condition. To work the face required endurance, ingenuity, knowledge and experience, as well as team co-operation; perhaps this is less true since the latest technological advances, but the aptitude must be the same in essence.

Pit loyalty was intense; lives depended on it. For all its hardship in the dark, mining is a social activity far more satisfying than working in a mass-production factory. The human being in a mine is not an accessory to a machine but a proud individual relying on himself and his comrades, none of whom would let the others down. It is a way of life, which explains why many miners hate to leave the pits for softer but less exciting occupations.

Some of the local party committee members were shocked when they saw Moorea and me on TV at Ascot beside Godiva's Pink Flower as he stood in the place marked 'Second'. Not the miners. They were delighted, as they were at anything that was fun, like their brass bands, which is one of the few branches of music which appeals to me.

As a famous *Panorama* television performer, I was on a Labour Party Committee chaired by Anthony Wedgwood Benn to prepare the 1959 election TV broadcasts. I was fond of Tony, who had not yet lost his balance and his bearings. I was also fond of his pretty, vivacious wife, which, though our friendship was wholly innocent, caused Tony to leave messages on their pillow, 'Go away, Woodrow'. I used to go to his house near Notting Hill Gate, once taking my own television set to make sure of seeing myself on a TV programme, which amused them. Then they were fans of my strong anti-Communist activities in the unions.

At that time Tony was an admirer of Hugh Gaitskell and was moderate politically, seeing power as a means of getting things done energetically and quickly, an attitude of which Attlee would not have disapproved. When I was holding up the nationalization of steel in the 1964 Parliament, he was not censorious, commenting to me, as we stood at the side of the platform at the 1965 Labour Conference, 'My family has never believed in nationalization.'

The fanaticism was the child of his burgeoning ambition. Tony had observed how Wilson got the leadership by sucking up to the extremists, who put their considerable powers of intrigue and persuasion into getting him the votes of the Parliamentary Labour Party. Tony began to see that the PLP would never make him Leader, so he agitated for a wider suffrage for the leadership elections. The demoralized PLP, weakened from within and without, collapsed and surrendered.

The preposterous system by which Labour MPs now have a minority say in who shall lead them in the Commons was ceded to extremists of the Left egged on by Tony Benn who, to retain their adherence, was and is compelled to make ever more lunatic noises, of which before he reached a prematurely self-induced dotage he would have been ashamed. A sad tale of not tempering ambition with commonsense. However, Tony was approximately normal in 1959, though Tony Crosland told me I overrated his intelligence and warned me not to be taken in by his exaggerated self-regard. His eyes had not yet acquired their curious staring and he was full of charm and jokes. I looked forward to seeing him.

Labour's TV broadcasts each began with an introduction by Tony Wedgwood Benn and ended with a challenge by me to the Tories. All but the last ran for twenty minutes. Tony, Christopher Mayhew and I were interviewers, presenters, compilers. I discussed our pensions plan with Dick Crossman, talked about general policy with Hugh, went into industrial relations and the unions with Bill Carron, President of the AEU, and interviewed Wilson on how Labour's programme was to be paid for. I made Wilson sound sincere and reliable, though it went against my inclinations.

The programmes, made as they were by professionals, were as entertaining as any current affairs programme on BBC or ITV. They moved fast, were convincing and a smash-hit. The Tories were rocked. I met Oliver Poole, Deputy Chairman of the Conservative Party, halfway through the campaign. 'You've got us on the run,' he said seriously. 'I think you may win.'

The Tories smartened up their TV broadcasts. At the end of

271

their third programme Iain Macleod deliberately imitated my style and, in his effective, acid way, issued a personal challenge to Hugh to explain how Labour's programme could be paid for. In modern terms this was not extravagant, but Hugh overestimated the public's understanding of economics when he said, and believed, that it could be paid for out of the growth in the economy and that extra taxation would not be necessary. If he had said *some* but not much extra taxation would be needed, more of the public would have been convinced and we might have won. It was ironic. Harold Macmillan, using public money to buy votes, helped set us on the road to massive inflation, but was able to appear as a guardian of financial probity.

The mood changed in the last few days of the campaign as it frequently does. We could feel the victory of which we had been confident slipping away. Maybe the pattern of the three weeks before polling is always apt to be confusing froth on top of a current. In the polling-booth most voters return to their original intentions. When the early results showed we had lost, I rang Hugh in Leeds, where his constituency was, to comfort him. 'I thought you and I would be having a very different telephone conversation,' he said sadly. He meant he was going to make me Secretary of State for War.

I was not as thrilled to be back in the House as I had expected. After the excitements of the wider world (until 1955 I had always been in closed institutions: school, Oxford, the Army, Parliament), it seemed tamer than I remembered. I had an immediate disappointment. Hugh told me that Bert Bowden, Opposition Chief Whip, had insisted that I should not be an official spokesman or shadow minister again. The jealousy of me as a TV performer and the hostility aroused by my campaigns to defeat the Communists in the unions were so great, that the trouble caused by my being allowed to speak for the Party would not be worth it. Hugh was shamefaced but asked me to put up with it. I had no option but I was restless, wondering what the point was of my sitting at the age of forty-one in a place where I was forbidden to do anything other than hope to catch the Speaker's eye for a rare, unreported speech from the back benches and to ask questions if I were lucky.

The trade union group of MPs with whom I had been friendly

before were especially bitter. They thought it presumptuous of anyone not of their number to say anything about the unions. I had exposed weakness, corruption and Communist infiltration in the unions. If they had been bigger men they would have welcomed what I had done and used it to campaign to make the unions clean. But they were little men in receipt of subventions from their unions and beholden to the union leaders who authorized them.

I was a disturbing anti-hero to my colleagues in the House and they did what they could to block me, which was just what the Communists and their allies hoped they would. I was a little wounded, too, by my friends in the ETU playing down in public the part I had had in getting them where they now were. The Communists had put it across that to be associated with me was to sup with the Devil. Les and Frank were anxious to prove that being opposed to Communist corruption did not weaken desire for all-out socialism. I did nothing to embarrass them.

The coldness which greeted me on my return to the House was another indication of how fast the Labour Party was falling into the grip of the Marxists and Broad Left. Hugh understood that. That is why he fought so hard to push them back. He despised Wilson for his trimming, and would tell me how Wilson would say nothing in a Shadow Cabinet meeting when argument raged over some behaviour of the left wing inimical to the Party, and would then come out of the meeting and tell the left wingers how hard he had battled for them. 'That man,' he would say to me, 'will only become Leader over my dead body.' That is what happened.

Hugh feared Wilson would let the Marxists and their friends swarm all over him in return for their support for the leadership. At the famous Scarborough Conference in 1960, when the resolution to dispense one-sidedly with nuclear weapons was carried against the platform, Hugh made a great speech finishing: 'There are some of us who will fight and fight and fight again to save the Party we love. We will fight and fight and fight again to bring back sanity and honesty and dignity . . .' Wilson sat motionless, not clapping, throughout Hugh's speech. When most rose to applaud Hugh, some with tears of emotion, Wilson remained expressionlessly fixed in his seat. He was signalling to the CND supporters and their Marxist friends that he was really on their side. Yet Wilson had firmly committed himself to the official defence policy.

After the conference Wilson's friends, Dick Crossman, Barbara Castle and others, urged him to stand against Hugh for the leadership when Parliament met again. He was afraid to. Then Anthony Greenwood, a dripping-wet CND supporter, announced that he would run against Hugh. Greenwood was popular with the Left and did well in the elections to Labour's National Executive from the constituencies section. He was always available to address a meeting, however small or remote, happy to fill in when a more important speaker dropped out. He went to hundreds of constituencies every year. He told me he kept careful notes of the Christian names of the chairman, secretary, treasurer and anyone who seemed locally influential, together with details about their families. Every Christmas he would send out torrents of Christmas cards with little messages: 'I hope Enid's back is better'; 'I hope John likes his new job'; 'Best wishes to your mother for a speedy recovery from her operation'; and so on. The system was foolproof and commendable for the application that went into it.

Anthony Greenwood was a polished creep, not at all like his robust, hard-drinking father, Arthur Greenwood, who set the Beveridge welfare state in motion for the War Cabinet, but he was pleasant and would take any amount of insults with a smile. When Wilson heard Anthony Greenwood was going to challenge Hugh he was alarmed. Greenwood would get all the left wing votes, many of which might be permanently lost to Wilson. Wilson persuaded Greenwood to stand down and promised to carry the banner for the Left himself. Greenwood agreed. He lost nothing. He got Cabinet rank, of which he was scarcely deserving, in 1964 and later a life peerage. Wilson got eighty-one votes from the left-hand side of the PLP, half as many as Hugh, but they were votes he could not risk forfeiting and were something to build on. Having declared himself against one-sided nuclear disarmament, Wilson had to produce another explanation for his contemptible disloyalty to Hugh. It was that the Party Conference decision on the subject must be observed, as all Party Conference decisions should be, and Hugh had announced he would take no notice of it, as Attlee would have done.

Hugh told me Wilson was not brilliant as an economist, though he got a first in the subject at Oxford. Despite that, and his doubts about his reliability, Hugh thought it politic to keep Wilson as Shadow Chancellor of the Exchequer until October 1961, with a lien on the post in the next Labour government. Hugh's commitment to Wilson enraged Roy and Tony. They told Hugh that they would not serve in his government if Wilson were Chancellor of the Exchequer. However, it turned out that Wilson was not Chancellor in the next Labour government but Prime Minister, and he gave them office.

During the 1959 Parliament I began to annoy Hugh. Having nothing else to do I used the system of Ten Minute Rule bills to ensure that, when I wanted to make a speech, I had to be called with a fair number of MPs present. Ten Minute Rule bills were taken immediately after Questions, and were usually well attended. With the aid of the clerks in the Public Bill Office they could be knocked out quickly and could, in the improbable event of the House and Government permitting, have become law after the long processes entailed. I should have been surprised if any of mine had.

Hugh was particularly irritated by one I introduced in February 1961, which proposed relief for surtax payers by increasing the level at which it began from £2000 to £6000. This would still not have matched inflation, as £2000 had been made the starting-point before the war. During the debate someone shouted, 'How would that help a miner on £20 a week?' to which my answer was, quite a lot if he had a wife going out to work as a teacher.

A few Labour MPs who paid surtax quietly agreed, but the rest jeered. In presenting my Bill I said that if surtax paying were brought up to date there would also have to be a Capital Gains Tax for the first time, which would catch the very rich. I remarked that Mr Charles Clore had made £10 million without, unlike the unfortunate middle classes, paying a penny in tax. (Mr Clore issued a statement that evening, not to contradict me but to explain that his £10 million was in shares, not cash!) I apologize to those who have suffered from Capital Gains Tax for setting the fuse to the tinder. I have often wished I had not.

After the mover of a Ten Minute Rule Bill has spoken, an opponent is called. Hugh hoped it would be Tony Crosland, but the Speaker called Gerald Nabarro, a rollicking cowboy of a Tory MP, a former quartermaster-sergeant with huge moustaches and a talent for making effective digs. He was naturally in favour of my Bill but was pretending not to be, so that he could make a commotion. He described me as the socialist leader of the Leicestershire coal miners, which sent most of the Labour benches berserk and made the rest of the House laugh. He followed that by saying: 'I believe this is a kite being flown on the instructions of the Leader of the Opposition.' Hugh angrily jumped up, on a bogus point of order, demanding from the Speaker that such a slanderous accusation, which Hugh said Nabarro knew to be untrue, should be corrected. So the fun went on.

Hugh said to me afterwards that my Bill had put back the sensible reform of surtax for years, but it had not. When the subsequent budget gave the relief my Bill proposed, Harold Macmillan, the Prime Minister, told me the Tories would never have dared do it if I had not first moved my Bill. It would have more truly reflected Hugh's views and done more good for the Labour Party in the country if he had backed my Bill and not attacked it.

Another Bill Hugh disliked, in April 1961, was a requirement that the Government should accede to the Treaty of Rome, or Common Market. That was the first time anyone had put the proposition in the Commons. Some Labour MPs, of the kind Hugh approved, supported me. I had always thought Britain should have been in at the beginning, when we could have shaped the Common Market much more to our liking. If the House had supported me when I introduced my Bill, Western Europe would be a stronger force today. Hugh thought differently, being fundamentally a Little Englander in the Attlee mould. His last major speech laid down impossible conditions for our entering the Common Market and he talked unmitigated claptrap about abandoning 'a thousand years of history'. Maybe after two exhausting battles, one to remove the albatross of Clause 4 from Labour's Constitution on which he was defeated, and the other to reverse the 1960 Conference Resolution in favour of one-sided nuclear disarmament, which he won, he was too tired to engage the Left in another titanic struggle.

The accumulation of my waywardness prompted Hugh to ask me to lunch at the Garrick for a serious talk. The food was all right, the wine was good, the atmosphere was friendly, changing to grim. Wouldn't I stop embarrassing him with my Ten Minute Rule bills, which made me ridiculous? Hugh's main point was that everyone knew that I was close to him and it was mistakenly thought that my ideas were always the same as his. Would I please shut up. Otherwise my future would be bleak. We argued for some time.

'Why should I deal in bromide?' I asked. 'I'm in my early forties, which is supposed to be the prime of life. I'll never be more vigorous. I spoke for the Party when I was in the House before. For reasons I understand, you won't let me do that. I've nothing else to do. It's not in my nature to be a Trappist monk. It's not fair to ask me.'

Hugh's face became kind and pleading: 'Won't you do it out of loyalty to me?'

I gave him an answer I have regretted ever since. 'No, why should I? You probably won't be Leader of the Party a year from now.'

I did not believe it. I was confident that Hugh would get the Scarborough resolution on nuclear disarmament reversed at the October 1961 Conference. But I was angry and wanted to hurt him. It was unforgivable.

In November 1961 our relations became still more edgy. It seemed that Harold Macmillan had conned the country so cleverly (Profumo and Macmillan's illness were yet to come) that 1964 would see thirteen years of Tory rule extended to seventeen or eighteen. That, still hoping for office as I was, did not appeal to me. There was an anti-Tory majority in the country but a reluctance to vote Labour because of the growing influence of the vituperative left wing. I suggested in the *Guardian*, much read by Liberals, and in a week-end speech, that there should be short-term arrangements for Liberal and Labour candidates not to stand against each other in Conservative seats where the Tories had won with the minority of votes cast. There had been an understanding of this nature between the two parties in 1906, which increased the Labour Representation Committee MPs to twenty-nine and secured a reforming Liberal government. There had been other partial pacts in 1921 and 1931. Why not one now? Even if the Liberals added twenty seats to their current six it would be worth it to ensure a solid Labour government.

Hugh angrily condemned my idea in a public statement, but a National Opinion Poll in the *Daily Mail* on 27 November indicated that the public liked it very much. Of Labour supporters, 56 per cent agreed with me and only 27 per cent disagreed; while 40.5 per cent of Liberal supporters agreed. It would have been enough on which to have founded a Lib-Lab electoral pact if the leaders of the parties had taken it up. A number of people I thought would be hostile wrote to journals and newspapers suggesting my idea should be explored.

Hugh rang me in a fury. I was standing in Moorea's bow-fronted bedroom at Tower House. 'Why don't you get out of the Party and stop embarrassing me?' he demanded.

I thought his behaviour was irrational. So did Roy, who said to Jennifer, 'Woodrow has more political sense than Hugh sometimes.' Twenty years later Roy was to adopt a similar arrangement between the SDP, largely headed by former Labour MPs and supporters, and David Steel's Liberal Party.

It seemed to me a disservice to democracy that such a reasonable idea should be suppressed without an airing. The opinion polls and my own instincts convinced me that millions were interested. I discussed it with John Freeman, then Editor of the *New Statesman*. He was still much on the Left, but he was a friend of mine and thought there was good journalism to be had for the *New Statesman*, which would stimulate readers and help the Labour Party to make up its mind whether it wanted pure socialism more than power. His strong dislike of Hugh, left over from when he had resigned from the Government with Bevan and Wilson, was by no means his main motive, though he was probably not averse to sticking a pin in him.

I wrote a long and detailed piece for the *New Statesman*, somewhat in the manner of the article which had been the launching agent for the dethronement of the Communists in the ETU. It had tables with the votes in ninety-seven constituencies held by Conservatives, and proposed that the Liberals should stand down in favour of a Labour candidate in sixty-one of them and vice versa in thirty-six. The result it predicted was a comfortable overall majority for Labour, with the Liberals having a reasonable number of seats more in accord with their voting strength in the country. I conceded that an agreement on a broad policy programme for Parliament would be necessary. That would be excellent, as mild Liberal restraint would reassure the electorate that Labour would not be able to do anything violently extreme, such as the nationalization of steel.

My article in the *New Statesman* was closely argued and found persuasive by many, including Jo Grimond. In a long editorial John Freeman wrote of it: '. . . an important and serious proposal seriously advanced. It cannot be dismissed out of hand because Mr Wyatt is unpopular in some parts of the Labour Party; nor more disreputably should attempts be made to silence Mr Wyatt because some of his parliamentary colleagues find his views embarrassing as well as challenging'.

Attempts were made to silence me before the article was even published on 26 January 1962. The week-end before, I was staying with Jakie Astor. The butler said a Mr George Brown wanted me to ring him urgently. I ducked. George Brown was Deputy Leader of the Party and I dreaded tangling with this man, who could be either charming or brutal. I knew which he intended to be.

'It's Mr Brown on again, Sir,' said the shaken butler a little later. 'He says he must speak to you.'

I held the telephone away from my ear, waiting for the artillery fire to cease. 'It's no good, George. It's all set in type and made up in the pages. I couldn't take it out now even if I wanted to.'

Another barrage of dark threats, blasphemy and curses. It was the end of my career. No one would speak to me. To suggest that Labour might not win on its own was the grossest disloyalty. I would be thrown out of the Party. Hugh was livid. I was a shit and a swine. If I told them I wanted to withdraw it, the *New Statesman* would have to take it out. They could easily put something else in its place. He had always stood up for me; never again. It was an utterly disgraceful article. How could I have written it? If he had been in the room with me, George

279

could have terrorized me into surrender. A hundred flying pickets with bicycle chains would seem preferable.

'I don't want to take it out,' I repeated lamely.

Finally the receiver banged down at the other end and I asked the butler for a strong drink.

The day of publication was the day of the Bosworth party's annual dinner. Our friendship had become sufficiently strong again for Hugh to have agreed some time previously to be the guest of honour. Extracts from what I had written were prominent in the Press that morning. I thought Hugh might be so disgusted that he would cancel his appearance, but that was not his way. When he arrived he nodded to me with half a smile. All watched us intently, wondering what would come out of this strange evening. I was terrified.

The dinner eaten, I introduced Hugh and spoke first. With genuine feeling I lauded Hugh, saying truthfully, as one of his staunchest supporters, 'more and more we have come to realize that he is our greatest electoral asset'. I said my suggestions, however much they displeased him, were designed to help him become Prime Minister, though some of the things I said might cause him to say, 'If he is my friend, God save me from him.'

Then, in front of the miners and the assembled dignitaries of the local party, Hugh tore into me. It was a reasoned onslaught but it was an onslaught. He argued that my pact would help the Tories more than Labour. 'You cannot possibly say that most Liberal voters would vote Labour rather than Tory if there were no Liberal candidate.' Liberal candidates, he argued, split the Tory vote. Proposing my pact now would create the maximum dissension in the Labour Party, antagonize the electorate, 'and undermine our hopes of victory'. It was irresponsible of me to 'spoil the great effort we are now making to persuade our fellow-citizens of the urgent need for a Labour government', and so forth and so on. When he sat down I said quietly, but audibly, remembering Galileo, 'but still it moves'. Hugh was the more displeased.

The following Monday, Morgan Phillips, General Secretary of the Labour Party, wrote me on behalf of the Labour National Executive: Either I must drop my advocacy of a Lib-Lab pact or be expelled. So I dropped it. I had made my point. Hugh was in favour of the warning given me. Ian Mikardo, Tom Driberg, Anthony Greenwood and Barbara Castle were opposed, which amused the other members of the Executive. They were hardly supporters of mine but doubtless thinking of their own right of dissent. Harold Wilson, whom I met in a TV studio, said, 'It shows how much we love you, Woodrow. Otherwise we would have expelled you on the spot, as some of them wanted.'

When Labour won the 1964 election with a majority of five Wilson might well have wished my Lib-Lab pact had been in operation. It would have got him a much bigger majority. It would have forced the Labour Party into a more sensible direction, with a wider appeal to the electorate. In 1974 Harold Wilson had more or less to exist on the sufferance of the Liberals, and Callaghan was defeated by their withdrawal of support in 1979. If a proper Lib-Lab pact had been organized when I proposed it, all would have been different.

Some of the miners tried to stop me being Bosworth's Labour candidate for the next election. I wrote to all the members of the local Labour Party, setting out what I had been aiming at. That, added to my regular monthly current affairs speeches to the management of executive committees, enabled me to survive without difficulty. I made friends with Hugh again. He knew I loved him, and his old warmth for me was beginning to return.

I stayed with Kenneth Galbraith, US Ambassador in Delhi, in the autumn, and on my return reported to Hugh on what I had seen and heard, including Kenneth's note to Kennedy, for which I made minor suggestions, urging him not to get dragged militarily into Vietnam. Hugh looked so tired that I was worried, and I pressed him to stop rattling round the country; he had done all he needed. He took no notice. Within a year of his public rebuke to me at Coalville he was dead of a strange virus, eventually described as lupus by the baffled doctors. It was so strange, indeed, that I am not altogether convinced that it entered him naturally. When the Bulgarian, Markov, was murdered by the injection of a mystery virus through the sharp tip of an umbrella, it made me wonder whether Hugh, too, had been murdered by the Russians or their agents. The idea of Hugh as a Labour Prime Minister was anathema to them. He would have been an unshakeable opponent; he would have made social democracy work so well that the contrast between that and Communism would have been internationally damaging to the Russians. This may seem fanciful but it is not impossible. Hugh was a mere fifty-six and might have done the Russians immense harm for another fifteen years. They knew any successor to Hugh would not approach his stature.

I was staying with Philip Dunn when the news came that Hugh had died after weeks of struggle, which made the nation spontaneously realize how much they needed him. Philip could be very sensitive. He patted my back saying nothing as I went silently to my room. That night I cried myself to sleep and did so every night for a fortnight. It felt like something torn from my side. As I drove down Regent Street I would say to myself, 'Darling gallant Hugh will never see this again', and I would say the same of every place I saw for months. I reproached myself for the difficulties I had made for him. I thought of him perhaps more as a father than any other man, which may account for why I was sometimes wayward with him. His death was a bad day for Britain.

# CHAPTER XIII

———— ❪❫ ————

# Some Dirty Work

THE DEATH OF HUGH GAITSKELL closed my prospects in the Labour Party. I might have kept them alive if I had acceded to the suggestion of the malevolent George Wigg. He was Harold Wilson's campaign manager, with Dick Crossman, in the subsequent leadership contest. He had long hated Hugh for the illogical reason that he had replaced George's hero Manny Shinwell as Minister of Fuel and Power after the fuel shortages of the severe winter of early 1947. George was never able to grasp that it was Attlee's decision, not Hugh's, to move Manny to the War Office. I liked Manny, a fierce patriot despite his bouts of class prejudice, and capable of kindness and intelligent action. That did not save me from George Wigg's intermittent resentment of me as a friend of Hugh.

However, with Hugh gone, George said to me, 'Harold's going to win. Don't be an idiot. Support him and you'll get a job in the next government. Otherwise—'

'I can't, he's so dishonest.'

'He's no worse than you. You're not so honest yourself. You're a fool.'

And George stalked off.

To see the man Hugh despised filling Hugh's shoes was repellent. I championed George Brown. George envied intellectuals like Dick Crossman, Tony and Roy because they had been formally educated and he had not. Yet he had a better brain than any of them, understanding a brief or a situation with sharp quickness, making usually good decisions with commonsense and unafraid to implement the unpopular. To win an argument against George was difficult for the cleverest. His mind was untutored but it was up to the best. He was brave, willing to take on the left wing and rout them. The Broad Left would never have got into his government as they did into Wilson's. He cared more about Britain than himself. He could be rough sometimes, almost treacherous, but he had emerged from an East End and trade union background where strong words and in-fighting were customary.

Stories were rife of George's erratic conduct. How could we have a prime minister who could not hold his liquor, who flared up unpredictably, was always ready with an insult? None of that mattered to me. He could be a bully but he was not a coward like Wilson; I thought we would all sleep easier in our beds with George as Leader. If George had been more balanced he would have won comfortably, as Alfred Robens would have if he had not been tempted out of Parliament into the Coal Board by a cunning Harold Macmillan in 1961. Either George or Alf would have been superior to Harold Wilson. I was surprised Tony Crosland did not see this, but gave his backing to James Callaghan, who split the right and centre vote, attracting wobblers nervous of George. But Tony rarely stood firm after Hugh had gone and not always when Hugh was there.

George was ahead on the first ballot but not far enough to beat Wilson in the run-off. Seeing how well Wilson had done, the wobblers were off to join him. On the Friday morning after the first ballot I met George in the Smoking Room and we had a drink.

'Why do you think it went wrong?' a deflated George asked.

'You must face it. It's because you're so dreadfully rude to people when you're drunk, George.'

'What makes them think I'm rude to them just because I'm drunk?'

It was a splendidly defiant answer in defeat. When the final verdict came, the wounded George disappeared for a while in a sulk.

Harold Wilson inherited a party healthier than when Hugh became Leader. Hugh had routed the one-sided nuclear disarmers and, with the support of the moderate trade union leaders, had stopped the advance of the lunatic Left. The PLP was sound, apart from the fifty-seven or so varieties always engaged in making left-wing noises against the leadership, though initially they gave Wilson a quiet time: he had propitiated them and they had voted for him. The Party was in good shape, thanks to Hugh. For the election which could not be delayed beyond October 1964 it had only one real albatross in its programme: the nationalization of steel.

Harold Macmillan was not beaten yet. His 'Night of the Long Knives' had given a spring-clean to his government, dismaying some of his supporters but not the public who like the drama of executions in high places. He was spending more than the country could afford, which made everyone feel cosy. He ducked doing the stringent things needed to make us competitive again, because that would have changed the comfortable atmosphere. The British are lazy and self-indulgent; they dislike being prodded into hard application. As Macmillan remarked, 'There's a lot of ruin in an old country', meaning Britain could overspend for a long time before the money ran out, by which time Macmillan would be gone.

Edward Boyle, Minister of Education, told me one day as we stood in the corridor by the tape-machine outside the Members' Smoking Room, of what to him was a strange exchange he had had with No. 10. A message had come asking him to put in his proposals for supplementary estimates. He had replied that he did not need any extra money, his department was well within its budget for the year. Another message came back from No. 10: 'Don't you realize this is an election year?'

Macmillan was as cynical as Wilson. That is why they liked and admired each other so much. They put their own interests first, and were deceptively cunning about it, though Macmillan cared more about the country than Wilson, being greatly affected by the loss of so many friends in the First World War and by his own considerable service as a minister in the Second. Macmillan had one achievement to be proud of: he was midwife to the H-bomb Test Ban Treaty. He could also claim credit for pulling the Tory Party round, after Eden went and Macmillan had skilfully disposed of Butler, who let it be known he was opposed to the Suez fiasco from the start while Macmillan gave apparent loyal support to Eden until he saw the moment to change tack. When Butler asked me why I thought the Tories rejected him for Macmillan, I answered, 'Because they didn't trust you.'

My difficulty in writing about Macmillan is that I have known him and his family too long to be unkind to him. His gentle, clever son, Maurice, who made up songs about mussels, and poems, for my daughter, Petronella, when he stayed with us in Italy and would happily read for hours in front of the Tuscan view under the pergola, would persuade Petronella to sing in the car, and would amuse us by swimming with his hat on, was a special friend I had known at Oxford, where, he said improbably, I frightened him. His father was friendly to me from the time he confided to me early in the 1945 parliament that he minded the fact of the Labour Government less than seeing the common people who ran it. He was always a snob, extravagantly pleased at marrying a daughter of the Duke of Devonshire. But scratch most people, including me, and you will find a snob nestling underneath pretending not to be one. Snobbishness can be a virtue, the creative aspiration to be among the best and to be the best yourself, the most obvious manifestation of which is the general regard for the upper reaches of society and power. Snobbishness has propelled many useful careers and was valuable in Macmillan's. He genuinely felt for the less lucky and the unemployed, on the pattern of Plantagenet Palliser, in whose image Macmillan undoubtedly sees himself. I like the old charmer, who deserved well of his country more for the entertainment he gave it than the good he did it. His failure to rouse Britain from her lethargy to meet the new competition in the world was a dereliction of duty.

Macmillan's ship was sailing on serenely until the summer of 1962 when it hit the iceberg of the Profumo affair. Jack Profumo was an agreeable, inconsequential, Secretary of State for War, lucky to have risen so high. Rumours had begun that he had been having a sexual association with Miss Christine Keeler, amorously connected with an attaché at the Russian Embassy. There had been naked swimming and wild parties at Cliveden attended by Jack Profumo, Miss Keeler and Mr Stephen Ward, a procurer of pretty girls. I now understood what Bill Astor had meant when I was staying with him one week-end at Cliveden. As we walked beside the river he pointed to a little house, saying, 'I let Stephen Ward use that house.' Then he giggled a lot. Damn it, no one has ever asked me to an orgy. I suppose, like Camillo, the hosts all thought me too square.

As the scandal developed, the vulture Wigg scented carrion. Profumo, he said, must be a security risk, as he had enjoyed the same girl as a serving Russian officer. Wigg knew that was nonsense: a secretary for war not in the cabinet has no great secrets worth Russian interest; he was not privy to the details of nuclear or other secret weapons. Wigg knew, too, that even if he had known any secrets, Profumo was a patriot who would never have passed them on while fornicating with Miss Keeler, whether at the height of enthusiasm or by way of post-coital small-talk, and that if he *had* done so, Miss Keeler was too dumb to have understood or remembered them accurately. Subsequent enquiry showed no breach of security was involved or ever likely, as Wigg knew.

Once Wigg had succeeded in mixing up the Government's reputation with Jack's harmless but indiscreet escapade, Profumo should have resigned, but he had gone too deep into deception to own up. Unfortunately for Macmillan he had an unsophisticated Chief Whip, Martin Redmayne, who questioned Jack and believed his denial, though it was obvious to anyone who had ever been inside a night-club that Jack Profumo and Miss Keeler were not platonic pen-pals associating because of their love of arts or literature. The former Tory Chief Whip, James Stuart, told me he could not believe whips could be such fools. If James Stuart had not ceased to be Chief Whip in 1959 he, with his long experience of the sexual habits of people like Jack, would have rumbled Profumo at the first hint of trouble for the Government and told him the game was up.

It was lovely for Harold Wilson. George Wigg had done all the dirty work needed. Poor butterfly Jack was broken and Macmillan had been brought low. Wilson's liking for Macmillan did not extend to missing a chance to destroy him and take his place. Grave nonsense about morality was the ordure of the day. I was sorry for Jack. I wrote an editorial in the *Banbury Guardian*, read by many of his constituents:

> Mr John Profumo fought bravely for his country through long years of war. He has served it well in peace. Many of his constituents are our readers. They know that he was devoted to their welfare, that he is fundamentally a good man. . . . The

great majority do not think that one peccadillo suddenly makes him a bad man. . . . The *Banbury Guardian* will cast no stones. It will not join with some hysterical Conservative MPs in suggesting that certificates of sexual moral rectitude must be furnished at regular intervals if a man is to continue to hold office. On this basis England would frequently have gone headless and gutless. Palmerston? David Lloyd George? Instead we feel this is more an occasion for sorrow than for jeering. . . . We hope that Mr and Mrs Profumo will feel consoled, when all the fuss has died down, in the knowledge that the bulk of their constituents – who knew them best – never rejected them in their hearts.

Jack lived close to me in Regent's Park. When my copies of the *Banbury Guardian* arrived on 20 June I took one round and dropped it in his letter-box, an action observed by some of the Press ghoulishly waiting outside. It had been a shabby episode, in which bogus morality had flourished its ugly face. George Wigg was not handsome and some years afterwards was prosecuted for persistently accosting women near Marble Arch.

Macmillan was stricken by illness in the autumn, accentuated by the sickening Profumo affair in which he had behaved with scrupulous honour and done no wrong save being over-trusting, which is more a virtue than a fault. He had to be operated on. He was still in hospital when the Conservative Conference began. Physically weak and temporarily demoralized, he gave in to the foolish pressures in his party for a new look and resigned, a decision he regretted many times when his health, vigour and mental alertness returned. He was sixty-nine, younger than many successful prime ministers and many world leaders. After a period of convalescence he would have been back to top form, good for several years more. The election was still a year away, plenty of time for the accomplished old performer to regain his magic hold over the British. Damaging to them though it was, it was less damaging than Wilson's was to be.

In 1964 I left a jolly party given by Edna O'Brien at her house in London, alone after midnight. I was somewhat drunk and therefore drove in my tiny Austin Healey sports car towards our house in Wiltshire the faster and more confidently. Somewhere the other side of Newbury I was hurtling along merrily at around ninety-five miles an hour, when I took a corner slightly on the wrong side and hit an oncoming car. My victim's car was damaged but it could move. The little Austin Healey was buckled and immobile. The other driver was pardonably cross and insisted on waiting for the police. I had no option: I had to wait for a breakdown vehicle. I walked about trying to sober up.

A senior police officer arrived, a superintendent or inspector. He asked the other driver, after surveying the scene, 'Do you want to prefer charges of dangerous driving?'

'I certainly do', and the angry man weighed in with a long and roughly accurate description. At the end the officer turned to me. I was standing a short distance away in the dark.

'Your name?'

'Woodrow Wyatt,' hoping there was no smell of alcohol.

'Oh.' He looked at me closer and shut his notebook, turning to the other driver. 'I wouldn't go on with this. These things are always six of one and half a dozen of the other.' And to me: 'I should be more careful in future, Sir.'

If I had been a masochist I should have demanded to be prosecuted. I was grateful at my undeserved luck at meeting a fan and did not demur. Sometimes policemen who recognized me when stopping me for a motoring offence felt hostile and preferred charges instead of giving me the caution I might have got if they had never heard of me. I had nearly killed the other driver and myself, so I was doubly lucky. His insurance did not cover the total cost of repairing his car. I was happy to pay the difference. Annie Fleming, fearful of another gap in Hugh's old circle, warned me anxiously that life was too short to risk driving drunk again (which I never did) and sent me a garden scythe for my birthday: apt symbolism, whether intentional or not. The incident had an English quality.

I had met the lively Edna O'Brien, whose party was nearly my undoing, through Nell Dunn, Philip's younger daughter. An open, pretty, fair-haired girl, she had some of the unselfconscious eccentricity of her grandfather, Sir James Dunn. When I took her to Salisbury Races she wore a circular piece of cardboard on her head. She told me it was a cut-out for a hat and was indifferent to the surprised looks in the paddock. She disliked the rich life and went to live in Battersea to get to know the poor, and ordinary people untainted by the jet set. With beautiful observation she wrote *Up the Junction* and other exceptionally appealing semi-fiction. Her play *Steaming* is a meticulously accurate minor masterpiece. Somehow she has drifted out of my life (too square again?), as people do. I miss her sunny face and the laughter she made.

The little Austin Healey (for *aficionados* 300 Mark II) had been mended in time for a visit we paid to Russia and Eastern Europe in August and September. (Nearly twenty years later a man from Scotland wrote to tell me he had just bought it. I was glad to hear it was still going after its experiences). I had wondered whether I would get a visa. Three years earlier a visa had been cancelled by a telegram: 'Woodrow Wyatt not acceptable in Hungary.' The Communist grapevine had been active and the Foreign Office had to make the Hungarians restore my visa by protesting that refusing admission to me was not a suitable inauguration for the cultural exchanges Hungary had recently asked for.

Russia was all friendliness, though it was difficult to shake off an interpreter guide who often travelled perched uncomfortably on the bucket seat. I pitied the people cheated by Communism of the prosperity on its way to them before 1914, but as total censorship prevented them knowing what they had missed, it was probably not so important as I thought. However, some of the young had a glimmering of understanding that life in the outside world was more pleasurable than their masters said. I saw a low standard of living but little grinding poverty, though accommodation was shoddy and cramped and large villages depended on one pump in the main street for their water.

I had no sense of anyone wanting war – I think that remains true today – but of some apprehension induced by Kremlin propaganda that the West might want one. My prevailing impression was of a vast, slow-moving society almost strangled by bureaucracy, with Gogol's Inspector-General to the fore. To get a tyre blown up entailed an hour and a half of form signing. It was the only country in which I have been asked to show my passport on the road, more than once and without any irregularity in my driving.

We drove 2500 miles in Russia, sometimes between towns

on forbidden roads without a guide, seeing dilapidated little wooden houses with apparently contented inhabitants. The countryside seemed better off. Before 1914 well-fed Russia was a huge exporter of grain. Give half the land, instead of 1.3%, to the peasants now, and she would be again. Russia could quickly be made a rich country if the Communist ropes were untied.

The Russians, like the British, are certain that they are superior to anyone else. They are more than our equal in kindness. Motor-cyclists would go miles to show us the way, the police guided us to petrol pumps often sixty miles apart. Between Smolensk and Borodino I saw at a filling station that a tyre was flat with a puncture. Fortunately there was an interpreter who explained the problem to a group of lorry drivers who came to help. They asked for a jack. Short of space for luggage I had none; I was not much good at using it when it was on board. Six burly, amused men lifted the car and held it in the air while the wheel was changed. They inspected the engine admiringly and patted me on the back, delighted with the Biro pens (then rare in Russia) which I distributed. But, they asked the interpreter, why did I carry no tools?

'It is the business of the wealthy man to give employment to the artisan,' I answered, quoting Belloc.

The interpreter must have made a good translation. There were roars of laughter from the small crowd now assembled. At last a real-life capitalist with more money than sense and not breathing fire from his nostrils. A thousand miles farther on I had a second puncture. Motorists and bystanders rushed to help and one of them had a jack. Visiting politicians and newspapermen see little of the ordinary Russians. I think I saw a fair sample. If the men in the Kremlin reflected their outlook we could get massive disarmament, but Russian rulers have always been paranoic and imperialist and the Russian people have never sought to influence their rulers.

We came back in time for the election campaign. If I had not known already that I had nothing to expect from Wilson, an incident during that campaign would have confirmed it. The BBC asked me to appear on a peak-time discussion programme. I agreed and cancelled two meetings arranged for that night, explaining why to the Bosworth voters. When the announcement was made, frantic calls came from Labour headquarters. John Harris, then aide to Wilson, told me that Wilson refused to allow me to appear. When I said that he could not stop me, I was told that the Party would be gravely embarrassed if I made a public scene. If I insisted, the Party would exercise its formal right with the BBC to choose which of its candidates should appear. It was a nasty slap in the face which caused me mild humiliation in Bosworth when the Press got hold of the story. It was very different from the 1959 campaign, when my appearance was demanded in every official Labour TV broadcast.

I did better in Bosworth than 1959 because of the national and regional swing. My majority advanced from 1393 to 5751, more than Arthur Allen's in 1955. I hoped that Bosworth was becoming a really safe seat. As usual I had not rushed around night and day, week-day and week-end. This displeased some of the local enthusiasts, so I asked the National Opinion Poll to examine the swing in Bosworth compared with elsewhere and got the comforting reply that it was 3.8 per cent to Labour and 'you did at least five times better than the Labour candidates around you and certainly far better than the national average'. My critics were unconvinced, never understanding how little local candidates have to do with winning general elections.

# CHAPTER XIV

————◖◗◖◗————

# The Government
# Shall Not Pass

WHEN WILSON WAS FORMING his government I wondered what I should say if he asked me to join it. I resented his being at No. 10. My distrust of him was the same as always. I felt he had weak principles, scarcely any that took precedence over his single-minded self-interest. *Après moi le déluge* was his motto, and no provision for umbrellas. Yet I did not dissuade George Brown from asking Wilson to include Desmond Donnelly and me in the Government. It is amazing how quickly the mind can adapt. Christopher Mayhew was profuse with denunciations of Wilson and said he would never serve under him. His anger rose as more appointments were filled without any summons to him from No. 10. In the very last batch he became a minister for the Royal Navy. Next day he told me how marvellous Wilson was; we had not understood his difficulties; he had saved the Party. Christopher had changed his view of Wilson back to his original one when he resigned in 1966.

I like to say to myself that I should have sternly resisted any approach from Wilson, but the truth is that I should have done the same as Christopher. I was faced with no crisis of conscience: the question did not arise. But what was apparent was that a resolute back-bench Labour MP with his government dependent on a knife-edge majority could have more power than if he were a minister, especially if he had a friend he could rely on. Wilson must have disliked me a lot to have missed that point. For instance, in 1965 the Tory speaker Hylton-Foster died.

Wilson wanted another Tory to keep the Labour majority intact. The Speaker cannot vote except in a tie and then it must be for the *status quo*. A Labour Speaker meant reducing the fractional Labour majority by one. Horace King, Deputy Speaker, was in line to be Labour's first Speaker and there was sympathy for him in the Party, though they were prepared to do as they were told and vote in another Conservative: it is always easy to find a Tory for such an agreeable job, and enough of them supported the Government's wish to give it to a Tory. Charles Pannell, a prominent Labour MP, said publicly that this would be unfair to Horace. Desmond and I (in a Press article) did the same and we told the whips we wanted Horace. They had to give in. Reducing the Government's majority was an important factor in giving us more power.

On 20 October Jo Grimond, the Liberal leader, came to lunch at Tower House with Desmond Donnelly. He gave us his assurance that the Liberals would back us in anything we did to stop 100 per cent steel nationalization. Desmond was against doing anything to tamper with steel. I was in favour of a 51 per cent BP government shareholding solution to meet the Labour Party's wish to have more control of the industry but not to destroy it.

As early as November 1959 I had begun to discuss with Sir Cyril Musgrave, the Chairman, and other members of the Iron and Steel Board, the possibility of a compromise between State and private ownership which would end the damaging seesaw of alternate governments. The Government actually had all the powers, through the Iron and Steel Board, that it could ever reasonably need. No nationalization was necessary to give the Government control over output, investment, the location and types of new plant, because they already had it. My compromise would keep the companies intact and the profit motive alive, and stop the inevitable slide to subsidy and huge job losses.

I had said as much in a *New Statesman* article in January 1962, so this was no opportunistic leap at a chance to embarrass Wilson. For a long time it had been my settled intention to do what I could to stop Labour lumbering itself and the nation with a gratuitous disaster, and I said so at election meetings at Bosworth. With the Liberals and Desmond Donnelly, and the Government's effective majority down to four, it could be done. With Jo's help we drafted a letter to Wilson. It began with a nice hypocrisy, 'we wish you every success in your difficult task', and went on:

In the hope that it may be of help to you in formulating your plans we thought we should let you know straightaway that we will not be able to support nationalisation of steel if it were done in a manner similar to that used for the Railways, Coal, Electricity. We feel that any attempt at old style nationalisation of steel would alienate middle of the road opinion in the country and that it would be seen to be a waste of Parliamentary energies irrelevant to more pressing economic problems. It would, therefore, be certain of losing us the next Election. We believe that there are compromise solutions possible which would not only be acceptable to the Liberals but might take steel out of the political battle altogether. There are others in the Parliamentary party who are of the same opinion as ourselves.

Jo was going down to the House and offered to put the letter in the mail to be sent over to the Prime Minister. Absent-mindedly, he gave it to an official Liberal Party messenger, who delivered it separately to No. 10 and was observed to do so, as Wilson caustically observed in his reply to me. Perhaps that was a good thing: Wilson knew that the threat was serious.

Desmond Donnelly was a large, lumpy man with an ugly but not repulsive face. He had ability and energy and was a good, unpolished speaker. He had strong enthusiasms, sometimes sustained and sometimes not. He was devoted to Nye until he saw that Bevanism was opening the road to a lunatic Left take-over of the Labour Party. At a Labour Party Conference he tipped off the Press and photographers that he was about to make a speech announcing that he had changed sides. Dramatically pointing his arm towards an astonished Bevan and his friends, he did so. He had courage and verve but was not assiduous in studying details, so his writings and speeches lacked content. He became a strong adherent of Hugh's, always in attendance. He was an encouraging friend to have around.

He loved publicity more than most politicians. When he wanted his name in the papers Desmond dispensed with the formality of addressing a meeting. He would send for a local reporter and, standing at his garden gate in Pembroke, would read out a statement starting, 'Labour MP Desmond Donnelly speaking in his Pembroke constituency said . . .' and ensure that his 'speech' got on to the London tapes. He lived rumbustiously and extravagantly, dreaming up schemes to make money which came to little. He had a keen interest in women which got him into tangles. He was a full if not steady character. Apt to be boastful, he talked too much. Once he blurted out to a pressman the details of behind-the-scenes negotiations I had been having with the Iron and Steel Federation (the steel-owners) and the Government. I had impressed on him the essential need for secrecy. When I exploded he said engagingly, 'You know I am a compulsive talker. Please don't tell me anything confidential again.'

I did not. Wilson distrusted him so much that he would never speak to him, only to me whom he did trust, whatever his other feelings about me. But Desmond was the only supporter I had on whose bravery to fight to the end I could rely. Others like George Strauss, who as Minister of Power introduced the first steel nationalization Bill in 1949, were against the present proposal but were frightened to say they would vote against it.

Desmond Donnelly later formed a party of his own and eventually joined the Tories, but they would not give him a safe seat to fight. The Tories rarely welcome converts. Winston, who started as a Conservative, joined the Liberals and rejoined the Conservatives, only just made the passage. Reg Prentice did for a while. Evelyn King and Aidan Crawley, former Labour ministers who became Tory MPs, attained no office. Disappointed Desmond, for whom political life meant everything, haunted by money and other worries, committed suicide. He did not realize that, so far as money was concerned, there would have been willing friends to help him. He killed himself in the Trust House Forte Post House Hotel at Heathrow. Every time I drive past it I think of him and metaphorically raise my hat to that unquiet man who was on the side of good.

Nationalization of steel was the centre-piece of the Government's legislation. The very Left regarded the Government's firmness on this issue as a test of attachment to true socialism: and on this issue were supported by many moderates. Wilson was scared of antagonizing them. Were Desmond and I really serious? A war of nerves began. Soon after our letter we saw George Brown, Secretary for Economic Affairs. I told him I would vote against any 100 per cent nationalization, and Desmond said he would at least abstain. George previously had not been keen on total nationalization but was now committed to it to keep on-side with the Left. He wanted to get 'the unpleasant thing over with quickly', which I told him I should not allow.

To get the Press buzzing I had a series of lunches at Tower House with Desmond present. Among those who came were Peregrine Worsthorne, Terry Lancaster of the *Daily Express*, Walter Terry of the *Daily Mail*, Nora Beloff of the *Observer*, John Boyd of the *Guardian*, Wilfred Sendall of the *News of the World*, William Rees-Mogg, Deputy Editor of the *Sunday Times*, James Margach, chief political writer on the same paper, and so on. Our means of putting across our case were not so good as Wilson's, but they were not bad. Steel nationalization, despite our warning, had gone into the Queen's Speech. The Government had to deliver. George Brown asked for another meeting on 10 December. We told him we would not budge.

After Christmas rumours, originating from No. 10, began that when it came to the point we would chicken out. There was another gambit. At a party at the end of January Ivan Yates, a political correspondent of the *Observer*, well in touch with No. 10, spoke to me. He hinted at an important job or a peerage, indicating that he was bearing a message.

'To keep me quiet about steel?'

'Yes.'

'They would have to modify the Steel Bill first.'

'You mean Wilson will have to eat his words if you won't eat yours?'

'Tell him he's had more practice at it than I have.'

Doubtless my reply was reported. When stories circulated, not from me, that I had been offered a peerage, Wilson denied them when questioned in the House. He moved in cunning ways his wonders to perform.

The Steel Bill was daily awaited. To remove all possible doubt I invited to lunch the Chief Whip, Ted Short, who now has a redolent name, Lord Glenamara. He came on 3 February 1965. He was put out to see Desmond, but I thought it advisable to have a witness, and he was my partner. Patrick Gordon-Walker had lost Smethwick in the General Election but had been made Foreign Secretary without a seat in the House. Reg Sorensen was made a peer to make way for Patrick in a by-election at safe Leyton, but Patrick had just lost that, too. The majority was down to three. I told Ted I would definitely vote against 100 per cent nationalization and he should be in no doubt about it. Donnelly said he would at least abstain. That would mean a dead heat, with the Speaker obliged to vote against to maintain the *status quo*. So goodbye to the Steel Bill. Ted was not surprised. He said I would not be endorsed as a candidate at the election which would follow immediately if the Government were defeated on steel.

'I am trying to make you understand,' I said, 'that our deterrent is credible. It might destroy us both but it would work, so why precipitate a general election by doing something foolish?' I knew that Wilson would not call a general election without strong signs of a Labour recovery from its current slump in the opinion polls.

Short had been waiting for a chance to speak to me alone. He got it when Desmond went to the lavatory. Then he said something he could not have said without Wilson's approval: 'Would you take a good job before the Steel Bill?'

I longed to ask what job it would be, but that would have seemed like discussing the price at which I would sell my principles.

'Not unless the Steel Bill is modified.'

'Will you at least abstain if I promise to convey any memorandum of yours to the Prime Minister and the ministerial committee responsible for the Bill?'

'That's no bargain at all. I can send them what I like any way.'

The last shot was to canvass my reactions to a trip as a one-man delegation to any part of the world, preferably the most distant, so that I should not be in England when the vote came. An isolated Donnelly would at the worst abstain, possibly not even that, if I were not at his side. The Government would have a guaranteed majority of at least one, maybe more. I was not in a travelling mood.

Suspecting that the Chief Whip might one day pretend this conversation had never happened — governments and prime ministers do not like their murky deals behind the scenes exposed to the light – I made a careful note of it in the diary I kept for this period. I also reported it to Desmond as soon as Ted Short had gone; I did not want Desmond to think I had been making deals behind his back. When years later Ted Short made evasive noises about the bargain he had tried to make, Desmond wrote a letter to *The Times* confirming the details I had immediately given him of my conversation. Perhaps Ted's memory was hazy. Mine was not. I might have got my political career going again if I had accepted some formula for papering over the cracks, which was another reason why I recorded the conversation.

Towards the end of February the Bill was still undergoing its birth pangs, not ready to meet the world. I chanced on George Wigg, Paymaster-General and Wilson's trouble fixer, in the corridor and endured a bout of blustering bullying, ending with a threat to stand against me at Bosworth. This would have been silly of him as he had a safe seat at Dudley. On my telling him to calm down he executed a volte-face and asked me to put forward a compromise which would save everyone's face. I drafted a paper and asked him to lunch on 10 March, to read it. George liked it a lot and asked for some rejigging so that he could give it to the Prime Minister. I sent it to him on Friday 12 March.

It was four thousand words long. I can reread it with pleasure but it is too boring to retail here. It was acceptable to the steel industry. It would have met Labour's manifesto pledge that 'private monopoly of steel will be replaced by public ownership and control' by providing for 51 per cent ownership. It would have appealed to the middle-of-the-road voters and neutralized opposition. It would have taken steel out of politics and enabled steel to operate commercially, like BP, unhampered by continuous destructive interference from governments asking for the impossible. It would have preserved jobs. It would have saved the taxpayer hundreds of millions of pounds in compensation and billions of pounds in losses, which were still persisting at £1 million or more a day in 1984. It would have given the Government control over the whole industry, not merely over the thirteen major companies to be nationalized. It would have got everyone off the hook.

But imbued with the bigotry of the big enders and little enders encountered by Gulliver (which end is the morally correct one from which to eat a boiled egg?) the opposing forces were resolute in their fervour. A majority of the Cabinet saw the folly of 100 per cent nationalization, but to a large element of their followers it was an article of faith. The following Tuesday a small victory was signalled. Wilson announced that the long-awaited Bill would now be preceded by a White Paper, to be followed by a Bill later in the session. Next day I told the Chief Whip that I hoped the Government was not taking up rigid positions from which they could not withdraw.

'Would you like to see the PM?'

'That's not for me to propose. I am willing to see him if he would like to see me.'

Desmond and I met George Brown that same afternoon. He was at his most abusive.

'I'm going into Bosworth to start fighting you now [his constituency, Belper, was not far away]. If you make the Government give in over steel, which you won't, I shall leave the Government. I have told Wilson I am seeing you and am going to make you take a different attitude. You bring the Government down and destroy me and I'll destroy you', and much more irrelevant nonsense. I laughed uproariously, which set him off again: 'You don't take the Labour Party seriously.' Well, neither of us is in it now.

The following day at 6.15 I saw Wilson in his room at the House. The strong man of the day before was replaced by one oozing butter and charm. I was pressed to have whisky or the brandy Wilson was getting fond of in those days. For nearly half an hour he talked about Vietnam and India, laying it on thick about my great knowledge of the latter country. At last he said, 'I have read your memorandum, I really have read it and studied it very carefully. I have two objections.' They were both trivial and procedural, touching on the delicate rule of hybridity, and readily surmountable, as I pointed out. Wilson made me repeat the advantage of the 51 per cent scheme. 'I said to George Brown when I read your paper, "Oh, Woodrow is more of a socialist than the rest of us. He wants us to go further."' Plop, plop went the butter.

Wilson was totally cynical. As he walked round and round the big table he kept saying, 'I'm a pragmatist'; then, 'I don't think there are ten votes in the country in steel one way or another but I'm stuck with it. I think you are anti-ideological, too. If I could prove to you that 100 per cent nationalization is anti-ideological, you'd support it.' He was attracted by my scheme and felt it might be extended to the machine-tool and other industries. Indeed, it has since been used elsewhere, notably in British Aerospace. 'My mind is open,' he repeated several times. And, suddenly: 'This is going very well. I've conceded a number of points and you have conceded some.'

When I said my model would get through the House much more smoothly he replied, 'I'm not going to discuss with you which way you are going to vote. I can't run a government on that basis. I should be blackmailed by everyone. You are only the second deputation I have received since I became Prime Minister.' Then he corrected himself hastily: 'But of course you aren't really a deputation because I invited you to come.' But he would not have invited me if he had not been terrified that I might use my vote to bring his government down.

It was a jolly, apparently frank conversation ending: 'We will have another talk.' I warmed to him, as I had in the past before his ambition incited him to let Attlee down, but he was stringing me along. I met him again on 12 April, the day before he went to America. We went over the ground once more. Wilson proudly said that the narrow majority had not prevented him governing effectively. The flattery was 'Your Lib-Lab pact is coming from below. There is no need for any Labour candidate to stand down. They maybe needed in the future. Your ideas are coming more to pass.' Would I please talk to Fred Lee, Minister of Power?

I did so for an hour and a quarter. It was like talking to a piece of wood. A trade unionist, formerly smiled on by Stafford Cripps, Lee was too dim to understand any of the essential points. I saw him again, with no result. I realized the imminent White Paper would be back to square one.

When it came on 30 April, it was. The thirteen major companies were to be nationalized. The debate on the White Paper to decide whether the Bill would be presented, and hence the fate of the Government, was to be taken hastily on 6 May. Wilson wrote me a long, flattering letter, which I received on 4 May: 'I know . . . disappoint you . . . very full consideration the points you have made . . . assure you that your wishes have been seriously taken into account and the decision against your scheme was in no sense a doctrinaire one.' Ha! Ha! The battle was in two days. Who would run away? The Press and political world wondered.

I had two letters from Ted Short, the Chief Whip. On 3 May he wrote:

> I should like you to understand quite clearly that the government will stand or fall on the result of the division. The Liberals have announced that they intend to oppose us. This means that we have a maximum majority of four. But we also have three members who are seriously ill, and in two cases there will be a definite danger to their lives if I insisted on them coming to vote. It is because of this I must ask you – in spite of your feelings on the matter – to support the government in the Division Lobby.

In the second letter, dated 4 May, Ted Short wrote:

> I would like you to see a letter I have had from the wife of one of our members. He is confined to bed with severe heart strain and has been told by his doctor that he must not travel for the next three weeks: none of this is public knowledge. However, if you are going to abstain this is the type of case that I would have to bring in to cover you.

Both letters had 'copy to the Prime Minister' at the bottom. That is how chief whips twist backbenchers' arms. The frighteners were on. Wilson's smile had gone.

It was to be an unusual debate. The Press was in a turmoil of speculation. Reporters and photographers were massed outside my house as if I were on the way to deliver something as important as a budget speech, which perhaps it was in its way. It was a rare occasion in which two ordinary MPs had their own Government's future in their grasp. It had not happened before in a hundred years or maybe ever.

Desmond and I were determined not to give in. The Gallup poll in the *Daily Telegraph* that morning recorded a swing in one week, because of the steel White Paper, from a 2 per cent Labour lead to an 8 per cent Tory lead. Having an immediate election with steel as the issue would be fatal to the Government. Illnesses made calculation difficult. If Desmond and I voted against the White Paper, the Government would certainly be out. If we merely abstained, the outcome was still hazy.

The House was full. Fred Lee opened with a pedestrian, unconvincing speech. Iain Macleod made a sharp, effective reply, with good jokes about the White Paper being an exercise in public relations within the Labour Party which would not get a hundred supporters if the House were allowed a free vote. 'We know perfectly well that Members who are too sick to be out of bed are to be brought here tonight to vote . . . that men and women who have been on their country's and their own business have been brought back from the other end of the world.'

George Strauss said the Government's plan for steel was absolutely wrong but he would vote for it just the same. The speech everyone was waiting for was mine. Before I spoke I had an urgent message to see George Brown in his room after I had finished. I guessed that meant the Government was cracking. I got up at 6.58 and recited my arguments plainly and without rhetoric. Sydney Silverman interrupted me when I said that I had repeatedly warned the Prime Minister and the Government that I would not vote for 100 per cent nationalization. 'If anything goes wrong in the Division tonight it is as much their responsibility as mine,' I added.

'Is it their responsibility because they don't allow my Honourable friend to dictate to them?' asked Sydney, the harasser of Labour governments.

'My Honourable friend,' I replied, 'has spent most of his life trying to dictate to the Government. Why shouldn't I?'

My joke lightened the sombre atmosphere.

I finished: 'If a steel bill is introduced on lines which are no different from those laid down in the White Paper I shall have to vote against it. . . . But today we haven't got the Bill in front of us. We are voting only on the White Paper. I shall not vote against it, but so far I have heard nothing which makes me think I can vote for it.' The crucial words were 'so far'. I had spoken for thirty-seven minutes to a partly stony but extremely attentive House.

I hurried off to see George Brown. The heat for Wilson and

303

his government had become too fierce and they were melting like chocolate soldiers. Rattled George had a concession to offer. The Government were prepared to say that the White Paper was not their final word. If the steel industry agreed to the government control that he and I thought necessary, the Government would listen to the industry's proposals for less than 100 per cent nationalization. If he announced that at the end of his winding-up speech (he wanted to leave it until the end, when time left for the debate could be counted in seconds: an earlier announcement would cause uproar on the Labour benches), would I vote for the Government and ask Desmond to do the same?

It was a famous victory. Once the Government committed themselves to this deviation there could be no Bill for 100 per cent nationalization in that Parliament. If they tried to wriggle away and produce a Bill for 100 per cent nationalization after all, Desmond and I could still stop it by voting against it, and would have the greater moral force behind us if the Government had betrayed us. Though I knew some would believe or pretend that Desmond and I had given in, George and I both knew it was a Government surrender. I accepted it as such. George and I agreed his exact words. The plan was for me to get up as he finished reciting them and ask him to clarify them again.

Desmond was making his speech when I returned to the chamber. He told me later that during Michael Foot's speech he had accounted for my absence by saying that I was answering 'the calls of nature', an explanation which wore thin after half an hour. When Desmond sat down I whispered to him that after my talk with George we should vote for the Government: with instant loyalty he backed me.

After making a show of disagreeing with me, 'he and I are great personal friends. But in this issue . . .', George described at some length what he understood my position to be, his eye on the clock. Then he reached the fateful words: 'I am prepared to say that if the industry and its friends in the Tory party will come to us and say that they are prepared for the Government to assume the control which we and my Honourable friend [Mr Wyatt] agree is essential, we shall, of course, listen to what they have to say.'

A pleasant smile from Harold Wilson before the storm

Pericles, son of my third marriage, at three

Just married to Verushka, December 7th, 1966

Verushka's Great Uncle
Emile in his regalia

My daughter, Petronella, dreaming at sixteen

A constituent's problem at Bosworth

Henry Porchester, the Queen's Racing Manager, accepts the trophy for the
Tote Bookmakers' Handicap in May 1979 on behalf of the Queen who won
with Buttress. Verushka looks no older than when I married her

Photographed by Diane Lever on her balcony in Eaton Square, Summer 1984

As arranged, I got up: 'Do I understand my Right Honourable friend to say that if the industry will come forward and concede the control which we both agree is necessary on something less than 100 per cent, he is prepared to listen? If so, I shall vote for his White Paper.'

George replied, '"Listen" is the word. "Listen", certainly.'

George had departed slightly from what we had agreed and which had been typed in his room by his secretary. Originally he was to have said, 'The White Paper is not the last word but is the Government's present approach.' I was to have said, 'What does that mean?'

He was to have replied, 'What I mean by that is that we will genuinely take into account the views of my Honourable friend, the Member for Bosworth. I make no promises but the vote tonight does not preclude further thought.' It was slightly different but not much.

The clock struck ten. The last words of this unique debate had been spoken. The Division was called. Despite Ted Short's lurid blackmail, none of the sick and maimed died. The Government won by four votes. There was pandemonium. The Tories and Liberals shouted that Desmond and I had lost our nerve. Michael Foot, Tom Driberg, Ian Mikardo and others on the outside Left quickly guessed that the betrayal of principle was on the other foot. Moorea, Desmond and I went to eat at the Savoy Grill.

The next morning George sent round a letter:

I, more than anybody else, know what it cost you to do what you did last night. No matter what the press have said (and at the time of dictating this I have not seen the papers), or what your friends have said – I simply want to say it was tremendous.

I want to repeat that, if the Industry and its friends, the Tory Party, would come to us and say they are prepared for the government to assume the control which you and I agree is essential we shall, of course, listen to what they have to say.

These are the words on which you and I met. I shall not go back on them and I know you will not.

After hearing on the news how the debate had ended, Randolph Churchill sent off a telegram from East Bergholt at 11.30

p.m. (I was lucky not to be rung in the middle of the night as I, and many of his friends frequently were, when he was excited): 'Think you have made great mistake in neither going half hog nor whole hog Stop No one except myself will ever forgive you Stop Randolph.'

He must rapidly have rung his political sources in the morning. The day after he prematurely blew off his telegram, he wrote:

> I hasten to apologise for, and to withdraw the exceedingly foolish telegram I sent to you after last night's steel debate. I have been abroad for most of the last three months and have seen very few people since my return. On fuller consideration this morning and after talking to some of my friends, it seems to me that you have behaved with cool and crafty cunning and that you may pull off one of the most extraordinary political coups of the century. You have already made Wilson, Brown and Mikardo look extremely foolish and did so in public. This is quite an achievement in itself. I think you will probably kill the Steel Bill for this session. If so, much else will follow. . . .

That was more like it.

I got to work with my friend Julian Pode, Chairman of the Steel Company of Wales. He was a prominent member of the Iron and Steel Federation, the steel-owners' organization. Through him I had met the members frequently and now continued to do so. Most of them were political troglodytes. I had won them a marvellous opportunity to keep their industry intact and they threw it away. They realized I had stopped Wilson's Bill, so that they were safe for this parliament. The opinion polls had turned so badly against Labour that they thought the Tories would be back at the next election. Why bother to parley about handing over 51 per cent of their shareholdings? They took no thought for the morrow.

The chairmen of the thirteen companies slated for nationalization issued a statement on the Wednesday after the debate. They suggested a new authority with stronger powers than the old Iron and Steel Board to supervise the whole industry, including the 220 companies hitherto free of control from any government body. They said 'fully adequate control is obtainable without the need for state-held shareholdings in the individual

306

companies'. It was logical, but the fools had ignored the religious feelings of the Labour Party. The crucial point was to keep the companies' structures intact whatever rationalization leading to mergers their boards might agree on. The statement was the best I could do with this group of backwoodsmen. The wiser ones agreed with me, but the majority blindly carried them all to their destruction.

I battled on with George Brown and Harold Wilson, and worked on the steel-owners. If Wilson had been taken at the flood, the industry could have been saved, but he was losing interest. He knew I would not allow a 100 per cent nationalization Bill and was gearing himself to leave it out of the November Queen's Speech. As he wrote in his book, *The Labour Government, 1964–70*: 'It was clear that with a majority of three, even if we were able to maintain that majority, we would have the utmost difficulty in carrying the Bill through every stage of a legislative process. I was not prepared to become a hostage of Messrs. Donnelly & Wyatt, to say nothing of their possible allies. We preferred to wait until we had an adequate majority.'

My last meeting with Wilson on the topic was on 6 July. I told him that I had persuaded the steel-owners to agree to the disbanding of the Iron and Steel Federation, to have government directors on each board, and to consider special government voting shares. This interested him and he asked for a note to be sent, with top security, through Marcia Williams, quickly changing the channel to George Wigg (Wigg was increasingly resentful of Marcia's participation in affairs he thought did not concern her). I sent it to Wilson and that was about the last of the affair.

Most of our conversation was on other topics. We talked about getting Liberal support for the Government. Wilson was attracted by the alternative vote and was having some research done on it. He thought the best approach to get Liberal backing was to say to them that they would never get the alternative vote, which might give them thirty seats, from the Tories, but could do so from Labour so if the Government were defeated their last chance would be gone. I named a Liberal MP, a lawyer, who might be opposed to such a deal between the Liberals and the Labour Government.

Wilson grinned: 'He'd make a good judge, don't you think?'

I named another Liberal lawyer, who might be doubtful.

Wilson grinned again: 'He would make a good judge, too.'

Wilson asked me why I was so certain that the public would be behind the things I advocated.

'Because I am the average man,' I said.

He pondered this for a while and looked at me quizzically. 'No, I don't think you are the average man, but you know how he thinks.'

A considerable compliment.

In March 1966 Labour won a thumping majority and Wilson was free to do as he chose including the 100 per cent nationalization of steel. The foolish steel-owners saw their industry ruined and the country suffer the appalling losses I had forecast. In 1980 a three months' strike added to steel's tribulations. My relations with both sides, from my past interest in steel, were such that I was able to arrange secret meetings at my house between the union leaders and senior officials of British Steel, which led to the appointment of Harold Lever as chairman of a committee which brought the strike to an end. British Steel gave me a decorative plate.

The first Chairman of the nationalized Steel Corporation was an old friend of mine, Julian Melchett. He had not been there long before he said, 'You were right about that 51 per cent. We're getting such constant government interference we can never make steel work. If we'd only had a 49 per cent private shareholding the Government couldn't have stopped us running it commercially.' He said the same when Verushka and I had dinner alone with him and his perennially youthful and elegant wife, Sonia, at their house in Tite Street a few weeks before Julian died of a heart attack in June 1973 at the age of forty-eight. So another of my dearest friends vanished prematurely.

It was not Julian's first heart attack. He expected to die young but was not deterred from working and playing hard, perhaps cramming in all he could in his last years. As he was the senior male descendant of the great Alfred Mond, through whom ICI was founded, he was thought to have inherited a fortune. In fact he got almost nothing; his unpleasant mother saw to that. Julian made his own way by work and inventiveness.

He enjoyed spending his money on such amusements as flying his own aeroplane to the sizeable and successful farm which he bought in Norfolk. I can see him now, standing in his upstairs drawing-room laughing at some joke, his face half-turned as he opened a bottle of champagne (a position I often saw him in). He loved parties and having friends around him. In Majorca the grounds in the beautiful house he built dropped down to the sea. He was keen on midnight naked bathing parties in the moonlight, forcing the girls to frolic in the warm sea. When a pretty one – now respectably married – refused, he said, 'Good Lord, she's been to bed with every man in London and now she jibs at swimming with nothing on.'

I was in the West Country when I heard on the car radio that Julian had died. I stopped the car and cried. He was about to announce a profit made by British Steel: the prelude to the deluge of losses when he had gone.

# CHAPTER XV

# As One Door Closes

I HAD SOME TROUBLE at Bosworth over steel. A section of the miners wanted a different candidate for the next election. Frank Smith, the Secretary/Agent of the Leicestershire area of the mineworkers' union and a sturdy friend, wrote to tell me that the miners had decided to withdraw their support and money from the constituency party. I commissioned an opinion poll in Bosworth. It demonstrated that my attitude towards steel was overwhelmingly supported by the voters, including a majority of miners, and that no other Labour candidate would do as well. My continuous reports to the local party on what was happening, and why, also paid off. The rumpus subsided.

In the March 1966 election I got my best majority in Bosworth – 7773, an increase of 2000 over 1964. I was the only Labour candidate not to mention Harold Wilson from start to finish at my meetings or in my election address, save for a tiny reference that I would be speaking at his rally in Leicester, which I could hardly avoid. He was no more pleased to see me than I was to see him.

My next four years in Parliament were a waste of time. I teased Wilson sometimes. When Nixon was elected in 1968 Wilson told the House of his wish urgently to go to Washington to see the new President. He wanted to be first in the queue of Western leaders. 'Why this unseemly rush?' I asked. 'Doesn't the Prime Minister realize that when the President wants to see him he'll send for him?' The House dissolved in laughter at Wilson's discomfiture.

At a Party meeting in May 1966 I was attacking our outdated East of Suez policy, maintaining forces and bases we could not afford and which were inconsistent with our foreign policy – a last echo of a vanished Empire. The reason we maintained it, I said, was because the Americans had told us we would not get any money from them if we did not do so.

Wilson jumped up furiously: 'I have denied that five times.'

I retorted, 'There may not be a written agreement but there is certainly a verbal understanding.'

Wilson jumped up again: 'This is absolutely monstrous. It's totally untrue.'

'Well,' I said, 'if we are not even getting paid for it, the policy is even barmier than I thought it was.'

The Party meeting was not used to seeing Wilson squashed and loved it, roaring with laughter. Wilson sat sullenly silent for a while and left the meeting without saying anything further. Party meetings were supposed to be secret but the Government was in the habit of leaking doctored versions to lobby correspondents. I was irritated by the bogus impression they gave of this East of Suez debate, so on 2 June I published an accurate account of it in the *Daily Mirror*, openly breaking the rules.

There was fury and artificial horror. Ted Heath asked the Prime Minister in the House whether my account were true. Wilson repudiated it, but no one believed him. There were funny cartoons in the papers, making Wilson look silly. I was hauled before the Party Liaison Committee chaired by Manny Shinwell; I was threatened by my old enemy the Chief Whip, Ted Short. I was told I would be censured and disciplined by the Parliamentary Party. I laughed. At the Party meeting I turned the tables on the Government by referring to their leaks in breach of the secrecy rule, citing among others the activities of Gerald Kaufman, then the Parliamentary Party's Press Liaison Officer. I asked what the fuss was about. Wilson had repudiated my account (which all present knew to be accurate), so I could not have been leaking anything from the Party meeting, could I? The Government retreated and the matter was dropped. It was harmless fun.

Denis Healey was Secretary for Defence and soon withdrew most of our forces from East of Suez, which were big enough to be an irritant in their neighbourhoods but not big enough to impose British policy. Denis was an excellent minister; he had the respect of senior officers and was able to persuade them into sensible economies which saved money without wrecking the effectiveness of the Services. But for the erosion of the Party by the Broad Left (Marxist extremists) he would have become its leader. He trimmed considerably to get their support to neutralize them, but he could not pretend to believe in our abandoning our nuclear defences, and throwing out US nuclear bases, while Russia kept hers. He made anti-American noises, but unconvincingly, upsetting his friends who knew he did not mean them without winning over his enemies.

Denis knew more about the intricacies of politics abroad than anyone in Parliament and used his compendious knowledge for good or harm largely in accord with what he saw to be his personal advantage. As Chancellor of the Exchequer he often did things harmful to the economy to ingratiate himself with the Marxist Left. It was sad to see him prostitute his brain and still not get the prize he was after. That the Labour Party should prefer first the amiable man of no political substance, Michael Foot, and then a lightweight trendy like Neil Kinnock, is another proof of its deterioration. Denis was always a poor orator, meandering lengthily, but he was a good debater and much more likely to get the better of Mrs Thatcher than Callaghan, Wilson or Kinnock. When Denis saw that the minnows were taking over he should have opted for an international job, like President of the European Economic Community, Secretary-General of NATO, or head of one of the greater inter-governmental institutions. He would have been admirable in that kind of work, relieved of the burden of adjusting to internal Party intrigues, able to do and say confidently what he believed.

Callaghan was not in the same class as Denis. He was an inept Chancellor of the Exchequer, an indifferent Home Secretary, a poor Foreign Secretary and an unsuccessful Prime Minster. When we were first in Parliament together I used to have lunch with him on Sundays with his family at Blackheath and enjoyed it. When our seniors intrigued against each other he said, 'We of our generation are never going to behave like that.' He forgot that precept as he grew older.

Wilson was not always without courage. He backed America over Vietnam and the Nigerian Government over Biafra. His bravest action was his attempt to get some trade union reform. Callaghan had promoted himself with the trade union leaders as having a special link with them because of his own trade union background. He joined the Civil Service when he was seventeen, spent the war commendably in the Navy, and then went back to his white-collar union in a part-time job. It was a thin connection with the great industrial and labouring unions, but Jim worked it up. It had got him the important job of Treasurer of the Labour Party in 1967, which he held until 1976, and he banked on trade union support to get him the leadership, which it largely did in 1976. In 1969 Callaghan saw that by opposing trade union reform he could not ingratiate himself further with the trade union leaders, few of whom had been elected by the individual votes of all their members.

These unrepresentative trade union leaders, all-powerful on the General Council of the TUC, were accustomed, whenever the Labour Party had weak leadership, to control the policies of the Party through the autocratic use of their block votes and indispensable role as paymasters. Attlee and Gaitskell did not let them get away with it; Wilson seemed a push-over, which in general he was. But in 1968 he appointed a spirited and still attractive lady, Barbara Castle, as Secretary for Employment. Barbara had bouts of commonsense and an intelligent woman's desire, similar to that of Mrs Thatcher, to clean up messes. As a minister she was energetic and brave.

Strikes, mainly unofficial, were tangling the machinery of industry and terrorizing employers into excessive wage payments, at a time when full employment made labour hard to get. Agreements were more freely broken than ever by unions. Even Wilson could see the damage to the balance of payments and the potential electoral backlash. It was not difficult for Barbara to persuade him that something should be done.

In January 1969 she produced a modest White Paper, sentimentally called *In Place of Strife* after Nye's shallow proclamation of faith *In Place of Few*. It proposed legislation providing, *inter alia*, for a twenty-eight-day cooling-off period for unofficial strikes; for the Secretary for Employment to have the power to order a ballot before an unofficial strike; for unions to have proper rules about the election of officials, strike ballots and the protection of members from arbitrary executives.

The union leaders were angry at Wilson's unexpected temerity. Callaghan, a member of the inner Cabinet, openly supported his union patrons on Labour's National Executive against the Government when a resolution was put condemning the legislation. Attlee would have fired him immediately. The fearful Wilson pretended nothing had happened. The emboldened Callaghan went public again just over a month later, in May. It seemed impossible to anyone but Wilson that he could stay in the Government; Wilson merely told him that he hoped he would not resign, but would he mind not being in the inner Cabinet? The Government was on the run.

Barbara, and to some extent Wilson, fought nearly to the end, almost isolated in the Cabinet. The surrender to the unrepresentative union leaders in return for worthless promises of good behaviour was announced in mid-June. Callaghan's intentions had been fulfilled, to be rewarded in 1976.

One of his first acts as Prime Minister was to throw Barbara, by then Secretary for the Social Services, out of his Cabinet, where he would no longer have to face her scornful eyes. I liked Barbara, despite disagreeing with her on most major issues. She was a jolly girl and no prude, ever ready for a party and a laugh. Shamelessly and sensibly she trapped her male adversaries with her exceptional feminine charm and banged them on the head with a brain as good as theirs. If she had led Labour against Mrs Thatcher the contest would have been amazing.

Callaghan, when Prime Minister, told Tony how sad he was not to have had a university education. Neither Tony nor I could see how it would have helped him get any further, but the lack of it made him feel inferior and inclined to bluster and bully. It also gave him an impetus to prove he could get to the top. Attlee thought him over-ambitious and refused, to Jim's annoyance, to make him more than a junior minister saying, when Callaghan protested, that no one had a prescriptive right to promotion. Callaghan had a residual patriotism. So did Wilson; they have both displayed it more since leaving office than when they were in it.

Two things primarily lost Wilson the 1970 election: his running away from the union leaders and his own conceit. He toured the country, cockily assuming the election was already won, asking people to have tea with him at No. 10 after it was over. Being Prime Minister does not stimulate humility; the electorate enjoy punishing hubris and those who take them for granted. If Labour had won, I think Wilson would have resigned soon afterwards. He was bored with politics. He hung on until the election of 1974, to convince himself that he had not lost his gift for bamboozling the people and could become Prime Minister again. There were dark suspicions about his resigning in 1976 at the unusually early age of sixty. Was some fearful scandal about to break? There was no scandal; Wilson was just world-weary. His resignation was nice for his sweet wife Mary, who loathed the tawdry atmosphere of political intrigue. Wilson should never have been Prime Minister and I liked him better when he gave it up and started to be a more wholesome man. When those who were obsequious to him in power turned to kicking him when powerless, I attacked his detractors. When I meet him now he sometimes says plaintively, 'You never understood what I was trying to do', but I think I did.

The worst hit by his resignation was Marcia Williams, who began to work for him as his personal Political Secretary in 1956. She loved the power and bolstered Wilson's courage when she favoured action on which he was weakening. He depended on her and she was his principal confidante, influencing Wilson so blatantly that many resented it. I understand the hold Marcia had over Wilson. She has a lively brain, adores the political scene, stays loyal and pretty. Wilson was lucky to find her.

I owed nothing to Wilson. Several times he urged the Mirror Group to stop my column and tried to prevent my readoption at Bosworth. He was a disastrous Prime Minister, shielding the British from the inevitable meeting with reality, hypnotising them into voting for him, to a worse degree even than Macmillan. It is his fault that the Labour Party, sound when he inherited it from Hugh, turned so rotten that the Marxist element became dominant and the SDP emerged. But despite what I have written, I like him.

On the last day of the 1966 Parliament I went into the Members' Smoking Room. There was no business to draw me to the House. I must have had a touch of Arthur Koestler's extra-sensory perception and gone subconsciously to say goodbye to the familiar chamber, the corridors, the Barry masterpiece where I had enjoyed the gossip, made friends, seen some excitement, but achieved little in twenty-five years since I first entered Parliament. The hopes, the dreams of July 1945, were dead leaves. I was fifty-two. A Tory MP said to me, 'You've got no worries. Your majority is nearly 8000, isn't it?' I agreed, but not with the confidence I should have had.

At Bosworth in 1970 there was no Liberal candidate, as on the previous occasions. That made me a little nervous, as Bosworth was an area where Liberal candidates tended to draw more from the Conservatives than Labour. Since 1966 there had been an influx of owner-occupiers from Leicester into agreeable new houses and housing estates in the Bosworth countryside who knew nothing of me and were natural Tory voters. The younger miners (in Leicestershire miners do not automatically vote Labour or go on strike with the rest of the NUM) were complaining about high taxes on their high wages and hinting at voting Tory. For the first time in history a miners' band had recently played at a Tory Party fête. There was a movement in the air which suggested a smaller majority but not defeat.

A few fanatically Marxist left wingers, newly resident for the purpose, had infiltrated the respectably staid management committee. They were hostile to me, saying that many voters thought I was a Tory. They were not placated when I retorted that that was why we had such a big Labour vote in a sprawling county constituency which normally would have gone Tory years ago. My internal opponents were not important, putting off only a few voters with their talk of pure socialism.

More worrying was the appearance at meetings of self-styled 'Paki-Bashers', a term new and abhorrent to me. There had been substantial coloured immigration in Leicester but none in Bosworth and in the country areas. Enoch Powell, who won Wolverhampton West with a more than doubled majority in 1970, had worked up the fear that coloured immigrants would soon flood the Midlands and elsewhere, spreading all over Britain. Heath had sacked Enoch Powell from the Shadow Cabinet for saying, 'Like the Romans, I seem to see the River Tiber foaming with much blood', and talking of other horrors to come from the coloured influx, but without the assistance of

Powell's anti-immigrant speeches Ted Heath might not have won the election.

The opinion polls remained set fair. Nothing could go wrong. Our eve-of-poll meetings were as crowded and as friendly as before. As usual the star speaker was Bernard Levin, long a treasured friend. He tends to have insomnia, so he can be rung at all hours for advice, comment, jokes and general conversation. When I first met Bernard, Randolph Churchill said, 'Look out, he's got the most remarkable brain and memory I have ever encountered. He will trip you up if he doesn't like you.' For consistent brilliance as a journalist no one has surpassed him, and that includes his hero H.L. Mencken. As a friend to weep with or laugh with, I could not do without him: I am glad that in the nature of things I shall die before he does.

My fondness for Bernard once annoyed my present wife, Verushka. Before we were married he stayed in a house we had taken in Spain. The day he arrived she asked me, 'Would you rather talk to Bernard Levin than to me?' 'Sometimes,' I said, thinking it obvious that men do like to talk to old men friends. When we settled down to the political implications of what we read in the English newspapers, something which did not interest her, her hostility rose to the point of refusing to get out of the car to look at an exceptionally beautiful cathedral. Bernard noticed nothing, but it was some years before the legacy of my tactlessness evaporated and she was pleased to see him.

Bernard and I have few disagreements on serious matters, though I suppose Bernard thinks music is serious. We have moved, politically, in parallel, or stayed the same as others have moved around us. In 1970 we both felt the same about Wilson: that he was still just the better bet. At the eve-of-poll meeting Bernard made his customary brilliant speech. As the final cheers and cries of 'It's in the bag' died away I was more sanguine of the morrow than Richard III the night before his battle at Bosworth.

It was my ritual to visit all the committee-rooms near the polling-stations. Everything seemed fine, with polling around normal for the time of day and the usual number saying they had voted Labour. But as I drove through the fields, stopping to pay my respects at the chapel where King Dickon said his last mass, I had another acute attack of extra-sensory perception. Against the evidence, the premonition settled upon me that I would never again see the fields and villages, the grammar school in Market Bosworth where Dr Johnson once taught. At about eight o'clock reports came in that large numbers in council-housing estates solid for Labour, who always left their voting late, were saying they could not be bothered this time. Frantic last-minute efforts by helpers were of no avail. Previously I would have rushed to rally and encourage them, but I thought a fate was working; anyway, there was little I could do, dashing back and forth in a thirty-five-mile-long constituency of some seven hundred square miles. So I had my dinner.

Next morning when our count began, the news had already come of slashed Labour votes in safe seats now lost in the Midlands. I was hopeful until I saw boxes which were usually two or three to one for Labour coming out almost level. Turn-out was down 3 per cent, nearly two thousand votes, confirming the apathy among the traditional supporters. Still, I could not believe we had lost. I was out by just under a thousand. I asked for a recount. I was out by just over a thousand.

The Marxist Broad Left put it down to my being too much of a Tory. I was quickly dropped and a very left-wing candidate chosen in my place. He was defeated by a bigger majority in February 1974 when the pendulum swung and other Midlands seats in the neighbourhood returned to Labour. Bosworth was held by the Conservatives in the second 1974 election and has been becoming safer for the Tories ever since. So much for the theory that the purer the socialism, the greater the support for Labour.

On my way back from Bosworth I stopped at the printing works in Banbury. There was a message from the kind and thoughtful Hugh Cudlipp, in control of the *Daily Mirror*, that my no longer being an MP made no difference to my weekly column. The column had begun early in 1965. Hugh had come to lunch at Tower House and asked how I would spend my time now I was not in the Government. 'I'm going to write a book,' I replied. I had in mind some pompous work intended to explain the workings of politics better than Bagehot.

'What do you want to write a book for? No one will read

it. It will have no influence.' He stopped. 'You'd do much better to write a column in the *Daily Mirror*. Dick Crossman had a lot of influence with his.'

Hugh was Chairman of Daily Mirror Newspapers at the time. I admired him enormously. Better even than Beaverbrook he knew instinctively what to put into a popular newspaper. I would call on him for the amusement of seeing him take a large piece of white paper and a thick pencil and in seconds lay out the front page complete with lively headlines. His bold flair told him when it was the moment for an unusual approach – he would even lead the front page with a column by Dick Crossman or myself or another writer if he thought it was arresting enough. He played with newspapers as a great impresario. In his hands they could not be dull, nor could those who worked for them. He ran the Mirror Newspapers in the Labour interest far more effectively than his brother Percy, hampered by direct union and Party interference, could run the *Daily Herald*. As elections approached, Hugh made it seem to the uninitiated that his papers were undecided, had many criticisms of Labour, were carefully weighing the pros and cons, before coming out with a brilliant, simplified conclusion that Labour it must be.

Hugh was right to engineer the coup which dethroned Cecil King as Chairman of IPC in 1968. King was suffering from Harmsworth megalomania, without the Northcliffe flair and without a majority shareholding. His canvassing for and attempts to organize a government of non-politicians and un-elected businessmen with himself prominent were ridiculous – he even tried to involve Mountbatten. When I was staying the week-end at Harry Walston's, Cecil King assured me with a straight face that his own board would man for man make a better cabinet. He wanted a peerage, but was prepared to accept a life peerage only if it were a life earldom.

However, King was better at operating a large business than Hugh, who found himself in difficulties and had to be bailed out by Reids, run by a man called Ryder, a former editor of the *Stock Exchange Gazette*. It was a miserable affair. Hugh was humiliated and resented Ryder being above him. He gave up editorial control of the Mirror Newspapers in 1973 when he was sixty and with at least ten more years of good newspaper-man left in him. The loss of Hugh's ever young and fresh outlook, though he was surprisingly prudish about nudes and displayed them half-heartedly, contributed to the *Sun*, acquired in 1969 by Rupert Murdoch, overtaking the *Daily Mirror* as the daily paper with the largest circulation.

I had more influence writing weekly in the *Daily Mirror* than as an MP. The small circulation quality papers have some effect on ministers, politicians and civil servants. The mass-circulation papers reach the voters in millions and help to form impressions which carry over into the ballot-box. At the February 1974 election the Tories lost to Labour in ten seats by less than 550 votes apiece. Geoffrey Finsberg, a Tory MP closely associated with Conservative Central Office, told me they had worked it out that if I had urged my readers to vote for Heath, instead of equivocating, the Tories would have got an extra handful of votes in each of the ten seats and have won at least five of them. The score would have been Conservatives 301, Labour 296, not the other way round, and Heath would have survived.

Readership surveys showed that more read all the way through my *Mirror* articles than those of the famous Cassandra (William Connor). Cassandra, despite the occasional vitriol in his pen, was a kind man pretending to be hard-boiled, very fond of cats and often writing and broadcasting about them. In one broadcast with him I argued the superiority of dogs. He became passionate. He was still writing two columns a week for the *Mirror* when I joined, but he died at fifty-eight two years later. He was a traditional Fleet Street drinker.

I could not hope to match his brilliance: I think I matched his audience because his subjects were sometimes esoteric with no concession made to the less educated. I geared myself to explain what was happening in short, simple sentences to readers interested in, but not obsessed by, politics. Fine phrases, even if I were capable of them, would have obscured the message and eaten into the short space, forcing me to leave out some of the things jostling to be said.

I preached a weekly sermon – but the congregation could walk out at any stage without embarrassment. If the sermon stayed too long on any one subject I lost the audience, so I began to cram five or six different items into nine hundred to a thousand words to give variety. Each week I thought how I could engage the attention of the ordinary housewife and keep it; nevertheless, more men than women read the column. Hope of power and to be somebody were two of the motives which directed me into politics. The third had been the compulsive urge to persuade Britain to do what will make her prosperous and stay among the leading nations, and for each, down to the smallest in the land, to have the freedom and cultural resources of the eighteenth-century gentleman, whether he wishes to use them or not. Democratic elections in the trade unions; joining the Common Market; stopping debilitating nationalization; the self-destructive nature of strikes; reducing waste caused by mal-administration in the public services; exposing the nature and consequences of the Marxist and Militant (Communist) Left take-over of the Labour Party; the dangers of one-sided nuclear disarmament; the importance of standing by the Americans; the cutting of taxation to encourage people to earn more, to the general good: these are among the matters I have vehemently canvassed with my readers.

The huge audiences I have had in the *Daily Mirror* (1965–73), *Sunday Mirror* (1973–83) and now the *News of the World*, the largest circulation Sunday newspaper, have tolerated my proselytizing with remarkable endurance. Perhaps it really is, as Wilson said to me, that I think like the average man. My brain is not good enough to soar out of his reach, even if I tried.

I shall be immodest: I believe that my articles have influenced attitudes and voting patterns more than the total output of the grander and smaller circulation papers. To sneer at the mass-circulation papers is to sneer at the majority, an undemo-cratic attitude. Because my articles are plain and unembellished I get no journalistic award, but I get many letters which keep me aware of how ordinary people think, and many requests from trade unionists to publish the names of those for whom they should vote, to prevent their union being controlled by undemocratic gangs from the Broad Marxist Left. Writing my weekly column has been for the last twenty years the most important work I have ever done. I take immense pains with it; daily making notes from sound and television broadcasts, the newspapers, weekly journals; ringing economists, businessmen, trade unionists, politicians and ministries. The actual writing takes two to two and a half hours; the checking and alterations continue until the article is finally set on Saturday.

Popular newspapers are more meticulous about facts than those written in a more literary style. They feel a stronger responsibility in political matters not to mislead their readers. I have been rung in all parts of the world by sub-editors anxious to make sure there is no mistake in a figure, a quotation or a date: newspapers with a higher percentage of A1 readers are more careless. I share the concern of the popular newspapers. I have never knowingly written what is untrue or concealed my opinions from my readers, though they have frequently been different from the editorial viewpoint. The Labour-supporting Mirror Group were understanding about this. As the style of the Labour Party changed, so did my feelings towards it. There was no censorship, save from the occasional rumblings of the print unions which sometimes restrained me from writing what I thought about their rapacious behaviour by the fear that we might lose that edition of the paper.

Bob Edwards, Editor of the *Sunday Mirror*, firmly defended my right to journalistic freedom, but during the 1983 election I detected some restlessness on his part over my detailed analysis of the Marxist approach of Labour's manifesto. It was evident that a parting was on its way. It was a natural progression to write for a newspaper owned by my old friend Rupert Murdoch. But it was a wrench to leave the *Sunday Mirror*, where some readers enjoyed hating me but more were in accord with my views. It was a fine pulpit from which to preach to many who were politically in the centre or slightly left of centre.

# CHAPTER XVI

———— ❈❈❈ ————

# A Dream Vanishes

I HAVE BEEN FASCINATED by newspapers ever since I first read the old mimeographed *Buzzings from Bonython* produced by my father and his brothers over a hundred years ago. The tiniest newspaper or journal generates its own romance. It is alive and it can kick. It can persuade and it can goad the mightiest. It can amuse and enrage. It has potency, however light. To add to the fun of running it, there is the possibility of making money.

Beaverbrook said to me one day in the garden at Cherkley, 'You will never make any real money in politics and writing articles. You have to have a business.' In 1961 Beaverbrook's advice surfaced in my mind. I wanted to build something which I could go on running and make money from when there was nothing left for me in politics. Provincial newspapers were buoyant. They seemed like a combination of business and entertainment. I knew Roy Thomson. He was strong in provincial newspapers and becoming stronger. I asked him what to do.

'Ask every reasonable-looking provincial newspaper if they are for sale. There's often a price they will sell at.'

I rang the owners of local newspapers, which did not belong to a chain, and were within seventy miles of London. Repeatedly I was told that they would not sell at any price. 'Not even a million pounds', I would ask despairingly. 'Yes, but you'd be an idiot if you paid it.' At last a response of guarded interest came from the *Banbury Guardian*. I took the balance-sheets to Roy Thomson. 'It will be worth it if you can get it for around £60,000,' he pronounced.

Using some of Moorea's money we bought it for £50,000. It had assets and saleable machinery which were sold off for £10,000, so the purchase price was really £40,000. The circulation was around 18,000. The *Banbury Guardian* had no rival to speak of in its area. Its advertising rates were low and its commercial potential unexploited. Roy Thomson, amused by the venture, helped. He sent advertising experts to tell us how to expand the classified advertising. I boldly raised the advertising rates to heights which terrified the management but which we got without losing advertisers. I enjoyed freshening up the old-fashioned journalism and layout of the pages. The *Banbury Guardian* began to hum and gently to increase its size and circulation.

The press the *Banbury Guardian* was printed on was an ancient Cossor flatbed, perhaps seventy years old. It took all week to print it badly and we could not cope with expansion. We needed a new press. Roy Thomson said, 'You must try to print colour. With all this colour television coming in, all newspapers will have to do it for their advertisers eventually.'

I asked the main British printing-press manufacturers if they had a press suitable for printing a small provincial newspaper with colour, not for pictures but to make splodges of different colours known as spot colour. They thought I was mad. British printing-presses once flooded the world but the innovative flair had gone. The nearest I could find to what I wanted was an ancient, discarded *Daily Mirror* press which would put a blob of red on the top right-hand corner of the front page. Then I happened to meet J. Morley Tonkin, an engineer who owned a printing plant in Wales on which he printed local newspapers. He told me that the Goss Company of Chicago had a new press designed for small newspapers which could do spot colour, and reproduce black-and-white pictures of a quality far superior to those of the old-fashioned newspaper presses still used in 1985 in Fleet Street except by the Communist *Morning Star*, whose type and reproduction of pictures are by far the best of the national dailies in Britain.

I flew immediately to Chicago to call on the Goss Company. In the waiting-room I saw an up-country local newspaper with an advertisement in full colour, not from a photograph but a kind of water-colour. It had been printed on the new Goss press. 'So it *will* print full-colour pictures, not just spot colours?' I asked.

'Mr Wyatt, we are not selling it to you to do that. It took

hours to set up that full-colour advertisement. It couldn't be done regularly in the normal run of the paper.'

'Oh,' I said airily, 'whatever American printers can do, British printers will do three times as fast and better.'

I bought the press and told Alan Mole, in charge of the printing works at Banbury, that the first time it printed the *Banbury Guardian* I wanted a full-colour picture on the front page. I then thought no more about it.

The following year, 1962, the Goss press was installed and ready to go. It worked on the continuous web litho offset principle and did not need heat to dry the colours – hence its clumsy name, non-heat set web-offset. Mole, unable to convince me of the difficulties, had juggled with the controls and made ingenious adaptations. The first time the *Banbury Guardian* was printed on the new machine it carried full-colour pictures of the Banbury Cross and of guardsmen marching in Whitehall. They were not on special paper but on the same rough newsprint as the rest of the paper. The printing industry was amazed. One expert from the great paper merchants, Bowater, who watched the first run said of me, 'If he'd known anything about printing, he would have known it was impossible.'

Never before in Britain or America had a newspaper printed full-colour pictures from photographs as part of the ordinary run of the paper. It led to the web-offset revolution in printing local newspapers. Roy Thomson was among the first to install the new-style machines, impressed by the product of the Banbury one. Goss gave me a handsome discount, and part of the deal was that we let prospective buyers see the press working. They came from all over the country. Some of the local journals which put the same press in were disappointed that they could not get such good results as Mole and his Banbury team who used unorthodox methods and attachments. Mole's work caused Goss to improve their machines so that they could be sold with the guarantee of full-colour pictures to be printed in their normal working.

The new type of printing obviated the ancient need for type-setting and making corrections with lead carried in heavy trays. We had obstruction from the printers in establishing what is still called in 1985 the new technology, not yet universal in

Fleet Street but established in the provinces for twenty years. The unions would not let us employ women who could have learned to use the new equipment, similar to a typewriter, as well or better than the men in a few weeks and would have been happy to do so for a third of the absurdly high wages successfully obtained by the unions through the power of their closed shops. Nevertheless, the modern manner of type-setting was an improvement. But for the unions' Luddite grip on the newspapers, it could cut production costs by two-thirds.

The quality of our printing brought us much acclaim. Our Goss press could print the *Banbury Guardian* in a few hours. I thought commercial customers would beat a path to our door to fill the free time on it. As they did not, I tried to buy some more local newspapers, but none were for sale at a tolerable price. I was dreaming of starting a newspaper empire. Roy Thomson was over sixty before he began to build his in Britain; I was only forty-four. Surely if he could do it, I could. But he had Scottish TV, with what he described 'as a licence to print money'. He had no feel for the content of newspapers but he had an acute business sense, poring over balance-sheets short-sightedly through his pebble-shaped spectacles.

I was over-confident, too vain and impatient. I rushed ahead with too small a base and started new weekly papers in Swindon, Birmingham and Coventry. With their bright appearance, beautiful printing and full-colour pictures they quickly achieved good circulations, but the advertising was slow to come. Their long-established rivals had equally long-established advertisers unwilling to shift to us. Though more money was put in, it was not enough to hold out for the four or five years needed to build up strong and reliable advertising revenue. They had to be sold to our rivals who closed them down, or else closed by ourselves.

This was not fatal. The *Banbury Guardian* was spinning money in larger quantities. Commercial work was building up and we bought new presses. It seemed a matter of waiting until old-established local papers in solo monopoly positions came on the market at manageable prices and the business had generated enough money to buy one or more. Then the break with Moorea came. She naturally wanted to take out her money and, in Anthony Rubinstein, had a very good lawyer. I needed several hundreds of thousands of pounds or I would lose the entire business. A merchant bank took over Moorea's 50 per cent shareholding, but that did not provide enough to enable me to produce the money I had to have.

They were traumatic days. The solution was to sell my beloved *Banbury Guardian*. I sold it for over four times the original purchase price, which was good after I had owned it for only five years. It was a melancholy day when I went to say goodbye to the staff in their offices near Banbury Cross, and had to abandon what I had dreamed of as the foundation of an expanding newspaper business. I should have been cast very far down if it had not been for the fighting spirit of Verushka, whose husband had died in the summer of 1965. She bolstered my optimism, a quality which leads me into rashness but is valuable in set-backs, keeping dreams alive without which there is no attraction in the future. It was a time for me to look at my horoscope again and comfort myself that the distant scene was bearable.

I had first seen Verushka at a little dance in Wimpole Street given, I think, in June 1962 by John Cronin, a surgeon and Labour MP. Verushka was small and entrancing, with curls bubbling over her head. I stifled my fear of looking foolish on the dance-floor and asked her for a dance. We danced a long time, perhaps three quarters of an hour, while she laughed at my ineptitude. I asked her for her telephone number, which she mischievously gave me.

When we sat down, what looked to me a very tall man stood stiffly in front of me. 'That was my wife you were dancing with.'

I was terrified. Verushka's husband, a baron in Hungary and a distinguished asthma specialist in England (possibly the only person able to cure asthma twenty years ago and whose book on asthma was a standard work), appeared formidable and quite capable of challenging me to a duel. He was twenty-eight years older than she was but strong and erect. I danced no more with Verushka, but I rang her several times at the number she said I could get her on. Each time her husband answered and I put the telephone down in panic. I saw her at a distance in Marylebone High Street and thought of her before I went to sleep. Hugh Gaitskell must have felt a similar pull. He invited her for walks in the park. Once he called at 12 Devonshire Street (now the Chilean Embassy) and asked for her, hoping to see her in her apartment at the top of the house.

On hearing the name Gaitskell, Dr Banszky came out of his ground-floor consulting-room. 'Oh, Mr Gaitskell, how nice to see you. What can I do for you?'

Politicians think quickly but not always well: 'Er, I was just passing by and I wondered whether you could arrange for me to meet the Romanian Ambassador.'

Dr Banszky was surprised. A leader of the Opposition can see any ambassador he wants, and an émigré from Communist-controlled Hungary was not the channel he would be most likely to choose for the purpose.

In November after Dr Banszky died I again met Verushka at a dinner at the Cronins. She had asked not to sit next to me, as she had decided I was too aggressive and conceited. My mother disliked my father, or thought she did, when she first knew him, and they were happily married until he died, so this was not entirely discouraging. We met again in February 1966 and matters progressed unevenly. The young widow had many admirers. Afraid of my incurable willingness to plunge into marriage, I urged her to take no notice if I asked her to marry me; it meant nothing. Fortunately, after the third or fourth time of asking, she disregarded my advice and we were married in December 1966. It is by far the longest and happiest marriage I have had, and the thought of life without her is desolation.

Verushka came to England by herself, just as the Communists were making their final take-over of Hungary. The rest of her family stayed behind to await disaster. During the fighting in Budapest, which began at Christmas 1944, Verushka had already had harrowing times. Their house was fought over and occupied alternately by Russians and Germans. When it was the Russian turn for occupation they made her help bury the German dead in the garden.

The Russians were sometimes monsters, sometimes children, washing their hands and faces in the lavatory-bowls. When they thought the family were unfriendly they locked them in the drawing-room and peed in the hall until streams of urine flowed in under the door. Then at a sudden whim they would hand out food. Verushka's grandmother saved herself from being raped by saying in Russian that she was an undercover NKVD agent, which absurdity was believed. The house was occupied by Russian soldiers for several years before it was confiscated by the Communist Hungarian Government. A Russian colonel billeted in it declared that after living there he wanted to be a capitalist. Would Verushka marry him when she grew up?

Verushka's family had been eminent lawyers and judges for centuries, as well as landowners. After the Communist take-over her father was allowed to make a small income from translating plays, though his property was confiscated. Two of her uncles high in the government service were given long prison sentences, followed by deportation to work in the fields. Her elderly great-uncle, Emile, who had been Minister of Justice in Admiral Horthy's government, was imprisoned and then sent to work as an agricultural labourer in his old constituency. The Communists believed their own propaganda and expected him to get rough handling from his former constituents. Instead they would not tolerate the great man working in the fields and fed and hid him in the most comfortable quarters they could find.

Great-Uncle Emile and his family lost everything, including the right to practise their professions. He was rich: for acting for him in one case alone Prince Esterhazy gave him 500 hectares (1250 acres), on which he grew lavender for its valuable oil. He was a powerful and turbulent political journalist as well as having a large law office similar to a New York practice, combining advocacy with solicitors' work. Of independent nature he challenged the Prime Minister, Count Bethlen, to a duel over some dubious share dealings in which the Prime Minister was engaged. The duel with the Prime Minister did not take place, though an associate of the Prime Minister took up the challenge, withdrawing at the last minute on the strange grounds that Emile fenced left-handed. Emile, who exposed the affair publicly, resigned from being Minister of Justice.

He had a magnificent house on a plateau in and overlooking Buda, with large grounds containing another house. This was stolen by the Communists. When I saw his property in Buda it housed dozens of families, turning it into a slum: the swimming-pool and tennis-courts no longer heard the laughter

329

of Emile's family and their friends. Towards the end of the war, Emile, as a notorious anti-Nazi who wanted Britain to win, had to go into hiding from the German occupying authorities. The good man, who stood for truth and justice, was persecuted by both sides in the ideological conflict. When he died in 1952 the Communists had a twinge of remorse. They paid for a grand funeral for the man they had imprisoned and brought to the direst poverty, and published long tributes to him as a great son of Hungary, especially praising his brave and skilful efforts in saving many Jews from concentration camps.

Great-Uncle Emile was legal adviser to the Belgian Princess Stephanie, the wife of Crown Prince Rudolf. She told him the true story of Mayerling and he told it to his niece, my mother-in-law. The pretty seventeen-year-old Vetseva was a readily available girl from a poor family on the outer fringes of the court. The promiscuous Rudolf had an affair with her, of which he soon tired. She, passionate and hurt in her pride, tried fiercely to hold him. She chased him uninvited to Mayerling, where he had gone to hunt, to plead with him. Rudolf could not be moved. She begged for one last night with him and he consented. During the course of it the unbalanced girl took his cut-throat razor and slashed off his penis, probably while he lay asleep and uncovered, before he had time to realize what was happening. Rudolf, aged forty-one, was not the kind of man who could contemplate life without a penis. He shot her and then himself.

There was no romantic suicide pact between lovers who preferred to die in each others' arms rather than never be married. There was no plot to assassinate Rudolf, on the grounds that he was too sympathetic to rebellious elements in Hungary. There was nothing more than the fury of a discarded mistress. The Emperor, Franz Josef, understandably wanted the squalid nature of his only son's death covered up. With his autocratic powers, no investigative journalists, and a censored Press, that was easy. When the Chief of Police died, his widow received a pension and went to live in Paris. Whenever she ran short of money she threatened Franz Josef with the revelation of the true story of Mayerling, and her demands were always met. Who should know the truth better than Rudolf's widow, the former

Crown Princess and Franz Josef's daughter-in-law? All the romantic novels about Mayerling are tosh.

I wanted Verushka to like my friends. She, with feminine contrariness, resented the implication that she ought to like them because they *were* my friends. She was wary of and almost hostile towards them and I lost some and nearly lost others. She determined to choose for herself which furniture and friends from my previous existence appealed to her. Two friends I was sorry to see on the blacklist were Raimund and Liz von Hofmannsthal, more particularly the latter. Liz was the most precisely beautiful woman I have ever seen. Face, features, form were classically perfect, as was her elegance in stillness or in movement. Her brain was quick, her loyalty deep, her humour sharp, her vanity small. She would say with glee in her later years that when Princess Margaret asked who was the most beautiful woman in London, to the reply 'Liz von Hofmannsthal' the Princess answered, 'No, I mean now.'

Raimund von Hofmannsthal was the son of the famous Hugo von Hofmannsthal who collaborated with Richard Strauss. They had a schloss, Prielau, at Zell-am-See, in Austria. In the summer we played tennis. In the winter some skiied, and others like Raimund and myself ambled round the taverns drinking goulash which, correctly, is a soup not a stew. I owe to Raimund the important knowledge that opened bottles of champagne put into the fridge keep their fizz for days. Late in the evenings Liz would assemble us in her large kitchen and heat red wine with cloves and other ingredients, in England called mulled claret but in Austria *gluwein* – excellent for sending you to sleep. Many amusing people went through that house: Sacheverell Sitwell, brother of Osbert who had been kind to me during the war and after; Diana Cooper, forever beautiful; Laura Charteris, whose husband Michael Canfield was rumoured to be an illegitimate son of a royal duke – he certainly looked Hanoverian.

When Liz was in her last illness, cancer, Verushka's tender heart melted. Liz came to a family lunch with my two children present. She looked ill but lovely and all was sweetness which made me, at least, happy. When she could no longer get out of bed I would go to see her. The day before she died I held her hand and said, 'I never saw you look more beautiful.' She smiled her old radiant smile and we parted almost as cheerfully as if we had just had lunch together.

With all the financial settlements arranged with Moorea's lawyer, prospects for the Banbury printing works seemed good. We led in the quality of our colour printing, winning numerous awards and customers. At one time we printed over a hundred house journals, many of them for the biggest firms in Britain. We printed numerous give-away newspapers for the forerunners of the weekly free sheet publishers that drop their publications unasked through the letter-box. We had a number of lucrative contracts, bought additional machines and decided to float ourselves on the Stock Exchange in 1973. I should, for my future financial well-being, have sold a slice of my 51 per cent shareholding then (at one time it was worth in 1985 terms several million), but with my usual optimism and with some grounds for confidence I believed I could make the company grow and grow and get back to running newspapers which I cared far more about than printing. I did not want to diminish my shareholding or lose control.

For several years after the public flotation we did well, turning out some good profits, but not well enough to get the big growth I was looking for. Though we had a high turnover, profit margins in this competitive industry were low. Small newspaper- and journal-owners bought the same relatively cheap presses as we had. After printing and selling their own publications at a profit, they might have two or three days a week with nothing to print, so they could afford to print at below the cost of the labour for outside customers. It was difficult for us to cope with this legitimate undercutting. We tried to upgrade ourselves by buying superior printing-presses and printing on better quality paper. We had some success in this but we were hampered by the past. Our printers were accustomed to newspaper style, not high-quality magazine techniques, and the grip of the unions on the industry meant that new printers could be recruited only with union consent. Dismissal of incompetent printers was impossible, involving threats of disruption. The unions also resisted changes in working practices. During our rapid expansion the management had accepted some new employees from London and elsewhere who had a disruptive, militant, even Communist slant, quite unlike the old Banbury employees. When I heard that one of them, later to become the Father of the Chapel, was selling the Communist *Morning Star* in Banbury market-place at the week-ends, I knew there was trouble ahead.

Still, all might have come right but for a period of exceptionally high interest rates and a rapid contraction in the printing industry. Some of our major jobs disappeared. We were printing millions of a free coloured journal for a giant dairy chain until the milkmen refused to deliver it without extra pay. We were printing a lucrative colour magazine for the *Evening News*, which stopped when it merged with the *Evening Standard*. The national Sunday paper colour magazines, for which we printed sections in web offset to add to their gravure printed sections, went through a long period of low advertising and did not need the extra pages.

We were misled at a critical point into incurring a bad debt of several hundred thousand pounds. The gods had turned against us. We were angling for a huge ten-year contract to print telephone directories, which would have given us a stable and highly profitable base, however bad the economic conditions. Indications were that we were front-runners for it because of the efficiency and cheapness with which we had already printed many millions of directories.

We had an outlying subsidiary at Daventry where the directories were bound. There were elaborate systems to ensure that the correct sections in the right order were in each directory. After final checking, these were loaded on to large clamped-down pallets to await delivery. Two recently employed youths thought it would be a lark to see if they could beat the checking procedures. Finding a time when the factory was closed and no supervisor was about they undid the fastenings and took a number of finally passed directories off a pallet, cut sheets from pornographic magazines to the same size and inserted them into the directories, which they replaced on the pallets whence they came.

Some two months later a housewife on the west coast of Scotland complained to the Post Office about the lurid contents of her telephone directory which she felt unsuitable for her children. The Post Office was in a frenzy. I explained how our defences against defective binding had been maliciously sabotaged and the precautions we were taking to prevent a recurrence, in so far as it is possible to thwart determined malefactors. The Post Office officials, timid by nature, were not mollified. Even the union (SOGAT) agreed with the sacking of the culprits, whose sense of humour I should have appreciated more if someone else had been the victim. The valuable flow of telephone directories ceased and the long-term contract we wanted so badly went to another printer, a subsidiary of an American conglomerate.

Whenever we tried to slim down excessive staff we were met with strikes, go-slows and overtime bans. Long-loyal customers began to drift away and new ones were put off. In May 1982, after a substantial expected profit for April was turned by union disruption into a thumping loss, we decided to bring the enterprise to an end. It had been going for twenty-one years: at one time it employed 650 people and was the largest web-offset firm in the country. Many of the employees who had been prevented by their leaders, by the threat of losing their union cards, from operating the cost-saving scheme which could have saved the company, were unable to find other jobs in the printing industry. The cost saving scheme, largely devised by the young financial director, Richard Rumble, could have worked. He struggled loyally sixteen hours a day to save the company. He fought cheerfully to the end and afterwards got a better job than I could give him.

Though at first I was crushed by the immensity of the loss, which savaged my prosperity base, I now regret the disappearance of the Banbury printing company less than I thought I would. It had absorbed much time in unproductive haggles with the unions, particularly in the latter years. It had given me nightmares whenever I heard the NGA were 'out on the bridge' over the canal cutting their throats and ours by stopping production. It was a relief as well as a shock when I could stop worrying how we were to get through the next month and, often, the next week. I now had time to do things besides running a printing works, which had ceased to be a possible base on which to build newspapers. To me the chief purpose of running papers was to propagate my views, and I have been able to do that in my weekly columns. If I had still been grappling with Banbury, though doubtless I would have been better off, I should not have had time to write this book. The reader may judge whether that is a beneficial outcome.

At Banbury we were innovators. The first-comer is not always the most successful. Banbury increased my respect for those who run factories and sell their products. They may not be exciting guests at a dinner party or know much about Jane Austen, but they have qualities of toughness, perseverance and ingenuity beyond the ordinary. In Britain, the home of the Industrial Revolution, they do not rank high socially unless they are very rich. Conscious of their social inferiority, generations of self-made industrialists have turned themselves into country gentlemen and given their sons a socially grander education than they had. We depend on trade, but talented young men would rather go into merchant banking or the professions. We have arranged our affairs so that the social pressures denude Manchester, Birmingham, Leeds and other industrial areas which need the able and imaginative, and we have filled the gentler and more, perhaps, over-civilized London and the South. The Americans have not yet made the same mistake.

It is a splendid thing to be a great industrialist. The most remarkable one I know is Arnold Weinstock. Arnold's company, GEC, employs more in manufacturing in Britain than any other and has more ready cash. Before he goes to work he listens to classical music until around 10.30. His headquarters is small and simple. He rarely visits a factory but his control is absolute. He operates a rigorous financial reporting system, examining the figures from his outposts. If a manager falls short of his agreed performance he is in trouble. At an outlying GEC factory an executive told me, 'We have a saying here, "If at first you don't succeed, your successor will."'

Arnold has been thought callous in eliminating surplus staff when taking over a new business or when factories falter. He has done it to save units and make them more efficient and prosperous. Eventually the result is more secure employment. He has an organizing brain of genius, abhorring waste. In his rapid progress through complicated details to the essential point he reminds me of Stafford Cripps. He has a similar impatience with the foolish, which makes him unpopular in Whitehall and the City.

It is supposed by the cynic that it is impossible to make vast sums without some element of sharp dealing. Arnold, upright and scrupulously honest, disproves this. He fights for his own business, but still harder for his country's interests, often advocating policies for the general good but harmful to the GEC. He is high in my class of those who mind above all else what happens to Britain. Through it all he has charm, which is another way of saying he is interested in whomever he is talking to.

Arnold is always at work, his brain buzzing over problems whether he is in his office or at the opera (a weakness I have to overlook in him, as in Bernard Levin). Or perhaps he is never at work, like a world champion chess player practising, playing, worrying ceaselessly about his performance, alternating between gloom and exhilaration, exhausting himself, recovering his energy again but not exactly working. He is free to talk on the telephone for half an hour or more at any time of the day on any topic from some government iniquity to the way one of his horses ran at Chantilly.

At dinner at my house, when TV-AM had just got their licence, Peter Jay asked Arnold how to run a business. Arnold told him patiently and at length, but Peter either did not believe him or could not understand what he was saying: very clever people frequently cannot grasp the simplicities of business, which often centre as much on the inadvisability of spending more than the company earns as offering a good product. If ministers and some of the leaders of nationalized industries had taken more heed of Arnold, industry would be in a much healthier state. Arnold could have reorganized the system of government administration, damming up the waterfalls of waste, if, as I wanted, he had been allowed to.

Many men successful in business are in it more for the power and the excitement of creation than the money. There comes a point when adding the odd £10 million is meaningless. I first began to know Rupert Murdoch after I rang him up suggesting we printed some free sheets for him when he started operations in Britain. I succumbed at once to his interest in everything that happens, to his smile, energy and enthusiasm. It has been fashionable to depict him as a crude, unpolished Australian from the Outback, brutally firing worthy editors and managers.

His father, Sir Keith Murdoch, was a distinguished journalist who forced the British Government to ameliorate the Gallipoli disaster in which Anzac troops were put at an unnecessary hazard, and who went successfully into the newspaper industry. Rupert's mother, made a Dame in her own right, was for years a trustee of the National Gallery in Victoria. Rupert was at Worcester College, the same college as mine. He is not short on education or knowledge of the values of Western civilization. But he is a tough businessman (soft businessmen usually fail) not ashamed to develop a potentially profitable situation, however disdainful the delicately refined may be. Putting nudes on page 3 of the *Sun*, filling it with accounts of how to make love, bringing sex out of dark cupboards, giving readers what they want to read in preference to what they ought to, was held to be a vulgar lowering of standards. The more the masses liked the *Sun*, the more the higher income classes disapproved of Rupert. Though he never said so to me, I could see that hurt him. It may have given him an added incentive to buy *The Times*, which he was able to do because the *Sun*, with the *News of the World* in the same group, was so successful. 'How do you like living on immoral earnings?' I sometimes ask friends on *The Times*, for which I now write. They are not always amused to be reminded that the paper would not have survived without the Rabelaisian *Sun*.

If I were not myself I should most like to be Rupert. He has newspapers and journals in three continents, as well as an airline and a television station and the temperament to enjoy them. He has the energy ceaselessly to fly back and forth, working as he goes. I have flown several times with him over the Midwest as he delved through papers, made frequent telephone calls, concocted new ideas for his latest deal and kept up a conversation with me. As he sits beside a swimming-pool he is ringing distant lands, listening, giving advice and instructions. When he walks into the local store at Old Chatham, in upstate New York, to do some household shopping (the details of which fascinate him), he buys a stack of newspapers, too, and thumbs through them as soon as he gets home. He has the exuberance of a small boy and perpetual curiosity, the basic ingredient of a good newspaper-man.

Rupert has gone beyond Beaverbrook and Northcliffe, though their power to influence was possibly greater before the wireless and television got going with news and current affairs programmes. Newspapers do have power but only so long as they echo and reinforce their readers' attitudes. Northcliffe did not unseat Asquith as Prime Minister in the First World War; Asquith's inadequacies did that. Beaverbrook could not sell the country Empire Free Trade, nor could Rothermere Mosley's Blackshirts. Nevertheless, there is real power in newspapers, and in evil hands they may do harm until the safeguard of affronted lost readership operates.

Rupert's approach is wholesome and straightforward. Once, he supported the Labour Party. His mounting disillusion with its changing character coincided with mine. He understands the interests of the West, and of ordinary people, and does not intend to lose touch with his readers. His rifts with his editors usually arise from his knowing how to edit better than they do. Rupert is a democrat with a generous nature who wants people to be happy as he is. I am always happy with Rupert and his beautiful, intelligent wife, Anna, of Estonian origin, and who, like mine, knows first-hand what Russian oppression means.

# CHAPTER XVII

─────◗❁◗─────

# Pastures New

FOR A FEW MONTHS AFTER I lost my seat in 1970 I thought of trying to get back again as a Labour MP. I was soon aware that the widening divergence between the current ethos of the Labour Party and myself made that impossible. I backed Labour in 1970 because I thought the Government had settled down reasonably well and I wanted to be in Parliament to urge it away from fatal courses, but I was uneasy. The member of the Bosworth Labour Party Executive who said after the count that my heart had not been in the fight was right.

I could not join the Tories because there was too much about the Tory Party I disliked. The Liberal Party was too diffuse and wishy-washy. I might have joined the SDP if it had existed then, but it was to be over ten years before it emerged. When I advocated a Lib-Lab pact in 1961 and earlier it was something of that kind I had in mind. Its natural leaders in 1970 were still forlornly hoping that the Marxist tide in the Labour Party could be pushed back.

Ted Heath's government had an early set-back. Iain Macleod, Chancellor of the Exchequer, died almost immediately aged fifty-six. He had been in pain with his back twisted and hunched for a long time, yet had stayed humorous and rational. He was sensitive about his contorted back and was mildly irritated when I asked him whether he had tried acupuncture, probably supposing as a former Minister of Health that it was a quack remedy. He was an excellent propagandist with a good brain and strong character. He would not have dissipated the advantages of the balanced budget handed over to him by Roy.

His successor, Anthony Barber, was a featherweight, easily towed along by Ted who thought that the more money that was injected into the economy, the higher would be production, the lower the unit cost of each item, the greater the exports and, hey presto, everyone would be better off. This attractive plan was a factor leading to the hyper-inflation of the mid-1970s, not brought under control until the late 1980s. Macleod, with his deft analytical mind and ability to argue forcefully, would never have allowed it.

Ted has been less condemned for his recklessness with the economy, which deserves condemnation, than for his 1971 Industrial Relations Act, which deserves praise. It did not provide for secret home postal ballots for the election of union officials but it did many other things Barbara Castle had wanted. It also set up an Industrial Relations Court with some effective powers. The union leaders were on the verge of accepting the Act as permanent, despite the strenuous disruption fomented by the Communist-led Liaison Committee for the Defence of Trade Unions. Then it all got swept away by the miners' strike and the change of government. But it was a good try. Even better was Ted's getting Britain into the Common Market. The credit for that can never be taken from him.

I have known Ted Heath not well but on and off for many years. He has lurking charm which an element of reserve and awkwardness held him back from using efficiently. The warmth in him has never got out properly. He has a sense of humour for jokes of the Oxford Union debating kind. He was an honest leader and Prime Minister telling what he felt was the truth and putting the country above his own immediate well-being. He was also brave.

Some weeks after the miners' overtime ban had forced the three-day week on industry he asked me to see him. I went to No. 10 on 30 January 1974 and we had a long discussion. While I was there he signed the letter to the TUC offering to refer the miners' 31 per cent wage claim to the Relativity Board. This body had the power to make awards in special circumstances in excess of the pay increase limits recently determined by law to ensure wage restraint.

'Why can't you pay the miners £2 a week on account of what the Relativity Board might award them and pay it straight away from March 1st?' I asked. This might have ended the strike.

'I'm not sure the Relativity Board will give them that much. Their case is not very strong.'

Ted was very firm about the Government's not breaching the law Parliament had recently approved by making offers beyond the limits it had set. I was startled when he told me he was going to call an election. He said he was aware of the danger that Labour might win and give in to the miners, with accelerating inflation when others successfully demanded comparable rises. But it had to be disproved that any union or group powerful enough to halt the nation could always defeat the Government.

'You do realize you might not win the election, don't you?'

I explained that I believed the mood of the country was very strange, moving backwards and forwards according to whether or not the public thought the Government was doing the right thing about the miners.

'Our information is that they want us to stand firm.'

'Yes, but maybe they won't want you to when it comes to the crunch. Supposing you win the election and the miners are still on strike in August, what will you do then?'

'Go to Cannes.'

'I admire your courage. You've got more guts than I have. I wouldn't dare do it.'

'Well, it's got to be done.'

As I was leaving I turned at the door and said again, 'I admire your courage.'

'Well, you've often been very brave, Woodrow.'

'Yes, but the stakes were not quite so high.'

The miners said on 5 February that they would call a national strike from 10 February. On 7 February Ted announced that there would be an election with polling day on 28 February. The miners put their case to the Relativity Board and on 21 February a left-wing member of the Board leaked that it had been discovered that the Government's calculation of miners' pay had been wrong and they could have had more all the time without fuss (this 'discovery' turned out, too late, to be false).

On 26 February Campbell Adamson, the Director-General of the CBI (Confederation of British Industry), trying to ingratiate himself with the union leaders, demanded the repeal of the

Industrial Relations Act, claiming without foundation that it had sullied all relations between employers and unions at national level. The country had lost its will to confront the unions, as I had told Ted it might.

Though the Conservatives got 1 per cent more of the total votes cast, Labour got four more seats than they did. All depended on the fourteen Liberals. Ted was morally and constitutionally justified in trying to cobble together a coalition, but the timid Liberals feared that it could be the death of their party, whereas it could have been the breakthrough from impotence to power.

I felt deeply for anguished Ted, whose gamble had cruelly failed, and sent him messages and letters of encouragement. On the evening of 4 March he gave up the struggle for Liberal support and resigned. On 6 March Wilson authorized the Coal Board to offer an outrageous 29 per cent increase to the miners, which they triumphantly accepted. They went back to work five days later. The inflation, for which Ted had been partly responsible, turned into hyper-inflation, as he knew it would.

I wished dearly that he had taken my advice that January evening in Downing Street and not held the election so soon. He had a majority of fifteen and eighteen months to go before his five years were up. Much could have happened to improve his position. As it was, he was done for when Labour scraped in again in the second 1974 election in October. That made three out of four elections he had lost as leader. The Tories are harsher with unlucky leaders than Labour and it was inevitable that Ted would go, old friends and recipients of his patronage deserting as they scented the smell of a decaying throne. Shakespeare has written it all, but that does not make it less bitter for the deposed king. For a proud and sensitive man like Ted there can be little solace. I cannot blame him if he seems ungracious: there is a noble soul there which has been grievously wounded.

I was hostile to Ted's successor. I had written in 1973 in *Turn Again, Westminster*: 'She vigorously displays that pernickety bossiness and prissy self-righteousness which is apt to disfigure women who enter an administration, and which is so irritating to their male associates.' I had observed her in the House but had hardly spoken to her except at dinner before an *Any*

342

*Questions?* broadcast in January 1960 a few months after she became an MP. Obviously she had not liked the look of me. One of the questions from the audience to the panel was, 'What did you discuss at dinner?' I answered first and, as I was finishing, Mrs Thatcher broke in with her best putting-down voice and withering smile, 'May I make one thing quite clear, Mr Chairman. We weren't discussing very much at dinner. We were mostly listening to Mr Woodrow Wyatt.' In the laughter I thought to myself: Ho, to that brassy blonde.

When she became leader of the Opposition in 1975 I was pleased that I could now attack the Tories in my weekly column in the *Sunday Mirror* with more zest than for a long time. Mrs Thatcher has always appreciated that the mass-circulation papers are far more important in forming public opinion than the small-circulation ones. She told John Junor, Editor of the *Sunday Express* and an old friend of mine, that she would like to meet me. 'Why don't you ask him to lunch?' he asked. 'I would be too nervous to' was the somewhat odd reply.

A meeting, not lunch, was arranged at her house in Flood Street. I found her much less scratchy than I remembered, more mature and broader in her mind, and pleasantly appealing with pretty legs and complexion. This time I was happy to let her do the talking. She won me over. The strength of her determination and the simplicity of her rational ideas uncluttered by intellectual confusion convinced me that she was the first party leader I had met, apart from Gaitskell, who might check Britain's slide and possibly begin to reverse it. She did not seem much like a Tory but she had the Tory Party to work for her, which was a useful start.

Mrs Thatcher is a radical of practical Manchester Liberal descent. She believes that Marx and other economic theorists have not extinguished Adam Smith's truths. Her feminine mind is seldom diverted by profitless essays into abstract thought. She deals in fact. She looks at old institutions and accepted methods with a new eye, demanding to know why. She is free of class snobbishness; to be of a grand family is no path to her patronage, almost indeed a handicap. This has distressed Tories, who thought their birth or wealth entitled them to the preferment they would have got from other Conservative prime ministers.

343

Some looked down on her, like the prominent Tory I urged, shortly after she became leader, to ask her to dinner. 'Oh, no. She's not the sort of person one has to dinner.'

Mrs Thatcher's radicalism is founded on commonsense. In Britain, to do what is obviously right is revolutionary. Traditional Tories dislike change and hope to jog along comfortably, avoiding trouble with timely concessions. Mrs Thatcher aims to shake the country out of its enfeebling complacency.

Holidays and week-ends without work are boring to her. Late to bed and early to rise is her recipe for health and productivity. If I telephone her it is usually between 7.30 and 8 a.m. Like Stafford Cripps she has an advantage over her ministers and civil servants by working 60 per cent more hours than they do. She works with the energy of one who knows there is too little time to do what must be done if she is to honour her responsibilities. She is quick to understand a new point; you can talk to her almost in shorthand. She covers the ground fast.

I have known all the post-war prime ministers. For eloquence and world renown Churchill towered above them all, but his gifts were not best suited to stirring a nation out of an economic torpor. The broad sweep was splendid when he was dealing with the President of the United States or the leader of the USSR: it was inappropriate to the detailed weariness of committees and their documents. Attlee was the man of his moment. The dignified withdrawing from Empire and the ending of the worst pre-war inequities were his achievement. The problems of the eighties would have been beyond him. Mrs Thatcher has had to puncture illusions and force unpleasant facts on reluctant listeners dreaming of a lazy Utopia, agreeable but unobtainable. So they call her strident. If she sometimes sounds it she can hardly be blamed, opposed as she is by lethargy in high places and the cosy post-war myth that governments can remedy any economic set-back by printing money. She longs to persuade everyone that her way is the right way, which it generally is, because she fears for Britain's future if we drift back to the old discredited and damaging ways.

It is said that she does not listen. I have not found it so, though she cheerfully and energetically feels a conversation between two people means that both should argue vehemently, and may the best man, or woman, win. When she says 'Let me finish', it is essential not to let her until you have made your case. She never resents being talked down. She is exhilaratingly unstuffy and, if you cannot keep up with her, that is your weakness not hers.

It is widely believed that she cares about Britain; but not about individuals. I talked to her frequently during the Falklands War. Every time sailors, soldiers or airmen were killed she was in acute distress and could think for a while of nothing else. She was stricken far more than a man would have been in her position, accustomed to and accepting war's sad but inevitable casualties. She felt them personally inside herself. The charge that she gloried in war, revelling in the added prestige it gave her, is not merely insulting but absurd. She has an unusual consideration for others. She steels herself to be an Iron Lady because she cannot do her duty unless she is. Sacking ministers is agony to her, and she stands by old friends and values them: she was badly hurt by Airey Neave's murder. But once she has decided a minister must go, or he has chosen to go, the decision is final and there is no return. She never looks back; for her it is always the future that calls.

She is no block of ice despite her exceptional courage. Her husband, Denis, has contributed immensely to her strength and confidence, as is clear when you talk to them together. He has commonsense, detachment, a balanced sense of humour and robustness. He is far from a cipher. A good biography of, or an autobiography by, Denis Thatcher would be of real historical interest. Without his help Mrs Thatcher would not have been able to start the counter-revolution in Britain, the benefit of which (unless the British foolishly abandon it) will be reaped for decades. Perhaps I am a bit in love with Mrs Thatcher, platonically of course. I shall write more about her one day.

She is the reason I did not join the SDP despite being sympathetic to many of its members and hopes, and in advance of them though I was. The SDP/Liberal Alliance had no chance of winning; but even if it had had one, it would not have been radical, clear-sighted or resolute enough to do what Mrs Thatcher had the boldness to start in 1979. The SDP's role is to force the Labour Party to drop its harsh nineteenth-century

345

Marxism, or to replace it, or maybe both. The time must come when the sensible left-hand side of the nation has a commonsense democratic party to represent it. The differences between the SDP and Mrs Thatcher are akin to those between Republicans and Democrats, which is as it should be if a country is to be united in making itself prosperous.

I was sorry I could not come out in my newspaper articles for the SDP and Roy Jenkins, but for me the moment had passed. I think Roy was hurt that I did not back him, but he never reproached me, understanding why I believed Mrs Thatcher's attitude was what Britain needed. I have never attacked Roy and never shall. His ideas are very similar to mine and much more similar to Mrs Thatcher's than either realize or would concede. Roy's achievement in launching the SDP looks likely to be of lasting benefit and one day offering that much-needed genuine and effective non-Marxist alternative to Labour.

Roy persuaded me when he was Home Secretary to become Chairman of the Tote in 1976. Roy was worried that the Tote, for which the Home Office is responsible for appointing the Board, might be heading for collapse. I was hesitant at first, recommending someone else, but Roy insisted. I had always been amused by the racing world and thought the Tote could be an interesting public office.

Before becoming Chairman I was a board member for a few months and was astonished by the dismal prospects unfolded by the then Director-General. The Tote board had been badly hit by the Government's legalizing of high street betting shops in 1961 but refusing to allow the Tote to own them unless they offered Tote dividends only and not the starting-price odds offered by bookmakers. This was ridiculous in a country accustomed to starting-price odds, which give the punter some degree of certainty as to how much he might win. Tote dividends come from a pool in which the Tote retains a fixed proportion; but there is no knowing how the punters will bet against each other, so the dividends may be over or below the starting price.

In 1972 the law was at last changed to allow the Tote to own betting shops offering SP odds like the privately owned bookmakers' shops. By this time there were some 13,000 of them. When the Tote applied for licences to open new betting shops, the magistrates rejected the applications because there were already enough betting shops in their areas. The Tote had to buy existing shops, which were mainly discards from bookmakers who had found them unprofitable and were glad to get rid of them.

When I became Chairman in 1976 the Tote had a chain of loss-making betting shops, a rocky credit business, and a cash business on the Tote machine at racecourses badly in need of computer modernization and steadily losing more and more of the on-course market. The Tote as a whole could show a profit only by courtesy of the big bookmakers paying some £350,000 a year for the authority to offer Tote dividends to their customers. They did this not to make money but as a public relations exercise; to ward off suggestions that there should be, as in other racing countries, a Tote monopoly; and to keep the Tote ticking over at a low level as a harmless rival. Since the Tote became a success those subventions from the bookmakers have been slashed by five-sixths and are made only when a bookmaker wants to offer Tote dividends out of commercial necessity.

In 1976 the Tote was worth £1.3 million, and profit forecasts were more a loss forecast. There were far too many staff and a general feeling that the place could amble along as a kind of public servants' relief-station. Reducing the permanent staff by half was unpopular among those of the old guard displaced or who feared they would be, giving rise to discontent which was troublesome for a while. Now the Tote must be worth £15 million or so, if the sale value of the betting shop chain is included. The betting shop business has become very profitable and the return on it favourably compares with that made by the leading bookmakers with their betting shops.

Our credit business is now the largest in numbers of customers but probably not in money. The big gamblers tend to put their £5,000 to £50,000 bets on with the big four bookmakers. Most of our credit customers bet in small amounts, but we have enough for the now well-managed credit business to succeed. The totalisator machine side is computerized and run with little waste, adding considerably to the strength of the business. From a dismal outlook of near-collapse in 1976 the Tote now sees good and steady profits. Credit is due to all

347

concerned, from Brian McDonnell, the Chief Executive, with whom most days I eat a picnic lunch in the office when reviewing our affairs, downwards.

When the Banbury printing works collapsed after twenty-one years I was determined to prove that I could successfully run and expand a business. Doing so at the Tote restored my confidence, though it is much easier to run a business without union problems than one in which short-sighted and politically-influenced union power has you by the throat.

My life has not happened as I intended. Achievement has been woefully short of ambition. I have attempted more than I was capable of and have made many foolish mistakes, largely out of vanity. I have been cast into despair from which I saw no escape but have been brought out of it by something Bertrand Russell said to me: 'Think of the very worst that could happen. Consider it carefully, and you can say to yourself, "Well that's not so bad after all."' He had another good piece of advice: 'If you have a problem, think about it before you go to sleep. When you wake up you will find your brain has solved it for you while you were asleep.'

I am glad I knew Bertrand Russell. I made a television series with him about the meaning of philosophy and other topics which is still shown on educational programmes. He had much wisdom and his silliness was occasional, as when he abandoned the idea he used to put to me (when we had the A-bomb and the Russians did not) that we should use the threat of nuclear war to force Russia out of Eastern Europe in favour of nuclear disarmament. But by then he was getting old and thought the end of the world might coincide with his own. The knowledge that I have lived most of my life does not make me believe the world will be so foolish as to blow itself up in honour of my departure.

I met Bertrand Russell through Rupert Crawshay-Williams, who lived with his wife Ba in a little house at Portmeirion where we would argue late into the night about his theories that philosophers are bunk, always excepting Bertrand Russell, his neighbour, about whom he wrote an excellent book, *Russell Remembered*. Though he was a philanderer, Rupert doted on his wife who cooked excellent cakes and bread and was tolerant of his infidelities. She became incapacitated and the doctors insisted on her going to die in hospital.

Neither Rupert nor Ba could bear the thought of being separated. Just before they came to take her away Rupert left a note downstairs to tell the cleaning woman not to go upstairs but to ring the police. They then climbed up the difficult stairs to their bedroom, took out their favourite books and read them as they lay together waiting for the sleeping pills to kill them. It was a sweet and noble exit, though I do not think I would ever be brave or pessimistic enough to do the same.

I have unlimited, sometimes irrational, optimism. 'Good, another day,' I say to myself when I get out of bed, unless something unusually unpleasant is scheduled for it. I gave up hope of making a splash in politics in the early 1960s, but I found other ways of making a small impact on events, not always publicly. I think I am happy, so I must be. It is a matter of temperament and health and I have rarely been ill. My character has changed little since I was a boy; all the original imperfections remain, with some accentuated, suggesting to me that one is born what one is and can only chip away at the material provided. Some, like Roy Jenkins, do better than others.

I have been lucky in having many friends who have made days cheerful and helped me in trouble and I am sorry that I have not always kept up with them as much as I would have liked or should have. Thinking of friends, old and new, dead or alive, seen recently or not, as they sit in my mind as part, willingly or unwillingly, of the furniture of my life, is like being in a library of always fascinating and rewarding books which supply entertainment and knowledge.

My daughter Petronella, born in May 1968, is still at home. As I move with her in the changing phases of her growing maturity, I am reinforced in my conviction that there is no generation gap, the divisions are between minds and temperament. She is cleverer than I; her school, St Paul's, teaches better than mine did, and keeping up with her forces me to stay mentally alert and aware of shifting trends. Probably I get more from her than she from me. I miss my son Pericles, born in August 1963, since he went to America at eighteen. He is not academically clever but, as he writes to me, is a 'survivor'. He is independent and sturdy and will make his own future. My wife Verushka has the gift of youth and laughter. When she is not in the house I miss her and the rooms feel empty till she returns. For her, like many central Europeans, the family comes first and must be fought for. Her son, Nicholas, has inherited her charm.

If with the benefit of hindsight I could have my life again I should plan it differently. I should have sought, as my mother once suggested, to make money before going into Parliament. By the time I had tried to do that the 1945 Labour Government would have completed its major reforms and the Conservatives would have accepted them. With Labour restlessly moving towards Marxism, hunting for fresh industries to nationalize and for new ways of punishing the wealth creators for their impudence in making money, I might have gone into Parliament on the Conservative side. There, it is likely I would have been more successful though probably I should not have been able to do so much about the trade unions: changing their nature is at the root of whether Britain goes up or down. However, there doubtless would have been other things to tackle.

I should not have diversified the Banbury enterprise into commercial printing. I should have stuck patiently with my precious *Banbury Guardian*, waiting for opportunities to expand in newspapers which I was better equipped to deal with than commercial printing. Staying small in printing we could have relied on local employees unaffected by imported troublemakers.

I suppose I should not have married so often, and have waited longer before I did, but I cannot help being susceptible to women and marriage. Something of interest emerged from each marriage, for me if not for my partner. I should certainly try to be a more considerate husband, but unless my nature changed that would be very difficult. I do not believe that out of the countless women in the world a miracle will always guide you automatically to the only one from which maximum happiness will emerge on both sides. It took me four marriages. I imagine it might be the same again; nor could I exclude being attracted by other women on the way. Perhaps I have a feminine romantic element.

At times I have taken myself too seriously, unwilling to laugh at myself as much as I ought to have done. I should try to avoid that. It is hard if you are ambitious and vain and plagued by raging desires to put the world to rights. If you do not take those seriously, who will and what would be the purpose of being alive apart from enjoying it? For someone of my mental composition, impregnated by Victorian values, life cannot be enjoyed unless one tries to do some good in it.

I should try to be less dismayed by adversity, having learned that one usually survives if the will is there. The main advantage of being alive is enjoyment, which can be had in numerous ways and at any age so long as the mental faculties are in order. At one of George Weidenfeld's parties Rose Macaulay, then nearly seventy, remarked to me that she felt the same enthusiasms and had the same attitudes as when she was eighteen: merely, the body had changed. The same with me.

I cannot complain of my life. So far it has been good, full of interest and amusement, with the black patches heightening the pleasure of the bright ones. Lord Reith told me that he was always unhappy after he stopped being Director-General of the BBC. He had found nothing to stretch his abilities and felt useless. I hope I am some way from that. Tomorrow is another day, with new sensations and new adventures.

# APPENDIX

━━━━◦❭❬◦━━━━

## Horoscope cast in January 1945 in India by K.P. Sharma, whom I never met

Born at Esher in Surrey on 4 July 1918 at noon

Planets ex-precession

Ascendant: Virgo     Mars – Virgo

Ascending Node: Scorpio     Moon – Aries

Venus and Descending Node: Taurus

Mercury, Sun and Jupiter – Gemini

Saturn – Cancer

Balance of Sun's cyclic period at birth: four years nine months.

A | This is a remarkable horoscope with the very auspicious combination of Mercury, Jupiter and Sun in the mid-heaven or the tenth house and Saturn in the eleventh house. The combination in the mid-heaven indicates a prominent public career, important positions in the Government of the country, particularly after the fortieth year of age, when you will reach the peak of fame and power. Love of arts and literature, association with learned men, love of authorship, influential friends, penetrating intellect, a generous heart and popularity. The royal planet in the tenth (viz. the Sun) also indicates titles and honours in the latter half of life.

B | Jupiter here is particularly indicative of a happy married life, its influence particularly starting with the fortieth year.

C | Saturn in the eleventh will create interest in problems relating to labour and industries. You will be able to do much constructive work in these directions. The planet is very good for

352

investments in industries and agriculture. It is fond of gardening and travel. The only defect that can be associated with it is a slight nervous pain, perhaps in the leg or ear late in life.

Venus in the ninth combined with the Descending Node of Moon is good for financial prosperity, especially after the thirtieth year of age. Venus here indicates some long travels, a critical attitude towards religion and a very optimistic outlook on life.

Mars in the Ascendant gives abundant energy and a fighting disposition. It assures success in each fight.

The Ascending Node in the third house gives courage. Moon in the eighth is indicative of inheritance and also some digestive troubles late in life. Troubles from cold should also be guarded against.

|  |  | years | months | days |
|---|---|---|---|---|
| | Age on 15 July 1945 | 27 | 1 | 10 |

|  |  | years | months | days |
|---|---|---|---|---|
| | Balance of the cyclic period of the Ascending Node on this date | 12 | 7 | 20 |

|  |  | years | months | days |
|---|---|---|---|---|
| 15 Aug. 1945 to 17 Mar. 1947 | Balance of Saturn's sub-period on this date | 1 | 7 | 2 |

*Saturn's sub-period* As Saturn is favourably placed in the eleventh house, being friendly with the Lord of the Ascendant, Saturn's sub-period indicates success in career, new associations, travel and a position in the Government. Saturn indicates influential friends. A new career is to be predicted. The second half of 1945 is good, as Saturn is in the third house from Moon; but the period after 19 December (1945) should prove still better, with the entry of Jupiter into the seventh house from Moon.

|  |  | years | months | days |
|---|---|---|---|---|
| 17 Mar. 1947 to 4 Oct. 1949 | *Mercury's sub-period* | 2 | 6 | 18 |

This sub-period is better than Saturn's. Better position, more fame and literary interest are indicated.

353

|  | | | years | months | days |
|---|---|---|---|---|---|
| H | 4 Oct. 1949 to 22 Oct. 1950 | *Descending Node's sub-period* | 1 | 0 | 18 |

This is not a very good period. It indicates slight illness and some worries.

|  | | | years | months | days |
|---|---|---|---|---|---|
| I | 22 Oct. 1950 to 22 Oct. 1953 | *Venus's sub-period* | 3 | 0 | 0 |

This is again a very bright period. Good especially for financial matters.

|  | | | years | months | days |
|---|---|---|---|---|---|
|  | 22 Oct. 1953 to 15 Sept. 1954 | *Sun's sub-period* | 0 | 10 | 24 |

Success after a fight. High position. Popularity. Expenses.

|  | | | years | months | days |
|---|---|---|---|---|---|
| J | 15 Sept. 1954 to 15 Mar. 1956 | *Moon's sub-period* | 1 | 6 | 0 |

Anxiety. Travel. Expenses. Slight illness.

|  | | | years | months | days |
|---|---|---|---|---|---|
| K | 15 Mar. 1956 to 3 Apr. 1957 | *Mars's sub-period* | 1 | 0 | 18 |

Not good, being the end of the cyclic period of the Ascending Node. Here ends the period of the Ascending Node.

L

Apr. 1957 (Age 39) – 1973 (Age 55)

After the cyclic period of the Ascending Node the period of Jupiter will start. Duration sixteen years. Jupiter is very well placed on the horoscope and this period of sixteen years may prove the best part of life. During this period you should occupy a very high position in the Government with great power, influence, honour and popularity.

M

1973–85 (55–67)– 1985–92 (67–74)

Jupiter's cyclic period will be followed by that of Saturn. Duration of this will be nineteen years. Of these, the first twelve years will prove good, but the last seven years may not be as good for health.

# My Comments on Horoscope

A   The time-scale is a bit awry. I was in the Government when I was thirty-two but not afterwards. The astrologer may have confused the BBC TV programme *Panorama* with a government position. I was thirty-seven when I began it. Maybe he thought Labour would win the 1959 election. The rest is true, though I cannot be the judge of the phrase 'penetrating intellect, a generous heart and popularity'. I got a knighthood in June 1983, so he was not far out on that.

B   Since 1966 I have had a very happy married life. The reader can decide on the previous marriages.

C   The astrologer clearly refers to my campaigns for democracy in the unions. The investment in Banbury was good for nearly twenty years. The bit about agriculture baffles me. I have had no connection with it apart from keeping a flock of Jacob sheep at a house we had in Wiltshire. I dislike gardening but I have travelled a lot and enjoyed it. I have not had the 'slight nervous pain' yet and hope the astrologer may be wrong.

D   Broadly true, and I am very optimistic.

E   I have not had success in every fight. I lost out on inheritance, which the astrologer guessed I might have had. I have guarded successfully against colds by taking eight grams of ascorbic acid (Vitamin C) every day before breakfast.

F   The election at which I became an MP was in June 1945 and the result was declared in July. I went on a Parliamentary Delegation to India at Christmas and was Personal Assistant to Stafford Cripps on the Cabinet Mission in March 1946. There were long travels.

G   About right, if literary interest means writing articles in newspapers and magazines and editing *English Story*.

H   I got amoebic hepatitis from a visit to Burma. I was worried about money.

I   I was re-elected in 1950 and became Under-Secretary for War in April 1951. I earned more. I was re-elected in October 1951. I was doing quite well in the House.

J   I was anxious over losing my seat in 1955.

K   A slippage of dates here. I was prominent through TV and other activities in this period.

L   Roughly right except that I never occupied 'a very high position in the Government', though I have had some influence. How could the poor astrologer know Gaitskell would die so young and the Labour Party would drift towards Marxism? Perhaps he thought I would have the sense to change parties in time.

M   I am in this period now. It is broadly right apart from the collapse of Banbury. I do not like the last bit about my health, but he got it wrong earlier and optimistically I hope he has again. Otherwise prospects seem fair for a while, if that is not tempting providence.

## CONCLUSION

Allowing for Eastern flattery, not a bad shot forty years ago for Mr K.P. Sharma, court astrologer in the remote state of Bikaner with little knowledge of what happens in England. Mr Sharma, now dead, has kept me optimistic when the going has been rough. Is all astrology bunk?

# INDEX

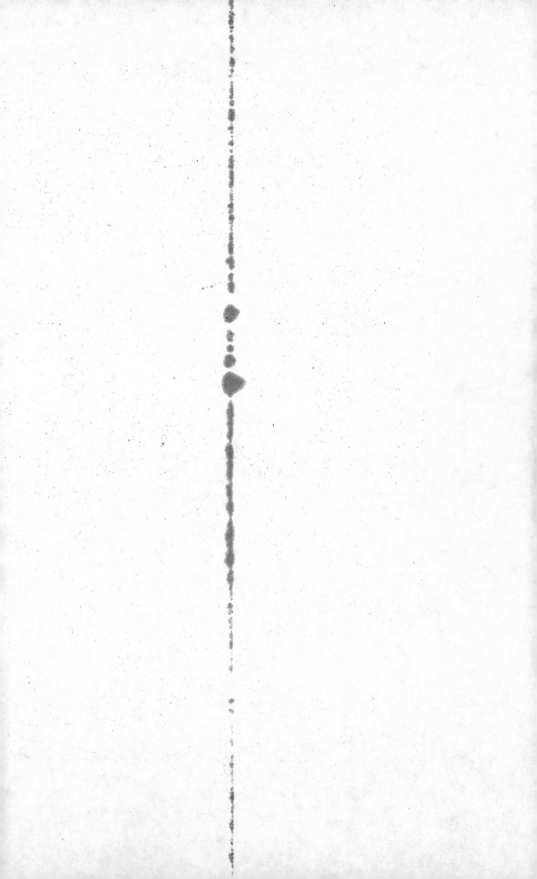